HARVESTING FEMINIST KNOWLEDGE FOR PUBLIC POLICY

Thank you for choosing a SAGE product! If you have any comment, observation or feedback, I would like to personally hear from you. Please write to me at contactceo@sagepub.in

—Vivek Mehra, Managing Director and CEO,
SAGE Publications India Pvt Ltd, New Delhi

Bulk Sales

SAGE India offers special discounts for purchase of books in bulk. We also make available special imprints and excerpts from our books on demand.

For orders and enquiries, write to us at

Marketing Department
SAGE Publications India Pvt Ltd
B1/I-1, Mohan Cooperative Industrial Area
Mathura Road, Post Bag 7
New Delhi 110044, India
E-mail us at marketing@sagepub.in

Get to know more about SAGE, be invited to SAGE events, get on our mailing list. Write today to marketing@sagepub.in

This book is also available as an e-book.

HARVESTING FEMINIST KNOWLEDGE FOR PUBLIC POLICY

Rebuilding Progress

Edited by

Devaki Jain and Diane Elson

International Development Research Centre
Ottawa • Cairo • Dakar • Montevideo • Nairobi • New Delhi • Singapore

www.sagepublications.com
Los Angeles • London • New Delhi • Singapore • Washington DC

Jointly published in 2011 by

 SAGE Publications India Pvt Ltd
B1/I-1 Mohan Cooperative Industrial Area
Mathura Road, New Delhi 110 044, India
www.sagepub.in

SAGE Publications Inc
2455 Teller Road
Thousand Oaks, California 91320, USA

SAGE Publications Ltd
1 Oliver's Yard, 55 City Road
London EC1Y 1SP, United Kingdom

SAGE Publications Asia-Pacific Pte Ltd
33 Pekin Street
#02-01 Far East Square
Singapore 048763

**International Development
Research Centre**
P.O. Box 8500
Ottawa, ON
Canada K1G 3H9
www.idrc.ca
info@idrc.ca
ISBN (e-book) 978-1-55250-545-8

Second Printing 2012

Published by Vivek Mehra for SAGE Publications India Pvt Ltd, typeset in 10/12pt Berkeley by Star Compugraphics Private Limited, Delhi and printed at Chaman Enterprises, New Delhi.

Library of Congress Cataloging-in-Publication Data Available

ISBN: 978-81-321-0741-5 (HB)

The SAGE Team: Gayeti Singh, Sushmita Banerjee, and Rajib Chatterjee

Contents

v

List of Tables, Figures, and Boxes

TABLES

FIGURES

BOXES

List of Abbreviations

ACFODE	Action for Development
ADWA	Asian Domestic Workers' Alliance
ADWN	Asia Domestic Workers Network
AGI	African Gender Institute
AJWRC	Asia-Japan Women's Resource Center
AT	Aid Transparency
AWID	Association for Women's Rights in Development
AWOMI	African Women's Millennium Initiative
BPL	Below Poverty Line
CAP	Coalition against Privatization
CBOs	community-based organizations
CDM	Clean Development Mechanism
CEDAW	Convention on the Elimination of All Forms of Discrimination against Women
CEO	Chief Executive Officer
CERs	Certified Emissions Reductions
CGE	computable general equilibrium
CMA	Conscientizing Male Adolescents, Nigeria
CMEA	Council of Mutual Economic Assistance
CODESRIA	Council for the Development of Social Science Research in Africa
COMESA	Common Market for Eastern and Southern Africa
CRP	common property resources
CSW	Commission on the Status of Women
CTT	currency transactions tax

DAW	Division for the Advancement of Women
DFID	UK Department for International Development
ECOSOC	Economic and Social Council
ECOWAS	Economic Community of West African States
EPMEWSE	Japan Inter-Society Liaison Association Committee for Promoting Equal Participation of Men and Women in Science and Engineering
EPZ	export processing zone
ESCAP	Economic and Social Commission for Asia and the Pacific
EU	European Union
FAO	Food and Agriculture Organization
FDI	foreign direct investment
FEMNET	African Women's Development and Communication Network
FGM	female genital mutilation
FLO	Fairtrade Labelling Organization
FMC	Federation of Cuban Women
FNV	Federation of Dutch Trade Unions
FVPF	Family Violence Prevention Fund, United States
GAD	gender and development
GATS	General Agreement on Trade in Services
GDP	gross domestic product
GEA	Global Employment Agenda
GEM	Gender Empowerment Measure
GGCA	Global Gender and Climate Alliance
GPAC	Gender Public Advocacy Coalition
GVA	Gross Value Added
HDI	Human Development Index
HIPC	Heavily Indebted Poor Countries
ICDS	Integrated Child Development Services
ICESCR	International Covenant on Economic, Social, and Cultural Rights
ICPD	International Conference on Population and Development
ICRW	International Center for Research on Women
IDS	Institute for Development Studies
IFI	international financial institution
IFPRI	International Food Policy Research Institute

IIED	International Institute for Environment and Development
ILO	International Labour Organization
IMAGES	International Men and Gender Equality Survey
IMF	International Monetary Fund
INSTRAW	International Research and Training Institute for the Advancement of Women
IPCC	Intergovernmental Panel on Climate Change
Isis-WICCE	Isis-Women's International Cross Cultural Exchange
ITUC	International Trade Union Confederation
IWYLG	International Women's Year Liaison Group, Japan
JAC	Japan Accountability Caucus, Beijing
JAIWR	Japanese Association for International Women's Rights
JAUW	Japanese Association of University Women
JAWW	Japan Women's Watch
JNNC	Japan NGO Network for CEDAW
JSA	Japan Scientists Association
JWEF	Japan Women Engineers' Forum
LAWPN	Latin American Waste-picker Network
LDC	least developed country
LGBTI	lesbian, gay, bisexual, transgender, and inter-sex
MARWOPNET	Mano River Women's Peace Network
MBOs	member-based organizations
MBOPs	member-based organizations of the poor
MDG	Millennium Development Goal
MFA	Multifibre Arrangement
MFN	Most Favored Nation
MNCR	Brazilian Waste-picker Movement
NABARD	National Bank of Agriculture and Rural Development
NCRFW	National Commission on the Role of Filipino Women
NEPAD	New Economic Partnership for Africa's Development
NGLS	UN Non-governmental Liaison Service
NGO	non-governmental organization
NSCB	National Statistical Coordination Board, Philippines
OECD	Organisation for Economic Co-operation and Development
OPEC	Organization of the Petroleum Exporting Countries
PERI	Political Economy Research Institute
PEVODE	Peoples Voice for Development

PRGF	Poverty Reduction and Growth Facility
PRSP	poverty reduction strategy paper
SAARC	South Asian Association for Regional Cooperation
SADC	Southern African Development Community
SAP	structural adjustment program
SAUR	Société d'Aménagement Urbain et Rural
SCJ	Science Council of Japan
SDE	Société Sénégalaise des Eaux
SERP	Society for the Elimination of Rural Poverty, India
SEWA	Self Employed Women's Association, India
SHGs	Self-help Groups, India
SONEES	Société Nationale des Eaux du Senegal
SPC	state-provided consumption
SNA	System of National Accounts
TAMWA	Tanzanian Media Women's Association
TINA	there is no alternative
TPDS	Targeted Public Distribution System, India
TRIPS	Trade Related Agreement on Intellectual Property Rights
UAF-A	Urgent Action Fund-Africa
UN	United Nations
UNCTAD	United Nations Conference on Trade and Development
UNDESA	United Nations Department of Economic and Social Affairs
UNDESA-DAW	United Nations Department of Economic and Social Affairs–Division for the Advancement of Women
UNDP	United Nations Development Programme
UNFCCC	United Nations Framework Convention on Climate Change
UNFPA	United Nations Population Fund
UNICEF	United Nations Children's Fund
UNIFEM	United Nations Development Fund for Women
UNRISD	United Nations Research Institute for Social Development
UNU-WIDER	World Institute for Development Economics Research of the United Nations University
WABAS	Women's Association for a Better Aging Society, Japan
WAD	women and development
WFP	World Food Programme

WHJ	Japan's Network for Women and Health
WHO	World Health Organization
WID	Women in Development
WIEGO	Women in Informal Employment Globalizing and Organizing
WRC	Workers Rights Consortium
WTO	World Trade Organization
WVS	World Values Survey

Foreword

Against the backdrop of the current financial and economic crises, the writing in this publication by some of the best and brightest thinkers working on women's rights, equality, and development today could not be more timely.

As the United Nations High Commissioner for Human Rights, and also as a committed and long-time advocate for women's rights and gender equality, I have learned that equality and non-discrimination on the basis of sex are not only goals in their own right, but they are essential for the achievement of human rights for all, the realization of sustainable human development, as well as the development of all societies. I have also learned that change comes not merely through individual endeavor, but through working collectively to achieve concrete progress.

More than 60 years have passed since the adoption of the UN Universal Declaration of Human Rights; three decades have elapsed since the Convention on the Elimination of All Forms of Discrimination against Women (CEDAW) set out legal obligations for States parties directed toward women's empowerment and rights; and in 1993 the Vienna Declaration and Programme of Action stated that the human rights of women and of the girl-child are an inalienable, integral, and indivisible part of universal human rights. That same year, the General Assembly adopted the Declaration on the Elimination of Violence against Women, and in 1994 the Commission on Human Rights established the first women-specific special procedure: the Special Rapporteur on Violence against Women. On December 10, 1999, the last human rights day of the 20th century, an Optional Protocol to CEDAW providing for individual petitions and inquiries was opened for signature, ratification, and accession. These tools have provided the framework for the development of international jurisprudence on the rights of women and girls.

There is no doubt that in this relatively short time-span we have also seen remarkable progress in the development and implementation of regional jurisprudence, as well as national laws, policies, and programs directed to promoting women's equality with men. Indeed, there is growing acceptance that human rights, as well as the development and security of all communities, depend on the full participation of women. To borrow from economists' parlance, violence and discrimination against women are "externalities" that the world can ill-afford. As Devaki Jain has pointed out, the degree and access women have to just development is a measure of the stage of development of a nation. It follows that women and their knowledge must be seen as growth agents.

Yet, women throughout the world remain among the poorest and most marginalized, with limited access to rights, resources, and opportunities. They continue to suffer multiple forms of discrimination and endure psychological and physical violence.

To fully tap into women's potential we must spare no effort to implement women's rights, to find practical and effective ways to relieve their suffering, but also—and more profoundly—to redress the injustice that hampers, belittles, and suppresses their contribution. To this effect, countries must live up to their international obligations, which enjoin them to repeal laws and stamp out discriminatory customs, harmful practices, and prejudices that negate or undermine the achievement of equality between women and men. That is an indispensable starting point for the creation of the level playing field for women and girls required for the achievement of substantive equality. It is also the precondition that underpins women's empowerment and their enjoyment of human rights.

The realization of women's rights is predicated on the removal of all factors that hold women back, frustrate their resourcefulness, and curtail their access to a fair share of the common wealth. It requires women's active participation in public life, their freedom of expression, association, and movement, as well as the enjoyment of their rights to education, adequate food, housing, and the highest attainable standard of health, including reproductive health. It demands firm communal commitments to defeating fear and want.

International human rights treaties prohibit discrimination on the basis of sex and include guarantees to ensure that women and men enjoy their civil, cultural, economic, political, and social rights on a basis of equality. I am very pleased to acknowledge that where CEDAW is concerned, 186 States are party to this treaty as of February 4, 2011, of which 100 are also party to its Optional Protocol. However, global and national realities indicate that there is a wide gulf between international legal obligations and their implementation. Women's human rights and entitlements must be ultimately locked into national policies fostering self-help, opportunities, and solidarity. Absorbing international standards into domestic law and enforcing them is of paramount importance and is indispensable to achieve women's equality in law.

In 2005, the Commission on the Status of Women conducted a review (Beijing +10) of the commitments undertaken by governments at the UN Fourth World Conference on Women in Beijing 10 years earlier. It concluded that women did not enjoy human rights on the basis of equality with men.

Inequality in the law exists in all regions of the world and in all legal traditions. In some countries married women are forbidden to keep their own names or pass their nationality on to their children. Their right to own land or inherit property may be limited, and their rights in marriage and divorce law are subjugated to the legal rights of their husbands. In other States, women do not have freedom of movement, and must be accompanied by male guardians. Their educational and employment prospects are heavily circumscribed, and they may be excluded from public office.

The Beijing +5 review established 2005 as a target date for the revocation of laws that discriminate against women, but this deadline has come and gone; that call remains unheeded. Many of these laws are still in force and continue to be applied to the detriment of women and girls. The next decade should see meaningful movement toward total repeal of iniquitous legislation. This would be a long overdue remedy to women's plight and a response to the plea of advocates all over the world.

Protecting women's rights in law and policies is particularly crucial when the economic going gets rough, as is the case now. Unquestionably, economic downturns jeopardize the full spectrum of women's economic and social rights. Women see their job opportunities shrink and are forced to accept more marginal and ill-paid employment to make ends meet. They are often forced to forego basic services to secure food and shelter. In June 2009, the International Labour Organization warned that the global financial crisis could add an increasing number of girls to the more than 100 million who are already involved in child labor.

Addressing the needs and critical vulnerabilities of women and girls caught in this recession is thus imperative. Economic stimulus packages must mitigate the effects of economic contraction as well as jump-start reforms in those public policy areas that address structural disadvantages. Thus, preventive initiatives, safeguards, as well as economic recovery and growth measures, must be designed to be gender-sensitive and non-discriminatory. They must be devised not only to address the immediate economic dire straits, but also to encompass longer-term measures to ensure that women's self-sufficiency and prosperity do not remain mere aspirations.

For example, all too often in many countries growth strategies have led to increases in the incomes of the bottom quintile or decile but at a lower rate than for top income groups, triggering even greater inequality. Indeed, today some of the countries that are among the strongest performers in economic growth are widely off-track on human development targets that directly affect women, such as maternal and child mortality.

Economic development strategies that do not seek to address asymmetries of power and status are both shortsighted and unjust. Conversely, a human rights approach to development helps to put communities and people themselves in charge of devising what measures are best suited to ensure that economic recovery is sustainable, evenly spread, and long-lasting. A human rights approach envisages such participation of the people affected and advocates evenhandedness, transparency, and accountability in policy-making.

Finally, human rights principles bring a stronger notion of mutual responsibility into modalities for development cooperation. While each State bears the primary responsibility for its own development strategies, all States have a responsibility to create a fair and favorable international environment for development. All development partners thus need to respect and promote fundamental human rights, equity, and social inclusion. They must integrate human rights principles and safeguards systematically in their policies and programs.

There are, of course, highly visible benchmarks of progress—women as heads of government, and in parliament; women leading the highest courts, and at the helm of businesses. Perhaps as a result, I see girls around the world growing up with a different sense of themselves than I and most women of my generation were given. Governments and international organizations must meet these girls' expectations and help them fulfill their goals. Empowering women and girls and creating an environment that is conducive to the realization of their full potential is a responsibility and a priority of the tallest order now and in the next decades.

The recent financial crisis provides a new opportunity for rethinking social and economic policies in all countries. This publication offers the viewpoints of a number of women activists and thinkers who envision a world that enhances and builds the capacities and creativities of all people through the establishment of more just and inclusive economies that respect, protect, and fulfill the entire existing spectrum of human rights. We must build on the progress achieved so far. Indeed, our past successes must be the prologue of our future advancement.

Navi Pillay
United Nations High Commissioner for Human Rights

Preface

The United Nations Development Programme (UNDP) and Canada's International Development Research Centre (IDRC) are delighted to be associated with this path-breaking new book.

Harvesting Feminist Knowledge for Public Policy emerged from a seed planted at a meeting in Casablanca, Morocco, where a group of influential feminist thinkers, scholars, and economists adopted the name "Casablanca Dreamers." They envisioned a world that enhances and builds the capacities and creativities of all people through new roads to progress and prosperity. Fourteen essays by these "Dreamers" have now been brought together in this volume by Devaki Jain, an internationally respected Indian feminist and founding member of Development Alternatives with Women for a New Era (DAWN), and Diane Elson, Professor of Sociology at the University of Essex, UK, who was named one of 50 key thinkers on development in 2006.

The editors quote a former governor of the Reserve Bank of India as stating:

> The financial sector has grown more rapidly than other goods and services in a way that made the growth of finance an end in itself and not a means to meet human needs such as food, fuel, health, and education. Excessive "financialization" often resulted in a redistribution of wealth in favour of a few, widening the gap between the haves and the have-nots. It was accompanied by excessive leverage, which means doing business with more of other peoples' money and less of one's own

money. And it was also accompanied by excessive risk-taking where individuals and institutions believe they can make gains without sharing in the losses.[1]

The essayists argue that the global financial and economic crisis that erupted in September 2008 is linked to a set of other crises—food, water, energy, climate change, and women's unpaid care work. They make the case that these crises are the accumulated outcomes of economic ideas, policies, and measures of progress that shifted the goals of national and international development from improvements in human well-being to increases in profits. Importantly, they go one step further, proposing that "rebooting (or returning to 'normality') is not an option," and putting forward workable recommendations to address the root causes and impacts of the crises.

As the development arm of the United Nations, UNDP promotes gender equality and women's empowerment through its capacity development, knowledge management, policy advisory, and advocacy services. These efforts are grounded in the conceptual and measurement work of the human development approach. In the 20th anniversary issue of its flagship publication, the global *Human Development Report*, UNDP reaffirmed the continued relevance of the core human development principles of equity, sustainability, and empowerment in today's evolving world, and launched a new set of measures including the Inequality-adjusted Human Development Index (IHDI), the Gender Inequality Index (GII), and the Multidimensional Poverty Index (MPI). UNDP's support for *Harvesting Feminist Knowledge for Public Policy* is in keeping with its tradition of evidence-based advocacy for sustainable human development and its strategic vision of a world free of gender inequality and poverty.

In 2010, IDRC celebrated its 40th anniversary of supporting innovative policy-relevant research in the developing world. IDRC has funded research on women in the informal economy, women's unpaid care work, gender-responsive budgets, and gender and taxation. These studies have demonstrated that economic policies assumed to be gender neutral tend, in fact, to have different impacts on women and men, and they may exacerbate gender-based inequalities. In supporting this very important book

---

[1] Devaki Jain and Diane Elson, in collaboration with the Casablanca Dreamers, "Vision for a Better World: From Economic Crisis to Equality," paper presented at the 54th Session of the UN Commission on the Status of Women, UNDP, New York, 2010.

by the Casablanca Dreamers, IDRC reaffirms its commitment to research that promotes concrete changes in social and economic institutions, policies, and practices.

Winnie Byanyima
Director, UNDP Gender Team, Bureau for Development Policy
United Nations Development Programme

Rawwida Baksh
Team Leader (former), Women's Rights and Citizenship Program
International Development Research Centre

Acknowledgments

*T*his volume of 14 chapters is one of the outcomes of a long journey. While some authors did not participate in every stop along the way, we all have a deep sense of gratitude both to those who set the process in motion and those who kept it moving toward this point.

The journey began in New York in 2000 at the five-year review of the Beijing Declaration and Platform for Action. With trepidation widespread that there might be backsliding on or dilution of the commitments made at the Fourth World Conference on Women, held in Beijing in 1995, a group of women led by Farida Allaghi met informally on the sidelines. They were Bisi Adeleye-Fayemi, Mehnaz Afkhami, Noeleen Heyzer, Rounaq Jahan, Devaki Jain, Thoraya Obaid, and Hilkka Pietilä. Mehnaz drafted a note out of the meeting that called for revisiting the women's movement and rethinking its approach to global initiatives and spaces, especially from the viewpoint of women from the South.

An opportunity to take the dialog forward was offered by the Eighth World Women's Congress in Kampala, Uganda, in 2002, which was attended by many of those who had been present at the New York meeting. A side meeting was also organized that expanded the base of the group, adding Thelma Awori, Eudine Barriteau, Laketch Dirasse, Stanlie James, Sakuntala Narasimhan, Nafis Sadik, Margaret Snyder, Zen Tadesse, and Aster Zaoude. Rhoda Reddock also joined for a time.

The aim of the discussions was to think together about the challenges with which the worldwide women's movement was grappling. The process was daringly named the Wise Women Process. The primary message that emerged was the need to upend the pyramid and use the messages being articulated by grassroots people's movements and the knowledge generated by their struggles as building blocks to shape the agenda for change. One of the considerations was for those present to document the women's movements in their countries or regions and to imagine what could or should be a global agenda for the United Nations to foster and universalize. Shubha Chacko drafted a brochure based on these discussions called "Revitalizing the International Women's Movement," which was widely distributed at the various UN meetings that followed, especially in 2005. We thank the Ford Foundation, New York, for enabling the side meeting, as well as all those who joined the journey up to that point.

Fatema Mernissi, the brilliant scholar and writer from Morocco (www. mernissi.net) and one of the founders of Development Alternatives with Women for a New Era (DAWN), then proposed a dialog in Casablanca, Morocco. She offered to host this along with a network called Caravan Civique, which worked with the women carpet weavers of the Atlas Mountains, whose oral history she was recording. The women's situation was a stark illustration of the impact of the negative aspects of globalization as their traditional skills of weaving carpets that told stories and represented many ideas were being effaced by the trend to produce carpets with machines. They inspired her to call the meeting "Women Weave Peace into Globalization."

Fatema named the process of bringing together the group the "Casablanca Dream," arguing that dreams are the human mind's creative spaces, where new ideas and visions are born. Dreams suggest traveling, and invoking Sinbad (the sailor). She argued that traveling is a valuable way of knowing and crossing boundaries, something that peace building requires. She challenged the group to work on solving the "enigma" of how to transform globalization into a voyage free of anxiety and fear.

At magical Casablanca, 12 primary participants, along with other supporters, came together and helped to frame the ethical and political horizon for themes elaborated within the pages of this volume. They included—besides Fatema—Nilüfer Cagatay, Shubha Chacko, Hope Chigudu, Yassine Fall, Nomboniso Gasa, Devaki Jain, Zanele Mbeki, Solita Collas-Monsod, Navi Pillai, Nafis Sadik, and Jael Silliman. The task was to unpack the biases of Eurocentric thinking and defining of the world, and to imagine and draw on the various threads to generate and create an integrated pattern for a different world.

The Casablanca group noted that the current situation, a result of aggressive free-market capitalism pursued in the past decades, calls into sharp question dominant—and even many of the so-called alternative— models for development. This translated to questions such as: If we were to replace the key issues or formats for programming and for monitoring from the Beijing Platform for Action or the Millennium Development Goals, what would they be? Could the women's movement capture an idea, like Gandhi's fistful of salt (a symbolic challenge to colonial rule), around which we could unite and bring to bear our collective power? Could it challenge global politics from a global perspective and move away from a masculinized worldview to one that is inclusive and respects plural ways of being?

The key theme or slogan identified was "Women, Water and Wealth: Getting the Fundamentals Right." This shifted the focus away from goals such as gender equality, mainstreaming gender, etc., and argued that the fundamentals—the basics——had to be dealt with first. The phrase "getting the fundamentals right" was also a dig at the neoliberal economists who are stuck in narrow policy reasoning. The other side of the argument was that besides getting the fundamentals right, we also need to get the fundamentalists out.

To Fatema and the Caravan Civique, which hosted the meeting with Najia El Boudali, our deepest gratitude. They brought to light the Northern African and Arab feminist visions——which are an expression of some of the most interesting and vibrant dissent of our times. To Heike Staff, who is a wizard at creating websites that promote a "concord of civilizations," thanks for giving life to the group by pulling together and designing a website on the spot called www.casablanca-dream.net. For supporting this meeting, we acknowledge the Ford Foundation—and especially Jael Silliman, at that time working at the Foundation—for trusting and encouraging the idea of a dialog located in Northern Africa. We also acknowledge the enthusiastic support of the Global Fund for Women and thank Kavita Ramdas for her trust, although alas she could not join the meetings as much as she wanted to.

The outcome of this exhilarating encounter was shared at many other platforms and forums, bringing new people into the fold. Nilüfer Cagatay was so inspired by the dialog in Casablanca and its potential that she invited the whole group to attend the Eighth International Conference on Engendering Macroeconomics and International Economics in Istanbul in 2007. This interface also brought into the group economists such as Lourdes Benería, Diane Elson, and Naoko Otobe—all authors in this volume—and provided an opportunity for a more structured set of chapters on thinking through the Casablanca dream. Nilüfer must be especially thanked for making possible this bridge between the two groups, while those who funded that conference are also to be thanked for the support they gave to her to bring us there.

Sylvia Borren, at that time with Oxfam Novib, was enthusiastic about the initiative and enabled a grant from that agency to support a research assistant to Devaki Jain, who was then coordinating the process. This was a most valuable contribution to the knowledge harvesting process and is gratefully acknowledged.

The quest found resonance with Winnie Byanyima, head of the gender team at the United Nations Development Programme (UNDP). Her support and commitment led to a colloquium on "Assessing Development Paradigms through Women's Knowledge," held in Rabat, Morocco, in 2008. This provided an opportunity to discuss a number of papers that UNDP had commissioned for a publication to look at economic reasoning and development models from very different spaces, as well as to build analysis and proposals that the gender team could take to various world conferences. We thank the UNDP gender team, and especially Winnie, for organizing and funding the colloquium and for starting the momentum for a book.

While the Rabat meeting had been planned to suit the timetable of the various partners, the Wall Street collapse took place just a few weeks before. Therefore, UNDP suggested that a paper might be drawn out of the larger set of presentations to provide the basis for a roundtable at the Beijing +15 meeting of the Commission on the Status of Women (CSW) in New York in March 2010. In order to finalize this synthesis paper, a meeting was called in collaboration with the South Centre in Geneva in July 2009. A draft was prepared and circulated to the larger group and a final paper entitled "Vision for a Better World: From Economic Crisis to Equality" was co-authored by Diane Elson and Devaki Jain and presented at the CSW.

For enabling the meeting in Geneva and supporting the colloquium in New York in partnership with the UNDP gender team, we thank Rawwida Baksh and the International Development Research Centre (IDRC). We thank the South Centre, especially Martin Khor and his team, for their lively and warm support to the meeting. We are also grateful to Justice Pillai and her colleagues in the office of the UN High Commissioner for Human Rights for providing the keynote address to the meeting and the foreword to this book. In addition, Nafis Sadik deserves special mention as, despite holding high office, she found ways of participating in all the events starting with New York, through Uganda, Casablanca, and Rabat, and back to New York again.

While the process of preparing for the CSW was taking place, there was also a move to get the papers ready for publication. At this point the UNDP and IDRC leadership agreed that the latter would take over the management of the process, and IDRC then funded and enabled further work on preparing the essays for publication as well as providing an editor, Tina Johnson. At IDRC, we are particularly grateful to Rawwida Baksh and Navsharan Singh and thank Bill Carman for providing support toward publication. Tina has been a sensitive and patient editor, putting up with many wrinkles, and a very special thanks to her for bringing us so far.

Shubha Chacko provided solid research and organizing support, and was then ably succeeded by Divya Alexander. We gratefully acknowledge their inputs, which have been critical to bringing this project to fruition. Thanks also to Perce Bloomer, who has steadily maintained continuity as Devaki's secretary.

The perspectives presented in this volume have emerged through a process of participation, critical reflection, and engagement with and inclusion within many "women's tents" (meetings, conferences, and networks) over the last 11 years. The basic premise is that we need to call on feminist voices and tools to negotiate what we aspire to achieve—a world of equality, peace, and justice. The central driver of this endeavor is the idea of building knowledge from the ground as a way to redefine the concept of "progress." It is a product of a strong feminist community. The hope is that the volume will draw attention to women's knowledge and its value to the macro policy spaces and rethinking that is taking place after the crisis.

So, as we flag the various milestones, we once again gratefully acknowledge the many traveling companions who have been part of this exciting voyage as well as the funders for trusting this venture. The website www.casablanca-dream.net provides the hub for the continuation of this process, this journey bridging across differences, and is now being nurtured and moved forward by (African Women's Millennium Initiative AWOMI: www.awomi.org), a feminist network with headquarters in Senegal. Many of those acknowledged here will be working to communicate our messages to and encourage UN Women, the new United Nations women's agency, to take up the challenge of facilitating a new vision of development for the whole world.

Introduction

DEVAKI JAIN AND DIANE ELSON

This volume brings together 14 chapters, by feminist thinkers from different parts of the world, reflecting on problems of current patterns of development and arguing for political, economic, and social changes to promote equality and sustainability. The chapters were written in the context of the "triple crises" of food, fuel, and finance (2008–2009) and the underlying deep-seated problems of growing inequality, squeeze on time to provide unpaid care to family and friends, and environmentally unsustainable patterns of economic growth. Their analysis remains relevant even though the immediate drama of bank failure and bailouts has passed. Indeed, at the time of writing, not only are food and fuel prices once again rising rapidly, but there are emerging threats of financial instability in many countries, as well as civil strife due to the pressures on citizens. The outlook is bleak for poor people around the world.

The chapters draw on the diversity of socioeconomic experiences of women in different countries. The policies and priorities that they suggest emerge from an engagement with the State, the United Nations, and the women's movement. The chapters argue for new ways of thinking about development, and offer ideas for reformulating development to secure social, economic, and political justice.

All the contributors agree that gender inequality has to be situated within the context of other forms of inequality, and that efforts to promote gender equality should not be divorced from efforts to promote a more equal world for all. It is not enough to call for the participation of women in existing patterns of market-based production, or for the empowerment of women within existing paradigms of development, or for gender mainstreaming within existing configurations of institutional power. It is the forms of production, the paradigms, and the institutions themselves that need questioning and transforming, both through changes in the ideas that generate economic policies and through social mobilization. This volume argues that the very approach being taken to understanding and measuring progress, and planning for and evaluating development, needs rethinking in ways that draw on the experiences and knowledge of women.

The different contributors address these issues in a variety of ways, with some drawing their examples from many countries and others rooting their arguments in a particular country. This introduction first offers a very brief overview of key themes in the various chapters, and then presents some key public policy alternatives distilled from these chapters and the process of discussion that produced them.

Key Themes from the Chapters in This Book

The chapters by Elson, Seguino, Benería, Otobe, and Castañeda and Gammage engage with some of the broad trends of contemporary development; those by Fall and Jain both focus on the problems of market-driven agricultural development, in sub-Saharan Africa and India respectively, to reveal the flaws in contemporary development paradigms. All these chapters argue for far-reaching changes in economic policy, not just an attempt to restore "normality" after the recent crises and their impact.

Elson focuses on how to reframe understandings of development, stressing the need for a greater role for social investment, production, and consumption. She argues for working toward a socially just economy that respects individual rights to use collectively owned resources; that is maintained and expanded through decentralized, democratic, and egalitarian tax and expenditure systems; that supports diverse ways of producing and using goods and services; that is regulated in ways that prevent harmful spillover effects; and that is guided by obligations to protect, promote, and fulfill human rights.

Seguino discusses how the neoliberal macroeconomic policies set in motion since the early 1970s have undermined the goals of dignified work, security, and inter-group equality, focusing in particular on the liberalization of the financial sector and reorientation of central banks away from employment creation. She argues that these policies contributed to the financial crisis and must be changed. She offers examples of policies for reform of the financial sector and central banks to make them capable of supporting the equitable creation of wealth and jobs, and the equitable enjoyment of human well-being.

Bería examines key challenges regarding labor market trends, including the changing organization of labor processes, the growth of the informal economy, and the reorganization of the care economy through the feminization of international migration. She challenges the acceptance of the informal economy, pointing out that it relies on cheap labor and does not provide decent work. She departs from the usual idea of simply offering targeted support for women in the informal sector, instead arguing that there needs to be an improvement in labor conditions built into macroeconomic policies. She raises fundamental questions of how labour markets would need to be restructured if gender equality is to be achieved.

Work and labor markets are also the subject of the chapter by Otobe, who reviews the gender dimensions of work in a globalized economy in the context of the standards and procedures agreed through the International Labor Organization. She argues that gender structures the division of labor and leads to the over-representation of women among the poor. She calls for economic recovery programs to bail out the working poor, not just the large banks, and argues for stronger efforts to build decent work.

Castañeda and Gammage explore the impact of climate change on access to food, water, and energy, discussing how women and men are differently affected, and how gender inequalities intersect with adaptation and mitigation strategies. They stress the importance of building on local knowledge in efforts to conserve ecosystems, recognizing that women and men have different kinds of knowledge, and critique gender biases in policy measures that rely on the creation of new market mechanisms.

Access to food and water are central to Fall's analysis of the costs of market-driven policies for agriculture and water provisioning in Africa. She shows how these policies, in which officials and corporations collude, are curtailing the realization of the right to water and the right to food, and deepening women's economic insecurity. She notes that women have been protesting against these policies at the local level, and calls for policy changes in both developing and developed countries, such as removing farm subsidies for rich farmers.

Jain is also concerned with the inequalities produced by market forces, and critically examines India's economic success through the lens of food security. She argues that entering into the liberal paradigm has shifted the emphasis in promoting GDP from agriculture to export-oriented sectors such as services and tradables. In her analysis of what lies behind the Indian paradox: "mountains of food and millions of starving citizens," she points out that that despite the large, State-managed food distribution system to households below the poverty line, the power of the corporate sector and the objective of enhancing foreign capital inflows has moved land use away from food production to real estate as well as non-food agriculture. She calls for more proximate production systems, especially led by women farmers, as an insurance against food insecurity for poor households.

Monsod, Hara, Chen, and Núñez Sarmiento consider the pressures that have limited realization of gender equality in development, drawing on the experiences of their respective countries: the Philippines, Japan, China, and Cuba.

Monsod argues that unless all of women's contributions to the economy are recognized, women will continue to be second-class citizens. She discusses the attempts to measure unpaid work and include it in the GDP of the Philippines, charting both progress and setbacks. She concludes that new economic measures that take into account women's unpaid work cannot be established without a strong, politically motivated, and united push by the women's movement.

Hara shows how successful economic development in Japan has not led to broad-based achievements in gender equality. She discusses the efforts of women's non-governmental organizations (NGOs) to secure greater voice for women, to advance the position of women in science and technology, and to secure new gender equality laws. She also identifies some of the challenges they face in sustaining their efforts.

The gender dimensions of rapid economic development in China are discussed by Chen. She argues that this development continues to be influenced by patriarchal gender norms, using as examples the impact in the country of the global economic crisis and the counteracting economic stimulus plan that was introduced in 2009. She points out that although women have been active in some local level protests, there are still few ways for them to have a voice in development policy.

The Cuban experience of development is analyzed by Núñez Sarmiento, who highlights the substantial achievement of providing free access for all to basic services, and the rapid increase in women's participation in the labor market, including in technical and professional work.

She notes that by the early 1990s, women accounted for two-thirds of the country's technical and professional workers. However, she shows that Cuban women still carry the burden of the second shift of unpaid work, which constrains their abilities to take leadership roles.

The remaining three chapters, by Jhabvala, McFadden, and Silliman, focus on feminist or women-led mobilization to achieve equality. Drawing on her experiences supporting the organizing of women informal workers in the Self Employed Women's Association (SEWA) in India, Jhabvala emphasizes that women workers in the informal sector—even though they are not protected by labor laws—can change their circumstances through collective organizing. She notes the difficulties involved in trying to scale up local-level organizations in ways that retain women's autonomy.

McFadden identifies the challenges facing feminists in Africa and calls for women's organizations to reclaim political agency. She considers the 2009 crises as a wake-up call, because the agenda for gender equality in Africa has been hijacked by donor-driven "gender mainstreaming," and there has been a resurgence in conservative ideas about women's roles. She calls for feminists to regroup and decide how the feminist movement can be rebuilt and strengthened.

Silliman points to the emergence of various types of "progressive masculinities" in some parts of the world, and discusses how this may provide a resource for women's struggles, particularly in relation to violence against women and reproductive rights. She calls for a reconceptualization of gender justice in ways that transcend a rigid binary divide between the two sexes.

All the chapters, in diverse ways, offer proposals for alternative strategies to address the limitations and contradictions of currently dominant ideas and practices in development, and move towards the creation of a socially just and egalitarian world.

KEY PUBLIC POLICY ALTERNATIVES

From the chapters in this book, and the discussions that produced them, the following seven points have been distilled as those that should be in the forefront of future thinking about development.[1]

---

[1] These points are explained in more depth in a paper presented by the authors at a panel organized by the United Nations Development Programme (UNDP) in New York in March 2010 (Jain & Elson, 2010).

Reforms in Economic Reasoning

It will be difficult to design the kinds of policies needed to secure equitable, just, and sustainable economies without fundamental reforms in economic reasoning. The measures by which policymakers judge progress need to become more varied to include not just increases in GDP and indexes of the value of shares, but also indicators of well-being, such as a decline in rates of malnutrition and unemployment, and indicators that incorporate unpaid as well as paid work.

The kind of reasoning that has dominated policy in the last 40 years ignores the issue of equality of outcomes. The criterion of success is maximizing the output to be obtained from available resources; the distribution of the output is a secondary matter. In future, the costs of inequality (not only in opportunity but also in outcomes) need to be factored in.

In addition, both inputs and outputs need to be judged in holistic terms, including non-market as well as market inputs and outputs. This idea has gained ground in relation to natural resources and pollution, but not yet in relation to unpaid work in households and communities, and the services this work produces. Here a new tack might be tried. Along with pressure for national level time–use surveys and satellite accounts, there might be a call for every appraisal of new investment, or reorganization of production and delivery, to include an assessment of whether the investment or reorganization is likely to reduce or increase the amount of time that has to be spent on unpaid work. In considering poverty, it is critical to get beyond simply looking at income to recognize the multi-dimensional, gendered experience of poverty.

Growth That "Bubbles Up" Rather Than "Trickles Down"

The process of poverty removal can itself be an engine of growth, leading to growth that "bubbles up," rather than "trickles down." If growth were led by the broad base of those at the lower end of the economy—and by the demand generated by increases in the wages of ordinary workers and the earnings of small and medium farmers, small and medium businesses, and the self-employed—it would rebalance the structure of production, both in terms of the types of goods produced, the types of organizations that produce them, and the way that they are distributed. It would help to ensure that employment provides decent work, with enough income for an adequate standard of living, and respect for worker's rights. Mere jobs are not enough. Pro-poor growth is all too often defined in terms of enabling poor people to work in production that creates profits for rich people, without providing any scope for fair shares in that process. The bedrock of fair shares has to be fair earnings and a pattern of output geared to meeting the needs of low- and middle-income people.

A new approach to agriculture and the food economy must be at the heart of new growth strategies. The liberalization of international trade in food, and the privatization of agricultural marketing and distribution of agricultural inputs, has jeopardized the livelihoods of poorer and smaller farmers, promoted the expansion of large-scale commercial agriculture, and enhanced the power of international agribusiness corporations. Moreover, an increasing amount of land has been diverted into non-food uses such as tourist resorts, shopping malls, and business parks.

In many developing countries, women make up over half of the agricultural workforce. In some countries they are the majority of farmers. Women farmers are particularly active in food production, but all too often they are not recognized as farmers in their own right, and have been denied secure land rights and access both to training and productive inputs and to stable markets with fair prices. The distribution of land rights, and of public investment and regulation of markets (including international markets), needs to be reoriented to support women farmers to enable them to improve the productivity of their land and labor. It will not be enough simply to distribute more land to individual women farmers. Without a complete reorientation of agricultural policy, they will be vulnerable to indebtedness and may end up having to sell their land. In the space of a couple of decades, land would be concentrated in the hands of large commercial farmers. Better land rights for women need to be embedded in a system of equitable public support, and the collective organization of small farmers.

Industry and manufacturing need to be reoriented to focus less on the production of fashionable goods (with built-in obsolescence) for individualized, competitive, private consumption, and more on good quality, long-lasting goods, affordable by all, and designed to meet needs rather than advertising-induced wants. The focus on the private car in many places as the lynchpin both of the transport system and of people's aspirations for a better life needs to be questioned. Individualized transport systems built around the privately owned car are a significant contributor to climate change and the fuel crisis. Moreover, they exclude those who cannot afford cars (even so-called cheap ones).

Control of the production and distribution of water and energy by large corporations also needs rethinking. Privatized production and distribution of clean water for profit risks excluding remoter regions and poorer people from improved access to this vital resource. Corporations can make more profit by distributing to those who can pay higher costs and are concentrated in urban centers. Public systems for water can be funded by taxation as well as by user charges that provide a basic allocation of free water. In such an arrangement, the better-off contribute to affordable access by poorer people. Public funding can also support people with information, training, and equipment to themselves become producers and distributors of water, harvesting, treating, and reutilizing it.

Strategies for growth that bubbles up must look beyond the market economy. They must have at their heart a concern with the unpaid economy. Work in the unpaid economy must be recognized and made visible through the collection of time–use data on a regular basis. The amount of unpaid work that has to be done, especially by poor women, must be reduced through public investment in infrastructure to provide fuel and water, and in social infrastructure, especially health services and care services for children, frail elderly people, and people with disabilities. The remaining unpaid work must be redistributed so that men and boys contribute more, and enjoy the delights as well as the challenges of care work. Both women and men should be able to reconcile and balance, on an equal basis, their paid and unpaid work. Both women and men should be equally recognized as earners and as carers. Everyone needs time free from unpaid work (especially the kind that is drudgery), and also enough time to care for families, friends, and communities.

The details of a "bubbling up" growth strategy will, of course, vary from country to country, but in each case the control of money and banking, the determination of public expenditure and taxation, the operation of markets (including international markets), the enjoyment of rights to resources and to work, and the reasoning on which economic policy is based, would need to change. Some ideas of the kinds of changes that are necessary can be gained from the many practices and concepts developed by women in their struggles for equality.

Socially Useful Banking and Finance, at Macro as well as Micro Levels

"Socially useless" banking needs to be replaced by "socially useful" banking. Women have a lot of experience with the creation of small-scale, self-organized savings and loan groups in their local neighborhoods, and women's organizations like SEWA have created cooperative banks for their members. The emphasis on putting finance at the service of social goals needs to be extended throughout the banking system, from the micro level to the macro and international level, including commercial banks and central banks.

Many progressive economists have set out proposals for improving the regulation of commercial banks, including the splitting of deposit-taking activities from speculative trading in financial assets; but there has been less emphasis on creating or supporting large-scale banks based on the principle that they operate to the mutual benefit of depositors and borrowers, and not to make profits for shareholders. Such banks did flourish in some countries before financial liberalization, and in some they continue to exist. More of such banks should be encouraged. In addition, central banks should change the way in which they operate to become promoters of employment creation, not simply guardians of very low rates of inflation. To do this, they need to explicitly set goals for employment creation as well as inflation control, and continue to sustain the expansionary monetary policies that many of them adopted immediately after the financial crisis, until their economies are on a path of sustained job-creation. This will need to be supplemented by proactive development banking, of the kind that does exist in some countries of the South, but with steps taken to ensure that loans are available to women on an equitable basis with men.

To make socially useful banking feasible, and to create stable conditions for the creation of decent work, it is important to reduce the volatility of financial flows in and out of national economies. Governments can introduce capital controls and stop inflows and outflows of short-term speculative funds. Malaysia did this during the Asian financial crisis of 1997, and as a result was one of the first countries to recover from that crisis. Brazil has embarked on a similar exercise following the 2007/2008 crisis. It is vital that the International Monetary Fund (IMF) changes its policy and supports such moves, rather than encouraging developing countries to keep larger reserves of foreign currency to tide them over periods of volatility. The latter policy is like requiring all motorists to carry higher levels of accident insurance rather than putting traffic lights at road junctions.

Just and Democratic Public Finance

To complement socially useful banking, there must be just and democratic public finance. This means fair taxation and equitable public expenditure, with citizen participation in determining priorities and monitoring and evaluating outcomes. Women scholars, activists, and elected representatives have done much to try to transform government budgets in the 16 years since the Beijing Platform for Action called for gender-responsive budgeting. There have been some successes in getting women more voice, and in reorienting public finance to address women's poverty and gender equality, especially at the local level.

However, gender-responsive budgeting has not as yet fully engaged with the macroeconomics of budgets at the national level, with the issues of how tax systems can be equitably reformed to generate more revenue, with how high public expenditure should be, or with what is the appropriate policy on budget deficits. These kinds of policies determine how much is actually available for allocation at the places where women have won more voice—at local level. This is the next frontier and will require more collaboration between progressive feminist economists, activists, and elected representatives.

Taxes need to be fair not only in terms of gender and class, but also in terms of the relative contributions of households and individuals on the one hand and businesses and banks on the other. All over the world there has been a shift in the balance of contributions, with businesses and banks, especially large ones, paying a smaller and smaller share, and taking advantage of tax havens. Many governments are not raising enough tax revenue, and there is an urgent need to stop tax avoidance and evasion. Rather than simply campaigning for tax breaks for women's businesses, feminists need to raise their voices in the emerging campaigns for tax justice to raise more revenue at national and international levels: the G20 has begun to tackle this issue, but it is vital that momentum is not lost.

Gender-responsive budgeting also needs to engage with questions of fiscal expansion and fiscal austerity. The response to the financial crisis in many countries was an expansion of the deficit as part of a stimulus package. But now, in a large number of countries in both North and South, deficit reduction and fiscal austerity have priority. Claims that there are no alternatives to expenditure cuts need to be evaluated, and governments reminded that well allocated public expenditure can reduce inflationary pressures by relieving supply bottlenecks. Of course, there is a risk that public expenditure will not be used in ways that support equitable and sustainable development, and so there must be continued pressure for women, especially low-income women, to have more say in its allocation and evaluation.

Socially Responsible Markets and Fair Trade

Markets are a critical component of a just and equitable economy, provided they are fair and balance competition with cooperation. Too many markets, national and international, have become dominated by large businesses that act as intermediaries between producers and consumers, taking the lion's share of the price that consumers pay. But many women's organizations have experience of markets built on direct links between small-scale producers and consumers to the mutual benefit of both: face-to-face via village markets where farmers and craftspeople sell their goods; and online via the Internet, enabling networks of small-scale enterprises (including cooperatives and the self-employed) to take advantage of economies of scope and scale. There is a need to scale up such marketing alternatives, by building larger-sized retailers and distributors that operate on principles of mutual benefit to producers, consumers, and traders, rather than on the principle of making profits for shareholders.

Fair trade in international markets requires changes to the regulation of international trade. Women's organizations have stressed that trade liberalization is often at odds with livelihood security, fostering destructive competition rather than prosperity for all. Trade liberalization definitely means a rise in imports; it may, but does not necessarily, lead to a rise in exports. There is no guarantee that low-income people who lose their livelihoods through competition from cheaper imports will gain new employment in export sectors. If there are to be more equitable forms of development, new trade agreements must be preceded by credible and properly funded systems of social protection, so that any low-income person who loses her or his livelihood is fully compensated.

More equitable development also requires rethinking the non-discrimination provisions in international trade agreements. In these agreements, non-discrimination is defined in terms of the principle that the same rules should apply to all businesses, irrespective of whether they are domestic or foreign owned. However, as is well recognized in human rights agreements, the application of formally equal rules to very unequal actors tends to institutionalize discrimination and lead to substantively unequal outcomes. Women organizing for human rights point to the Convention on the Elimination of All Forms of Discrimination against Women (CEDAW), which allows "special measures" that treat women and men differently in order to overcome women's historical disadvantage. The same principle needs to be recognized in international trade agreements, allowing governments in poor countries to treat domestic firms differently from foreign firms, so as to enable the former to improve their productivity. Demands for developing countries to liberalize imports need to be put on hold until their business owners, workers, and farmers have been able to develop the skills and acquire the technology that would enable them to match the productivity in developed countries.

Support for Equitable Property Rights

A just and egalitarian economy needs property rights (associated not only with ownership, but also with tenancy and use of communal resources) to be much more widely dispersed. This can take place not only through redistributing title to land, but also through support for small businesses, as well as support for collective forms of ownership and management, including cooperatives, employee-owned enterprises, municipally owned enterprises, and local committees for the management of natural resources. In all cases, support needs to be given to women to have rights, and exercise them, on the same basis as men. Moreover, formal title to individual property is not enough. It has to be supported by access to public services, infrastructure, and credit; by contracts to supply the public sector; and by collective organization.

The main, and often only, property of the majority of people in many countries is, of course, their own capacity for work. Labor rights must also be strengthened, including rights at work and to organize collectively. Women have been at the forefront of developing new forms of workers' organizations that include informal as well as formal workers.

Economic and Social Rights as an Objective of Economic Policy

An important way to reorient economic policy in support of equitable, just, and sustainable development is to put the realization of economic and social rights at the forefront of such policy. Governments have an obligation to progressively realize economic and social rights, using the maximum available resources, under the International Covenant on Economic, Social, and Cultural Rights (ICESCR). But these obligations are not in the forefront of the minds of ministers of finance, who may not even know of their existence; even if the ministers are aware of them, they may think that promoting economic growth will take care of them. The crises of finance, food, and fuel have shown how far that is from being the case.

It is necessary for finance ministers to pay direct attention to the realization of economic and social rights. States that are parties to the ICESCR are under an obligation to ensure the satisfaction of, at the very least, minimum essential levels of each of the rights in the Covenant. This means that a State party in which any significant number of persons is deprived of essential foodstuffs, of essential primary health care, etc., is prima facie failing to meet its obligations under the ICESCR. Even in times of severe resource constraints, States must ensure that rights are fulfilled for vulnerable members of society.

There is a strong presumption that retrogressive measures on the part of a State are not permitted. An example of a potentially retrogressive measure would be cuts to expenditures on public services that are critical for the realization of economic and social rights, or cuts to taxes that are critical for funding such services. If such retrogressive measures are deliberate, then the State has to show that they have been introduced after consideration of all alternatives and to justify them "by reference to the totality of the rights provided for in the Covenant and in the context of the full use of the maximum available resources" (ICESCR, 1990). For example, cutting government spending on health and education, while not cutting expenditure on arms, will likely violate the principle of non-retrogression.

The importance of the rights to food, to work, to an adequate standard of living, and to social security has been particularly highlighted by the crises. These rights cannot be fully realized overnight, but progress can be made everywhere in their realization, giving priority to those who least enjoy them and introducing new laws to entrench these rights as legal entitlements, available to women as well as to men.

CONCLUSION

Even though the immediate drama of the financial crisis has died down, the need for alternative thinking has not gone away. Many developing countries in Latin America and Asia experienced a slowdown in economic growth, rather than a recession, and their GDP growth has recovered (though employment growth has lagged behind). A few developing countries, such as Brazil, China, and India, emerged as new global powers and joined the G20, the main economic council of wealthy nations, and/or formed their own clubs as "successful" developing countries—such as IBSA (India, Brazil, and South Africa) and BRIC (Brazil, Russia, India, and China)—to pursue their interests. But despite these shifts in the global balance of economic power from the North to the South, there has been a dispiriting trajectory toward returning to the same public policy stances and practices that were in place before the crises erupted.

This book does not aim to offer panaceas. The process of changing development paradigms is not easy, and the conditions for bringing about equality and sustainability vary across the world. It is right that there should be vigorous debate about how to organize and what alternatives to propose. However, this book does insist that feminist analysis and women's voices should be in the forefront of these debates, putting forward ideas not about how more women can participate in economic and political spaces as they are, but how those spaces can be transformed to become more equal and sustainable for everyone. There is no one path to the creation of equitable, just, and sustainable development. But women's organizations in many countries have begun to create a path by walking it. Goals and targets may help us get there, but only if they are embedded in a fuller vision of what development should be and may become.

References

CESCR (Committee on Economic, Social, and Cultural Rights). 1990. *General comment 3: The nature of States parties obligations* (Art. 2, para. 1 of the Covenant). December 14. UN doc. E/1991/23.

Jain, D., & Elson, D. (in collaboration with the Casablanca Dreamers). 2010. *Vision for a better world: From economic crisis to equality*. New York: UNDP.

Economics for a Post-crisis World
Putting Social Justice First*

DIANE ELSON

If post-crisis economies are to meet the goals of social justice and environmental sustainability, more will have to be changed than the international financial system.... Measures to end the crisis will fail if they simply seek to restore growth and greed.

INTRODUCTION

The financial crisis that began in the United States and parts of Western Europe in 2008 had by early 2009 become a global recession encompassing loss of jobs and incomes in all parts of the world. It has called into question neoliberal macroeconomic policy; Keynesian economics has been rediscovered. Fiscal stimulus and regulation of finance are again on the agenda to try and ward off a worldwide economic depression. There is more space now for alternative thinking. Indeed, the *Financial Times* has been hosting a discussion on what a new form of better-regulated capitalism should be built.

However, despite declarations that the Washington Consensus is dead, the G20 seem to see the way forward in terms of giving more power and

---

*This chapter draws on ideas first put forward in Elson (2001).

money to its architects: the International Monetary Fund (IMF) and the World Bank. And while the Commission of Experts of the President of the United Nations General Assembly on Reforms of the International Monetary and Financial System (Stiglitz Commission)—set up to reflect on the causes of the crisis, assess its impacts, and suggest adequate responses—has put forward some far-reaching reforms of international finance, more will have to be changed than the international financial system, if post-crisis economies are to meet the goals of social justice and environmental sustainability. As well as a financial crisis, there is a food crisis and a climate change crisis. We need to rethink what goods and services we want to produce and consume, and what criteria we are going to use to judge economic success. Measures to end the crisis will fail if they simply seek to restore growth and greed.

Across the world, an increase in privately produced and consumed goods and services has been used as the hallmark of success. The example of the United States has come to dominate, with its emphasis on individual purchases and market-based provision of even the necessities of life, such as health services, and a popular culture based on the commercialization of human beings and promotion of the cult of "celebrity." Women have been encouraged to understand emancipation in terms of being able to buy more and more consumer goods and transform themselves into more attractive sex objects, not in terms of becoming fully realized human beings. Instead of creating economies in which caring relations are valued, and the work of care is socially recognized and shared equally between women and men, care is being commercialized and delegated to low-paid women. In addition, time for care is squeezed in a drive to incorporate as much of both women's and men's time as possible in production for profit.

The goal of social justice has been forgotten, or it is considered only as an afterthought. The development that women are getting is not the development that women dreamed of when they struggled for equal enjoyment of human rights. Some forms of subordination of women have indeed weakened: typically the most visible forms of patriarchal power diminish as women enter labor markets and do paid work outside the home. But new forms of subordination of women are created, at new sites, and using new technologies (Elson & Pearson, 1981).

Neoclassical economics (the economics of the Washington Consensus) reflects and reinforces the idea that consumer capitalism can deliver the good life. However, there are some resources to resist these trends in several currents of thought that challenge the dominance of this thinking.

This chapter draws in particular on two: the human development current (see the annual UNDP *Human Development Report*) and the feminist macroeconomics current (see Elson, 1997, 1999; Elson & Cagatay, 2000). Another important resource is environmental economics, but that is beyond the scope of this chapter.

The human development approach challenges the merely instrumental treatment of human beings as factors of production in the service of economic growth. Similarly, feminist economics challenges the validity of the idea that everyone is a self-interested "rational economic man," and argues that unpaid time spent producing goods and services for family, friends, and neighbors is an economic issue, as well as a personal issue, all over the world (see, for instance, the journal *Feminist Economics*; Cagatay et al., 1995; Grown et al., 2000). This does not mean that human development and feminist economics try to force all countries into a "one-size-fits-all" economic and social policy. Rather, they encourage and help us to rethink the criteria we can use to evaluate economic and social policies and to construct better ones that are more likely to realize the dreams of social justice and women's rights.

This chapter puts forward an evaluative framework based on guaranteed social entitlements rather than the opportunity to go to the shopping mall, and it advocates for economic strategies that give a central place to social investment for social consumption rather than private investment for private consumption. It argues for a vision of a socially just economy in which people's economic rights would not be dominated by individual rights to buy, sell, and consume individually owned resources in disregard of others—a system that facilitates the growth of large corporations, able to manipulate people's choices. Instead, first place would be occupied by individual rights to use collectively owned resources, maintained and expanded through decentralized, democratic, and egalitarian tax and expenditure systems, supporting diverse ways of producing and using goods and services, regulated in ways that prevent harmful spillover effects.

There would still be room for other forms of economic rights—rights to buy, sell, and use individually owned resources—but they would not dominate and would operate in a context that ensures that people are guaranteed an adequate standard of living in their own right. Markets would be transformed from being masters to being servants; at the same time, state agencies would cease to be alien forms with ascendancy over people and would be transformed into agencies that seek to protect, promote, and fulfill human rights.

THE GOOD ECONOMY AND THE GOOD LIFE: FROM UTILITY TO CAPABILITY

Mainstream neoclassical economics assumes that the best—the optimal—economy is one that maximizes the utility that consumers get from buying goods and services in the market. Such an economy is judged to have achieved an efficient allocation of resources. To put it another way, it is assumed that policymakers should first try to maximize the economic pie, and then address social justice issues through redistributing the pie once it is baked. To maximize the pie, it is assumed that the best method is production by privately owned, profit-seeking businesses operating in markets that are regulated in ways that promote competition between such businesses.

Although, in theory, efficiency can be defined in relation to any set of rights over resources, in practice it has been defined in relation to the rights over resources characteristic of free-market capitalism. Thus the rights that count are property rights over land, equipment, buildings, etc., that can be bought and sold. All other rights (such as labor rights, indigenous people's rights over common land, welfare rights, etc.) are regarded as "distortions" that impede the efficient functioning of the market (for an insightful discussion, see Chang, 2001).

Efficiency and satisfaction of consumer wants are seductive concepts. No one is in favor of waste, or for settling for less than can be achieved, and shopping can be an enjoyable pastime—provided one has money to spare. But neoclassical economics gives particular meanings to these ideas. An economy is in the optimal state if no one can consume more without some consuming less, regardless of the distribution of consumption. The satisfaction of consumers' preferences on what and how much to buy are taken as the benchmark against which to judge outcomes regardless of how those preferences are formed (and distorted) by consumer culture and social norms.

The human development approach has a different aim: the emancipation of individual human beings from the constraints that prevent them from living a life that they have reason to value. This means having the capabilities to enjoy a rich set of valued functionings, far beyond the utility to be got from visits to the shopping mall, including being free from poverty and social exclusion and enjoying affiliation with other human beings (see, for instance, Sen, 1999; Nussbaum, 2002). This position might be described as one of ethical individualism, in that it does not take as its starting point the well-being of the nation, the community, or the household, but begins from the equal valuing of all human beings as celebrated in the Universal Declaration of Human Rights. The human development approach does not entail methodological individualism, however, a form of analysis that rips individuals from their social context and that is the foundation of neoclassical economics. Instead it recognizes that human well-being depends on relations with others, and that what people are able to do and be (their capabilities) depends not only on themselves but on the wider society. It supports an egalitarian mutual interdependence, rather than relationships in which some people are subordinate to others, or are alienated from others because their only connection is through profit-driven markets.

RETHINKING ECONOMIES, RECOGNIZING UNPAID WORK

Many feminist economists share the values of the human development approach, but they place particular emphasis on rethinking economies to include not only paid work but also nonmarket unpaid work. This unpaid work includes both care for members of families and communities, and also housework and subsistence production, like growing food for family consumption and collecting water and fuel. Most analyses of economies privilege production for the market—try to measure it, increase it, optimize it. The sphere of reproduction is taken for granted, rather like the "traditional sector" in the Lewis model of economic development. Feminist economics has challenged this exclusion, arguing that as well as the economy of the market and the state, we should take account of the unpaid economy in which people produce goods and services for their families, friends, and neighbors on the basis of social obligation, altruism, and reciprocity (and, in some cases, coercion—as expressed in domestic violence, for instance). In this unpaid economy, people produce food and clothing, fetch fuel and water, cook and clean, and take care of others, especially children, the sick, and frail elderly people (see Folbre, 1994, 2001; UNDP, 1995, 1999).

There are two reasons to include the unpaid economy. The first is that it is very important for human well-being. For instance, being required to do too much unpaid work while getting too little care from family and friends jeopardizes the possibility of living a satisfying life. The second is that though the unpaid economy is not properly measured and taken into account in economic analysis and policy, it affects the operations of the paid economy. It affects the quantity and quality of labor supplied for production in businesses, large and small, and the public sector and nongovernmental organizations (NGOs). It affects the quantity and quality of goods demanded from production. Its operations affect the stability of the social framework in which the market and state are embedded.

This interaction has been analyzed in a number of contexts relevant to development, with a particular emphasis on the gender relations that assign most of the responsibility for the supply of unpaid work to women. For instance, in the early 1990s I examined the interaction in the context of structural adjustment programs, arguing that their design implicitly assumed that unlimited supplies of female labor was available to make good any shortfalls in provision of public sector nontradable services (such as health, education, and water and sanitation) and to increase production of exports, while at the same time maintaining household food security and the social fabric of family and community networks (Elson, 1991). Adjustment theory does not confront this implication because it appears to treat labor as a nonproduced means of production and all consumption as discretionary.

Ignoring the implications of macroeconomic changes for the unpaid economy, in which most of the work is done by women, is tantamount to assuming that women's capacity to undertake extra work is infinitely elastic, able to stretch so as to make up for any shortfall in income and resources required for sustaining human beings. However, women's capacity for work is not infinitely elastic, and a breaking point may be reached. There may simply not be enough female labor time available to maintain the quality and quantity of human resources at its existing level This may not have an immediate impact on the level and composition of gross national output, but in the longer run, deterioration in health, nutrition, and education will tend to have adverse impacts on output levels (ibid.).

Further examples of analysis that takes account of the unpaid economy can be found in a special issue of *World Development* on macroeconomics and gender (Cagatay et al., 1995). William Darity (1995) constructed a two-sector model of a gender-segregated, low-income agrarian economy, in which one sector produced crops for export and the other produced subsistence food and care for the family. The model was used to analyze the gender-differentiated effects of one of the keystones of neoliberal agricultural reforms: measures to raise the relative price of export cash crops. The analysis shows how this means extra demand for women's labor in the export sector and extra income for their husbands who control the sale of the crop, given the prevailing pattern of gender relations in both sectors. If women respond to this demand, through some combination of compensation, cooperation, and coercion, output of food and care is liable to fall under reasonable assumptions, with potentially adverse impacts on the health and nutrition of women and children. On the other hand, if women are able to resist the demand, the supply response of the export crop is muted and the devaluation does not have the expected impact (a scenario explored by Warner and Campbell, 2000). Mainstream economics has now admitted that agricultural sector reforms have failed in a large number of countries; however, it continues to ignore the gender dimensions of agricultural production and the role of the unpaid economy in rural areas.

As more comprehensive studies of time use become available for developing countries, it will be possible to carry out richer empirical analyses of the interaction between the paid and the unpaid economies. Some examples that point that way can be found in the special issue of *World Development* on growth, trade, finance, and gender inequality (Grown et al., 2000). Fontana and Wood (2000) present a computable general equilibrium (CGE) model—using actual data to estimate an economy's reaction to external shocks or policy changes—that includes the unpaid economy (labeled "social reproduction"). The model is calibrated for Bangladesh and is used to explore the implications of different trade policy regimes. Lim (2000) examines the effects of the East Asian financial crisis on employment in the Philippines and, though the data on paid work is much richer than on unpaid work, is able to consider some of the interactions between the two in the aftermath of the crisis.

It is important to extend this approach to examining the current global economic crisis. Both women and men will lose jobs, and whether the loss is disproportionately male or female will depend on which sectors of the economy are hardest hit. In economies that produce a lot of garments, for example, it will be women who are hit hardest; in economies that produce a lot of cars, it will be men. Gender-based cultural norms about what is men's and what is women's work mean that men tend not to take up women's work, even if the availability of "men's jobs" decreases. Instead, a more likely outcome is unemployment and underemployment for men and overwork for women, many of whom try to compensate for loss of male income to the family by taking on more informal work, where the pay is very low. It is likely that this will be the effect of the economic crisis in many countries, with women asked to provide the ultimate safety net.

ENTITLEMENT FAILURE AND ECONOMIC SUCCESS

The neoclassical framework for judging how well economies are doing allows feast and famine to coexist without this being regarded as an economic failure. If, given the prevailing distribution of rights to resources, those who are experiencing famine cannot be given more food without reducing the amount available at feasts, then the economy is still judged to be in an optimal position from the perspective of neoclassical economics.

Amartya Sen (1984) challenged this idea by introducing the idea of entitlement failure in his work on famine. In effect, this provides a way of criticizing the prevailing distribution of rights to resources rather than taking it for granted. He defined entitlements as the totality of things a person can have by virtue of her/his rights to resources. What bundle of goods and services a person ends up with will, of course, depend on how s/he exercises these rights, which include rights to inherit and acquire assets including health, strength, skills, and property; rights to use this endowment to produce for one's own consumption or for sale; and rights to goods, service, and financial transfers from the state. Sen's concept of entitlements thus includes both production and distribution as well as legally sanctioned claims on fellow citizens via both market transactions and the state.

Sen argued that many deaths in famines occurred not because there was an overall insufficiency of food in the country as a whole, but because some people were excluded from obtaining food because they could not produce it themselves, could not pay for it in the marketplace, and had no institutionalized claim on the state to provide it for them. They died because of entitlement failure. In his words:

> Most cases of starvation and famines across the world arise not from people being deprived of things to which they are entitled, but from people not being entitled, in the prevailing legal system of institutional rights, to adequate means for survival. (ibid.)

As Fine (1997) points out, although entitlements were defined by Sen on an individual (micro) basis, he also gave the idea a social systemic (macro) dimension, referring to a network of entitlement relations (Sen, 1981). Famine occurred because entitlement failures were endemic in the prevailing social arrangements, so that episodes of bad weather or economic recessions led to a needless loss of people's ability to live a well-nourished life, which could have been prevented by a better system for sharing resources. A one-sided focus on the fall in food output obscured this important fact.

More generally, we might extend the idea of entitlement failures to cover all occurrences when the resources people can obtain through their existing entitlement relations are not sufficient to enable them to live a well-functioning human life: well-nourished, healthy, literate, able to take part in the life of their community, and able to define and pursue their own goals in life. Sen himself has not developed any precise definition of basic or essential functioning, though such an idea of a basic minimum in relation to being well nourished is implicit in his work on famine. Nussbaum (2002) has been less reticent and has proposed various lists for discussion. Economic progress could be judged in terms of success in ensuring that all citizens do achieve at least the essential functioning for a good life. Economies marred by widespread entitlement failures would not be judged a success, even though they might be growing fast.

Sen's entitlement approach has been criticized for putting too much weight on formal legal rights and not paying enough attention to the problems people with little power have in exercising these (Gaspar, 1993). It has also been criticized for leaving out the informal gifts of income and property within families and kinship networks to which people may feel they have moral entitlements (Gore, 1993). Gore suggests a concept of extended entitlements to include all of these ways of acquiring resources, through both moral rules and legal rights.

A key issue relevant to these comments is the importance of examining the processes through which people articulate and claim their entitlements and recognize their responsibilities, both legal and moral. In doing this, however, it is important not to lose sight of the core idea of the exercise of rights. To have an entitlement implies access to an accountable process in which the discretion of decision-makers is limited and in which they can be held to account—for instance, through courts of law. If my access to a resource is at the arbitrary discretion of a public official, or dependent on the favor of a patron, the goodwill of a husband, or the price-fixing power of a monopoly supplier, then I do not get that resource as of right. The notion of rights is at the heart of the notion of entitlements.

Worries are often expressed that a focus on rights and entitlements ignores, minimizes, or undermines reciprocity. These worries are shared by some feminist economists. van Staveren (1996), for instance, argues that an entitlements approach cannot deal satisfactorily with the provision of care for others. She contends that such care can only be partially provided through public and commercial services, suggesting that much of its value comes from it being given as a gift, without immediate recompense, in a context of mutuality. Of course, she recognizes that the reciprocal provision of unpaid care is far from symmetrical, with women providing more and receiving less than men. There needs to be a change to symmetrical reciprocity, in particular a redistribution of responsibilities between men and women. However, a problem with this redistribution is "that it cannot be forced by law or rules, as involuntary care giving would most probably result in bad care" (van Staveren, 1996, p. 6).

I think this problem can be addressed by the construction of entitlements in ways that promote the reduction of unpaid care work for women and promote an increase in unpaid care work by men, even if these changes cannot be prescribed. We need reciprocity as well as rights, but without rights, reciprocity is unlikely to be symmetrical.

In judging the effectiveness of an economic policy regime, we could examine how far the system of entitlement relations that it promotes has adequate safeguards against entitlement failures. Entitlement relations that operate through buying and selling in liberalized markets seem to have the advantage of autonomy; they seem to avoid the problem of dependence, either on the family or the state. However, the independence that markets seem to provide is an illusion, masking a many-sided dependence on people scattered far and wide whose only social bond is the market.

Moreover, such markets are inherently risky and volatile. There is absolutely nothing to guarantee that the prices a person gets for the goods or services he sells (including the labor) will be high enough to enable him to purchase the minimum levels of food, education, and health, let alone the other requirements for a well-functioning life. Nor is it clear who in the market can be held accountable. Responsibility is diffused through many buyers and sellers, none of whom has an overview of the market system, and different decisions made by any one of them acting alone will make no perceptible difference to the outcomes. Everyone can say with truth that they are merely offering the going rate for the good or service in question.

This diffusion of responsibility gives rise to the illusion that the outcome is a result of ineluctable market forces acting beyond human control, whereas in fact it is the result of human decisions to establish a set of entitlement relations that have no provision for mutual scrutiny of interactions of individual decisions and mutual assurance of social security. The only kind of security that markets offer is through the purchase of private insurance, which is beyond the means of those who need it most. This private security is in turn subject to the inherent risks of markets.

Of course, all other kinds of entitlement relations are also subject to risk, but they tend to be more stable and less volatile, and their failure is not so likely to engulf a large number of people simultaneously, as they do in a financial crisis or recession.

Neoclassical economists do recognize that competitive markets are risky, which is why they advocate state provision of narrowly targeted social safety nets. But there are several problems with this kind of residual provision. There may be no minimum standards; access is determined by means tests of various kinds; criteria is often complex and difficult to understand; and public officials may exercise such discretion that the claimant has very few, if any rights, so that the provision is not properly described as an entitlement. The effectiveness of such provision in meeting needs is also limited by the unwillingness of the better-off to pay taxes to finance services that they do not themselves make use of.

A minimal safety-net system accords greater moral value to making claims for resources on other people (outside one's family) via the market rather than via the state. This depends on the illusion (noted earlier) that exercising entitlements via the market constitutes providing for oneself, being independent, not being a burden on others; whereas making claims via the state entails being dependent. This ideological dimension of the neoliberal agenda has considerable social power and may result in a sense of social exclusion on the part of those who have recourse to the safety net. It also results in many people not claiming the resources to which they are legally entitled.

Universal state-based entitlements that are equally available to all members of a society are likely to be more accessible, more transparent, and more effective. Claiming such entitlements is not stigmatizing. It is not taken as a sign of failure or dependency. Universal entitlements are also more secure. While they can be changed by the political process and their real value may be eroded by rising prices, the majority of citizens have a stake in maintaining them, not just poor people. It is clear that the government has responsibility for these entitlements and must be held accountable for them. Such entitlements are a form of mutual assurance against entitlement failure and symbolize citizenship as a social bond. Of course, such entitlements do demand a society willing to pay taxes, but this willingness is more likely to be forthcoming if everyone stands to gain. Obviously the scope and modalities of such a system will depend partly on the wealth of a country. But we should recall that in the 1950s and 1960s, poor countries aspired to provide at least well-functioning basic education and health systems free of charge to all their citizens. Where resources are very scarce, there is a case for some targeting of resources, but within a firmly established system of universal provision of some basic services.

It is very important for women that entitlements are not constructed mainly on the basis of participation in paid work. If they are, as in so many social insurance systems that are based on payment of contributions from cash earnings, women are always at a disadvantage because of their lower rate of participation in the paid economy. Instead, women need systems that confer universal entitlements on everyone living in the jurisdiction.

Human Rights as an Anchor for Entitlements

The best anchor for such entitlements is the international human rights system because this acknowledges that people have human rights by virtue simply of being human and has been agreed by almost every country in the world as a legitimate benchmark. Particularly relevant are the standards set out in the International Covenant on Economic, Social and Cultural Rights (ICESCR) and the Convention on the Elimination of All Forms of Discrimination against Women (CEDAW). Human rights do imply duties. Article 29 of the Universal Declaration of Human Rights states, "Everyone has duties to the community." These duties are clearly specified for states that are parties to the Declaration and to the human rights treaties stemming from it. They are obliged to protect, promote, and fulfill human rights. They are held to account through the mechanisms of the United Nations Commission on Human Rights and other UN mechanisms, and also through the collective action of many social groups that campaign to claim rights and ensure that these do not just remain words without deeds.

The Committee on Economic, Social, and Cultural Rights has begun to identify the core obligations on states arising from the minimum essential levels of the rights to food, education, and health, and it has confirmed that these core obligations are non-derogable. In other words, there is an obligation to fulfill these obligations right now on the part of states and any others in a position to assist. It is not permissible to trade-off provision of the goods and services required to fulfill these rights against an increase in the provision of some other goods and services.

This Committee has also emphasized that:

> Critically, rights and obligations demand accountability: unless supported by a system of accountability, they can become no more than window

dressing. Accordingly, the human rights approach to poverty emphasizes obligations and requires that all duty-holders, including States and international organizations, are held to account for their conduct in relation to international human rights law. In its General Comment No 9, the Committee remarks upon mechanisms of legal accountability for States parties. As for other duty-holders, they must determine which accountability mechanisms are most appropriate to their particular case. However, whatever the mechanisms of accountability, they must be accessible, transparent and effective. (UN, 2001, paragraph 14)

The CEDAW is important for its insistence that women have to be treated as human beings with the same claims to dignity and respect as men. It provides an important corrective to readings of economic and social rights as applicable to male breadwinners and their dependents. The phrasing of the ICESCR does seem to allow that kind of reading, although its Committee has clarified that it should not be read in that way (for further discussion, see Elson and Gideon, 2004).

The idea of human rights is often understood as emphasizing individuality, but it is also at root an idea of mutuality: an idea of the interconnectedness of individual human beings. Writing in the tenth _Human Development Report_, Amartya Sen puts it this way: "To have a particular right is to have a claim on other people or institutions that they should help or collaborate in ensuring access to some freedom" (UNDP, 2000, p. 21).

The idea of human rights rests on a vision of a mutuality of active human beings who make demands of and owe duties to one another. As well as freedom, human rights entail accountability, culpability, and responsibility (UNDP, 2000). Human rights can be seen as claims to "a set of social arrangements—norms, institutions, laws, an enabling economic environment—that can best secure enjoyment of these rights" (ibid., p. 73).

Nor are individual rights necessarily in opposition to collective rights. Collective rights always have to be exercised by persons. The question is who are those persons, through what process they come to have the power to exercise those rights, and how accountable they are to the other members of the collectivity. Individuals can have rights to a say in how collective rights are exercised and to use collective property in stipulated ways. Individual rights should be distinguished from privatized rights, which consist of rights to exclude others from the enjoyment of something and are exercised in the market through buying and selling for commercial gain.

In some parts of the world, women are engaged in a complex reconstruction of the relation between individual rights and collective rights. An important example is Mexico, where indigenous women are intervening in the restructuring of rights at federal, state, and local level. This restructuring is taking place both through amendments to the federal and state constitutions (to some extent influenced by aspects of the human rights system, especially the International Labour Organization Convention on the Rights of Indigenous People), and through the reshaping of so-called "traditional" customary law (*usos y costumbres*), influenced by the new *usos y costumbres* introduced in the Zapatista Autonomous Municipalities. Indigenous women have taken up issues of domestic violence, forced marriage, equal participation in a wide range of political arenas, rights to housing, education, jobs, medical care, and land rights (Hernandez Castillo, 1997; Gutierrez & Palomo, 2000).

Some Mexican researchers have described this as "indigenous feminism," which attempts to protect indigenous people's rights and women's rights at the same time and which sees both as connected sets of individual and collective rights (Hernandez Castillo, 1997; Sierra, 2002). Indigenous women have also been organizing to stake claims to use land for themselves through the notion of collective indigenous rights (Stephen, 2003). There is in Mexico a national indigenous women's network dedicated to getting women's rights enforced through processes of enlarging the autonomy of indigenous communities. These women do not take their culture as static and univalent; instead they strategize to reshape it. They do not see a dichotomy between individual and collective rights; rather, they aim for a new social synthesis.

SOCIAL PRODUCTION, SOCIAL INVESTMENT, SOCIAL CONSUMPTION

In focusing on rights and entitlements, there is a danger that we ignore production and think only about distribution. This would be a mistake. We need to think about what kind of production systems will be supportive of a society that ensures no one suffers entitlement failure. The experience of the last 25 years suggests that it is very difficult, if production is dominated by private production for private profit, to build the kind of mutually supportive and solidaristic entitlement system that is needed. The growth of this domination, fuelled not only by privatization but also by market liberalization that intensifies the competitive advantage of large-scale for-profit producers, has been accompanied by growing inequality and a breakdown of solidarity.

Much more attention needs to be put on social production, investment, and consumption as the drivers of the economy. By "social," I mean a whole range of nonprofit institutions on all scales: cooperatives, credit unions, mutual savings societies, community enterprises, community management of forests and irrigations systems, community kitchens and childcare centers, municipally owned and operated enterprises, not-for-profit enterprises, state-owned enterprises, and all kinds of hybrids built on cooperation between them. For instance, municipalities can give contracts to cooperatives or community enterprises to provide care, cleaning services, and meals for schools. It is important to put the focus on "social," which implies the direct involvement of social groups, rather than "state," which can all too often mean control by a small group of officials.

Social production, investment, and consumption can take account of a wider range of objectives—and, in particular, can take account of non-market relationships—much better than profit-driven production. It is often argued that private production is more responsive to consumer demand, but the response is only to consumers with enough money. It is often argued also that social production will be operated for the benefit of producers not users, but strengthening the rights of users and developing direct links between producers and users can guard against this. Old-style state enterprises and state services were all too often run on a top–down basis. Social production must be operated in ways that allow for diversity and provide a new synthesis between individual and collective rights.

Social production and investment are vital to ensure a sufficient quantity of public goods, that is, goods whose benefits spillover to those who do not directly utilize them. Education is clearly one important example and so are health services, especially those directed to improving maternal and child health or reducing the incidence of infectious diseases. Others are good public transport systems, street lighting and paving, water and sanitation, and clean energy systems. A sustainable climate is one of the most important public goods, as is now becoming recognized. A sustainable system of care is also an important public good. This is something not yet properly appreciated, though in countries with rapidly aging populations or high levels of HIV and AIDS, governments are starting to develop the beginnings of an understanding. Leaving it all to be done unpaid and unsupported by women and girls is not sustainable.

There has been underinvestment in all types of goods and services that we use not as privatized consumers but as members of communities. Instead, economic growth and structural change have been driven by consumerism: private cars, apartments, electrical and electronic goods, based on privately produced communications networks and energy, depleting not conserving the environment, and creating unsustainable climate change.

The crisis should be used as an opportunity to change this, especially in the rich countries that pioneered consumerism and that contribute the most to the environmental crisis. It would be a mistake to think that an adequate response to global recession is to provide incentives for the better-off to go shopping again, even if it is for new, more fuel-efficient cars.

JUST AND DEMOCRATIC PUBLIC FINANCE

Fiscal and monetary policies set some of the key parameters that constrain individual entitlements and provision of public goods. If these policies are inappropriate, there can be macro-level entitlement failure in both markets and public provision. The neoliberal policy agenda prioritizes the danger of systemic entitlement failure through high rates of inflation. "Sound policy" is policy that minimizes this risk. But it downplays the risk of systemic entitlement failure through deflationary bias and embraces a miserly macroeconomics in which budget surpluses (or speedy deficit reduction) and high levels of foreign exchange reserves are seen as the top priority and lower levels of taxation and public expenditure are typically preferred (Elson & Cagatay, 2000). Of course, hyperinflation does erode entitlements, but it is usually the result of populist policies that fail to place sufficient emphasis on increasing revenue. The avoidance of hyperinflation does not entail massive reductions in social provision; rather, it requires building the social capacity to finance adequate levels of social provision.

A major problem in doing this is that macroeconomic policy in neo-classical economics is constructed as something beyond social dialog and public debate. Fiscal and monetary policies are typically a technocratic exercise in short-term balancing of financial flows, with key decisions increasingly handed over to independent central banks that have little political accountability. Bakker (2001) describes a high priesthood of economists wielding mathematical models, carrying the same message to every country as if the truth were carved in stone.

The argument is not that policymakers should not make macroeconomic calculations, but that these should be used as inputs into a democratic deliberative process. Instead of exercising judgment behind closed doors to tweak the results of running models or to decide the implications for policy in the face of an uncertain future, judgment should be exercised in a much more transparent way, with much more public debate. Some innovative approaches are being developed in a number of initiatives on participatory budget processes (Cagatay et al., 2000; for other examples, see http://www.internationalbudget.org).

Gender equality is being addressed through a wide range of gender-responsive budget initiatives in both developed and developing countries, some organized by women outside government and some by women inside government (Budlender, 2000; for numerous examples, see http://www.gender-budgets.org). However, many of these have become sidelined in making calculations of how much funding goes to women's projects or what share of the funding of different programs goes to women and girls. It is vital that gender-responsive budgeting should engage with the overall determination of macroeconomic policy and the degree to which there is adequate support for social investment and provision of public goods.

Until the current global economic crisis, the possibilities of determining macroeconomic policy through an open social dialog in which different interests can exercise voice, and in which entitlement failure and social investment can be explicitly brought into view, was foreclosed not by the technical requirements of macroeconomic policy but by fear of pre-emptive exercise of the exit option by financial capital (Cagatay, 2003; Elson, 2004). The ability to exit ("capital flight") is a result of the deregulation of capital markets. Ironically the openness of capital markets is conducive to an absence of openness in policy discussion, for fear that the wrong signals will be sent and the volatile capital markets will be disturbed. It is difficult to conduct a policy dialog when some of the key players have no stake in the outcome beyond the next few hours (a further reason for controls on international movement of capital).

It is critical that budgeting becomes reoriented to ensure that the new spaces opened up by the crisis are used to promote social investment for social consumption as the driver of economies all over the world. This is better for guaranteeing that there is no entitlement failure, that the unpaid economy and the environment are properly taken into account, and that there is social justice for everyone.

Of course, a just and democratic public finance needs a just and democratic international financial system. A few moves are being made in the right direction, especially the measures to regulate tax havens more effectively and reduce the scope they provide for tax evasion. The Stiglitz Commission has also developed some farsighted proposals for reform. While these are important steps forward, however, by themselves they will not bring about socially just economies. To achieve that also requires changes in the way that goods and services are produced, distributed, and consumed. This chapter has argued that this requires three key actions: recognizing the contribution of the unpaid economy; ensuring there is no entitlement failure; and developing social investment, production, and consumption as the core of the paid economy.

REFERENCES

Bakker, I. (2001). Who built the pyramids? Engendering the new international economic and financial architecture. Paper presented to the International Studies Association Annual Conference, Chicago, February.

Budlender, D. (2000). The political economy of women's budgets in the South. *World Development, 28*(7), 1365–1378.

Cagatay, N. (2003). Gender budgets and beyond: Feminist fiscal policy in the context of globalization. *Gender and Development, 11*(1), 15–24.

Cagatay, N., Elson D., & Grown, C. (Eds) (1995). Gender, adjustment and macroeconomics [Special Issue]. *World Development, 23*(11).

Cagatay, N., Kelik, M., Lal, R., & Lang, J. (2000). *Budgets as if people mattered: Democratizing macroeconomic policies.* New York: United Nations Development Programme (UNDP).

Chang, H. J. (2001). *Breaking the mould: An institutionalist political economy alternative to the neo-liberal theory of the market and the state.* Social Policy and Development Programme Paper No. 6, United Nations Research Institute for Social Development (UNRISD), Geneva.

Darity, W. (1995). The formal structure of a gender-segregated low-income economy. *World Development, 23*(11), 1953–1968.

Elson, D. (1991). Male bias in macro-economics: The case of structural adjustment. In D. Elson (Ed.), *Male bias in the development process* (pp. 164–190). Manchester: Manchester University Press.

———. (1997). Economic paradigms old and new: The case of human development. In R. Culpeper, A. Berry, & F. Stewart (Eds), *Global development fifty years after Bretton Woods: Essays in honour of Gerald K. Helleiner* (pp. 50–71). London: Macmillan.

——— (1999). Theories of development. In J. Peterson & M. Lewis (Eds), *Elgar companion to feminist economics* (pp. 95–105). Aldershot: Edward Elgar.

———. (2001). *For an emancipatory socio-economics.* Draft paper prepared for discussion at the United Nations Research Institute for Social Development (UNRISD) meeting on The Need to Rethink Development Economics, September 7–8, Cape Town, South Africa.

———. (2004). Engendering government budgets in the context of globalization(s). *International Feminist Journal of Politics, 6*(4), 623–642.

Elson, D., & Cagatay, N. (2000). The Social content of macroeconomic policies, *World Development, 28*, 1347–1364.

Elson, D., & Gideon, J. (2004). Organising for women's economic and social rights: How useful is the International Covenant on Economic, Social and Cultural Rights? *Journal of Interdisciplinary Gender Studies, 8*(1 and 2), 133–152.

Elson, D.; & Pearson, R. 1981. Nimble fingers make cheap workers: An analysis of women's employment in third world export manufacturing. *Feminist Review, 7*(Spring), 87–107.

Fine, B. (1997). Entitlement failure? *Development and Change, 28*, 617–647.

Folbre, N. (1994). *Who pays for the kids? Gender and the structures of constraint.* London: Routledge.

———. (2001). *The invisible heart: Economics and family values.* New York: The New Press.

Fontana, M., & Wood, A. (2000). Modeling the effects of trade on women at work and at home. *World Development, 28*(7), 1173–1190.

Gasper, D. (1993). Entitlements analysis: Relating concepts and contexts. *Development and Change, 24*(4), 679–718.

Gore, C. (1993). Entitlement relations and 'unruly' social practices: A comment on the work of Amartya Sen. *Journal of Development Studies, 29*(3), 429–460.

Grown, C., Elson, D., & Cagatay, N. (Eds). (2000). Growth, trade, finance and gender equality [Special Issue]. *World Development, 28*(7).

Gutierrez, M; & Palomo, N. (2000). A woman's eye view of autonomy. In A. Mayor (Ed.), *Indigenous autonomy in Mexico* (pp. 53–82). Copenhagen: International Work Group for Indigenous Affairs.

Hernandez Castillo, R. (1997). Between hope and adversity: The struggle of organized women in Chiapas since the Zapatista rebellion. *Journal of Latin American Anthropology, 3*(1), 102–120.

Lim, J. (2000). The effects of the East Asian crisis on the employment of women and men: The Philippine case. *World Development, 28*(7), 1285–1306.

Nussbaum, M. (2002). Women's capabilities and social justice. In M. Molyneux & S. Razavi (Eds), *Gender justice, development and rights* (pp. 45–78). Oxford: Oxford University Press.

Sen, A. (1981). *Poverty and famines: An essay on entitlement and deprivation.* Oxford: Clarendon Press.

———. (1984). The right not to be hungry. In G. Fløistad (Ed.), *Contemporary philosophy: A new survey* (pp. 343–60). The Hague: Martinus Nijoff.

———. (1999). *Development as freedom.* New York: Knopf Publishers.

Sierra, M. (2002). The challenge to diversity in Mexico: Human rights, gender and ethnicity. Working Paper No. 49, Max Planck Institute for Social Anthropology, Halle.

Stephen, L. (2003). The gendered dynamics of agrarian counter-reform and indigenous rights in Southern Mexico. Paper presented at a conference at the Institute of Latin American Studies, University of London.

UN (United Nations). (2001). *Substantive issues arising in the implementation of the International Covenant on Economic, Social and Cultural Rights: poverty and the International Covenant on Economic, Social and Cultural Rights.* Statement adopted by the Committee on Economic, Social and Cultural Rights, E/C.12/2001/10, United Nations, Geneva.

UNDP (United Nations Development Programme). (1995). *Human development report 1995: Gender and human development.* New York and Oxford: Oxford University Press.

UNDP (United Nations Development Programme). (1999). *Human development report 1999: Globalization with a human face.* New York and Oxford: Oxford University Press.

———. (2000). *Human development report 2000: Human rights and human development.* New York and Oxford: New York and Oxford.

van Staveren, I. (1996). Amartya Sen's entitlement approach and women's poverty. Paper presented at FENN Seminar on Countering the Feminization of Poverty, Utrecht.

Warner, J. M., & Campbell, D. A. (2000). Supply response in an agrarian economy with non-symmetric gender relations. *World Development, 28,* 1327–1340.

2

"Rebooting"* Is Not an Option
Toward Equitable Social and Economic Development

STEPHANIE SEGUINO

Wide gaps in income and well-being—that is, economic inequality between individuals, households, and social groups—conflict with the goal of broadly shared economic prosperity.... It is evident that the policies that have undermined the goals of dignified work, security, and inter-group equality have contributed to the crisis and must be replaced.

INTRODUCTION

Many feminist economists argue that a fundamental aim of economic policymaking should be to ensure the conditions that enable adults to provide for themselves and their families under dignified work conditions. Central to that goal are work opportunities that generate an adequate level of family income and economic stability. The latter is especially important; economic uncertainty and volatility are anathema to the goal of provisioning, not only because these conditions make it difficult for families to provide, save for retirement, and fund children's

---

* "Rebooting" refers to the common practice of hitting the restart button on computers after systems freeze or crash.

21

education, but also because of their contribution to psychological distress that undermines family well-being.

Wide gaps in income and well-being—that is, economic inequality between individuals, households, and social groups—conflict with the goal of broadly shared economic prosperity. Gender inequality, for example, is linked to unequal bargaining power for women in the household and in the paid jobs they hold. This has negative effects on women's agency and children's welfare. Legal inequalities in land ownership rights and access to productive inputs can harm agricultural productivity, as evidence from sub-Saharan Africa shows (Blackden & Bhanu, 1999). Thus gender inequality radiates, producing harmful effects economy-wide.

Racial/ethnic inequality contributes to social and economic exclusion. Apart from the negative effects of that exclusion on the well-being of subordinate ethnic groups, it contributes to a lack of political voice and, equally important, racialized state policies that frequently favor the dominant ethnic group. Accentuated household and individual inequality have similar effects: the dominant economic group (class) is able to wield disproportionate political power, often resulting in government economic policies that further reinforce the existing unequal distribution of income and wealth. The resulting intergenerational effects of inequality are well documented. Where the state fails to act to ensure equalizing distributive policies that provide for children's health and education, children in poor households face circumscribed life chances and income-generating possibilities.

In contrast, a central feature of equitable societies would be that intergroup inequalities are first attenuated and then eliminated over time. Further, economic mobility for children in low-income households would be maximized through state-level policies to ensure adequate social and economic investments. And importantly, the care burden women shoulder, at the expense of achieving material equality with men would be alleviated with the help of state-level policies that support men's care role, complemented by public expenditures on care for children, the elderly, the sick, and people with disabilities.

These basic guidelines offer an evaluative framework for national and international macroeconomic policies. Such policies shape the possibilities for provisioning; they influence both the size of the economic pie and the distribution of the pie itself across racial, ethnic, and gender groups as well as among countries. The right macro-level policies can enable rising living standards; the wrong policies can pitifully restrict families' array of options to provide for their well-being, and may result in a much greater care burden for women, at a heavy cost to their own economic agency and life choices.

This chapter explores the salient well-being outcomes of the set of macroeconomic policies set in motion since the early 1970s, known now as neoliberalism. To anticipate the results of this analysis, a consideration of trends in well-being makes it clear that "rebooting" the global economy—continuation of the same set of neoliberal policies with only minor adjustments—is not a fruitful option. Rather, it is evident that the policies that have undermined the goals of dignified work, security, and intergroup equality contributed to the crisis and must be replaced. As noted by Joseph Stiglitz (2009), "We have huge unmet needs in climate change, in poverty, in an economic system in which there is huge economic capacity…. If you can't solve those problems, that economic system is not functioning the way it should be."

In the penultimate section of this chapter, I offer some illustrative examples of policies for reform of the financial sector that support the goals of an alternative vision. I emphasize the financial sector because of the implications of policy reforms there for broadly shared well-being and equality. I hope that attention to that sector will elicit the interest of feminist economists to develop even more detailed proposals for reform. Armed with comprehensive analyses and policy proposals from a well-being perspective, feminist economists will be situated to assume a seat at national and international decision-making tables so as to have a voice in charting our global economic future.

THE ROOTS OF TODAY'S INEQUALITY AND GLOBAL ECONOMIC STAGNATION

The period 1945–1973 is sometimes fondly referred to as the "Golden Age" of capitalism—golden because, in many countries, wages rose in lockstep with living standards and the rate of economic growth. An era of low unemployment, combined with mild business cycles, provided relatively stable income in both developed and developing countries, underpinned in the former by social safety nets and social insurance programs erected in response to the economic havoc induced by the Great Depression. Governments were on the whole willing to regulate markets, especially the financial sector, so as to provide the conditions for society-wide economic security and job growth. As a result, more families were able to enjoy stable incomes and relative economic security. Indeed, it appeared that policies that permitted a redistribution of income to low-income households also stimulated economic growth, at least in industrialized countries. This win–win relationship can be labeled "equity-led growth," whereby the effect of a more equitable distribution of income stimulates economic growth, employment, and livelihood expansion, while increasing government revenues to fund social and physical infrastructure expenditures that further equalize well-being.

This was also a period when many countries became newly independent, and here, too, there is evidence of relatively rapid economic growth— that is, a growing economic pie and improvements in the quality of life, in part due to public expenditures on social and physical infrastructure that improved health and education.

Although governments had taken measures to promote economic security and to calm the volatility of otherwise erratic markets, their role was under attack by the time of the Organization of the Oil Exporting Countries (OPEC) oil crisis. A shift in macroeconomic policy that emphasized deregulation of markets began to emerge. The new macroeconomic regime of neoliberalism has had as a central goal reduction of the role and reach of government, arguing that an unregulated private sector is more efficient than a regulated economy and government intervention. Central tenets of neoliberal policies have included:

- *Trade liberalization*: Elimination of tariffs on imports and other forms of trade protection.
- *Investment liberalization*: Reduction of restrictions on foreign direct investment.
- *Financial liberalization*: Elimination of restrictions on cross-border movements of money.
- *Exchange rate liberalization*: The shift from fixed to flexible (market-determined) exchange rates.
- *Fiscal discipline*: Restrictions on government deficit spending, even in times of economic crisis.

Other features include deregulation (the elimination of regulations on economic activity, as well as in areas such as anti-discrimination and the environment); flexibilization of labor markets, including the elimination of trade unions; and privatization of basic social services and amenities such as water, electricity, and telecommunications, and the sale of state enterprises.

While the above list might suggest a return to Adam Smith and the full embrace of the "invisible hand"—that is, free and unregulated markets—such has not been the case. The growth of inequality enabled economic elites to use their political strength to further increase their wealth. This wealth helped them to secure political influence, resulting in governments directing economic rents (unearned profits) to them. Two key pieces of evidence exemplify the influence of economic power on the state to enact on the behalf of elites. Perhaps one of the most obvious, in the United States at least, is the impact on the tax rates of the highest income groups. The tax cuts enacted under George W. Bush in 2001 and 2003 disproportionately benefited high-income households. One analysis indicates, for example, that if the tax cuts are extended until 2018, the top 20 percent wealthiest households will receive 74 percent of the tax cuts' benefits, while the poorest 40 percent will receive less than 5 percent of the benefits (Aron-Devine, 2008).

A second example of the growing power of economic elites is reflected in the lobbying power of multinational corporations, whose greater ability to extract profits has come at the expense of the poor in developing countries. Prior to the signing of the Trade Related Agreement on Intellectual Property Rights (TRIPS) in 1994, for instance, pharmaceutical companies in a number of countries held patents for a period of 10 years on medications such as antiretrovirals to treat HIV and AIDS. Patent control essentially confers monopoly rights on the sale of a product, thus driving up the price that can be charged and corporate profits. TRIPS extended patent rights to 20 years for a variety of products, including essential medicines. Though presumably intended to encourage research, TRIPS legislates greater monopoly power in contrast to the neoliberal argument that liberalization is needed to promote competition and efficiency. Essential life-saving drugs have become increasingly expensive, restricting the access of the poor and uninsured (Kawachi & Wamala, 2007). It should be noted, however, that civil society advocates have successfully organized to oppose sanctions imposed by drug companies against some countries (for example, Brazil and South Africa) that permit lower-cost generic production.

TRENDS IN GLOBAL INEQUALITY AND WELL-BEING

Neoliberal proponents have argued that market liberalization and a reduced role for the state will produce more rapid rates of growth through the efficient allocation of resources. Higher per capita incomes, it is asserted, will provide the means for improved living standards and increased revenues for governments to spend on social investment.

Neoliberal "regime change" has, however, failed to yield the predicted improvements in well-being within and across groups. Instead, the new macroeconomics agenda ushered in the "Leaden Age," a period of widespread slowdown in economic growth, downward pressure on wages, and a dramatic increase in inequality. A number of Asian economies—Japan, South Korea, Taiwan, and later China—that refused to adopt wholesale the full array of neoliberal policies were an exception to this rule. They engaged in trade and investment liberalization but in ways that benefited their own economies in terms of technological innovation, employment growth, and stability (Amsden, 1989, 2001; Seguino, 2007; Wade, 1990). The state has played a pivotal role in these countries in managing trade and investment and in moving their economies up the industrial ladder to the production of sophisticated and high-tech goods. Key to growth in these countries has also been the regulation of financial markets, and central banks that adopted policies consistent with the development strategies of the state, allowing targeted investment at subsidized rates.

As the data in Table 2.1 indicate rates of economic growth globally in the neoliberal period are almost half those attained in the previous 20 years. In Heavily Indebted Poor Countries (HIPC), average annual growth rates since 1980 have turned negative, as they have also done in sub-Saharan Africa in general.

Table 2.1 Average annual per capita gross domestic product (GDP) growth rates, 1960–2005

Regions and groups	1960–1980	1980–2005
East Asia	3.5	6.6
Latin America and the Caribbean	2.9	0.7
Middle East and North Africa	5.5	3.7
South Asia	1.3	3.6
Sub-Saharan Africa	1.6	–0.1
Heavily Indebted Poor Countries	0.5	–0.2
Middle-income Countries	3.4	2.3
OECD	3.7	2.1
World	2.6	1.4

Source: Author's calculations from World Bank (2008).
Note: OECD is the Organisation for Economic Co-operation and Development.

Moreover, the trend has been unambiguously toward worsening income inequality since the 1970s (ILO, 2008; Milanovic, 2002, 2007). This movement is in evidence both within and between countries. A few statistics highlight the extent of the growing income gap. One measure of global inequality is the ratio of incomes of the richest 20 percent of households compared to the poorest 20 percent. That ratio in 1960 was 30:1; in just 45 years, it rose to 103:1 (see Table 2.2).

Table 2.2   Ratio of incomes of richest 20 percent of households to poorest 20 percent

Year	Ratio
1820	3:1
1870	7:1
1913	11:1
1960	30:1
1991	61:1
1997	74:1
2005	103:1

Source: Ortiz (2008), from United Nations Development Programme (UNDP) data.

Figure 2.1 suggests that the growth of inequality accelerated in the late 1980s, coinciding with the expanded adoption of neoliberal policies across the globe.

Figure 2.1   Accelerating inequality: The richest 20 percent share of global income relative to the poorest 20 percent

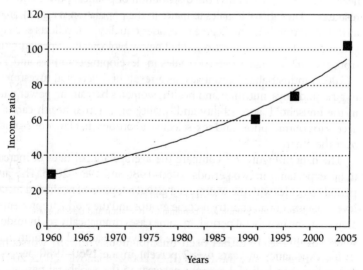

Source: Author's calculations with data from Ortiz (2008).
Note: The exponential trend line is estimated from the data, with an R^2 of 0.981.

Rich countries have not escaped these trends. In the United States, for example, the median family income rose at an annual rate of less than 1 percent a year between 1980 and 2007, only one-third as much as median incomes had risen in the previous 27 years. In contrast, the incomes of the top 0.01 percent of American families increased sevenfold during that same period (Krugman, 2009).

Chief Executive Officer's (CEO) pay in the United States shows a similar trend. While the wages of workers have stagnated, CEO's pay has increased dramatically over the last three decades: its ratio to average worker pay rose from 42:1 in 1980 to 500:1 in 2008 (Anderson et al., 2006; ILO, 2008).

GDP and other income measures are sometimes criticized on the grounds that income is a means to an end, and that to better understand trends in well-being we should measure the ends themselves. Three measures of well-being are helpful in painting a portrait of global progress: life expectancy, infant mortality rate, and the ratio of females to males in the population (see Weisbrot et al., 2008). Trends in life expectancy and infant mortality rates tell us something about the level of public investments in social infrastructure (health, education, care services, and so forth); subsidiary (positive or negative) effects of economic growth on health; and, more generally, the distribution of political power and thus resources. The ratio of females to males in the population is a good proxy indicator of trends in the degree of gender equality as it reflects society's valuation of females. The ratio can fall below biologically expected ratios (roughly 102.5 females per 100 males in developing countries and 105 to 100 in industrialized countries) as a result of differential investments in girls' and boys' nutrition and health, women's bargaining power within the household, accessibility and quality of maternal health care and access to contraception, and sex-selective abortions that favor one gender over the other.

The data in Figure 2.2 compare the average annual rates of increase in life expectancy in two periods: 1960–1980 and 1980–2006. The latter period coincides with the widespread global adoption of neoliberal macro-level policies. For all country income groups and the world, improvement slowed in the neoliberal period, in some cases dramatically so. In middle-income countries, for example, while the average annual rate of increase in life expectancy in years was 2 percent in the 1960–1980 period, it fell to less than half of 1 percent per year in the neoliberal period. We might expect that rates of improvement would slow for industrialized countries with already elevated life expectancy, due to biological limits.

Figure 2.2 Rate of average annual increase in life expectancy, 1960–1980 and 1980–2006, by country income group

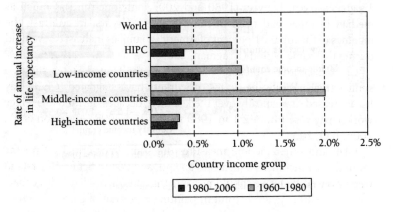

Source: Author's calculations with data from World Bank (2008).
Note: HIPC is Highly Indebted Poor Countries. Countries are categorized according to World Bank lending categories, based on countries' per capita gross national income. Low income is USD 975 per capita or less, and high income is USD 11,906 per capita.

But we would anticipate continued progress in lower-income countries. As the data in Figure 2.2 shows, however, the rate of improvement slowed significantly in lower-income countries, while remaining relatively stable between the two periods in high-income countries.

The infant mortality rate data in Figure 2.3 tells a similar story: rates of reduction in infant mortality have slowed in most regions, even in high-income countries. Only low-income countries managed to continue to reduce infant mortality rates in the 1980–2006 period at a similar pace to the earlier period (data for 1960–1980 are lacking for middle-income countries).

Progress toward gender equality also appears to have suffered during the neoliberal period, when measured as the share of females to males in the population. Figure 2.4 shows the percentage change in the ratio of females to males in the population for countries at varying income levels and across geographic regions, as well as for three rapidly growing Asian economies: China, India, and South Korea. This story—in some ways an astounding one, given the rise in the ratio of female-to-male educational attainment and employment during this period—indicates that the number of women as a ratio to men has fallen in most regions of the world and

Figure 2.3 Rate of average annual decline in infant mortality rates, 1960–1980 and 1980–2006

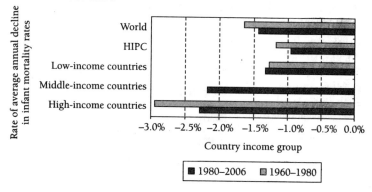

Source: Author's calculations with data from World Bank (2008).

Figure 2.4 Changes in the ratio of females to males (difference between average ratio in 1960–1980 and 1981–2006)

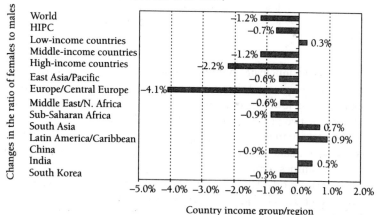

Source: Author's calculations with data from World Bank, 2008 (CD-ROM).
Note: The change in the ratio is calculated as the female-to-male population ratio, averaged across 1981–2006, minus the ratio averaged across the previous period, 1960–1980. South Asia includes Afghanistan, Bangladesh, Bhutan, India, Maldives, Nepal, Pakistan, and Sri Lanka.

countries at various income levels. The only exceptions to this negative trend are Latin America and the Caribbean and South Asia. In Europe and Central Europe, the decline has been especially precipitous.

The overall sex ratio is determined by sex ratios at birth and mortality rates by gender and age; given this, caution should be used in making cross-country or regional comparisons. Comparisons of trends over time, however, can be useful. The causes of declines in sex ratios from 1960–1980 to 1981–2006 are varied and include different rates of out-migration, sex-selective abortion, differential access to health care and nutrition, HIV and AIDS, and suicide rate differentials, among other causes. Given the way the ratio is calculated, it could also fall if male improvements in life expectancy exceeded women's; this occurred only in sub-Saharan Africa. Anderson and Ray (2010) found that a large number of missing women in India die as adults, while the majority of missing women in China are due to prenatal fetal deaths. Table 2.3 shows the female-to-male ratio in both periods by country income level and region.

Table 2.3 Ratio of females to males in the population, 1960–1980 and 1980–2006

	1960–1980	1980–2006	Change
World	0.992	0.980	-.012
HIPC	1.015	1.008	-.007
Low-income countries	0.955	0.957	.003
Middle-income countries	0.994	0.982	-.011
High-income countries	1.042	1.020	-.022
East Asia and Pacific	0.959	0.953	-.006
Europe and Central Europe	1.118	1.079	-.039
Middle East and North Africa	0.981	0.976	-.005
Sub-Saharan Africa	1.022	1.013	-.008
South Asia	0.921	0.927	.007
Latin America and Caribbean	1.001	1.010	0.009

Source: Author's calculations with data from World Bank (2008).

FINANCIAL LIBERALIZATION: AN UNDERMINING FORCE FOR GENDER EQUALITY AND WELL-BEING

I turn now to a more microscopic focus on the impact of financial liberalization. Because of its central role in the expansion of inequality and concomitant deterioration of progress toward improving well-being, this aspect of neoliberalism merits more attention.

Many years ago, economist John Maynard Keynes warned of the economic crises and instability created by financial liberalization, underscoring the tendency toward irrationality in decision making and perverse incentives that contribute to manipulation by insiders. The 1929 stock market crash and subsequent Great Depression were painful examples of these tendencies. Governments implemented a series of financial regulations in the wake of that catastrophe, including capital controls and the adoption of fixed exchange rates. The regulations were intended to maintain the health of the financial sector and to prevent excessive risk taking on the part of financial institutions. They also enabled countries to use fiscal and monetary policy to manage the level of economic activity and to prevent excessive volatility in prices, including exchange rates.

After a relatively long stable period after World War II, the 1970s witnessed the beginning of financial deregulation in the global North. In the United States, its roots were linked to the breakdown of the Bretton Woods agreement, resulting in the shift from fixed to flexible exchange rates, which exacerbated price fluctuations. Second, the inflation of the 1970s lowered real (inflation-adjusted) interest rates, inducing financial firms to find ways to circumvent regulations that limited their profit-making opportunities.

Government regulators and policymakers seemed prepared to ratify the desires of the financial sector. The United States played a lead role in this global shift, since its financial sector policies are often used as a model by other countries. The Glass–Steagall Act of 1933, which had regulated banks so as to separate investment and commercial banking activities, had been gutted by 1999 due to heavy lobbying by the financial sector. As a result, it became easier for commercial banks to engage in speculative financial activities, thus opening the financial sector up to greater volatility and risk, with potentially disastrous effects for the real economy, that is, people's livelihoods, jobs, and incomes.

In lockstep with the emergence of neoliberal economic policies and trends toward deregulation in the United States, countries across the globe have increasingly eliminated restrictions on capital mobility, making it easier for wealth holders to move money across borders. Wealth holders are now relatively free to "shop" the globe over for the highest rates of return on their investments, with little or no control on speculative behavior (countries that do have capital controls, regulating the speed at which money flows across borders include Chile, China, Malaysia, South Korea, and Taiwan). Neoliberals justify such deregulation by arguing that liberating the financial sector from regulations will allow capital to flow to investments yielding the highest rate of return; they equate this with the efficiency of investment. That is, capital will magnetically be attracted to the winners, as measured by high profits and thus high rates of return on investments, and will shun unprofitable, low-yielding projects.

A flaw in this analysis is the failure of neoliberals to differentiate between speculative and productive innovation-inducing investments. The former are destabilizing and costly to those who do not share in the profits; the latter produce beneficial spillover effects to the rest of the economy by potentially raising productivity growth and thus incomes.

Unfortunately, financial liberalization has created the condition for a surge in the types of short-term speculative investments that led to the Great Depression. The downsides of liberalization have been severe, with people increasingly finding their livelihoods determined by the whims and caprices of wealth holders. Apart from shifting the negative effects of speculative behavior onto those least able to navigate economic turmoil, the overall effects on national economies have been negative. Evidence of the inefficiency and waste associated with speculative investment can be found in the global economic growth slowdown since the 1980s (see Table 2.1). This slowdown is exactly the opposite outcome that neoliberals predicted would occur with financial liberalization.

Equally worrying and detrimental is the increase in wealth holders' bargaining power vis-à-vis governments. Now free to roam the globe in search of the highest rate of return on their investments, they play one capital-starved country off against another, frequently demanding concessions such as tax cuts that boost their profits. But their behavior imposes huge social costs.

I would like to trace out more explicitly the widespread and negative effects of unregulated capital flows on the macro economy. This is an important exercise because these effects are not immediately obvious if we only consider the impact on investment. Thus, it is important to look beneath the surface at subsidiary impacts to understand how they link to broadly shared well-being.

First, wealth holders prefer low rates of inflation. Low inflation ensures that inflation-adjusted returns on investment (the rate of return on the investment less the inflation rate) are high, which is equivalent to saying that the profits derived from owning money rise. Economists call profits obtained from holding wealth "rentier" income, rentiers being wealth holders. Epstein (2005) provides evidence that rentier income has risen substantially in the neoliberal period.

As a result, when finance is deregulated, countries competing to attract the pool of global capital are forced to take steps to quell fears of inflation (even if those fears are irrational). To do this, central banks have adopted inflation-targeting policies—in many cases, attempting to keep inflation close to zero. This goal perforce reduces their flexibility to use monetary policy to ensure adequate levels of employment, instead bolstering the profits of wealth holders. Inflation targeting is a case where ideology has trumped economic evidence. Central banks, in setting a low inflation target, argue that low inflation is required to stimulate growth. And yet a growing body of research, including the work of World Bank economist Michael Bruno, has demonstrated that inflation below 20–40 percent does not have a negative effect on growth, although the evidence does suggest that a policy focus on low inflation contributes to a redistribution of income to the wealthy (see, for example, Pollin & Zhu, 2006).

In order to lower inflation, central banks raise interest rates, thereby causing the cost of borrowing to rise. The result is that businesses (especially small firms) and households find it more costly to obtain loans. The net effect of higher interest rates is to cause economic and job growth to slow or turn negative.

Economists dub the cost of cutting inflation in terms of its effects on employment "the sacrifice ratio"—and it should be clear the sacrifice is the livelihood of low-and middle-income families to the benefit of wealth holders. In short, the cost of reducing inflationary pressures through monetary policy is the job and livelihood of ordinary people, worsening the unequal distribution of wealth and income.

The shortage of employment and livelihood opportunities has damaging effects on a household's ability to provide for its members. The viability of small businesses—including informal sector self-employment enterprises—suffers as well, because when jobs are in short supply, too few people have the income to spend on goods and services.

In a number of countries, women suffer disproportionately from job shortages, in part because gender norms continue to designate men as the legitimate "breadwinners." Data from the 2005–2008 wave of the World Values Survey for a sample of 65 countries find that 36.2 percent of those surveyed agree with the prompt "When jobs are scarce, men have more right to a job than women" (WVS, 2009). Women are also disproportionately concentrated in temporary, contingent jobs, suggesting a structural reason why they are more vulnerable to job loss during economic downturns.

A second means by which liberalization produces negative economy-wide effects is through the impact on government spending and fiscal policy. To enhance their credibility with wealth holders, many govern-ments have been forced to reduce their budget deficits. This is in response to the fact that wealth holders link such deficits to potential inflation. Again, the link may be real or imagined. Financial markets assume that budget deficits lead to inflation, perhaps under the assumption that output is fixed, so with more government spending—that is, with more money chasing too few goods—the only effect will be higher prices. This stance ignores that government spending can raise productivity and lower prices of production, and thus is not inflationary. Moreover, most government deficit spending occurs in the context of widespread unemployment, indicative of a great deal of unused capacity in the economy to raise output without inflation. In effect, due to financial liberalization, wealth holders across the globe have gained (undemocratic) veto power over a country's domestic fiscal and monetary policy, and by extension, long-term growth possibilities.

This is a debilitating constraint since government expenditures, even if funded by deficit spending, can improve health outcomes, educational attainment, the conditions of roads, and communications, to name just a few benefits. Expenditures on water and sanitation can make it easier for adults to provide caring labor for their families, a burden most heavily borne by women. Such gender-equalizing expenditures have the benefit of "crowding in" private expenditures—that is, they tend to lower the costs of production, given enough time, and raise the profitability of productive investment. Thus government expenditures, even if funded by borrowing, can reduce inflationary pressures in the longer run.

But financial markets that are liberalized suffer from "short-termism." Due to financial market deregulation, wealth holders engage in hyperac-tive speculative behavior, with capital able to move abruptly from one country to another instead of acting as "patient" capital, invested for the long term. The mobility of financial capital in response to deficit spend-ing short-circuits the beneficial effects that might ensue in time. It should be clear from this discussion that a short-term speculative focus benefits wealth holders, but it imposes huge costs on ordinary people. In contrast, long-term, patient capital can generate profits both for investors and for society as a whole.

A third effect of liberalization is the increased likelihood of financial panics. More common in the age of elimination of capital controls, panics can lead to rapid capital outflows, sharp declines in asset prices, bankrupt-cies, and recession. The Asian financial crisis of 1997 provides evidence of such effects (see Box 2.1).

Box 2.1 The effects of financial panic on Thailand

Considered to be on sound macroeconomic ground and a rising star in the Asian miracle, Thailand was the recipient in the early 1990s of large capital inflows (that is, financial investments that included loans by foreign banks to domestic banks, and direct investments by wealth holders in financial assets). It looked like a good investment prospect. Exchange rates were fixed, so foreign investors felt secure that the value of their investment would not decline as a result of devaluation of the Thai currency, the baht.

By mid-1997, however, Thailand had developed a trade imbalance—it was importing more than it was exporting—a situation that cannot continue for too long without provoking unease in financial markets. Many foreign investors saw this trade imbalance as evidence of an impending devaluation of the currency (so as to make exports less expensive and imports more expensive). It does not matter whether that assessment was correct or incorrect. What matters is that large investors sold off their Thai assets, exchanging the baht for dollars, yen, and euros, and driving down its value. The central bank struggled to maintain the value of the baht, but ultimately could not. The Thai currency was allowed to float (that is, instead of its value being maintained by the central bank, it became market-determined). As a result, its value fell 40 percent relative to the dollar in just a few weeks. Some banks that had borrowed from foreign banks in dollars went bankrupt; others were forced to call in bank loans owed by domestic firms, causing a wave of business bankruptcies, with a widespread increase in lay-offs. Moreover, due to the lower value of the baht, firms that relied on imported goods for production suffered a dramatic increase in costs, leading them to either close their doors and lay-off more workers or raise their prices. Thus, the panic led to not only the destruction of jobs but also inflation.

The gender effects of financial crises have been well-documented (Buvinic, 2009; Lim, 2000; Seguino, 2010; Singh & Zammit, 2002; Sirimane, 2009). Women are disproportionately affected for several reasons. Because recessions are accompanied by job losses and men are seen as the "breadwinners," women can experience higher rates of lay-offs. This is exacerbated by women's concentration in precarious jobs—temporary, part-time, contingent, or sub-contracting employment—and they are structurally likely to experience greater decline and fluctuation in earnings, especially in developing countries (Betcherman & Islam, 2001).

The most recent financial crisis that began in the United States in 2008 and then spread to the rest of the world is instructive with regard to the distributional effects of deregulation. Liberalization contributed to a wave of mergers, with the banking industry becoming increasingly concentrated, particularly in OECD countries. This consolidation not only meant fewer banks and thus less healthy competition, it also led to a preference on the part of the remaining large banks to fund wealthy borrowers, to the exclusion of smaller and less collateralized segments of the population, largely women.

A perverse exception to this trend, of course, is the targeting of subprime loans to people of color and female-headed households in the United States. The loan conditions, however, could be considered predatory. That is, many of these loans were originated under unfair, deceptive, or fraudulent practices. What I have described is a system of dual credit markets, one for the rich at favorable rates, and one for people of color and majority women. This has rightly been termed "financial apartheid" in recognition of the racial effects, although the gender effects should also be underscored (Montgomerie & Young, 2009). The trends in the United States offer an example of the negative distributional effects of the state's withdrawal from setting a credit strategy that can lead to rising living standards for all income groups, not just the wealthiest strata.

It should also be noted that the 2008 recession in the United States, induced by the subprime mortgage crisis, initially led to men losing jobs at a higher rate than women. This is because the first and hardest-hit industries were construction and durables manufacturing, industries that are male-dominated there in terms of employment. The full effects of the crisis on gendered unemployment may not be fully apparent, however. Many states are facing budget deficits and have plans to or have already laid off state workers. Education is particularly hard hit, as evidence from two major cities, Detroit and Los Angeles, demonstrates. School districts in these cities are reported to be planning lay-offs of 600 and 2,000 employees, respectively. Because women are concentrated in education and other publicly funded services (for example, health and childcare), state budget cuts are likely to disproportionately fall on women in the fugure. This suggests that the net gender effects in terms of employment may weigh more heavily on women over time.

Apart from the effect on access to paid work, the disproportionate impacts of crises on women—and the current crisis is no exception—are particularly evident in unpaid labor. As family incomes fall and public services are cut, families have to mobilize to provide care services that had formerly been purchased in the market (for example, prepared meals) or provided by government (for example, home health care aides). These tasks are gendered because women provide the bulk of caring labor and their work burden will rise disproportionately during times of economic crisis.

Further, as economist Sharmika Sirimane (2009, p. 5) notes:

When societies are in danger of collapse, for example, during severe economic turmoil as experienced by some Asian countries in 1997, there is evidence of significant rises in suicide and crime rates; abuse and violence against women; and ethnic tensions.... Women bear the brunt of these social fallouts.

The 2008 financial crisis is only the latest incarnation of a series of banking crises that have become deeper and more widespread since the 1970s, as evidenced by events in Mexico in 1994 and Asia in 1997. The most recent crisis, perhaps more so than the others, demonstrates that it is not financial liberalization alone that has undermined the well-being of ordinary citizens. Two other key factors are also implicated: the increased freedom of corporations to respond to local cost pressures by relocating factories overseas or outsourcing production; and, connected to this (as discussed earlier), growing income inequality in most countries across the globe (see Table 2.2). The mobility of corporations has weakened the bargaining power of workers, leading to a slowdown in wage growth and, in some cases, an absolute decline in real wages.

The growing "footlooseness" of multinational corporations has negatively affected wage growth in not only high-income but also semi-industrialized economies (Seguino, 2007). Women in various parts of the world have been particularly negatively affected because they are concentrated in just the kinds of labor-intensive export firms that are mobile.

This creates a macroeconomic problem: as wages fall, or wage growth slows, so does workers' consumption. Thus, the central predicament the global economy faces is one of insufficient global demand. Without sufficient buying power on the part of workers, businesses have little motivation to invest, expand output, or create jobs.

In the United States, a growing number of low- and middle-income households relied on borrowing to maintain their living standards as their wages were squeezed. The consequences of this are apparent in the subprime mortgage crisis. Unsustainable credit expansion was one way economic growth continued in the face of inequality. The wave of foreclosures in the United States, however, was a symptom of the bigger problem of stagnating incomes for workers and debt-financed consumption.

This summary of the effects of neoliberal policies on distribution and the incomes of ordinary citizens underscores that hitting the "reboot" button on the global economy will not work. That much is clear. But what is the alternative? The preceding analysis holds the seeds of an alternative policy agenda to rectify the negative effects of the global economic crisis. Key features of this are to: first, focus on full employment policies; second, increase the availability of credit to disadvantaged groups, including farmers, women, and ethnic minorities; and third, seek to resolve the problem of unequal income distribution that has led to insufficient demand. These three goals highlight the way forward.

ALTERNATIVE STRATEGIES: CREDIT POLICY THAT PROMOTES GENDER EQUALITY AND BROADLY SHARED WELL-BEING

The financial sector is an instrumental target for policies aimed at achieving the goals of full employment, economic growth, equitable income and wealth distribution, and economic stability. Numerous progressive economists have detailed mechanisms for its re-regulation. Proposals aim at dampening the tendency for the emergence of banks that are "too big to fail" and limiting the risk of system failure, that is, bank panics and asset bubbles such as occurred with the dot.com bubble of the 1990s and in the housing market in the 2000s (Crotty & Epstein, 2008; Morgan, 2009; Palley, 2008). But more is needed to promote well-being and gender equality. Several examples of policies that focus on provisioning, stability, and equality are given in the following lines. A key quality of any such policy would be to shift incentives that encourage speculative financial activities to support for long-term, patient investment. The maldistribution of credit also needs to be explicitly addressed. Complementary policies outside financial sector reforms are also important to promote well-being for ordinary people. For an example of a progressive, that is, equitable, proposal for economic recovery and financial reconstruction, see PERI (2009).

Central Banks as Engines of Employment Growth

Central banks abandoned their role of promoting employment growth and livelihood generation during the neoliberal era. Instead, their focus on inflation targeting has starved subordinate groups of badly needed credit. These groups, often overlapping, include people of color in ethnically divided societies, women, small labor-intensive enterprises, and the self-employed. A reformulated role for central banks should be focused on job creation and livelihood stimulus. In order to expand employment opportunities, central banks could utilize expansionary monetary policy, development banking, and credit subsidies. (For more on reform of central banks and monetary policy, see, Crotty & Epstein, 2008; Epstein, 2006; Palley, 2008.)

To undertake this effort, governments would have to begin by outlining national goals for investment. A comprehensive development banking plan focused on job expansion in high unemployment countries might include subsidized credit to small-scale agriculture, small- and medium-sized businesses, and large-scale businesses that can demonstrate their ability to promote significant increases in employment relative to their total spending. Women's enterprises and cooperatives could be targeted for such subsidies, and the cost to the public budget would be limited given women's strong track record in loan repayment. The set of goals outlined by the government would then determine the central bank's credit policy.

An example of credit policy tools that could be employed to attain a country's development goals is the combination of government loan guarantees with asset portfolio requirements—requiring banks to direct a certain percentage of their loans to targeted activities. (See Pollin et al., 2006 for an application of this approach to the case of South Africa.) The loan guarantees induce banks to lower their interest rates, since the government has agreed to absorb some of the risk of the loans. The lower interest rate makes credit more accessible to some borrowers. Social benefits are achieved when credit is directed to activities that stimulate job creation and raise productivity.

Capital Management Techniques for Economic Stability

Financial liberalization is one of the root causes of the increased economic volatility observed over the last three decades. Central banks can help stabilize their economies through the use of capital management techniques that help reduce the variability of financial flows, especially those associated with short-term portfolios or speculation. A good example of the benefits of applying capital controls is Malaysia, which was, as a result, one of the first countries to recover from the Asian financial crisis. Other countries that have adopted related techniques to regulate cross-border flows of capital and regulate domestic banks, with respect to external transactions (that is, transactions with foreign lenders), are Chile, China, Colombia, and Taiwan (Epstein et al., 2004).

There is a further benefit to capital management techniques. Developing countries have been forced, as a consequence of volatility, to hold high levels of foreign reserves in order to self-insure against a financial crisis. Reserves drain the economy by restricting the ability of governments to spend aid and loan money on the physical and social infrastructure needed to boost the domestic economy, create jobs, and invest in services to benefit poor households, and in particular, to reduce women's unpaid care burden. Capital controls help to alleviate this leakage of needed resources from the economy.

Currency Transactions Taxes and Social Insurance

A very small currency transactions tax (CTT) can provide resources to generate a pool of funds to be used for social insurance. This source of funding has several benefits. Globally, approximately USD 3 trillion is traded in foreign exchange markets daily, and only a very small percentage—less than 5 percent—is to facilitate trade. Speculative currency transactions increase financial and macroeconomic volatility, imposing costs on households not party to the transactions, especially in times of crisis. A second channel by which currency trading produces social costs, as noted above, is the higher level of foreign exchange reserves countries have been forced to hold to self-insure against a speculative attack. The opportunity cost of those reserves is roughly 1 percent of GDP.

A CTT would be similar to a pollution tax in the sense that it seeks to discourage behavior that can have negative social effects, but the cost of which is not captured in the existing cost of trading (and in any case is not fully borne by trading parties). The CTT would offer a disincentive to engage in short-term speculative transactions, and estimates of the response of trading to a modest tax are on the order of –0.43. Such a low tax may not quell speculative cross-border flows of money, however, suggesting that this option should be adopted in consultation with capital management techniques discussed earlier (Grabel, 2003). Rich countries would generate the bulk of the tax revenues and, more generally, the tax would be highly progressive.

Tax revenues generated from a global CTT could be pooled and earmarked for a variety of developmental purposes, including public investments in water and sanitation, a global insurance fund to respond to developing country budgetary constraints in times of economic crisis, and achieving the Millennium Development Goals (MDGs). The project of establishing a CTT will require international cooperation, and it should be at the top of the list of actions by developed economies as a means to fund social insurance, enhance macroeconomic stability, and discourage unproductive speculative financial activity by shifting the cost of the insurance to those who create systemic risk.

A global CTT could be a useful source of revenue to target gender-equalizing expenditures. Proposals for CTT rates vary from 0.005 percent to 0.25 percent, generating between USD 35 and USD 300 billion in revenues a year. Grown et al. (2006) estimate the cost of interventions specific to MDG 3 (on gender equality and the empowerment of women) and gender-mainstreaming in low-income countries at USD 47 billion per year, with an expenditure stream extending for five years. That amount could easily be funded by a CTT, with remaining funds used for a global insurance fund and other agreed upon investments in developing countries' physical and social infrastructure.

A CTT would make tax avoidance legal and socially useful as currency speculators could avoid the tax by reducing their transactions, a response that would have beneficial effects on families, especially low- and middle-income families, as well as women and people of color.

The State's Role in Maintaining Full Employment

The Great Depression taught us in no uncertain terms that capitalist economies are inherently unstable and, indeed, irrationally erratic. Since that time, Keynesian demand-management policies were routinely adopted by governments of a wide array of political leanings—until the 1970s, that is. Those policies entailed "leaning against the wind." In other words, during economic downturns governments would increase spending on goods and services to soften the blow of unemployment and recession, and conversely, cut their spending during inflationary periods when business and household spending exceeded the ability of the economy to produce. During the former, government budget deficits build up, and during the latter, surpluses amass, allowing the national debt to be paid down.

A return to these counter-cyclical policies is needed on a global scale. To be sure, industrialized countries have had no difficulty in adopting such policies in response to the current crisis because they have the fiscal space—the ability to borrow in order to deficit spend, due to credibility among lenders. But the IMF in particular has leaned heavily in the opposite direction via the conditionalities it imposes on poor countries that must borrow from it, rather than from private capital markets, during crises. Instead of supporting increases in government spending as a response to economic downturns, the IMF has required budget reductions in a number of developing and transition countries—for example, in Bosnia and Herzegovina, Djibouti, Ghana, Latvia, Mali, and Republic of the Congo, among others (Weisbrot et al., 2009). Apart from the irony that this is the opposite policy that rich countries are permitted to adopt, the costs in terms of lost services and employment are painfully high among those who have the least savings and assets to weather economic storms. Reining in the IMF, and tempering if not eliminating its ability to impose conditionalities that strangle growth and recovery, needs to be part of any humane global economic architecture that emerges from this crisis.

But that is not enough. Government spending can usefully be used to reduce inflationary pressures, especially in developing countries where the origins of the problem often lie with supply bottlenecks, not with citizens on a "consumption binge." A poorly understood fact is that the causes of inflation, especially in developing countries, are often on the supply side of the economy, not on the demand side. Inflation targeting is not the appropriate tool to address the source of a supply side problem. Targeted spending to reduce bottlenecks—in physical infrastructure, roads, and communications, as well as social infrastructure, such as spending on public health—can reduce production costs and therefore inflation.

Expenditures aimed at reducing their care burden, including fetching fuel and water, and again, public health expenditures, can provide women with more time to spend in income-generating activities to the benefit of families and especially children. This linkage is due to women's tendency to spend a larger share of their income on children than men do (UN Millennium Project, 2005). Policies that improve women's economic bargaining power in the household thus reverberate with beneficial effects on children. The productivity of the labor force improves and, as a result, costs of production fall, reigning in inflationary pressures. This implies the need not only for a return to the government's role in stabilizing the economy, but also for gender-enabling expenditures that improve women's bargaining power, thus promoting gender equality.

CONCLUSION

A fundamental guideline in economic policy-making should be that it ultimately serves the needs of ordinary people who are working hard to provide for themselves and their families. That goal is undermined by inequality and economic insecurity. In the wake of the global financial crisis that has now turned into a serious crisis for millions around the world, hitting the restart button and returning to the policies of the last three decades will not work. The roots of that crisis are traced to a variety of aspects of neoliberal policies, and in particular to investment and financial liberalization. Both have undermined the ability of the state to adopt equity-enhancing policies, to regulate, to tax, and to spend to ensure a social safety net and economic stability.

A transformative response to the crisis requires regulation of the financial sector and reforms that make key monetary institutions function on behalf of sustainable economic development and growth. The alternative way forward, described in this chapter, is one in which financial apartheid is ended, with adequate sources of capital delivered to those disadvantaged by neoliberalism, including women. Re-establishment of the state's role as an entity that facilitates provisioning, equality, and stability is the key to this shift. A step in this direction is the reregulation of capital, including controls on cross-border movements of money, and a reformed role for central banks.

Feminists, and in particular feminist economists, have much to contribute to the elucidation of detailed policies that follow these broad contours but take account of local conditions. For example, a central bank lending agenda centered on well-being will differ depending on whether an economy is heavily dependent on agriculture or not, the distribution of women and men in the labor market, and the degree of supportive institutions such as cooperatives. Similarly, details of the structure and allocation of a global social insurance fund derived from CTTs are necessary to give traction to this alternative.

All of these proposals are inconsistent with a return to the neoliberal agenda. Although feminists have only begun to venture into the territory of macroeconomic and financial policy, this moment represents an opportunity to shape a global economy that is consistent with the goals of dignified opportunities to adequately provision for our families, equality, and economic stability.

REFERENCES

Amsden, A. (1989). *Asia's next giant: South Korea and late industrialization.* New York: Oxford University Press.

———. (2001). *The rise of the "rest": Challenges to the West from late-industrializing economies.* Oxford: Oxford University Press.

Anderson, S., Benjamin, E., Cavanagh, J., & Collins, C. (2006). Executive excess 2006: defense and oil executives cash in on conflict. Washington, DC: Institute for Policy Studies. Retrieved April 6, 2010, from http://www.faireconomy.org/files/Executive Excess2006.pdf

Anderson, S., & Ray, D. (2010). Missing women: Age and disease. *Review of Economic Studies,* 77(4), 1262–1300.

Aron-Devine, A. (2008). *The skewed benefits of the tax cuts: With the tax cuts extended, top 1 percent of households would receive almost $1.2 trillion in tax benefits over the next decade.* Washington, DC: Center for Budget and Policy Priorities.

Betcherman, G., & Islam, R. (Eds). (2001). *East Asian labor markets and the economic crisis: Impacts, responses and lessons.* Washington, DC: World Bank.

Blackden, C. M., & Bhanu, C. (1999). *Gender, growth, and poverty reduction: Special program of assistance for Africa—1998 status report on poverty in sub-Saharan Africa.* World Bank Technical Paper No. 428. Washington DC: World Bank.

Buvinic, M. (2009). *The global financial crisis: Assessing vulnerability for women and children, identifying policy responses.* Paper presented by the World Bank at the 53rd Session of the United Nations Commission on the Status of Women, New York, March 2–13.

Crotty, J., & Epstein, G. (2008). *Proposals for effectively regulating the US financial system to avoid yet another meltdown.* PERI Working Paper No. 181.

Epstein, G. (Ed.). (2005). *Financialization and the world economy.* Cheltenham, UK: Edward Elgar Publishing Ltd.

———. (2006). *Central banks, inflation targeting and employment creation.* Mimeo. Amherst, MA: Political Economy Research Institute (PERI).

Epstein, G., Grabel, I., & Jomo, K. S. (2004). Capital management techniques in developing countries: An assessment of experiences from the 1990s and lessons for the future. G-24 Discussion Series 27. Retrieved April 6, 2010, from http://www.g24.org/un-egj04.pdf

Grabel, I. (2003). *Currency transactions taxes: A brief assessment of opportunities and limitations.* Policy memo prepared for the New Rules on Global Finance conference on the "Tobin Tax," Washington, DC, January 16. Retrieved April 6, 2010 from http://www.financialpolicy.org/financedev/grabel2001.pdf

Grown, C., Bahadur, C., Handbury, J., & Elson, D. (2006). *The financial requirements of achieving gender equality and women's empowerment.* Paper prepared for the World Bank High-Level Consultation on Promoting the Gender Equality Millennium Development Goal: The Implementation Challenge held on February 16, 2006 in Washington, DC. Retrieved June 22, 2010 from http://www.levyinstitute.org/pubs/wp_467.pdf

ILO (International Labour Organization). (2008). *World of work 2008: Income inequalities in the age of financial liberalization.* Geneva: ILO.

Kawachi, I., & Wamala, S. (2007). Globalization and health: Challenges and prospects. In I. Kawachi & S. Wamala (Eds), *Globalization and health* (pp. 3–15). Oxford: Oxford University Press.

Krugman, P. (2009, August 29). All the president's zombies. *New York Times.*

Lim, J. (2000). The effects of the East Asian crisis on the employment of women and men: The Philippine case. *World Development, 28*(7), 1295–1306.

Milanovic, B. (2002). Can we discern the effect of globalization on income distribution? Evidence from household budget surveys. World Bank Policy Research Working Paper 2876. Washington DC: World Bank.

———. (2007). *An even higher global inequality than previously thought.* MPRA Paper 6676, University of Munich.

Montgomerie, J., & Young, B. (2009). *No place like home? Gender dimensions of indebtedness and homeownership.* Working paper, Centre for Research on Socio-Cultural Change (CRESC), University of Manchester.

Morgan, J. (2009). The limits of central bank policy: Economic crisis and the challenge of effective solutions. *Cambridge Journal of Economics, 33*(4), 581–608.

Ortiz, I. (2008). *Social policy: The way forward.* Presentation at International Council on Social Welfare conference, Tours, France, June 30–July 5.

Palley, T. (2008). *Asset bubbles and monetary policy: Why central banks have been wrong and what should be done.* Macroeconomics Policy Unit (IMK) Working Paper, May. Retrieved April 6, 2010, from http://www.boeckler.de/pdf/p_imk_wp_05_2008.pdf

PERI (Political Economy Research Institute). (2009). *A progressive program for economic recovery and financial reconstruction.* PERI, Amherst, Massachusetts, January. Retrieved April 10, 2010 from http://www.peri.umass.edu/fileadmin/pdf/other_publication_types/PERI_SCEPA_full_statement.pdf

Pollin, R., Heintz, J., Epstein, G., & Ndikumama, L. (2006). *An employment-targeted economic programme for South Africa.* Cheltenham, UK: Edward Elgar Publishing Ltd.

Pollin, R., & Zhu, A. (2006). Inflation targeting and growth: A cross-country non-linear analysis. *Journal of Post-Keynesian Economics, 28*(4), 593–614.

Seguino, S. (2007). Is more mobility good? Firm mobility and the low wage-low productivity trap. *Structural Change and Economic Dynamics, 18*(1), 27–51.

———. (2010). The global economic crisis, its gender and ethnic implications, and policy responses. *Gender and Development, 18*(2), 179–199.

Singh, A., & Zammit, A. (2002). *Gender effects of the financial crisis in South Korea.* Paper presented at New Directions in Research on Gender-Aware Macroeconomics and International Economies: An International Symposium. Levy Economics Institute of Bard College, New York.

Sirimane, S. (2009). *Emerging issue: The gender perspectives of the financial crisis.* Written statement submitted by the United Nations Economic and Social Commission for Asia and the Pacific to the 53rd Session of the United Nations Commission on the Status of Women, New York, March 2–13. Retrieved April 7, 2010 from http://www.unescap.org/ESID/GAD/Publication/Others/IWD09_ESCAP-panelist-Sirimanne_CSW paper.pdf

Stiglitz, J. (2009). *Panel discussion: Exploring how G-20 policies affect our communities, and how we can change them.* Monumental Baptist Church, Pittsburgh, Pennsylvania, September 24.

UN Millennium Project. (2005). *Taking action: Achieving gender equality and empowering women.* Task Force on Education and Gender Equality. London: Earthscan.

Wade, R. (1990). *Governing the market: Economic theory and the role of government in East Asian industrialization.* Princeton, New Jersey: Princeton University Press.

Weisbrot, M., Baker, D., & Rosnick, D. (2008). The scorecard on development: 25 years of diminished progress. In K. S. Jomo & J. Baudot (Eds), *Flat world, big gaps: Economic liberalization, globalization and inequality.* London: Zed Books.

Weisbrot, M., Ray, R., Johnston, J, Cordero, J. A., & Montecino, J. A. (2009). *IMF-supported macroeconomic policies and the world recession: A look at forty-one borrowing countries.* Washington, DC: Center for Economic and Policy Research.

World Bank. (2008). *World development indicators.* Washington, DC: World Bank.

WVS (World Values Survey). (2009). *World values survey.* Retrieved October 9, 2009, from http://www.worldvaluessurvey.org/

3

Questioning Economic Success through the Lens of Hunger

DEVAKI JAIN*

Feminist constructions of thought have always drawn from the ground, from the experience of struggles and local initiatives. What is needed is to consolidate the revelations from these efforts into a strong, globally affirmed theory by feminists.

INTRODUCTION

*T*his chapter looks at how providing food security for all—or, to put it another way, ensuring freedom from hunger (Drèze & Sen, 1989)—can point the way toward a more humane political economy. Looking at the political economy through the lens of food fits well with the feminist concept of the intersectionality of disciplines; it falls under the human security rubric, as well as under human rights, sustainable development, and economic growth.

The meltdown of 2008–2009 has shaken the world in many ways. It was not just a global downturn in the GDP but a set of linked crises, some dimensions of which—relating to the food and fuel crises and climate

*The author would like to thank Divya Alexander for her assistance in preparing this chapter.

change—predate the financial crisis (Jain & Elson, 2010). It has exacerbated the challenges of feeding the world, of obtaining clean water, of having sufficient energy, and of global warming and ecological disasters (FAO, 2009; Simms, 2010). It has made clearer the tensions around access to and provision of care for households and communities.

Food has been a central issue in feminist explorations of identity, stigma, and intra-household power dynamics, and hence it offers space for feminist interrogation. Food is also central to political strategies of the state as well as the household. In both of these spaces gender dynamics get played out in various ways. Using India as the landscape, and food—or better yet, hunger—as the entry point, this chapter critically explores the reasons for what can be called the Indian paradox of "mountains of food and millions of starving citizens" and suggests that:

- measures of economic success—be they GDP growth rates, capital inflows, or trade values—that fail to recognize the various nonmarket, nonmonetized values mislead and misdirect national efforts to redress hunger and poverty; and
- without the underpinning of a political and ethical philosophy toward economic justice, massive inequalities will persist despite pro-poor and welfarist policies.

With so many serious threats to human security, it is an appropriate time to revisit the ideas that Mahatma Gandhi provided for economic growth and people's well-being. A holistic approach such as the one he offered to India and the world at the turn of the 20th century is needed to build a peaceful and just world.

GROWING GLOBAL INEQUALITY

A recent study by the World Institute for Development Economics Research of the United Nations University (UNU-WIDER) on the world distribution of household wealth (Davies et al., 2006) takes wealth (rather than income) as the parameter and finds resounding evidence that its distribution is highly concentrated, much more so than the world distribution of income. It has also been stated in unequivocal terms, "corporate globalization has been marked by greatly increased disparities, both within countries and between countries" (Edwards, 2006). A World Bank study reveals that between 1820 and 1992 the income share of the bottom

60 percent of the world's population halved to around 10 percent while the share of the top 10 percent rose to more than 50 percent (cited in Shah, 2008).

The rise in inequality appears to be the result of three factors: a shift in earnings from labor to capital income; the rapid growth of the services sector—particularly the finance, insurance, and real estate sectors—with a consequent explosion in demand for skilled workers but reduced demand for other workers, especially women in less formal work; and a drop in the rate of labor absorption. In India, this has been happening since 1993 with the liberalization of the economy.

The gender dimension further complicates this issue as women usually do not share equitably in the wealth of men, even within the same household or family (Deere & Doss, 2006). Therefore, the gender distribution of wealth matters. The asymmetrical nature of gender relationships leads women to experience greater inequality than men; not only are more women poor, but their experience of poverty is also markedly different.

FEMINIST ANALYSIS AND HUNGER—THE LINK

In a UNDP paper launched at the Beijing +15 meetings at the United Nations in March 2010, the informal group of Casablanca Dreamers (see http://www.casablanca-dream.net/index.html) proposed that the global crises of contemporary development were not only those of finance and employment but also deprivation of food, water, energy, fuel, and care as well as increasing environmental devastation—problems that had been growing for decades (Jain & Elson, 2010).

Responding to the devastating food crisis that also appeared in full fury in the same years as the financial meltdown, the Casablanca group pointed out that food economies are by and large led by women farmers, adding, "In many developing countries, women make up over half of the agricultural work force. In some countries they are the majority of farmers" (ibid.).

But there is a gender–caste system operating here, with the lack of recognition for women as farmers still a submerged issue. Women's association with the provisioning of food, not only as growers but as preparers, is considered one of their virtues, taken for granted, and seen as a cultural value in patriarchal societies. Thus even when a woman farmer commits suicide, it is not seen as "a farmer's suicide." The Casablanca group therefore continued:

It will not be enough simply to distribute more land to individual women farmers. There would be a need to direct the entire economy towards support to small farms and the kind of farming that women engage in. If the current trend is followed then in the space of a couple of decades, land would be concentrated in the hands of large commercial farmers. Better land rights for women need to be embedded in a system of equitable public support. (Jain & Elson, 2010)

In other words, they pointed to the link between women's roles and values in a political economy and the changes in macroeconomic policy that are required. A complete reorientation of the role/location/share of agriculture in GDP—and thus a revision in the selection and prioritization of the triggers of economic success as well as the political philosophy underpinning current policy—would be a necessary condition for freedom from hunger for all.

THE SITUATION IN INDIA

The Indian paradox is interesting to study not only because its economy has been witnessing very high rates of growth in the current decade but also because the State has engaged itself with the issues of poverty and hunger for decades. Further, despite deep flaws in its performance, it does function under the rule of law and continues to have space for the affirmation of rights, a free press, etc., that are characteristics of a democratic nation.

Real GDP in 2004 was 10.3 times of what it was in 1978. In the post-liberalization period since 1994, the country's rate of growth of GDP has gone up from a mere 5 percent to around 8.5 percent per annum. India managed to keep up a growth rate of around 6 percent even during 2009, and in 2010 is building up to reach 8 percent again.

However, India's excellent growth has had little impact on food security and the nutrition levels of its population (Saxena, n.d.). Per capita availability as well as consumption of foodgrains has decreased; the cereal intake of the bottom 30 percent continues to be much less than the cereal intake of the top two deciles of the population, and calorie consumption of the bottom half of the population has been consistently decreasing since 1987.

"The rich get hungrier," says Amartya Sen (2010), answering his own question, "... will the food crisis that is menacing the lives of millions ease up—or grow worse over time?" He adds:

Though the need for huge rescue operations is urgent, the present acute crisis will eventually end. But underlying it is a basic problem that will only intensify unless we recognize it and try to remedy it. It is a tale of two peoples. In one version of the story, a country with a lot of poor people suddenly experiences fast economic expansion, but only half of the people share in the new prosperity. The favored ones spend a lot of their new income on food, and unless supply expands very quickly, prices shoot up. The rest of the poor now face higher food prices but no greater income, and begin to starve. Tragedies like this happen repeatedly in the world.

India is now home to nearly half the world's hungry population, with the usual special assault on the female of the species. Although it has put in place a Targeted Public Distribution System (TPDS)—which caters to 65 million families below the poverty line and 115 million families above the poverty line—it is ranked 65th ("alarming") among 88 vulnerable countries in the 2008 *Global Hunger Index* (Von Krebmer et al., 2008). Its hunger record is worse than that of nearly 25 sub-Saharan African countries (ibid.). Around 35 percent of India's population—350 million people—are considered food-insecure, consuming less than 80 percent of minimum energy requirements (Adil, 2008).

Along with this situation of terrible food deprivation, there are also growing inequalities related very specifically to this post "reform" period. The narrow base of economic growth focused on the service economy has meant that trickle-down theories of the spread of prosperity have remained confined to the sphere of illusions, and the magnitude and rate of change of inequalities are quite substantial. Very sharp contrasts are evident between the rural sectors of the slow-growing states and the urban sectors of the fast-growing states (Sen & Himanshu, 2004; Sinha, 2005). This rise in the incidence of rural poverty and inequality has meant that, despite better growth, poverty reduction has been sluggish (Jha, 2000). Multiple inequalities lock in the income levels of poor, disadvantaged populations in backward areas, and the effects of growth are limited to the margins of the high-growing enclaves and urban conglomerations (Sinha, 2005).

These inequalities are reflected in a number of ways. For example, the poor rural population has 230 million undernourished people—the highest for any country in the world—and 50 million Indians under five are affected by malnutrition. Malnutrition accounts for nearly 50 percent of child deaths, and every third adult (aged 15–49 years) is reported to be unacceptably thin (body mass index less than 18.5) (Sinha, 2009). Rising food prices, UNICEF says, mean 1.5 to 1.8 million more children in India could end up malnourished (TheIndian News, 2008). More than half of India's women and three-quarters of its children are anemic, with no decline in the last eight years.

India has a high maternal mortality rate of about 230 per 100,000 births, and had the largest number of maternal deaths (63,000) in 2008 (WHO et al., 2010). And if we delve deeper again, the story of inequality becomes even more evident—for example, one study showed that over 67 percent of maternal deaths occurred among the oppressed castes and in indigenous populations; in another district it was noted that 48 percent of the women who had died had had no formal schooling (*Financial Express*, 2008).

High economic growth rates have failed to improve food security in India, leaving the country facing a crisis in its rural economy (WFP & MSSRF, 2009). The number of undernourished people is rising, reversing gains made in the 1990s. The slowing growth in food production, rising unemployment, and declining purchasing power of the poor are combining to weaken the rural economy (ibid.).

With a network of more than 400,000 Fair Price Shops claiming to annually distribute commodities worth more than 150 billion INR to about 160 million families, the TPDS in India is perhaps the largest distribution network of its type in the world (in 2010, 47 Indian rupees [INR] = 1 United States dollar [USD]). These shops distribute a total of 35 kg of wheat and rice to about 65 million families below the poverty line at 4.2 INR per kg for wheat and 5.6 INR for rice (the present market rate is about double the TPDS price). Another 25 million poorest families get 35 kg of food grains at a highly subsidized rate of 2 INR per kg for wheat and 3 INR per kg for rice. In addition, there are welfare schemes such as hot cooked midday meals for school-going children and supplementary nutrition for preschool children. Yet, the "targeting of BPL (below poverty line) households has been one of the more spectacular policy failures of contemporary India" (Sharma, 2010).

WHAT WENT WRONG?

The suggestion here is that this situation of gross inequality and of hunger and extreme poverty in India is the result of contagion from the disease that is the currently operating paradigm of progress: the globalized trade, finance, and GDP growth rate-led market and monetized value-led path to economic success. Belief in the rate of growth of GDP as the sign of success, and moving away from farms and farming, neglecting the masses, and ignoring the enormous increase in disparities, are the contagion from the ideas behind the management of the global economy not only in the decades since the 1990s, but a continuum of the "modernization" project, the paradigm of progress as designed by the global North, the "advanced" countries, springing from the approach of the colonial powers.

Currently, India is experiencing the pressures arising out of taking that imitative road; it has shifted its interest from the agricultural sector to services and other sectors. This shift in the share of the three sectors in GDP is a worldwide phenomenon, as can be seen in the Figure 3.1 and Table 3.1. Figure 3.1 shows the shift in the GDP composition of India from 1973 to 2010.

Figure 3.1   GDP by economic activity (percent)

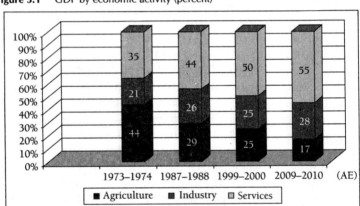

Source: Computed from Government of India (2010).
Note: The author would like to thank Divya Alexander for her assistance in preparation of the figure.

Table 3.1 reflects the same issue of shifts—from agriculture to services—in the composition of GDP at the global level from 1970 to 2001.

It will be noticed that in all the categories of countries, labor has shifted downward in agriculture, though more dramatically in the other regions than the developing countries. This movement away from agriculture, it is argued, has been responsible for the crisis in food security worldwide. The United Nations has estimated the total number of food insecure people at close to 3 billion, or about half the world's population (UN, 2008). The early years of the 21st century have seen hungry people

Table 3.1 Economic activity by sector (percent)

	Economic activity—agriculture (%)			Economic activity—industry (%)			Economic activity—services (%)		
	1970	1980	1990	2001	1970	1980	1990	2001	1970	1980	1990	2001
World	27	7	5	4	32	38	33	29	41	55	62	67
Developed countries	7	4	3	2	35	37	33	26	58	59	65	72
Developing countries	27	17	15	11	32	42	36	37	41	41	49	52

Source: UNCTAD (n.d.).

rioting in 37 countries. There is a shift toward greater market orientation at the macro level, which is also reflected at the micro level, with people increasingly moving out of subsistence production and into production for the market, which often means moving away from basic food crops to crops for the higher income classes. This trend is being reinforced by micro-level interventions, such as credit delivery programs that encourage poor households to engage in market-oriented production.

Within India this crisis in agriculture is a direct offshoot of the change in priorities during the early 1990s. Growing obsession with the so-called "new economy," information technology, media, and the urban consumer has led to the marginalization of the rural and agrarian sector, with respect to both private and public sector investment. Simultaneously, a greater proportion of the land used for agricultural purposes is now devoted to nonfood agriculture (Sundaram, 2008). One million hectare has gone out of cultivation in recent years in India and much more is threatened.

A recent example is the subsidies that the government of Maharashtra is offering for liqor production from food grains, especially sorghum—known locally as *jowar*—the cereal of poor households and also a dry land crop. This policy will turn *jowar* into a cash crop and divert huge quantities of food grains to alcohol production, creating scarcity and causing food inflation. Moreover, Right to Information (RTI) documents have revealed the falsity of the claims made by the government as to the project's benefits: distilleries are purchasing grains from dealers and not from farmers. Rather than focusing on the acute problem of malnutrition plaguing the state, the government is promoting a policy that is clearly meant to benefit only those with business interests (Tiwale, 2010).

The policies of economic liberalization have also required all sectors of the Indian economy to be opened up to global markets. Opening up the farm sector, in a country where the predominant structure of agricultural production is small-size holdings (as opposed to plantation economies), has undermined the viability of small farms and food farming. Corporate-driven agriculture, camouflaged with misinformation as to the threat that it posed, treated farmers as recipients and not as partners in the process (Ramprasad, 2008). The further erosion of the opportunity and space for small farmers is the argument that introducing retail trade chains—through what in India is called bringing foreign direct investment (FDI) into the food sector—will assist them in their marketing. Evidence from the United States and other countries clearly shows that this arrangement basically disempowers the farmers and is a profit-enabling mechanism for the retail chain (Chandrasekhar & Ghosh, 2009; DFID & IIED, 2004).

THE GENDER DIMENSION

This withdrawal from the food-driven economy, or land being used for food, as well as the intensification of inequality are acutely gendered. As noted earlier, food is central to political strategies of the state as well as the household. In both of these spaces gender dynamics get played out in various ways. Within the household, women's sense of accomplishment is linked to feeding her family a satisfying meal, even while she eats last or starves.

The agricultural sector is the largest employer of women in India. According to official statistics, women make up 32 percent of the country's total workforce, and of this 84 percent work in rural areas. Men have been steadily moving out of the agricultural sector into more diversified occupations; by 2004–2005, only 66.5 percent male workers were in agriculture compared to 83.3 percent female workers (Srivastava & Srivastava, 2009). This adds to the responsibility and strain on women to provide for the household, within an increasingly neglected part of the economy (Kanchi, 2009).

Given women's role in food production and provision, any set of strategies for sustainable food security must address their limited access to productive resources. Crucial to their access to resources is ownership of land; providing land rights for women is the very first need for food security for all. Women's limited access to resources and their insufficient purchasing power are products of a series of interrelated social, economic, and cultural factors that force them into a subordinate role to the detriment of their own development and that of society as a whole.

The volatility of prices of agricultural products and fuel due to the liberalization of international trade, the withdrawal of input subsidies and contraction of the public distribution system, environmental stress, and climate change are some of the other factors originating outside the sector that compromise women's capacity to ensure household food security (ibid.).

Inequity in access to common resources—water bodies, forests, and grazing grounds—affects women in cultivating, casual labor, and above all, landless labor households. A study in seven states in semiarid regions showed that common property resources accounted for 9 to 26 percent of household income of landless and marginal farmers, 69 to 89 percent of their grazing requirements, and 91 to 100 percent of their fuel requirements (Bandyopadhyay, 2008).

Restriction of access to community resources not only robs women of opportunities for diversification into livestock and collection of non-timber forest products, but also adds to their work burden by increasing the distance traversed and time required for collecting fuel for cooking and water for drinking. For women, agricultural work, informal work, landlessness, discrimination, and poverty mesh into a connected web.

WAS THERE ANOTHER WAY? THERE WAS

With independence in 1947, India inherited a heady cocktail of ideas for its regeneration. Inevitably, the economic exploitation-centered nature of colonial rule and consequent destitution of the people drove many political leaders of the liberation movement to try and free the masses from both the political oppression of the colonizer as well as the oppression of deep material deprivation. The latter was called the second freedom: freedom from economic exploitation. In this quest, there was a natural rejection of European culture and an affirmation of the country's own civilization, as well as its people's skills.

Like some of the leaders of freedom struggles in other countries, Gandhi wanted, when rejecting the colonial masters, to also reject their notions and strategies for progress. He had already described himself, in 1914, as "an uncompromising enemy of the present day civilisation in Europe" and rejected the so-called success story of industrialization and "modernization" (Johnson, 2006). When asked by a British journalist whether he would like India to have the same standard of living as Britain, he replied that considering that such a small island had to exploit half the globe to have this living standard, there were not enough globes for a big country like India (ibid.).

Revolting against the exploitative nature of the build-up of the West's industrial and technological strength, Gandhi argued that Indian ideas in Indian conditions were necessary to relieve the masses from the burden of economic oppression in the shortest time, with tools and techniques that were labor-absorbing and used minimum capital and energy. He was also, perhaps, one of the first to understand the nature of roving capital, and how it can not only exploit for self-advantage the resources of the colonies, but also subordinate the mind of the colonized and gain partners among them.

Gandhi suggested that production and consumption should be proximate and based as far as possible on local resources, "the first concern of every village republic will be to grow its own food crops and cloth" (Kripalani, 1970). To provide dynamic institutional underpinning to operationalize these ideas on the ground, Gandhi held that a unified political and economic strategy was required. This entailed the creation of an institution in the political realm, "village republics," to ensure that every adult had an equal share of political power as well as the duty to be an active custodian of political freedom. *Swaraj*, self-rule, was applied at all levels: *Hind swaraj*, self-rule for India; *gram swaraj*, self-rule for the village; and *swa-dharma*, self-rule for the individual. One could suggest that this was similar to or the same as affirming individual rights.

Interestingly similar ideals were put forward by leaders of freedom struggles elsewhere. For example, Julius Nyerere led a socialist economic program in Tanzania (announced in the Arusha Declaration), establishing close ties with China, and also introduced a policy of collectivization in the country's agricultural system, known as *ujamaa* (familyhood or extended family). He had tremendous faith in rural African people and their traditional values and ways of life. He believed that life should be structured around the *ujamaa* found in traditional Africa before the arrival of the imperialists.

The *kibbutzim* in Israel was a post-liberation idea using the same concept of collective ownership, attempting to efface inequality among Jewish settlers through collectivity (but not through force, as in the Soviet Union, but as a form of "voluntary mobilization"). So Gandhi's ideas for village-level governance really were resonating with what other leaders post-liberation were attempting: to bring back the community spirit of the pre-imperial days.

Initially, when India became independent in 1947, agriculture, the poor, employment, state intervention in ensuring security were the basis of policy. Land reforms, such that large land holdings were to be distributed and rights over land given to peasants, were also on the agenda. The Constitution guaranteed these rights.

However, as well as causing a move away from agriculture, the food distribution policies and practices did not work. Those who are trying to use the rights framework to correct India's wrongs to the poor and the hungry are now re-invoking Gandhi. First, the Supreme Court commissioner on the right to food in India, Harsh Mander, affirms that the paradox of a country with high growth producing enough food to feed all its people, and yet having greater hunger and malnutrition than much poorer countries, is due to the systematic destruction of the livelihoods of small producers—farm workers, artisans, and small traders—as well as great gender and social barriers (Mander, forthcoming). He suggests the relevance of Gandhi and his focus on the "last person," the least privileged (ibid.).

Second, research shows that small farms are capable of high productivity through intense husbandry and family motivation (OneWorld UK, 2009). Those who are promoting the alternative philosophy of "food sovereignty" favor local ownership and control of the full chain of resources. Small farms, they argue, can deliver the added value of reducing the contribution of agriculture to climate change. Low-input ecological or organic farming avoids fuel-dependent inputs in favor of soil carbon sequestration and sustainable water management (ibid.).

Third, support for the idea of greater control by local communities over the production, storage, and distribution of food is gaining ground everywhere, and many examples of how this is done are being invoked at all levels of knowledge. These include community grain banks to which farmers give grain in times of plenty and from which they borrow in times of need; seed banks to reduce dependence on moneylenders and local suppliers; local community food production planning by small and middle farmers; community irrigation schemes and *pani* panchayats, or water collectives, for the sustainable and equitable use of water for food production; ration shops run by panchayats or Self-help Groups (SHGs) of women; local procurement for the TPDS, and also other food-transfer schemes such as Integrated Child Development Services (ICDS) and midday school meals; and production and distribution of school meals as well as weaning foods as part of these services by women's SHGs—so many examples abound in India as they do elsewhere (Mander, 2009). One of them is described in Box 3.1.

Box 3.1 RUDI: A sustainable local procurement and distribution system

RUDI is the acronym for a project being run by the Self Employed Women's Association (SEWA) in Gujarat. Excess farm produce is procured at fair market prices from marginal farmers, and women then clean, grade, sieve, grind, weigh, pack, and label it. It is then sold in the villages at competitive prices. RUDI's portfolio of products is based on the needs of its rural consumers, and the products are priced according to the purchasing power of poor households. By procuring products locally, and processing them and distributing them locally, RUDI has created a sustainable ecosystem at the village and block level, a model that can be replicated and expanded seamlessly.

Following this experience, and the ideas drawn from Gandhi, SEWA critiques the current concept of the Right to Food Act and asks for proximate linking between producers and consumers. Through RUDI, SEWA argues for initiatives incorporating local procurement and distribution as this creates a sustainable economy at the local level, creates equitable access to essential goods, while at the same time generating the purchasing power required to purchase these goods.

Source: Note by Reema Nanavaty, Chair, RUDI.

However, there are questions and challenges in that the ways by which this can be achieved in the complex world of globalized markets are hard to find. This is where the recognition of the need for a sea change in global economic reasoning and policy becomes critical for the local to flourish as an alternative to the global—or as the basics, as Gandhi would have argued.

This idea of local initiatives and circulation of production and exchange is resonating in global reports too. The 2008 *World Development Report*, for example, says, "GDP growth originating in agriculture is at least twice as effective in reducing poverty as GDP growth originating outside agriculture" (World Bank, 2007). Moreover, the UN adds regarding Africa:

> ... the implementation and scaling up of initiatives to support improved agricultural productivity, particularly amongst smallholder farmers, will be critical to speeding growth, increasing incomes and improving the lives of the continent's people. With the assistance of the international community, rural producers who are the prime victims of the present crisis can become the prime actors of its solution. (NGLS, 2008)

These views bring back the relevance of the Gandhian package for freedom from hunger and the building of a just and equitable society. This is not fragmented to deal with specifics but is founded on an overall approach to what is economic and political progress, enshrining individual rights and sovereignty but ensuring that the basics—food, clothing, shelter, and the right for self-determination—are there. The measures of success are not the rate of growth of GDP or the value of trade but the spread of well-being. It is thus in direct conflict with the ideas that are now seen as leading to economic success.

Changing the Measurement of Progress

In his seminal work *Development as Freedom*, Amartya Sen (1999) contrasts the remarkable economic progress and wealth created in the last century to the devastating deprivation, destitution, and oppression suffered by billions of people worldwide, especially women and children. He argues for an integrative framework in economics that moves the focus from market expansion to the improvement of individual lives, which will invariably lead to sustainable economic growth.

The current crisis can thus be seen as an opportunity to move away from the export-led model in developing countries and focus on domestic and/or regional markets, especially the food segments where small-scale producers are concentrated. Whether sold or donated, cheap food from the West has almost always undercut, damaged, and skewed agriculture in poor countries by pricing local farmers out of the market. As a result, Western farmers and agriculture have political weight far beyond their contemporary economic importance.

But the debates—whether in the G20 or other global forums as well as within countries—continue to spin around exports, capital inflow of FDI, and rates of GDP growth as the health of a nation. Neither the hunger index nor the unemployment index nor the inequality index is being seriously used to measure progress, despite statements by high-profile economists such as Joseph Stiglitz:

> If we have poor measures, what we strive to do (say, increase GDP) may actually contribute to a worsening of living standards .... Statistical frameworks are intended to summarize what is going on in our complex society in a few easily interpretable numbers. It should have been obvious that one couldn't reduce everything to a single number, GDP. (Stiglitz, 2009)

Moreover, the Commission on the Measurement of Economic Performance and Social Progress (the Sarkozy Commission, created at the beginning of 2008 on the initiative of the French Government) has merely added a few more indicators to deepen the knowledge on what is happening, rather than decoding GDP. It is also not addressing the basic triggers of growth as currently used, namely capital-led, corporate-led, competition-led production and trade.

Feminists have also engaged with the idea of measures. Braunstein & Folbre (2001) and Eisler (2007), for example, do not discount the value of GDP as an economic indicator but argue that it does not give a full and accurate assessment of a country's economic production and condition. Eisler emphasizes the need to measure the status of women and children as fundamental indicators of the well-being and economic strength of societies. Her main critique of GDP is that it does not fully account for all economic activities, especially those that exist outside the realm of monetary exchange. For instance, GDP does not add in the monetary value of "the caring economy"—the unpaid care of households, children, the elderly, the sick, and the disabled—by family members, usually women.

Others have also noted that GDP does not take into account the work done within families and communities for free (Rowe, 2008). Still others argue that not only is GDP inadequate as an economic index, it simply fails as a measure of social welfare. But in all this work, the underpinnings of economic reasoning—the questions of for whom the economy is being run or developed and where is the trigger to start an engine that can lead to more widespread economic prosperity toward a just society—do not get addressed.

Yet this is what Gandhi did. We all know Gandhi's basic recommendation to start with the poor and his mantra on how we choose the path to shared prosperity. But whereas most economic progress theories begin with production and surplus from which distribution would take place, called the "trickle down" theory of growth and currently predominant in India, Gandhi's prescription could be seen as the "bubble up" theory of growth.

This approach would argue that the process of removing poverty can itself be an engine of growth; that the incomes and capabilities of those who are currently poor have the potential to generate demand that in turn will be an engine of production. However, this production would be specifically of goods that are immediately needed by the poor, which are currently peripheral in production. The oiling of this engine will bubble up and fire the economy in a much more broad-based manner. Unlike export-led growth, it will not skew production and trade into the elite trap, which is accentuating disparities and creating discontent.

Looking back from India's current situation of the striking exclusion of the poor from the agenda, as well as the co-option by the elite of the fruits of growth, and the subordination to the old paradigm of modernization and "progress," the value of Gandhi's economics is that it starts from distribution and leads through the foundation of individual freedom and individual rights to self-determination. Its formulae are very similar to the ones being put forward by those working for the right to food and for sovereignty.

While colonial Europe used to talk of rights in terms of rights over territory and the population of nation–states, the anticolonial struggles have turned the term against their colonial masters to stress the rights of the colonized to control their own political and economic structures and systems. The term is revisited now in an era of transnational powers to bring in notions of self-determination of communities and peoples, especially the marginalized.

Within the debate on food, the idea of sovereignty is linked to bio-politics. The global South has seen a huge rise in social movements contesting corporate globalization's control over food, even while confronted with accusations of backwardness and utopianism as well as the assumption that there is no turning back. The message from these struggles is basically of food sovereignty, affirming the right of every population to decide what to eat and how to produce it in a way that is equitable, just, and sustainable. Very clearly, those who control food production also control the political economy of the planet (Caffentzis, 2008).

One specific policy that could be put in place today to make India less punishing for the poor—and drawn from Gandhi's ideas—is that of localizing food self-sufficiency. Given that the major part of India's labor is still in rural areas, where 84 percent of the female workforce is toiling, and given that we have the germ or nucleus for *gram swaraj* in the panchayati raj institutions that were put in place by Rajiv Gandhi, it would not be impossible to start from the poor and follow a Gandhian program from the village upwards.

For example, a present-day Gandhian feminist, Ela Bhatt, makes a proposal to implement Gandhi's production/consumption cycle within a geographical space. She calls it the 100-mile principle for economic security for the poor (see Box 3.2). Putting it into general practice would require a total turnaround from what is catching the imagination of political leaders today. Yet it shows the way, and feminist movements and networks, working together, need to and can rewrite economic success through ideas such as this.

Box 3.2   The 100-mile principle for economic security

The 100-mile principle weaves decentralization, locality, size, and scale to livelihood. What one needs for livelihood as material, as energy, as knowledge should stem from areas around us. Seed, soil, water are forms of knowledge that need to be retained locally. Security stems from local innovations, not distant imports. The millennia-old link between production and consumption has to be recovered. 100-mile is a threshold principle. It shows when you export food or import seed you deculturate a community. Take food. Is it grown and cooked locally? How many energy miles has it consumed? Unless food is grown locally, you cannot sustain diversity. Food has to be grown locally, made locally. Ask yourself what happened to local fruits, local foods like barley, and local staples like cotton. But when food is produced locally and exported, the locality has no access to its own labor, to its produce. You grow milk and vegetables for the city and survive on less. Freedom is the right to your labor, your produce. Such a freedom needs a community. A community is autonomous when it controls food, clothing, shelter (*roti, kapda, makan*). This old cliché of *roti, kapda, makan* has to be within a 100-mile radius. The minute you extend the production cycle you lose control.

Comparative advantage might be good economics but let us leave well-intentioned economics outside communities. Otherwise, instead of freedom, we face obsolescence. When food is exported, when technology is centralized, when shelter depends on some remote housing policy, we lose our freedom as a community. 100-mile is a guarantee that citizens retain control, inventiveness, diversity. We could grow 50,000 varieties of rice because we followed the 100-mile principle intuitively.

Source: Bhatt (2009).

Much of India's industrial output comes from the informal economy—from home-based work with no security, either economic or legal, in terms of labor laws. A strong revivalism of the handmade product industries, as well as own enterprises, could both provide security as well as ensure GDP with justice. Such a thrust would require complex undoing of not only tax and credit policies, but also trade policies, approaches to infrastructure development, and licensing laws, to mention a few areas.

A village plan that starts with the poor mapping out the structure and shape of their existing sources of livelihood through products that are unique, including growing foodgrains that are appropriate to the local area, and enabling their circulation through local marketplaces, means beginning at the bottom. A strong push with backward–forward linkages to the industrial goods that hands make—handmade products that often are not only the major proportion of domestically used goods but are also exportable, such as diamonds or embroidered goods being produced in many other developing countries apart from India—would create another cycle of growth with employment.

Conclusion

A strong political move is needed by women to reclaim democracy and development through the mobilization of those engaged locally, through the concepts of the inverted pyramid and of "think locally and act globally" (not the other way around), bubbling up to become a tidal wave at the macro or global level (Jain & Chacko, 2007). By identifying ourselves with justice and inequality, with the downtrodden as Gandhi would say, or the discriminated against and the hungry, by having a vision, as many feminists have argued, and by superseding all the challenges to forging identity, such as gender or race, we may be able to build our voice. To challenge androcentric and eurocentric knowledge, we need to rebuild knowledge together as a bonding process for building political solidarity.

However, for this to replace the old model of production, of surplus then distribution—for it to give space both to environmental protection as well as economic security for the masses, especially women among them—the underlying principles of what makes for progress need drastic revision. Feminist constructions of thought have always drawn from the ground, from the experience of struggles and local initiatives. What is needed is to consolidate the revelations from these efforts into a strong, globally affirmed theory by feminists.

The Indian experience, both in its inspiration from Gandhi and its enslavement to the current impulses and measures of success, offers a lesson or a path for feminists building alternative economic models to consider.

References and Select Bibliography

Adil, A. (2008). *India's export ban on food grain: A measure to ensure availability of food for its poorest citizens*. California: The Oakland Institute.

Bandyopadhyay, D. (2008). Does land still matter? *Economic and Political Weekly*, March 8, 37–42.

Bhatt, E. (2009). *Citizenship of marginals*. Third R. K. Talwar Memorial Lecture, Indian Institute of Banking and Finance, Mumbai, July 23.

Braunstein, E., & Folbre, N. (2001). To honor and obey: Efficiency, inequality, and patriarchal property rights. *Feminist Economics*, 7(1), 25–44.

Caffentzis, G. (2008). Descrambling the "food crisis." *Mute*, August 26. Retrieved February 8, 2010, from http://www.metamute.org/en/content/decoding_the_food_crisis

Chandrasekhar, C. P., & Ghosh, J. 2009. Corporatisation of agriculture. *Lok Samvad*. Retrieved February 7, 2010, from http://loksamvad.org/e107_plugins/content/content. php?content.82

Davies, J. B., Sandstrom, S., Shorrocks, A., & Wolff, E. N. (2006). *The world distribution of household wealth*. World Institute for Development Economics Research of the United Nations University (UNU-WIDER), Helsinki, December 5.

Deere, C. D., & Doss, C. R. (2006). *Gender and the distribution of wealth in developing countries*. UNU-WIDER Research Paper No. 2006/115, October 2.

DFID (UK Department for International Development), & IIED (International Institute for Environment and Development). (2004). *Concentration in food supply and retail chains*. Working Paper, DFID, London. Retrieved August 12, 2010, from http://dfid-agriculture-consultation.nri.org/summaries/wp13.pdf

Drèze, J., & Sen, A. (1989). *Hunger and public action*. Oxford: Clarendon Press.

Edwards, P. (2006). Examining inequality: Who really benefits from global growth? *World Development*, 34(10), 1667–1695.

Eisler, R. (2007). *The real wealth of nations: Creating a caring economics*. Washington, DC: International Food Policy Research Institute.

FAO (Food and Agriculture Organization). (2009). *The state of food insecurity in the world: Economic crisis—impacts and lessons learned*. Rome: Economic and Social Development Department, FAO.

Financial Express. (2008, October 7). Maternal mortality: This India story is a shame! *Financial Express*. Retrieved February 3, 2010, from http://www.financialexpress. com/news/Maternal-mortality-This-India-story-is-a-shame/370599

Government of India. (2010). *Press note: Advance estimates of national income, 2009–10*. Press Information Bureau, Central Statistical Organization, February 8. Retrieved October 20, 2010, from http://mospi.nic.in/Mospi_New/upload/adv_rel_pressnote_8feb10.pdf

Jain, D., & Chacko, S. (2007). *Shifting our platform in response to current ground-level phenomena*. Paper prepared for Current Developments on Issues Pertaining to Rural Women, 4th World Congress of Rural Women, Durban, South Africa, April 23–26.

Jain, D., & Elson, D. (in collaboration with the Casablanca Dreamers). (2010). *Vision for a better world: From economic crisis to equality*. New York: United Nations Development Programme (UNDP).

Jha, R. (2000). *Reducing poverty and inequality in India: Has liberalization helped?* Paper prepared for the World Institute for Development Economics Research (WIDER) project on Rising Income Inequality and Poverty Reduction: Are They Compatible? Retrieved February 2, 2010, from http://rspas.anu.edu.au/economics/publish/papers/wp2002/wp-econ-2002-04.pdf

Johnson, R. L. (Ed.). (2006). *Gandhi's experiments with truth: Essential writings by and about Mahatma Gandhi*. Lanham, Maryland: Lexington Books.

Kanchi, A. (2009). *Women's work in agriculture—expanding responsibilities, shrinking opportunities*. ILO Working Paper. International Labour Organization, Geneva.

Kripalani, J. B. (1970). *Gandhi: His life and thought*. Ahmedabad: Navjivan.

Mander, H. (2009). *Fear and forgiveness: The aftermath of massacre*. New Delhi: Penguin Books India.

———. (Forthcoming). *A fistful of rice*. New Delhi: Penguin Books India.

NGLS (UN Non-governmental Liaison Service). (2008). Smallholder farmers hold solution to global food crisis. *Media Advisory*, September 16. Retrieved October 18, 2010, from http://www.un.org/millenniumgoals/2008highlevel/pdf/MEDIA%20ADVISORY_smallholder%20farmers.pdf

OneWorld UK. (2009). *Time to attack hunger's root causes—UN*. June 10. Retrieved November 2, 2010, from http://us.oneworld.net/article/364288-global-action-needed-food-security

Ramprasad, V. (2008, October 16). The polemic of global food economy. *Deccan Herald.*

Rowe, J. (2008). *Rethinking the gross domestic product as a measurement of national strength.* Testimony before the Subcommittee on Interstate Commerce, United States Senate Committee on Commerce, Science and Transportation. March 12.

Saxena, Naresh C. (n.d.). *Hunger, under-nutrition and food security in India.* Retrieved January 30, 2010, from http://www.dfid.gov.uk/r4d/PDF/Outputs/ChronicPoverty_RC/CPRC-IIPA44.pdf. Working paper 44, Chronic Poverty Research Centre, Indian Institute of Public Administration, New Delhi.

Sen, A. (1999). *Development as freedom.* New York: Knopf.

———. (2010, May 28). The rich get hungrier [Op-ed]. *New York Times.*

Sen, A., & Himanshu. (2004). Poverty and inequality in India—I. *Economic and Political Weekly,* September 18, 4247–4263.

Shah, M. (2008, October 21). Cutting off the chain of hate. *The Hindu.*

Sharma, D. (2009, July 17). Food for all? Not through the NFSA. *India Together.* Retrieved November 2, 2010, from http://www.indiatogether.org/2009/jul/dsh-nfsa.htm

———. (2010, October, 28). What size is your hunger? S, M, XL? *The Asian Age.*

Simms, A. (2010, January 25). Growth is good… isn't it? *The Guardian.* Retrieved January 29, 2010, from http://www.guardian.co.uk/commentisfree/cif-green/2010/jan/25/uk-growth-energy-resources-boundaries

Sinha, A. (2005). Globalization, rising inequality, and new insecurities in India. Retrieved February 2, 2010, from http://209.235.207.197/imgtest/TaskForceDiffIneqDevSinha.pdf

Sinha, K. (2009, February 27). India tops world hunger chart. *The Times of India.*

Srivastava, N., & Srivastava, R. (2009). *Women, work, and employment outcomes in rural India.* Paper presented at the FAO-IFAD-ILO Workshop on Gaps, trends and current research in gender dimensions of agricultural and rural employment: differentiated pathways out of poverty, Rome, March 31–April 2.

Stiglitz, J. (2009). *GDP fetishism.* Project Syndicate, September 17. Retrieved October 20, 2010, from http://www.project-syndicate.org/commentary/stiglitz116/English

Sundaram, J. K. (2008). *Statement by the UN Assistant Secretary General for Economic Development.* Press conference on World Economic Situation and Prospects, New York, May 15.

TheIndian News. (2008). *India has worst indicator of child malnutrition: Unicef.* May 14. Retrieved February 3, 2010, from http://www.thaindian.com/newsportal/india-news/india-has-worst-indicator-of-child-malnutrition-unicef_10048495.html

Tiwale, S. (2010). Foodgrain vs liquor: Maharashtra under crisis. *Economic and Political Weekly,* 45(22), 19–21.

UN (United Nations). (2008). *World economic situation and prospects (WESP) 2008.* New York: United Nations.

UNCTAD (United Nations Conference on Trade and Development). (n.d.). *UNCTAD handbook of statistics on-line.* Retrieved February 8, 2010, from http://www.unctad.org/Templates/Page.asp?intItemID=1890

Von Krebmer, K., Fritschel, H, Nestorova, B., Olofinbiyi, T., Pandya-Lorch, R., & Yohannes, Y. (2008). *Global hunger index: The challenge of hunger 2008.* Welthungerhilfe, Bonn; International Food Policy Research Institute (IFPRI), Washington, DC; Concern Worldwide, Dublin.

WFP (World Food Programme), MSSRF (M S Swaminathan Research Foundation). (2009). *Report on the state of food insecurity in rural India.* Retrieved August 11, 2010, from http://home.wfp.org/stellent/groups/public/documents/newsroom/wfp197348.pdf

WHO (World Health Organization), United Nations Children's Fund (UNICEF), United Nations Population Fund (UNPFA), & the World Bank. (2010). *Trends in maternal mortality: 1990 to 2008*. WHO, Geneva. Retrieved October 19, 2010, from http://whqlibdoc.who.int/publications/2010/9789241500265_eng.pdf

World Bank. (2007). *World development report 2008: Agricultural development*. Washington, DC: World Bank. Retrieved August 11, 2010, from http://siteresources.worldbank.org/INTWDR2008/Resources/WDR_00_book.pdf

4

Globalization, Labor, and Women's Work
Critical Challenges for a Post-Neoliberal World*

LOURDES BENERÍA

The paradigm tied to global capitalism and rational Economic Man, with its conceptual frameworks and economic policies, has failed us not only because it has brought some "development" while neglecting "human development" for all, but also because, despite progress toward gender equality at many levels, it has done so within a paradigm of social inequality that feminism needs to question.

INTRODUCTION

The focus of this chapter is on labor and globalization with the objective of providing an angle from which to assess some of the challenges facing the post-neoliberal and post-economic crisis world—in general and from a gender perspective. It begins with a brief critical evaluation of the neoliberal regime that has predominated during the past quarter century across the globe, with special reference to the consequences that this has

---

* Slightly modified in September 2009 from a paper prepared for the Colloquium on Assessing Development Paradigms, UNDP Gender Team, Rabat, Morocco, October 25–27, 2008.

had for unregulated markets, changing labor/capital relations, and working conditions. Following some questions about neoliberal globalization and the 2008 financial and subsequent economic crisis, the main bulk of the chapter focuses on some key challenges regarding labor market trends and on-going transformations at the workplace. In particular, it examines four areas that exemplify these transformations: (i) the changing organization of labor processes and the so-called new labor contract, (ii) working conditions and international labor standards, (iii) the informal economy; and (iv) the care economy and the feminization of international migration. These issues have been taken up not only to discuss their implications but also in terms of rethinking policy and action. The chapter concludes with a discussion of the extent to which a new gender order is being constructed, and of the crucial importance for gender equality of policies to balance family and labor market work.

QUESTIONING NEOLIBERAL GLOBALIZATION

During the initial stages of what we have come to call globalization, the predominant reaction was to view it as propelled by powerful economic and technological forces. These were seen as the result of the extension and deepening of markets—from financial markets and trade, to labor markets and even cultural trends. The transnationalization of production and exchange was intensified by the wide adoption of neoliberal policies; it was backed up by potent discourses about the magic of the market and its efficiency for the purpose of allocating resources, fostering development, and dealing with poverty and other economic and social problems. Strict structural adjustment programs (with high social costs) were imposed on developing countries during the 1980s and 1990s as a way to remedy debt problems and alleviate macroeconomic imbalances.

The slogan "there is no alternative," or TINA, became one way of justifying the imposition of market fundamentalism across countries. Capitalism had triumphed over attempts to construct alternative institutions for the production and distribution of resources; this was particularly emphasized after the post-1989 dismantling of the former Soviet Union. The "end of history," we were told, had arrived. Often framed in terms of the impact of the "global" on the "local," this discourse tended to project a notion of the local as passive recipient of these powerful forces. At the same time, however, the idea of top–down globalization was met by many objections to such an approach to development and social transformation. The last decades have witnessed the multiple reactions—local and global—that have repeatedly reminded us that "another world is possible." Rather than accepting passively the dictates of TINA, these have demonstrated the power of civil society to organize and affect the direction of change, and to reject both the policies imposed by the Washington Consensus and the dictates of the market (Hart, 2002). The global crisis has reinforced these tendencies.

Nevertheless, even the social democratic countries, which had gradually been building welfare states and regulated markets during the post-World War II period, have had to adjust to neoliberal trends. Global competition has forced them to regress in many of the social gains that had been obtained over the years—for example, in the area of labor rights. In the same way, it is a well-known fact that the real wages of blue-collar workers in high-income countries have tended to decrease or remain stagnant since the early 1970s despite increases in labor productivity (Krugman, 2009). In the United States, income disparities and inequality have continued to grow (Saez, 2008), and similar trends have been observed in other high-income countries (Seguino, this volume).

In developing regions, the informal economy has become a permanent feature associated with poverty and precarious working conditions, even in cases when the new industrialization and shift of production from high-wage countries has led to very significant levels of growth, such as in China and India during the past decades. Instead of improving labor conditions in the poorer countries, globalization has lowered those of the higher income countries, leading to a common deterioration of labor markets. The shift of investment to low-cost areas has been a constant threat that has resulted in the diminished economic and political power of labor relative to capital across countries; this is illustrated by the decrease in the share of labor in gross domestic product (GDP) in the majority of countries. As the International Labour Organization (ILO, 2008, p. 20) points out:

> Employment growth has … occurred alongside a redistribution of income away from labour. In 51 out of 73 countries for which data are available, the share of wages in total income declined over the past two decades. The largest decline in the share of wages in GDP took place in Latin America and the Caribbean (–13 points), followed by Asia and the Pacific (–10 points) and the Advanced Economies (–9 points).

The current economic crisis is likely to reinforce these tendencies and affect low-income groups disproportionately.

In the global search for low-cost production, lower-wage countries have attracted global investment, and some areas have industrialized at a rapid rate. Industrial enclaves, such as export-processing zones (EPZs), have developed and absorbed large numbers of new participants in the industrial labor force, with a high proportion of women workers. These enclaves have symbolized the contradictions of global capitalism. On the one hand, globalization has contributed to generating unprecedented levels of production of goods and services at the low prices required for mass consumption. Although with uneven regional results, this has contributed to increasing living standards for a proportion of the population—though unacceptable levels of poverty have remained a continuous feature in many countries (ILO, 2008). On the other hand, uncontrolled markets have generated periodic financial crises of major proportions—such as in Asia, Brazil, and Russia in 1997–1998, Argentina on several occasions culminating in the severe crisis of 2001–2002, and the major meltdown in global financial markets that began in 2007 with the subprime crisis in the United States, resulting in the collapse on Wall Street and global financial markets in 2008 and beyond.

In retrospect, we can see how the triumphalist market-oriented discourses of the 1980s and 1990s have been tamed, if not defeated, by these events. As illustrated by articles in the weekly *The Economist* in the early 1990s, the market was viewed as a "civilizing" force that would solve not only economic problems such as poverty and sluggish growth but also those having to do with the dangers of what Samuel Huntington (1996) has called the "clash of civilizations." In an editorial critique of Huntington, *The Economist* (1997) argued that the market and its homogenizing tendencies were more likely to bring people and cultures together than force them apart. At the same time, we became very familiar with the imposition of policies linked to the Washington Consensus, which assumed that freeing markets and privileging the private sector were essential to maximize efficiency and economic growth, often at the expense of social protection (ILO, 2004). Under TINA's banner, market fundamentalism and unregulated markets became an integral part of the hegemonic development model.

In many ways, the historical course that began with the events of 9/11 changed some of the initial optimism regarding neoliberal globalization. Perhaps Huntington was right in his arguments regarding the clash of civilizations. At the same time, evidence of the reaction against many of the negative consequences of globalization surfaced in the numerous and often violent protests that have taken place around international gatherings of the most powerful global forces, such as with the World Trade Organization (WTO) meeting in Seattle in 1999 and the annual G9 summits in different locations. Neoliberal globalization has brought to practice the theoretical pillars of orthodox economics based on the rationality of "Economic Man" (Ferber & Nelson, 1993) or its global version of "Davos Man" (named for the venue of the annual World Economic Forum of global bankers and business leaders) (Benería, 2003). What *The Economist* and free market promoters did not initially predict was that market failures on the one hand and unregulated markets on the other, would generate the multiple problems that have surfaced—from the persistence of poverty in the midst of plenty, to the abuses in the financial sector that resulted in the financial meltdown, and the misuse of the environment that has led to the current world environmental crisis.

This should have been enough to humble the initial triumphalist discourses regarding the magic of free markets and of globalization, but the 2008 financial meltdown in the United States and its global spillover have demonstrated that not only would neoliberal policies not achieve the positive results expected, they would in fact undermine the system on which they rely, thereby creating a crisis of immense proportions. As US Treasury Secretary Henry Paulson pointed out, one core issue was the "lax lending practices" that led to "irresponsible borrowing" (Nocera, 2008). In addition, uncontrolled risk taking and trading in financial markets generated the pyramids of credit that finally collapsed. With the advent of the crisis, this led even to the inability to determine the price of "financial products," to the extent that nobody could understand who owed what to whom—or whether they had the ability to pay.

In fact, it was the rationality of Economic Man that led to the enormous financial bubble that gradually and then suddenly generated the meltdown and the billions of "toxic assets." For example, insurance on debt reached a "nearly unimaginable" USD 45.5 trillion in 2008, up from USD 900 billion in 2001 (Schwartz, 2008)—and there have been higher estimates. James Cawley, the founder of IDX Capital, saw this escalation as a phenomenon based not on an understanding of the financial markets but on behavior tied to "let's make money when the sun shines and worry about details later" (ibid.). In addition, and as the *Report of the Commission on the Measurement of Economic Performance and Social Progress* has argued, it is clear that part of the economic performance of the period was a "mirage," representing profits that were based on prices that had been inflated by a bubble (Stiglitz et al., 2009).

If Davos Man has failed us in different ways, this is a perfect moment for everyone in general—and for women and feminist visioners in particular—to examine some of the challenges that have emerged. As the abovementioned report and many recent events have demonstrated, the financial crisis has led to some questioning and rethinking of standard orthodox approaches to economic theory and practice. For example, a new network of economists was launched in 2009 with the help of financier George Soros to reconsider some of the fundamental tenets of economics, with founding Advisory Board members including Nobel laureates such as George Akerlof, Sir James Mirrlees, A. Michael Spence, and Joseph E. Stiglitz, as well as other prominent economists (all male in its initial launch).

In the same way, and for the purpose of this discussion, we need to rethink the connections between our gender-based concerns on the one hand and the larger systemic frameworks that affect human development on the other. The paradigm tied to global capitalism and rational Economic Man, with its conceptual frameworks and economic policies, has failed us not only because it has brought some "development" while neglecting "human development" for all, but also because, despite progress toward gender equality at many levels, it has done so within a paradigm of social inequality that feminism needs to question.

LABOR MARKETS AND EMPLOYMENT: THE CHALLENGES FOR FEMINISM AND BEYOND

The processes of deep economic restructuring brought about by globalization and neoliberal policies have resulted in profound changes in labor markets, employment patterns, and working conditions across the globe, for both women and men but with important gender differences. The relocation of production from high- to low-income countries has led to the geographical dispersion of manufacturing, while trade liberalization has induced rapid changes in the international division of labor and in the location of employment. These processes have been widely analyzed and are well known. Although it is difficult to generalize—given the many differences related to specific local, regional, and national factors—the following sections represent an attempt to highlight some significant tendencies that have affected labor markets and women's work in order to identify current challenges for a post-crisis world.

The Changing Workplace and the New Labor Contract

Technological changes, the flexibilization of labor processes, and the decentralization of production tied to globalization and the age of high tech have resulted in the dismantling of what many authors have called the "old labor contract" that had prevailed in high-income countries and in the "modern sector" in developing countries during the post-World War II period. This contract, tied to the male breadwinner family model, was linked to the internal labor market within each firm and included stable working conditions, long-term contracts, trade unions and collective bargaining, relatively high wages, and predictable patterns of promotion. Employment was assumed to provide health insurance and other fringe benefits, while the internal labor market was instrumental in setting wages, promotions, and working conditions, especially in large firms.

By contrast, the "new labor contract" that has gradually been introduced during the past decades has been reversing many of these conditions. While Taylorism and Fordism implied "deskilling" for workers reduced to narrow tasks, the emphasis has changed to the building of skills for the new technologies that have been rapidly transforming the workplace. We have observed increasingly more individualized and less stable labor contracts, with many workers expected to shift regularly from job to job and often performing unrelated tasks (Benería, 2003; Stone, 2006). Rather than workers having long-term and stable employment, as was typical of large corporations and especially in some countries such as Japan, they have had to build skills that allow them to change jobs as needed. Downsizing and decentralization of firms has flattened out some of the old hierarchies by reducing middle management and supervisory jobs, "professionalizing" low-level skills, and reducing boundaries between them through teamwork and the diffusion of authority. In this sense, many authors have talked about the "boundary-less workplace" (Stone, 2006) in which job rotation among teams is a typical feature of the labor process.

These trends have affected industrial manufacturing as well as other sectors such as office and administrative work. They have also been accompanied by the growth of contingent work, with an increase in part-time jobs and temporary contracts, representing a shift of work to the margins of formal activities and with more insecure conditions. Parallel to these trends, we have witnessed an increase in women's labor-force participation rates across countries, which is partly a reflection of the inability of families to survive or keep their living standards with a single wage.

The fragmentation and individualization of labor contracts has affected different levels of the labor hierarchy and can be observed also for professional echelons. A common example is provided by the proliferation of short-term or even long-term individual "consultancies" so prevalent in international institutions; it can also be found among skilled blue-collar workers subcontracted on a short-term basis. Individualized labor contracts tend to make collective interests among workers less obvious, making labor unions and collective actions less likely. Thus, it is no coincidence that the importance of unions has gradually been decreasing in countries where they had played a significant role in the past (Katz, 2000).

These changes in employment contracts have been parallel to a clear tendency toward less stable employment, which can be observed at many levels—from the precarious conditions of informalized markets to the employment instability prevalent in a wide range of the occupational spectrum (ILO, 2004; Standing, 2004). For many countries with available data, job tenure has tended to decrease for different labor groups; the average worker, particularly among the young, has to change jobs and firms many times before acquiring any job security. Not surprisingly, women tend to have the lowest median job tenure (Atkinson & Court, 2002), and these trends are reported for most rich and poor countries (ILO, 2004, 2008).

To some extent, the new workplace is characterized by a more democratic management style and a diffusion of authority within firms. Likewise, the breaking down of rigid job ladders and promotion rules raises the possibility of opening up opportunities for reducing discrimination based on gender or other characteristics such as race and ethnicity. It appears to be more democratic and less hierarchical and thus, to the extent that women tend to be less aggressive than men in working toward their advancement and promotion, might represent a positive step for them. For example, Salzinger's (2003) research on US–Mexico maquiladora industries, which includes an interesting account of factories with different types of labor organization, shows how women workers can benefit from teamwork and rotating responsibilities.

Yet, these advantages may be turned around if cases of discrimination surface and if labor unions are not available. The new labor contract implies that job descriptions are harder to compare, and having workers operating in teams with rotating responsibilities implies that any type of discriminatory behavior—whether based on gender, class, or any other form—might be diffused among team members and hard to prove. Given that job ladders and promotion criteria are less clearly defined, it is less straightforward for workers to show that they are being treated differently. As Stone (2006) has argued for the case of the United States, individual workers have found it difficult to provide evidence of racial and gender discrimination under conditions in which responsibilities are shared and thus not well defined, and "the new employment practices have made conventional civil rights remedies problematic" (ibid., p. 258).

This suggests the need to develop new forms of assessing and dealing with discrimination and exclusion at the workplace. Stone (ibid.), for example, mentions the need for "accessible and flexible" mechanisms to deal with cases of sexism and racism. While she suggests that class action suits presented by a group of workers have a better chance of winning (ibid.), such practices are not very developed in many countries and work situations. To the extent that the individualization of contracts and discriminatory practices can also affect professional workers, the search for solutions is a significant issue for all the echelons in the labor hierarchy; the case of the glass ceiling for women is a notorious example.

The World of Work and International Labor Standards

The search for the lowest possible production cost and its correspondent lowest common denominator in labor conditions has brought to the surface the asymmetry between labor and capital regarding global mobility across countries. Transnational corporations can discipline workers with threats of moving to another country; capital mobility is used as an instrument of labor control, or as a way of dealing with labor unrest and pressure for higher wages. An example of this is the Pico Korea case, in which some 300 workers, almost all women, lost their jobs when a US-based multinational electronics company suddenly shut its subsidiary in South Korea in February 1989 in violation of a collective bargaining agreement and of Korean laws requiring notice, severance pay, etc. (see Liem & Kim, 1992).

On the other hand, labor does not enjoy the same privileges of mobility. With the exception of highly skilled labor, workers have met with increasingly tougher obstacles—such as restrictive immigration policies and high transaction costs—and to migrate to higher income countries. Likewise, capital has been able to use the threat of mobility as a bargaining chip to obtain tax and other concessions by host country governments, such as in the case of the many EPZs where taxation and labor regulations are lax or not applicable (ILO, 2003; Wachtel, 2004). As is well known, from the maquiladora industries on the US–Mexico border and elsewhere in Latin America to the new industries and manufacturing centers in China and India, production has been organized under the dictates of this "low road" to development. While there are differences according to local conditions, many studies have illustrated the exploitative ways in which workers are treated, particularly unskilled, low-wage workers in labor-intensive production with a high proportion of women (Hsiung, 1995; Fussell, 2000; Pizarro, 2006; Ngai, 2007).

It is for these reasons that the debates on international labor standards have taken a new twist under globalization. Global competition and the race to the bottom have rendered some of the existing national labor legislation meaningless. At the international level, the ILO had traditionally played an important role in setting standards through its conventions adopted over the years (see Otobe, this volume). With globalization, many of these conventions, even if ratified at the country level, have been ignored in practice. For this reason, in 1998 the ILO adopted the Declaration on Fundamental Principles and Rights at Work as "a universal reaffirmation of the importance of social progress" in order to "set the basis for social justice in the workplace and provide a framework to ensure that people fairly share in the wealth that they have helped generate" (ILO, 2007). However, the ILO has no power to enforce these principles unless national governments are willing to collaborate, hence the importance of labor and other social groups pressing for compliance at the country level.

This is not an easy task given the resistance of many firms to complying with labor standards to the extent that they increase labor costs. Many of them have argued for and even adopted voluntary codes of conduct, but these do not guarantee compliance. The opposition to international labor standards has been voiced especially by newly industrializing countries, which argue that they are not ready yet to impose the standards prevalent in high-income countries, pointing out that the latter did not apply these when they themselves industrialized (Lee, 1997).

The basis for this argument is twofold. First, to the extent that higher labor standards can result in increased costs of production, their adoption might imply that lower-wage countries lose their competitive edge in global markets. Second, countries fear that the adoption of such standards will lead to the loss of foreign investment to noncompliant countries. Naila Kabeer, for example, has suggested that their imposition in Bangladesh could lead to the loss of many jobs for women in garment and textiles production. She and other authors have argued that, rather than focusing on trade and labor standards, living conditions could be improved through social programs that provide a "social floor" for all citizens (Razavi, 1999; Kabeer, 2004). The fear of job losses is one of the reasons behind the lax policies regarding labor practices in many countries, as in the case of the maquiladora industries employing large number of women in Latin America; this has been intensified by the loss of investment to China and other Asian countries (Watkins, 2002).

There are two types of responses to these arguments. The first is that higher labor standards do not need to result in a loss of competitiveness and exports if proper measures are applied, as Berik and Rodgers (2008) have shown for the case of Cambodia. They contrast the Cambodian experience with that of Bangladesh, where low wages and poor working conditions have persisted without attempts to comply with labor standards. In both countries, garment production is the main source of women's employment—women represent 90 percent of the garment industry's labor force in Cambodia, for example (ILO & World Bank, 2006); both are very poor countries, with precarious working conditions, and face strong competition from China and from world markets in general; and both have managed to increase their exports of garments since the expiration in 2004 of the Agreement on Textiles and Clothing and of the Multi-Fiber Arrangement trade regime.

However, Cambodia has done so while improving its labor standards through the "Better Factories Cambodia" program, the result of a 1999 trade agreement with the United States that called for compliance with the country's labor laws and international labor standards, with the ILO acting as the monitoring institution. In 2006, the ILO reported "fairly good compliance" with several labor standards, such as child labor and gender discrimination, while Bangladesh continued its "poor employer compliance" with the country's own laws. While the ILO report points out that compliance in Cambodia was poor in other areas such as health and safety, a subsequent ILO and World Bank (2006) report mentions improvements in health and nutrition among women workers. What this example demonstrates is that it is possible to improve labor standards without negative consequences for working conditions, production, or export performance.

A second response to the fears of loss of investment and jobs is that the approach should be global. If the strategy were focused on the need to raise at least the core labor standards across countries, the incentives for capital to move to areas with lower standards would disappear. This strategy requires international agreements and an effective monitoring system. Although this would be difficult, it is not far-fetched to think that this is possible if there is political will, particularly since it can be argued that employment security would increase in all countries, especially those threatened by the loss of capital. In the Cambodian case, monitoring costs have been shared between the Government, the United States, and the country's Manufacturing Association; these costs have been kept down thanks to hiring local monitors at wages that were low by international standards (Berik & Rodgers, 2008). At the global level, the ILO could play the crucial role of engaging member countries in negotiating a global agreement. However, this will require cooperation on the part of all country governments, and it may only happen if it is linked to trade incentives, as was the case in Cambodia. Additionally, the ILO would need more resources to take up this task.

Rethinking Informalization and Precarious Work

For almost four decades, development "experts" have been discussing the nature and significance of informal work in developing countries. From its initial conceptualization in the 1970s as the "informal sector" to its pervasive extension as the "informal economy" in more recent times, the literature has discussed widely its characteristics and the extent to which informality has been, and continues to be, an obstacle to or a stimulus for development (Portes & Castells, 1989). The high proportion of women involved in the informal economy makes it imperative to incorporate it in any discussion on development paradigms from a feminist perspective. For women, informal activities often provide an important way to combine income-earning activities with their work in the household and the care of children and family. To be sure, informal work represents highly heterogeneous forms of production and "degrees of informality," generating different income levels and living conditions (Benería & Floro, 2006). However, the bottom line is that a large proportion of it consists of activities with poor, unstable, and unregulated working conditions at subsistence levels.

The nature of informality has been analyzed by a number of authors who have questioned the role it plays in the wider economy. It might be useful to briefly revisit the different conceptualizations in the earlier 1970–1980 debates for the purpose of reexamining current tendencies. Predominant in the 1970s were dualistic representations such as formal/informal and dominant/marginal; the "informal sector" was viewed as a temporary phenomenon of marginality that would gradually be absorbed by the "modern" economy, and thus eventually disappear as a country developed (ILO, 1972). However, the 1980s generated critiques of this initial view by those who saw informality as the result of structural factors and as an integral part of a segmented and socially unequal/uneven capitalist economy. Hence, they rejected the dualistic view separating the "formal" and "informal" while emphasizing the linkages between the two (Benería & Roldán, 1987).

A third position, developed from a neoliberal perspective, is typified by the Peruvian economist Hernando De Soto (2000), who conceptualized informal activities as the result of government overregulation tending to choke individual initiatives and thus limiting economic growth. His prescription of regularizing and embracing informal work for the purpose of fostering development represented a formula highly compatible with the pro-market policies of the past decades. And indeed the pro-market privatization processes of the 1980s and part of the 1990s in Latin America did result in a resurgence of activities that seemed to back up De Soto's arguments. However, there was market saturation in the 1990s, and chronic problems of employment and underemployment continue in the region (Pérez-Sáinz, 2006).

Under globalization, informal activities have become increasingly linked to global production. In this regard, it is useful to distinguish between the "informal economy" and "informalization." While the former relates to the existence of informal activities on the ground, the latter is a process tied to the shift of production to lower cost, more precarious, and more decentralized activities. It is also tied to technological change, since high-tech production has made possible the industrial flexibilization and labor process fragmentation that has intensified these tendencies. As noted above, the informal sector was initially described as a remnant of the premodern conditions found in traditional economies. It would be difficult to argue that this is so for many cases now. While the old sector can still be found—for example, in the type of subsistence activities typified by street vending in urban areas—this is not true of informal production generated by global networks, such as through subcontracting and the so-called value chains, or home-work producing goods for global markets. We can then say that in many ways informality in modern production, rather than being a remnant of the past, has become an integral part of the national and global economy, providing jobs at the margins of subsistence for many workers (Dicken, 2007).

Informalization has also contributed to the crisis of social protection that has accompanied globalization. As Standing (2004) analyzed extensively, economic insecurity has resulted in different forms of social insecurity that have lead to rethinking social protection. In many ways this is also a consequence of the growing inequalities that emerged under neoliberal globalization calling for rethinking distribution. Given the importance of the informal economy in many areas, raising its standards from the bottom–up would affect a large proportion of the world's poor populations. This importance varies across countries, but the estimated proportion of the population engaged in informal work reaches levels as high as 50 percent in many African, Asian, and Latin American economies. For poor countries like Bolivia and Ecuador, it has reached levels as high as 65 and 55 percent of the working population respectively (Benería, 2003). More recently, it has been estimated at 50 percent for Bolivia, compared with 36 percent for Latin America as a whole (ILO & UNDP, 2009).

A key question is how informality can become "formalized" and working conditions upgraded. One possibility is to rely on economic growth, increase in productivity, and high levels of employment. This can create the conditions for upgrading labor standards, especially if there is an effort on the part of labor to press for these demands, and if governments back-up such a process. But relying on growth is far from sufficient. A complementary route can result from efforts to regularize informal activities. This has been illustrated—even though not with outstanding success—in the case of Italy, with an underground economy estimated at 27 percent of its gross national product (GNP). The government introduced measures to promote the regularization of informal activities such as waiving taxes for firms deciding to legalize while penalizing those remaining underground (Busato et al., 2005). Although the case of Italy might differ substantially from that of other countries, it nevertheless points to the possibilities that can be explored. The ILO's "decent work" campaign also represents a global effort in the same direction, as do the many efforts carried out by activists, academics, and NGOs such as the Workers Rights Consortium (WRC) and the Fairtrade Labelling Organization (FLO).

Improving labor conditions also depends on raising productivity, and this points toward factors such as the need to press for more educational opportunities, better access to microfinance and credit in general, technological help for small firms, and improved access to information regarding markets. Ultimately, these measures need to be placed within a macro distributional effort favoring the lower echelons of the labor hierarchy, with special efforts to eliminate gender differences and reverse the trends that have privileged capital.

During the past decade, the ILO has emphasized the discourse of "decent work" as a way to call attention to the poor working conditions under which many people labor. As described by Juan Somavia, the organization's 9th Director General elected in 1998:

> Decent work ... offers a way of combining employment, rights, social protection and social dialogue in developing strategies.... Reducing the decent work deficit is the quality road to poverty reduction and to greater legitimacy of the global economy. (Quoted in Hughes, 2002)

These general goals are highly relevant, even if somewhat vague, for the informal economy. The main challenge is to find ways to make them more specific and applicable at the national and international level.

The Care Economy and the Feminization of International Migration

During the past two decades, international migration has become a hotly debated issue, and the asymmetry in the mobility of labor and capital has created tensions and challenges for policy at the national and international levels. Part of these debates, particularly since the 1990s, has been the feminization of migration (Herrera, 2006; Parreñas, 2005; UNDP, 2009; UNFPA, 2006). In Latin America, for example, women have represented the clear majority among the total migrant population to Spain during the past decade (Benería, 2008a). The female proportion among those who emigrated to Spain in 2006 reached levels as high as 70 percent for Nicaragua, 66 percent for Honduras, 65 percent for Paraguay, and about 56 percent for several countries such as Brazil, the Dominican Republic, Mexico, and Venezuela. For Latin America as a whole, the proportion of 54.62 percent was estimated for a total of over 306,000 women migrants for 2006 (Benería, 2008a). As they are based on official statistics, these figures do not include undocumented migrants.

These increasingly female migrant populations differ from earlier migration flows in Latin America, which were predominantly male and whose main destination tended to be the United States (Herrera, 2006). Women are now in many cases the first family members to move, before men do, with mothers often leaving their children behind. In countries such as Ecuador and the Philippines, the massive migration of women to multiple destinations has generated a national debate about the social loss that this represents and about its social effects, particularly on children and families. These trends are, however, likely to shift under the current economic crisis, and some changes, including a decrease in the number of migrants and in remittances, are already under way (Ratha et al., 2008).

The main reason behind the trends prior to the financial crisis was that migrant women tended to find jobs more easily than men, particularly in the service sector and in a wide range of activities such as care work within families and in the tourism and prostitution industries. To illustrate, the shift of Latin American female migration to Western Europe has resulted from a combination of well-known factors. First, on the demand side, the crisis of care has been felt strongly in countries with a significant increase in women's labor force participation since the 1990s, such as Italy, Spain, and other Southern European countries with inadequate public policies to deal with the problems of balancing domestic and labor market work. This leads to time and cost pressures in households to deal with domestic activities. Second, the care crisis is also due to the aging of the population resulting from the fall in fertility rates and the gradual rise in life expectancy. This has led to further "nuclearization" of the family, with reduced extended family networks to turn to for help.

The deficiencies in services for care provision have been met with immigrant labor hired by individual families. For middle- and upper-class households, immigrant women provide the help needed to deal with their own care crisis and to carry out the tasks of social reproduction, such as looking after children, the sick, and the elderly, and doing domestic work and other family-related chores. Based on her study of Ecuadorian women in Spain, Herrera (2006) reports that nine out of ten immigrant women were engaged in paid domestic work, the proportion being higher among those without legal papers. The jobs pay relatively low wages with respect to those prevalent in the receiving country, but high enough to provide an incentive to migrate. In this sense, they are an integral part of what we can call the "globalization of reproduction."

On the supply side, growing inequalities between high- and low-income countries provide another economic reason to migrate. Other incentives have to do with the sense of insecurity, vulnerability, and instability resulting from economic crises, poverty, and unemployment affecting a proportion of the population in many developing countries. For women, there are also gender-related factors behind their decision to migrate, such as the wish to leave abusive relationships, family conflicts, and different forms of gender discrimination (ibid.). Migration also takes place within the Latin American region, with Bolivian, Ecuadorian, Paraguayan, and Peruvian women working in Argentina, Brazil, and Chile. A variety of studies have shown that women often assume that the family will follow them eventually; when this is not the case, they engage in some form of "international mothering" (Parreñas, 2005). As argued by Parreñas (ibid.) for the case of the Philippines, the export of women's labor generates a "depletion of care resources" for the family left behind. Households have to negotiate who will be responsible for domestic chores and for the children and other family members, including the involvement of men and others in the process, and the extent of transnational mothering. Even if fathers left behind become responsible for taking care of the children, women (especially grandmothers) tend to do a significant proportion of care work. This places a heavy responsibility on older women, who have to carry on mothering roles at an age when their physical health is declining. In any case, it is obvious that there are hidden costs of migration that are not easily captured by economic estimates, including the psychological costs of the dislocation of families and communities that are very difficult to measure.

The geographical dispersal and fragmentation of families with migrant mothers does not only imply a significant shift in gender relations; it is also part of the new gender order associated with globalization through which women's roles experience contradictory changes. On the one hand, there are role reversals, symbolized by their decision to migrate and find employment abroad before men do; likewise, they take on a new role in family maintenance through the remittances sent. Both represent an increase in women's individual and financial autonomy and responsibility that can contribute to a process of "undoing gender" (Benería, 2008b). On the other hand, the prevalence and intensity of transnational mothering also implies a continuity of women's traditional roles; although subject to changes in time and space, there is evidence that migrant women's care of their children does not stop when they physically leave them (Fenstermaker & West, 2002). In her study of children growing up in homes of migrant mothers in the Philippines, Parreñas (2005) illustrates the extent to which the experience of children is different in mother-away versus father-away households. In the first case, children not only feel deprived of their mother's presence and love, but also her absence is socially more difficult for them to accept than that of the father because it goes against conventional social norms and traditional gender roles.

Likewise, Herrera (2006) makes reference to an Ecuadorian mother who is saddened by the fact that her children are resentful of her absence and have not understood her decision to leave. My observations in Bolivia also show that the effect of mothers' migration on children is expressed in contradictory terms. Older children in particular understand the complex reasons behind the mother's decision to emigrate while at the same time they manifest feelings of loss and even anger. Their reactions are also tied to their relationships within the extended family. These examples speak of tensions between role reversals on the one hand and continuities on the other, and between the persistent ideology of women's domesticity and the de facto transformation of gender relations.

Hochschild (2002) has referred to the extraction of care resources from the South by the North as "emotional imperialism," and she has compared it to 19th century imperialism's extraction of material resources. This extraction, she argues, is not done by force or through colonial structures; it is the result of choices that result from economic pressures constituting a different form of coercion. However, while growing North–South inequalities and the problems of development in the South are at the root of these decisions, the issue is more complex, and the comparison with 19th century imperialism is interesting but not totally warranted. Rather than being linked to an institutionalized form of Northern colonialism, the extraction of care resources is the result of world inequalities and of decisions taken by individual households responding to their perceptions of conditions in emigrant and immigrant countries, including the perception that they will benefit from migration.

The solution is not only to be sought in the systematic improvement of economic conditions in the South and the elimination of North–South inequalities, but also depends on the shift of policies in immigrant countries toward the provision of social services that can meet the care needs of individual households. This implies a new turn in policy toward more collective approaches to social provisioning and a shift beyond the dictates of neoliberal regimes. In addition, part of the solution depends on achieving a higher degree of equality in the gender division of labor within households so that men take up their share of care responsibilities. In this sense, charges of emotional imperialism might tend to intensify North–South tensions rather than illuminate the fact that both share the need to counter the consequences of neoliberal policies.

CONCLUDING REMARKS

The current world financial crisis presents an interesting opportunity for women to discuss the challenges around labor and globalization, examined in this chapter, and to ask what makes a good society. A key issue has to do with the extent to which the free market is capable of meeting the needs of all people while eradicating gender inequality along with other forms of discrimination. The debates generated by the crisis have raised important questions along these lines, and I want to focus on three of them: How free—or, to put it differently, how regulated—should the market be? Can a society rely on the role of economic rationality and even greed for the purpose of meeting people's needs and fostering human development? And can gender equality be constructed under capitalism or does it require more egalitarian social structures conducive to dealing with distributive justice and discussing what constitutes a "just society?"

From different circles that include pro-market tendencies and conservative politics, criticisms of the financial meltdown have interpreted it to imply the beginning of the death of laissez-faire economics. As reported in a *New York Times* article, French President Sarkozy declared, "a certain idea of globalization is drawing to a close with the end of financial capitalism that imposed its logic on the whole economy.... The idea that the markets are always right was a crazy idea" (Berenson, 2008). Even economist Lawrence Summers, well-known for his rather controversial pro-market ideas, said, "... problems cannot be addressed by market solutions alone" (ibid.). The result might be the rejection of unregulated markets promoted by the fundamentalism of the Washington Consensus and the acceptance of a tamer and more regulated capitalism. To be sure, opposition to market regulation has already surfaced, especially in the United States and particularly from the financial sector (Krugman, 2009). In any case, it is timely to reexamine feminists' contributions to these questions. This chapter argues that labor market challenges represent one of the key areas that feminists need to discuss in order to build gender equality within more egalitarian societies.

A different but somewhat connected issue concerns the role of economic rationality in human behavior. Orthodox economic thinking and pro-market policies are based on the premise that people are moved by self-interest and individual maximizing behavior regardless of its consequences for others and for society as a whole, a premise that has been questioned by feminist economists and others who see that people are also moved by more altruistic social objectives (Benería, 2003; Ferber & Nelson, 1993). The 1980s represented a historical shift from the more idealistic visions of the 1960s generation, from which modern feminisms emanated, to a world of neoclassical economics. This was the world of financial liberalization and "yuppy" behavior that accompanied globalization, in which there was no room for a social contract in search of collective well-being.

We might be at another turning point and, as another *New York Times* article put it, "greed, to put it mildly, is no longer good" (Steinfels, 2008). The abuses that led to the current systemic crisis seem to have raised many questions about the basic assumptions behind orthodox economics. Milton Friedman's assertion in 1979 that all societies run on greed and the claim (by the character Gordon Gecko in the movie *Wall Street*) that "Greed works... [and] marked the upward surge of mankind."

It is interesting to note that, together with this critique of greed and of the enormous salaries drawn by the CEOs, there has been a new interest in "frugal life styles" and "frugal behaviour" (Hoffman, 2008). At the same time, this turning point, if it lasts, might become a test of whether citizens are ready to accept a "new social contract" that would, for example, call for greater fiscal responsibility (Muñoz, 2009).

Finally, the current crisis presents an opportunity to discuss the extent to which gender equality can be constructed within a system such as capitalism that is based on social inequality. Since the early days of modern feminism, there has been a tension between different points of view in this regard. The past decades have witnessed positive steps toward gender equality, even within the confines of neoliberal globalization. We have observed advances for women at many levels of society, ranging from their higher degrees of representation in politics and the professions to greater financial autonomy and an increase in bargaining power within households.

Yet, we have also been aware of the limits of this progress, symbolized, for example, by the glass ceiling facing women in the professions, the feminization of poverty, the persistence of discriminatory practices in the workplace, and the problems of social protection (UNDESA-DAW, 2009). This chapter has raised this question of limits by looking at how unregulated labor markets generate inequalities that place women at the bottom of labor market hierarchies in global production. The implication is that gender inequality needs to be contextualized within the wider system of social inequalities.

REFERENCES

Atkinson, R. D., & Court, R. (2002). *The new economy index: Understanding America's economic transformation*. Washington: Progressive Policy Institute.

Benería, L. (2003). *Gender, development and globalization: Economics as if all people mattered*. New York: Routledge.

90 Lourdes Benería

Benería, L. (2008a). The crisis of care, international migration, and public policy. *Feminist Economics, 14*(3), 1–21.

———. (2008b). Globalització, mercats de treballo i la transformació dels rols de les dones. *Revista Catalana de Geografia,* Fall.

Benería, L., & Floro, M. S. (2006). Labor market informalization, gender and social protection: Reflections on poor urban households in Bolivia, Ecuador and Thailand. In S. Razavi & S. Hassim (Ed.), *Gender and social policy in a global context: Uncovering the gendered social structure of "the social."* Basingstoke: Palgrave.

Benería, L., & Roldán, M. (1987). *The crossroads of class and gender: Homework, subcontracting, and household dynamics in Mexico City.* Chicago: University of Chicago Press.

Berenson, A. (2008, October 5). How free should a market be? Week in Review. *The New York Times.*

Berik, G., & Rodgers, Y. (2008). Options for enforcing labor standards: Lessons from Bangladesh and Cambodia. *Journal of International Development, 22*(1) (published online November 4). Retrieved September 10, 2009, from http://onlinelibrary.wiley.com/doi/10.1002/jid.1534/pdf

Busato, F., Chiarini, B., de Angelis, P., & Marzano, E. (2005). *Capital subsidies and the underground economy.* Economics Working Papers No. 2005–10, School of Economics and Management, University of Aarhus.

De Soto, H. (2000). *El misterio del capital.* Lima: Empresa Editoria El Comercio.

Dicken, P. (2007). *Global shift: Reshaping the global economic map in the 21st century.* London: SAGE Publications.

Economist, The. (1997, February 1). In praise of Davos man: How businessmen may accidentally be making the world safer [Editorial]. *The Economist.*

Fenstermaker, S., & West, C. (2002). *Doing gender, doing difference: inequality, power, and institutional change.* New York: Routledge.

Ferber, M., & Nelson, J. (Eds). (1993). *Beyond economic man.* Chicago: University of Chicago Press.

Fussell, E. (2000). Making labor flexible: The recomposition of Tijuana's maquiladora female labor force. *Feminist Economics, 6*(3), 59–79.

Hart, G. (2002). *Disabling globalization: Places and power in post-apartheid South Africa.* Berkeley, California: University of California Press.

Herrera, G. (2006). Mujeres ecuatorianas en las cadenas globales del cuidado. In G. Herrera & M. Moreno-Ruiz (Eds), *Cohesión social, politicas conciliatorias y presupuesto público: una mirada desde el género.* Mexico City: United Nations Population Fund (UNFPA) and GTZ.

Hochschild, A. (2002). Love and gold. In B. Ehreinreich & A. Hochschild (Eds), *Global woman: Nannies, maids, and sex workers in the new economy* (pp. 15–30). New York: Holt.

Hoffman, J. (2008, October 12). The frugal teenager, ready or not [Sunday Styles]. *The New York Times.*

Hsiung, P. C. (1995). *Living rooms as factories: Class, gender, and the satellite factory system in Taiwan.* Philadelphia: Temple University Press.

Hughes, S. (2002). Coming in from the cold: Labor, the ILO, and the international labor standards regime. In R. Wilkinson & S. Hughes (Eds), *Global governance: Critical perspectives* (pp. 151–168). New York: Routledge.

Huntington, S. P. (1996). *The clash of civilizations and the remaking of world order.* New York: Simon and Schuster.

ILO (International Labour Organization) (1972). *Employment, incomes and inequality: Strategy for increasing productive employment in Kenya.* Geneva: ILO.

———. (2003). *Employment and social policy in respect of EPZs.* Papers of the Governing Body, 286th Session. Geneva: ILO.

———. (2004). *Economic security for a better world.* Geneva: ILO.

———. (2007). *Declaration on fundamental principles and rights at work.* Retrieved October 15, 2008, from http://www.wiego.org/stat_picture/www.ilo.org/declaration/langen/index.htm

———. (2008). *World of work report 2008: Income inequalities in the age of financial globalization.* Geneva: ILO.

ILO, & UNDP (United Nations Development Programme). (2009). *Trabajo y familia: hacia nuevas formas de conciliación con corresponsabilidad social* (Joint report). La Paz.

ILO, & World Bank. (2006). *Cambodia: Women and work in the garment industry.* Phnom Penh: ILO Better Factories Cambodia and World Bank Justice for the Poor Program.

Kabeer, N. (2004). Labor standards, women's rights, basic needs: Challenges to collective action in a globalizing world. In L. Benería & S. Bisnath (Eds), *Global tensions: Challenges and opportunities in the world economy* (pp. 143–159). New York: Routledge.

Katz, H. C. (2000). *Converging divergences: Worldwide changes in employment systems.* Ithaca, New York: Cornell University Press.

Krugman, P. (2009, November 29). Taxing the speculators. *The New York Times.*

Lee, E. (1997). Globalization and labour standards. *International Labour Review, 136* (Summer), 171–189.

Liem, R., & Kim, J. (1992). The Pico Korea workers struggle. *Amerasia Journal, 18*(1), 49–68.

Muñoz, R. (2009, April 4). Avaricia, sí; pero no con mis impuestos. *El País,* pp. 34–35.

Ngai, P. (2007). Gendering the dormitory labor system: Production, reproduction, and migrant labor in South China. *Feminist Economics, 13*(3–4), 239–258.

Nocera, J. (2008, October 20). A hail Mary pass, hoping to find a receiver in the end zone. *The New York Times.*

Parreñas, R. S. (2005). *Children of global migration: Transnational migration and gendered woes.* Palo Alto, California: Stanford University Press.

Pérez-Sáinz, J. P. (2006). Labor exclusion in Latin America: Old and new tendencies. In N. Kudva & L. Benería (Eds), *Rethinking informalization: Poverty, precarious jobs, and social protection.* Cornell University e-Press.

Pizarro, R. (2006). *The ethics of world food production: The case of salmon farming in Chile.* Paper presented at the Cornell Conference on International Development, September 15–16.

Portes, A., & Castells, M. (1989). *The informal economy.* Baltimore, Maryland: The Johns Hopkins University Press.

Ratha, D., Mohapata, S., & Xu, Z. (2008). *Outlook for remittances flows* (Development Brief, no. 8). The World Bank, Washington, DC.

Razavi, S. (1999). Export-oriented employment, poverty and gender: contested accounts. *Development and Change, 30*(3), 653–683.

Saez, E. (2008). Striking it richer: The evolution of top incomes in the United States. *Pathways Magazine,* Winter, 6–7. Retrieved September 15, 2009, from http://www.wiego.org/stat_picture/www.stanford.edu/group/scspi/pdfs/pathways/winter_2008/Saez.pdf

Salzinger, L. (2003). *Genders in production.* New York: Routledge.

Schwartz, N. D. (2008, September 20). Uncharted territory led to a new kind of crisis. *The New York Times.*

Standing, G. (2004). Globalization: Eight crises of social protection. In L. Benería & S. Bisnath (Eds), *Global tensions: challenges and opportunities in the world economy* (pp. 111–133). New York: Routledge.

Steinfels, P. (2008, September 27). Modern market thinking has devalued a deadly sin. *The New York Times,* p. A19.

Stiglitz, J., Sen, A., & Fitoussi, J. P. (2009). *Report of the commission on the measurement of economic performance and social progress.* Retrieved September 15, 2009, from http://www.wiego.org/stat_picture/www.efta.int/content/statistics/StatData/stiglitzreport-140909

Stone, K. (2006). The new face of employment discrimination. In J. Fudge & R. Owens (Eds), *Precarious work: Women and the new economy* (pp. 243–264). Oxford: Hart Publishing.

UNDESA-DAW (United Nations Department of Economic and Social Affairs–Division for the Advancement of Women). (2009). *World survey on the role of women in development.* New York: United Nations.

UNDP (United Nations Development Programme). (2009). *Human development report 2009: Overcoming barriers—human mobility and development.* New York: Palgrave Macmillan.

UNFPA (United Nations Population Fund). (2006). *The state of world population 2006: Women and international migration.* New York: UNFPA.

Wachtel, H. (2004). Tax. In L. Benería & S. Bisnath (Eds), *Global tensions: Challenges and opportunities in the world economy* (pp. 27–43). New York: Routledge.

Watkins, R. (2002). Mexico versus China: Factors affecting export and investment competition. *Industry Trade and Technology Review,* July, 11–26.

5

Removing the Cloak of Invisibility
Integrating Unpaid Household Services in the Philippines' Economic Accounts

SOLITA COLLAS-MONSOD

One of the conclusions at Casablanca was that unless women's contributions to the economy are recognized and accepted, women will continue to be second-class citizens, with all the negative implications of this. And nobody but women can be relied on to push for that recognition and acceptance.

UN SCHIZOPHRENIA AND THE INVISIBLE WOMAN

*T*he United Nations (UN) system is at the forefront of efforts to achieve gender equality, the elimination of discrimination against women, and gender mainstreaming. The system includes the Commission on the Status of Women (CSW), which had its 54th session in 2010; the Committee on the Elimination of Discrimination against Women (CEDAW Committee), which had its 47th session in 2010; the Division for the Advancement of Women (DAW) in the United Nations Department of Economic and Social Affairs (UNDESA); as well as the United Nations Development Programme (UNDP), International Research and Training Institute for the Advancement of Women (INSTRAW), United Nations Development Fund for Women (UNIFEM), and International Labour Organization (ILO), among others.[1]

---

[1] Several of these entities (DAW, INSTRAW, and UNIFEM) had been amalgamated by the time of publication into UN Women.

The UN designated a decade for women (1976–1985) and organized four world conferences on women. The first of these, in 1975, recognized the need to measure and value women's unpaid work. Ten years later, at the third, the UN Economic and Social Council (ECOSOC) endorsed a package of strategies, with a recommendation that the value of household goods and services be included in countries' GNP:

> The remunerated and, in particular, the unremunerated contributions of women to all aspects and sectors of development should be recognized, and appropriate efforts should be made to measure and reflect these contributions in national accounts and economic statistics and in the gross national product. Concrete steps should be taken to quantify the unremunerated contribution of women to agriculture, food production, reproduction and household activities. (United Nations, 1985, paragraph 120)

There are also eight Millennium Development Goals (MDGs), the third of which aims to "promote gender equality and empower women." The MDGs are a road map for implementing the Millennium Declaration, agreed by 189 governments at the September 2000 UN Millennium Summit in New York. The Declaration commits governments "to promote gender equality and the empowerment of women as effective ways to combat poverty, hunger and disease and to stimulate development that is truly sustainable" (UN, 2000). Most recently, on July 2, 2010, the General Assembly voted unanimously to create a new entity—to be known as UN Women—to accelerate progress in meeting the needs of women and girls worldwide.

Yet, all these efforts are being undermined in another part of the UN system: the Statistics Division (also part of UNDESA) and its System of National Accounts (SNA), which gives the guidelines and procedures for estimating a country's GDP and national income. Introduced in 1947, this national accounting system was "based essentially on the model of an advanced industrial economy in which transactions in money are dominant" (Bos, 2005, p. 202).

Since then four major revisions have taken place (1953, 1968, 1993, and 2008), but there is one constant according to Bos: "they all exclude unpaid household services, do-it-yourself activities, voluntary work and the services of consumer durables. These types of production are ignored despite the existence of paid counterparts that are counted as production" (ibid., p. 203).

Thus have the majority of the economic contributions of women in households been rendered invisible by a statistical cloak provided by the

SNA. This is supremely ironic given that the word "economics" is derived from the Greek word "oikonomia" meaning "the management of family and household." The efforts of the Dr Jekylls in the UN system have been negated by the Mr Hydes in the same schizophrenic system. What follows is an examination of the narrow, inadequate, erroneous definitions and concepts that are used to weave that cloak of invisibility and ultimately lay the basis for a hidden, and therefore even more virulent, type of discrimination against women. The chapter then discusses what is needed to remove the cloak of invisibility, and the Philippines experience in that regard, before ending with a look at the road ahead.

THE SNA, WARTS, AND ALL

Originally, the so-called production boundary of the SNA excluded not only the value of services but also the value of goods produced at home for own consumption. Slowly, over time, exceptions were made for certain kinds of goods (for example, primary products and their processing), until in 1993 all goods produced for home consumption were finally allowed to enter the national accounts. But the exclusion of services—household members producing household and personal services for own consumption (that is, cleaning, meal preparation, caring and instruction of children, caring for the sick) and volunteer workers in non-profit institutions serving households—has remained, as mentioned earlier, a constant.

Nonmarket, Therefore Noneconomic

The articulated reasons for the non-inclusion of these activities are as follows:

- Large nonmonetary flows of this type would obscure what is happening in the market and thus reduce the usefulness of the SNA.
- The inclusion of the production of personal services by household members for their own final consumption would imply that such persons were self-employed, thus "making unemployment virtually impossible by definition…" (ISWGNA, 1993, paragraph 1.22).
- The activities have a limited impact on the rest of the economy.
- It is difficult to obtain market prices to value these services.
- There are differences in their economic significance for analytical purposes.

All of the above are used to highlight the need to "confine the production boundary in the SNA and other related statistical systems to market activities or fairly close substitutes for market activities" (ISWGNA, 1993, paragraph 1.22).

I have been teaching economics for almost 40 years and never once have I come across a definition of "economics" that equates it with markets. There are "command economies" and there are "nonmarket economies." The basic fact of economics is scarcity, not markets. The SNA's dictum is that only what is marketed is economic (which is more descriptive of developed countries). This exclusion of the household economy from the total economy has distorted the macroeconomic picture—at best giving only a partial one, particularly in developing countries not far removed from the subsistence level.

But the non-recognition of the contribution of women to the economy and society in national statistics has also implicitly perpetuated gender inequalities.

> Official non-recognition of contributions to the national as much as to the household economy obviously leads to non-recognition in policy-making, planning, allocation of resources, the provision of support services and information, and of course in the distribution of the benefits of development. The failure to recognize much of the work that women do is therefore a failure to take women into account in all these areas. (APCAS, 1994)

Producers of Non-marketed Services Are Therefore Not "Economically Active"

There is a devastating corollary: since nonmarketed services are invisible in GDP, the efforts that went into producing these goods inevitably became invisible as well. How? Again, by definition. According to the ILO, to be a member of the labor force, or to be "economically active," one must not only be above a specified age (working age), but must also be engaged in the production of economic goods and services—as defined by the SNA. And, since the SNA-defined economic services exclude production for home consumption, those involved solely in the latter—mostly women—are automatically excluded from the labor force. These producers are considered economically inactive, which is the greatest irony since it is the work they do at home and in the community that makes it possible for husbands and children to participate in the economy as consumers and producers (now and in the future). Arguably, it is this labor that allows the rest of the economy to function, yet those who are doing it are considered to be "at leisure" or "dependents."

The SNA Reasoning in a Nutshell

Reduced to its simplest terms here is what the SNA would have us accept: if a service is not marketed, it is not economic; if it is not economic, the producers cannot be considered to be economically active (that is, they cannot be part of the labor force). The alternative would be to classify them as self-employed, which would render unemployment virtually impossible—and that is a no-no. In other words, for the high priests of the SNA, it is better to make unpaid labor services in the home invisible than to rethink employment concepts—a case of the tail wagging the dog.

The "Unemployment Virtually Impossible" Card

Let us examine this assertion a little more closely. Assume a conventional labor force of 100, with 90 employed and 10 unemployed, and therefore an unemployment rate of 10 percent. Now assume that the inclusion of unpaid household services will increase the labor force by 50, or 50 percent. The unemployment rate would decrease (to 6.7 percent) but the number of unemployed would remain the same, unless it is further assumed that all those who were considered unemployed under the conventional system (those not working but seeking work) are all producing household services.

In this "worst case" scenario, attention would shift from unemployment to employment in general and underemployment (those working but seeking more work) in particular, which, given the present realities, is what should have been done in the first place. For example, the present protocol considers a person to be employed if she has spent at least one hour of the past week in "productive" work, such as feeding chickens, but does not consider her to be part of the labor force if she has spent 40 hours in the past week in "reproductive" work, such as feeding and caring for her children.

As regards underemployment, it is clear, looking at the statistics on poverty and employment, that it is not the quantity so much as the quality of employment that is important. The general view is that unemployment and poverty are closely connected. That is a myth. In a country like the Philippines, the poor cannot afford to be unemployed. Family poverty incidence in the Philippines was 26.9 percent in 2006, using national standards. Where the head of household was self-employed (using ILO norms) it was 34.3 percent, while where the head of household was unemployed it was a much lower 11.6 percent. The self-employed group, by the way, makes up over half of the total number of poor families in the Philippines. It is they, the self-employed, who deserve at least as much attention as the unemployed. And, if they now include those who labor without pay to produce goods, there should be every reason to also include those who labor without pay to produce services that are so necessary for basic survival and quality of life.

In any case, because of the kind of thinking behind the SNA, we are left with this conundrum: why is it that when we pay for childcare and house-cleaning, when we eat out, when we buy milk for our babies, or when we call in the mechanic or the plumber, these add to GDP and count toward economic growth and progress; but when we look after our own children, clean our own house, cook our own meals, breastfeed our babies, tune up our own cars, and fix our own leaking faucets, these have no value in our current measures of progress?

Sometimes statisticians will even go to great lengths to try to measure illegal activities in the economy, as in the following:

> Informal Activities: Countries should try to make estimates from both the value added and expenditure sides of all the economic activities covered in the SNA production boundary. These include both informal and illegal activities where these are considered to be significant. Where an informal activity is known to be going on at a significant level, the worst estimate is zero but this is implicitly the estimate that is being made if the informal activity is simply ignored. *Even a very crude estimate will improve the accuracy of the accounts.* (ICP, 2003, p. 2; emphasis in original)

Thus, we are urged to include illegal activities (since they are within the SNA production boundary), but we are not allowed to include the nurturing services that shape our very future. Another irony is that as the household economy shifts to the market economy, this is registered as growth in GDP, even though no additional production is actually performed. Such nonsense.

Is a Satellite Account the Answer? No, It Is Not

In what is considered by many to be a major step forward, the 1993 SNA recommended the use of special satellite accounts that can be linked to but are separate from the SNA accounts, in recognition of the limitations of the central framework in addressing specific aspects of economic life important to a particular country. Satellite accounts, the 1993 SNA stated, "expand the analytical capacity of national accounting for selected areas of social concern in a flexible manner, without overburdening or disrupting the central system ..." (ISWGNA, 1993, paragraph 21.4). The terms used are "augmented," "expanded," and "enhanced" GDP. This has been regarded by many as a "realistic" compromise between the advantages of tradition and the adaptation of new economic, social, and political requirements.

Certainly, including unpaid household services in a satellite account is better than excluding it completely, but there are disadvantages to this. First, relegating women's contribution to GDP to an adjunct, supplemental position violates the concept of gender equality—if women and men are to be treated equally, they should be equally visible in the national accounts. An "augmented," "expanded," "enhanced" GDP (such patronizing terms) is not the answer. What is needed is an accurate picture that reflects the reality on the ground. Why should women not be included in the "central system"? Second, insisting on a truncated GDP—and it is truncated, as we all know from various estimates (Appendix 5.1A) of just how much unpaid work contributes to the economy—and then "enhancing" it is like amputating a person's leg and then throwing a stick at her.

Third, the reference to the "advantages" of tradition versus new economic, social, and political requirements may be misplaced. The cavalier treatment of women's caring services at home has not always been the norm. Over 200 years ago, in the population censuses in England and the United States, housewives—or, more accurately, "women whose work consisted largely of caring for their families"—were considered to be productive, gainful workers. Unfortunately, over time, that view of the role of women slowly changed, so that by 1,900 housewives were no longer considered productive workers; they were formally relegated to the census category of "dependents" (which included infants, young children, the sick, and the elderly)—mouths, rather than hands. This situation was partly due to the influence of Alfred Marshall, the greatest economist of his time (Folbre, 1991).

Fourth, as mentioned previously, "economic" and "market" are not, never have been, and never should be interchangeable. Certainly economies in developed countries are primarily market economies, but imposing that as a criterion for the developing world makes no sense. We should remind ourselves that GDP is the measure of the market value of all final goods and services produced in a country during a year; it is not the market value of only those final goods and services that are bought and sold in a market. Using the latter definition, for fear of being overburdened, is, to borrow an analogy, like looking for one's car keys one block away from where one lost them because the light is better; it may be brighter, but you will not find the keys.

Undoubtedly, the valuation of unpaid work is difficult, but experiencing difficulties is at par for the course in national income accounting, or for that matter in any endeavor where measurement is involved. Prior to its publication by UNDP, Mahbub Ul Haq's Human Development Index (HDI), a comparative measure of living standards in countries worldwide, was the subject of savage criticism (come to that, it is still being criticized), and he was advised not to use it until the problems were ironed out. If Ul Haq had followed that advice, the HDI would still be unpublished today and the world would be the poorer for it. Instead, he took the plunge and, with the HDI being constantly finetuned, it is still a work in progress. What was important was that the methodology used was transparent, the need for improvement was recognized, and constructive criticism was welcomed. Following the UNDP lead, many countries are now estimating intranational HDIs.

More to the point, it is not as if unpaid work in the national accounts is uncharted territory. The Norwegian national accounts for the periods 1935–1943 and 1946–1949 included estimates of the value of unpaid household work, as apparently did other Scandinavian countries (Aslaksen & Koren, 1996). This begs the question: if it could be done 60 or 70 years ago, why not now?

In summary, the SNA cloaks the contribution of women to the economy with invisibility by using narrow, and at the very least inadequate, definitions. But that cloak of invisibility can and should be removed, and including women's contribution in satellite accounts should not be considered a final and permanent solution but rather a preliminary and temporary one.

Slow Progress

If it is indisputable that women's contributions to the economy are statistically invisible, it is at least arguable that time-use data, either from full time-use surveys or from time-use questions included in regular household surveys, are indispensable in counting the paid and unpaid work of women and men. Time-use data are therefore a necessary first step in removing that cloak of invisibility. The second step would be to use the time-use data to create monetary measures of the value of nonmarket production to facilitate their integration into the GDP figures—in the current environment, through the use of satellite accounts. The third step would be to create the satellite accounts and to institutionalize them (to prevent them from being one-shot deals). The final step would, of course, be the full integration of unpaid labor into a country's national accounts.

Much work has already been done with regard to the first step. A 1999 report (Horrigan et al., 1999) lists some 57 time-use surveys undertaken by 38 countries from 1924 to 1999 (the first was conducted in what was then the Soviet Union). The UN Statistics Division website (http://unstats. un.org/unsd/default.htm) features a map and a list of countries and areas that conducted time-use surveys between 1990 and 2004—20 in all; seven from the developed and 13 from the developing world. The UN Economic and Social Commission for Asia and the Pacific (ESCAP, n.d.) reports that 95 time-use surveys were undertaken in 19 of the 58 member countries between 1960 and 2003. It also reports that at the world level, 82 countries have carried out at least one time-use survey. Along the way, many conceptual, methodological, and measurement problems have been ironed out, and many lessons learned.

However, of these 82 countries that have undertaken at least one time-use survey, not many have used the data gathered to value the time spent on unpaid household labor. Even fewer countries have started or developed household satellite accounts. And just a handful have institutionalized the survey (that is, conducted it on a regular basis).

Why is it that the majority of countries do so little follow-up in terms of integrating unpaid work into the country's national accounts? One reason could be that the learning curve is a steep one, notwithstanding the enormous research and training efforts by organizations like INSTRAW (1995, 1996) and ESCAP (ESCAP & UNDP, 2003), as well as by national institutions. Then there are the usual problems related to lack of financial resources, particularly in developing countries.

But resolving the technical problems involved in time-use surveys and the valuation of the unpaid work that they generate is still not sufficient to achieve the goal of integrating unpaid work into national accounts and macroeconomic policy. The support of policymakers and stakeholders has to be mobilized, which requires that they are made aware of the benefits to be derived from this integration. Without that support, the valuable data gathered and analyzed may be confined to academic interest, or worse, left to molder on library shelves.

REMOVING THE INVISIBILITY: THE PHILIPPINES EXPERIENCE

In this regard, the Philippines experience may be instructive. As far as gender empowerment goes (and it does not go very far), the Philippines has been shown to be better off than some other countries in East and Southeast Asia that boast of higher per capita incomes and a higher HDI. As can be seen from Table 5.1, it has the lowest GDP per capita and the lowest HDI of those listed, but the highest Gender Empowerment Measure (GEM), a measure that focuses on the participation of women in political and economic decision making as well as power over economic resources (UNDP, 2006).

Table 5.1 Per capita income, human development index (HDI), and gender empowerment measure (GEM), selected countries, 2004

Country	Per capita GDP purchasing power parity (ppp) USD	HDI rank	GEM rank
Malaysia	10,276	0.804 (61)	0.506 (55)
Thailand	8,090	0.784 (74)	0.486 (60)
South Korea	20,499	0.912 (26)	0.502 (53)
Philippines	4,614	0.763 (84)	0.533 (45)

At the same time, the country is one of four (with Canada, Ghana, and India) cited as good-practice case studies in the development of gender-sensitive indicators in a Commonwealth Secretariat reference manual for governments and other stakeholders (Beck, 1999). It is not coincidental that a majority of the high-level personnel in the Philippines Statistical System are women. In short, the Philippines would have to be included in any list of developing countries in the forefront of women's visibility-raising activities.

Effects of the International Conferences on Women

It must be said that much of the success the country has had in advancing the status of women and moving toward gender equality is due to the galvanizing effects of the preparations for, and the aftermaths of, the UN international conferences on women. The National Commission on the Role of Filipino Women (NCRFW), the first national machinery on women in Asia, was established by Presidential Decree at the beginning of 1975, in time for the First World Conference on Women in Mexico City. The 1985 Nairobi conference caused another flurry of activity, this time focused on mainstreaming women's concerns in policymaking, planning, and programming of all government agencies. This led to the launching of the Philippines Development Plan for Women, 1989–1992 (which may have been the first of its kind), and a successful lobby for legislation ensuring women equal rights in all areas (Women in Nation-Building Act). The Philippines Plan for Gender-responsive Development (1995–2025) was adopted under Executive Order 273 as the country's main vehicle for implementing the Beijing Declaration and Platform for Action from the Fourth World Conference on Women in 1995. The Beijing Platform outlines the policies, strategies, programs, and projects that governments must establish to enable women to participate in, and benefit from, national development.

The numbers to support all the great words were provided by an Inter-Agency Committee on Women and Statistics, which published the first edition of *Statistics on Filipino Women* (National Statistics Office, 1992). The best of these efforts was to empirically measure the contribution of women to the economy in terms of the SNA-type GDP, but more importantly, their share in a GDP that more accurately reflected all productive activities in the economy.

Promising Start

Scarcely two years after the Beijing conference, the country's National Statistical Coordination Board (NSCB) proceeded to construct satellite accounts. These identified the distribution of economic production by sex in accordance with the SNA production boundary; identified, measured, and included unpaid housework services of those in the labor force, also by sex; and included the unpaid work of those not in the labor force (that is, those not considered economically active in the SNA).

Of course, there were problems that would have discouraged the faint-hearted. The proposed national time-use survey project, the first to be conducted nationwide and the results of which were to be the used in the NSCB's valuation attempts, fell by the wayside—a victim of a change in the executive directorship of the NCRFW and an accompanying change in priorities (in favor of an all-out push for programs and projects to eliminate violence against women).

The attempt to distinguish the contributions of females and males to the "conventional" GDP also met with problems. For example, GDP by employment reflects the number of employed persons by sex but not by labor input (and the one-hour per week definition of employment complicates matters). Other problems included underestimation due to the fact that unpaid housework is also done by persons younger than 15 years of age, as well as problems associated with classification and valuation of the different types of unpaid labor (it is noteworthy that the value assigned to housework was assumed to be equal to that of janitors, using the so-called generalist approach).

Undaunted, the NSCB decided to press ahead using data generated from previous time-use surveys. This in itself posed some challenges, namely the need to validate the data and their shortcomings (for example, surveys were not nationwide, and volunteer work and travel related to unpaid work were not included in any previous survey).

Still the effort was an excellent start toward removing the cloak of invisibility of unpaid labor as far as the economy was concerned. The work was completed in 1998 and the results, covering the years 1990 to 1997 and subsequently updated to 1998, are summarized in Tables 5.2–5.5 (taken from Virola & de Perio, 1998).

Table 5.2   Percentage distribution of GDP by sex, 1990–1998, at current prices

Year	Men		Women	
	Employment	Hours of work	Employment	Hours of work
1990	63.5	63.2	36.5	36.8
1991	62.7	62.3	37.2	37.7
1992	62.9	63.1	37.1	36.9
1993	61.9	62.3	38.1	37.67
1994	61.5	62.3	38.5	37.7
1995	61.8	61.8	38.2	38.2
1996	61.7	62.5	38.3	37.5
1997	61.5	61.4	38.4	38.6
1998	64.5	60.5	35.5	39.5
1990–1998	62.5	62.2	37.5	37.8

Women in the Philippines Economy

Briefly, the findings were as follows:

- The share of women in the "conventional" GDP (including only SNA activities), as measured by employment and by hours of work, ranged from 35–39 percent (Table 5.2). In the more accurate GDP, which includes unpaid work (the NSCB calls it the "adjusted" GDP), women's contribution increases to 48–53 percent (Tables 5.3 and 5.4).
- With the inclusion of unpaid household services, GDP itself increases by 27–40 percent over the nine-year period (Table 5.5).
- Women perform about 90 percent of the total unpaid hours of work (which is much higher than the 65–68 percent share in a developed country like Canada during roughly the same period). Among the employed and unemployed, women do about 71–73 percent of total unpaid hours, but this goes up to 91 percent among those not in the labor force according to SNA–ILO definitions (Table 5.5).

Table 5.3 Percentage distribution of GDP and GNP adjusted for unpaid household services by sex using hours of work, employed-opportunity cost, unemployed, and not in the labor market price, in million pesos at current prices

Year	GDP adjusted			GNP adjusted		
	Total	Men	Women	Total	Men	Women
1990	100	51.9	48.1	100	52.7	47.3
1991	100	49.3	50.7	100	50.1	49.9
1992	100	48.5	51.5	100	49.3	50.7
1993	100	49.5	50.5	100	50.3	49.7
1994	100	49.0	51.0	100	49.7	50.3
1995	100	49.8	50.2	100	50.3	49.7
1996	100	50.2	49.8	100	51.0	49.0
1997	100	48.7	51.3	100	49.5	50.5
1998	100	47.3	52.7	100	48.3	51.7
1990–1998	100	49.4	50.6	100	50.1	49.9

Table 5.4 Percentage distribution of GDP and GNP adjusted for unpaid household services by sex using hours of work, employed, unemployed, and not in the labor market price, in million pesos at current prices

Year	GDP adjusted			GNP adjusted		
	Total	Men	Women	Total	Men	Women
1990	100	52.1	47.9	100	52.9	47.1
1991	100	49.5	50.5	100	50.3	49.7
1992	100	48.6	51.4	100	49.4	50.6
1993	100	49.7	50.3	100	50.5	49.5
1994	100	49.2	50.8	100	49.8	50.2
1995	100	49.9	50.1	100	50.5	49.5
1996	100	50.3	49.7	100	51.1	48.9
1997	100	48.8	51.2	100	49.6	50.4
1998	100	47.3	52.7	100	48.4	51.6
1990–1998	100	49.5	50.5	100	50.3	49.7

- In terms of economic activity, the contribution of women to unpaid hours of work in sectors making up about 80 percent of GDP (that is, agriculture, fisheries, and forestry; manufacturing, wholesale, and retail trades; financing, insurance, real estate, and business services; and community, social, and personal services) is greater than that of men (Table 5.5).

These results were presented nationally in the National Conference of Statistics and internationally in the International Statistical Institute biennial meetings in 1999 in Helsinki (where it was the only paper dealing with the contribution of women to the economy).

Table 5.5 Percentage distribution of total unpaid hours of work (housework services) by sex, employed, unemployed, and not in the labor force

	1990		1991		1992		1993	
	Male	Female	Male	Female	Male	Female	Male	Female
A. Employed	27.46	72.54	27.30	72.70	27.98	72.02	27.26	72.74
Agriculture, fishery, and forestry	13.14	14.97	13.38	14.63	13.60	16.19	12.99	15.75
Mining and quarrying	0.24	0.09	0.27	0.10	0.26	0.09	0.22	0.08
Manufacturing	2.44	8.90	2.60	9.72	2.79	9.98	2.59	9.27
Electricity, gas, and water	0.15	0.16	0.17	0.14	0.15	0.11	0.17	0.13
Construction	1.92	0.17	2.00	0.22	1.98	0.20	2.03	0.20
Wholesale and retail trade	2.57	22.12	2.23	23.15	2.31	23.30	2.40	23.12
Transportation, communication, and storage	2.47	0.40	2.44	0.43	2.57	0.52	2.76	0.52
Finance, insurance, real estate, and business services	0.61	1.66	0.57	1.51	0.58	1.54	0.60	1.72
Community, social and personal services	3.91	24.09	3.65	22.80	3.74	20.10	3.49	21.94
B. Unemployed	25.98	74.02	27.35	72.65	27.93	72.07	28.40	71.60
C. Not in the labor force	8.93	91.07	8.44	91.56	8.53	91.47	8.94	91.06
Total	10.49	89.51	10.14	89.86	10.26	89.74	10.64	89.36

No Effect

While the paper was of interest to professionals in the field, it made no dent whatsoever on the consciousness of policymakers or Filipino women, much less on the public consciousness. Actually, it never reached them at all. The results were as invisible as the unpaid work that was being measured, and therefore could not have made a difference.

A time-use survey conducted in 2000 by the National Statistics Office initially met the same fate. In spite of all the methodological and conceptual advances both in time-use and valuation processes, there seemed to be no felt need for a national time-use survey, so the proposal was scaled down to "pilot" status covering only two areas, one urban and one rural. Even then, the results did not seem to have captured the attention of, or made any impression on, the major stakeholders, although they were used by the NSCB to update the "adjusted" GDP figures for 1999 and 2000.

No further work was done from 2001 to 2007 on measuring women's contribution to the economy and the integration of unpaid labor into the national accounts. In 2007, though, efforts were renewed in the aftermath of a meeting that was held in Casablanca as part of an attempt to revitalize the feminist movement and put forward an alternative vision of progress that stresses social justice (see www.casablanca-dream.net/meetings/casablanca_2007.html).

Post-Casablanca Developments

One of the conclusions at Casablanca was that unless women's contributions to the economy are recognized and accepted, women will continue to be second-class citizens, with all the negative implications of this. And nobody but women can be relied on to push for that recognition and acceptance. This was what spurred me to contact the Secretary General of the NSCB, Dr Romeo Virola, to get a better feel of what it would take to pursue the goal of integrating women's unpaid labor into the macroeconomic picture provided by our national accounts, and perhaps even set a time frame for achieving this goal. Dr Virola was supportive of the idea, and welcomed my concern. He told me of the efforts he had already made—and abandoned—in this regard (as recounted earlier). But he assured me that he and his staff would be eager to resume those efforts—if there was a demand for it. At the time of writing, re-estimates of the national accounts to include the contribution of household labor by sex have been carried out for the period from 2001 to 2009. And preparations are being made for a national time-use survey to be conducted in 2011.

Although there are still many conceptual technical, methodological, and measurement problems to be ironed out, Dr Virola did not agree with the conventional (read UN SNA) thinking that these constituted the main obstacle to estimating women's contributions to the economy in general, and the integration of unpaid work into the national accounts in particular. These could be overcome, and to a certain extent, the results of the NSCB's earlier efforts demonstrated this. What had caused Dr Virola to abandon his efforts was a lack of demand. As he said, "How can we continue to produce statistics that are not being asked for, or used, when there are calls for other data to be generated?"

What is behind this lack of demand? There may be a lack of understanding of how the statistics can be used for more effective decision making (on the part of the policymakers) or how they can be used as tools in influencing these decisions (on the part of the policy advocates). To overcome this, what is needed, according to Dr Virola, is "capacity-building of the users of the statistics."

But the demand constraint may arise not only because of a lack of ability on the part of the "consumers," but also because of a lack of desire or willingness on their part as well. As Benería (1999) makes clear, there are those who think that it is worth neither the time nor the effort to measure unpaid labor, who do not see how such information could be of use to the poor exploited woman who is the subject of such information, and who think that resources would be better spent on other activities that would benefit her directly. These views, held as they are by some feminists, cannot but weaken the efforts to integrate unpaid labor into the macroeconomy. In the case of the Philippines, they could explain why the NCRFW leadership shifted focus from unpaid labor to violence against women.

There may be another reason, though never articulated, for this unwillingness to pursue the issue of integrating unpaid labor into the macroeconomy: the preservation of the status quo, where women remain invisible, exploitable, and unable to widen the choices open to them.

Renewed Efforts

In any case, what is important is that Dr Virola and the NSCB give the effort a second go. As mentioned earlier, the conventional and "accurate" GDP accounts were updated to 2009, based on the 2001 time-use survey, and these were presented again to the 2010 National Convention on Statistics. In the latest results, unpaid work added between 38.4 and 79.8 percent to GDP, depending on the metric used; women's share in conventional

GDP increased by 4.6 to 9.5 percentage points; women accounted for 60 percent of all unpaid work; and over 55 percent of this contribution was performed by women not in the labor force.

Unfortunately, once again, very few people aside from the statisticians either know or care that the data are available, although Dr Virola reports that his plan of integrating women in the national accounts was received enthusiastically by the NCRFW. Such enthusiasm notwithstanding, the hard fact is that some 15 years after Beijing—and after the proposal was first made to create satellite accounts measuring the contribution of unpaid family work to the economy—this is still not a reality. In contrast, satellite accounts for environment, tourism, and health, which were suggested much later, have already been constructed.

According to Dr Virola, this is because there are joint international efforts to come up with a methodological framework for environment and tourism. For environment, the UN has created a "City Group," called the London Group, which makes recommendations on how the accounts will be compiled. In the case of tourism, the World Trade Organization (WTO) is spearheading the work on methodological studies (and has, in fact, come up with a revised framework for tourism satellite accounts). No similar efforts seem to have been undertaken for unpaid work, other than a guide to producing time-use statistics (UNDESA, 2005).

THE WAY FORWARD—TOWARD A TIPPING POINT

Three overall conclusions can be drawn from the foregoing. First, it is the SNA that threw a cloak of invisibility over women's contributions to the economy, by using narrow and inadequate definitions. That cloak can and should be removed. Segregating women's contributions in satellite accounts should not be considered a final and permanent solution but rather a preliminary and temporary one.

Second, given the present SNA reality, the full integration into the macroeconomy of unpaid work (which we have established is done mostly by women) can be accomplished as a sequence of steps: gathering time-use data, valuing that unpaid work, creating the satellite accounts, institutionalizing them (estimating them regularly), and finally, integrating them as part of the "central system" of the national accounts. To date, to the best of my knowledge, less than half of the world's countries have gathered time-use data, and about half of that half (mostly developed countries) have begun valuing unpaid work. Even fewer are creating satellite accounts, and only one or two have begun institutionalizing them.

Third, the slowness of this progress is not just a problem of technical, supply constraints, but also one of demand—potential users and even potential beneficiaries lack either the ability or the will (or a combination of both) to carry it forward. This is not to belittle the supply constraints; and our statistical system must be supported, particularly financially, in its attempts to push the envelope in identifying and integrating the contribution of women in our national accounts. But the demand side, like the second blade in a pair of scissors, has to be addressed as well.

What can be done to increase, or even create, the demand for data that will allow women's contributions to be visible? Here, we have to reach out to other disciplines, other professions, for help and guidance. In a nutshell, what is required is a series of consciousness-raising activities. It is not enough that data are produced, and that the producers of the data know that they have a gold mine. It is not enough that user capacity should be increased. The public should be on the side of the angels—should also want the data to be produced, want to know the results, and want their leaders to make use of those results—because it is the public that can exert the necessary level of pressure on reluctant policymakers, technocrats, organizations, or anybody else who is in the way.

In other words, the effort to integrate unpaid work into the macroeconomy must include not only time-use surveys, valuation processes, and satellite accounts until the final goal is reached, but also a proactive effort to get the public interested in what is being done or should be done. Not only should the public demand that data, but preferably the nature of that demand should reach "epidemic" proportions so that the only possible outcome is the desired one.

How did epidemics get into the picture? In a fascinating book (which may not cross the path of economists and statisticians), Malcolm Gladwell (2000) posits that ideas, messages, and behavior spread like viruses in epidemics. And an epidemic has three characteristics: the virus is very contagious, little causes have big effects, and tipping points occur.

Three factors are involved in reaching a tipping point. First, there is the "law of the few," which says that the success of social epidemics depends on the degree of involvement of a few people with a particular and rare set of gifts. These are the connectors, who are at the hub of a large network of people from different walks of life and who can connect these people with each other; the mavens, who are to information what connectors are to people; and the salespeople, who can sell ideas or products because they can communicate their belief in these ideas or products.

Second, there is the "stickiness factor," which ensures that once a person gets infected (buys the message), she stays infected. To make something "sticky," one has to find a way of packaging information that under the right circumstances will make it irresistible. For example, a communications expert (a woman, naturally), who was asked for top-of-the-head suggestions, came up with the following: "Hot on M.A.M.A" (Measure and Account for Mother's Accomplishments or Movement to Account for Mom's Accomplishments); Mothering: a 24/7 Job Without Pay; H.O.M.E. (Homemaker Output Measurement in the Economy); and even one in the vernacular, playing on the double meaning of the word "*kita*" ("to see" and "salary"), *Kawawang Ina, Di Nakikita, Di Kumikita* (Poor Mothers. Unseen. Unpaid). One can only imagine what could be achieved if she and other experts really put their minds to producing a national or international campaign.

Third, there is the "power of context," which posits that people's behavior is affected by circumstance rather than any innate set of values. Gladwell (2000) illustrates this by recalling the so-called Stanford Prison Experiment, a simulation study of the psychology of imprisonment conducted at Stanford University in the United States in 1971, in which 24 normal, ordinary students turned into either sadists or nervous wrecks depending on whether the role randomly assigned to them was to be a guard or a prisoner. The experiment had to be stopped after only six days (Zambardi, n.d.).

Clearly, the integration of unpaid work into macroeconomics has not yet reached that tipping point. What is needed to achieve this are people—researchers, economists, statisticians, feminists—who have the talents to be either connectors or mavens or salespeople, with a message that will not be forgotten (here is where the talents of advertising and marketing agencies can be tapped, as illustrated earlier, and where it is clear that research budgets should include a component for information and education), and an environment that will shape the behavior of people in a major way.

Unless these requirements are met, integrating unpaid work into the macroeconomy and removing the invisibility of women's contributions to the economy from their homes, will remain an idea whose time has not yet come. But we can all take heart from the last lines of the Gladwell (2000, p. 259) book: "Look at the world around you. It may seem like an immovable, implacable place. It is not. With the slightest push—in just the right place—it can be tipped."

Appendix 5.1A. Valuation of Unpaid Work, Various Countries

Country	Time series	Results	Data source	Remarks	Institutionalization	Link/Source
United Kingdom	1995	Value of unpaid work was estimated at between 40 and 120 percent of GDP, depending on the method of measurement.	1995 General Household Survey	Experimental household satellite account.		http://www.radstats.org.uk/no074/article2.htm Developing Gender Statistics in the UK (Linda Murgatroyd)
Finland	2001	GDP is increased by 40 percent and household consumption by almost 60 percent when production excluded from the national accounts is included in the figures. The highest gross value added (GVA) figure was recorded for housing.	1999–2000 Statistics Finland's Time-Use Survey; 2001–2002 Household Budget Survey	Finnish Household Satellite Account compiled in compliance with Eurostat and SNA93 guidelines.		http://www.kuluttajatutkimuskeskus.fi/files/4919/2006_household_satellite_account.pdf Household Production and Consumption in Finland 2001: Household Satellite Account
Germany	2001	Using the generalist rate, the GVA of household production for 2001 amounted to 820,000 million euros. This was roughly the equivalent of the combined value added of the trade, hotel and catering, and transport segments.	1999–1992 and 2001–2002 time-use surveys	Household satellite system compiled on the basis of the time-use surveys.		http://www.genderkompetenz.info/eng/gendercompetence/subjectareas/employment/unpaid/aspects Gender aspects in the area of unpaid work

Australia	1992, 1997	Unpaid household work accounted for 91 percent of the estimated value of total unpaid work in 1997. The value of total unpaid work in 1997 was estimated to be about USD 261 billion (48 percent of GDP), compared with about USD 225 billion in 1992 (54 percent of GDP). Women contributed 63 percent of the estimated value of total unpaid work in 1997 (65 percent in 1992).	Time-use surveys conducted in 1992 (pilot) and 1997	Results released as a "satellite account" to the national accounts.	The Australian Bureau of Statistics conducted the 2006 TUS and data from the survey was expected to be publicly available in 2007. Results were to be used to update the monetary value of unpaid work (that is, for 2007).	http://www.oecd.org/data oecd/23/18/2508574.pdf Aspects of Sustainability: Australian Experience (Barbara Dunlop, Australian Bureau of Statistics)
Canada	1961–1992, 1992–1998	The estimated value of unpaid work in Canada in 1998 was USD 297 billion. Between 1992 and 1998, the value increased by 18.3 percent (in nominal terms). As a percentage of GDP, however, it fell 3 percentage points, from 36 to 33 percent.	Major time-use surveys conducted in 1986, 1992, 1998	In the case of non-marketed goods and services, the national accounting approach is to assess value in relation to costs.	Publication on Households' Unpaid Work: Measurement and Valuation is being published by Statistics Canada.	http://www.statcan.ca/ english/conferences/ economic2003/ hamdad3c.pdf Valuing Households' Unpaid Work in Canada, 1992 and 1998: Trends and Sources of Change

(Appendix 5.1A Continued)

(Appendix 5.1A Continued)

Country	Time series	Results	Data source	Remarks	Institutionalization	Link/Source
		Women who were not employed contributed the greatest proportion in the value of households' unpaid work with 36 percent in 1998. Those employed contributed 27 percent.				http://www.swc-cfc.gc.ca/dates/whm/1998/index_e.html Women's History Month 1998: Canadian Women Making an Impact
Bulgaria	1988	The value of production in non-SNA activities is 47 percent and 71 percent of GDP based on net wages and gross wages, respectively. Estimates based on labor costs are 13 percentage points higher than those based on gross wages (84 percent).		Value of labor and value of production at cost of inputs in non-SNA activities (as percentage of GDP)		http://unstats.un.org/unsd/publication/SeriesF/SeriesF_75v2E.pdf Household Accounting: Experience in Concepts and Compilation (United Nations)

			See above		See above

Denmark 1987

The value of labor inputs in non-SNA activities based on labor costs is 37 percent of GDP, which is 16 percentage points higher than those based on net wages (21 percent).

The value of production in non-SNA activities based on labor costs is 43 percent of GDP. If GVA for owner-occupied dwelling is included, the value rises to 50 percent.

See above

France 1985

The value of labor inputs in non-SNA activities based on gross wages and labor cost is 33 and 36 percent of GDP, respectively.

See above

(Appendix 5.1A Continued)

(Appendix 5.1A Continued)

Country	Time series	Results	Data source	Remarks	Institutionalization	Link/Source
Norway	1990	The value of labor inputs in non-SNA activities using labor cost is 38 percent of GDP.		See above		See above
	1992	Using an opportunity cost approach, specialist method, and generalist method, the value of unpaid work was estimated at 39, 38, and 37 percent of GDP.		Based on a study by Dahle/ Kitterod.		http://www.unescap.org/ stat/meet/wipuw/wipuw-01.pdf
Korea		The value of unpaid work took up 30–40 percent of GDP and 70–90 percent of total annual wage.				http://www.unescap.org/ stat/meet/wipuw/wipuw-01.pdf
						Economic Evaluation of Unpaid Work in Republic of Korea
Netherlands	1990	Using an opportunity cost approach, the value of unpaid work was estimated at 108 percent of GDP. Using specialist method, it is estimated at 82 percent of GDP.		Based on a study by Bruyn-Hundt.		See above

Austria	1992	Using an opportunity cost approach, the value of unpaid work was estimated at 138 percent of GDP.	See above
Switzerland	1997	Using an opportunity cost approach, specialist and generalist method, the value of unpaid work was estimated at 49, 41, and 52 percent of GDP.	Based on a study by Sousa-Poza.
Japan	1996	Using an opportunity cost approach, specialist and generalist method, the value of unpaid work was estimated at 23, 15, and 20 percent of GDP.	Based on a study by M. Fukami.

(Appendix 5.1A Continued)

(Appendix 5.1A Continued)

Country	Time series	Results	Data source	Remarks	Institutionalization	Link/Source
New Zealand	1990	Using an opportunity cost approach, specialist method, and generalist method, the value of unpaid work was estimated at 66, 42, and 51 percent of GDP.		Released by Statistics New Zealand.		See above
	1999	The value of productive unpaid work by New Zealanders aged 15 years and over was 39 percent of GDP.		See above		http://www.stats.govt.nz/ products-and-services/ Articles/unpaidwork-Jun01.htm

Notes: Other countries that are mentioned in some references as having started or developed satellite accounts of unpaid work are listed below. Further research is needed on the main documents for each of these countries describing the methodology as well as presenting the resulting estimates. See also work for Social and Political Economy of Care project of the UNRISD, which covered six countries: Argentina, India, Nicaragua, South Africa, South Korea, and Tanzania (Budlender, 2010).

- Integrating Women's Unpaid Work into Economic Indicators (Lee, 2005). See website http://www.undp.org.my/uploads/files/unpaid_work_women.pdf

  The EU statistic agency, Eurostat, began developing a harmonized satellite system of household production under a pilot programme which allows the calculation of unpaid household labour.… Countries participating in the pilot include the Basque region, Finland, Italy, Luxembourg, and Slovenia.…

- Time-Use Data for Policy Advocacy and Analysis: A Gender Perspective and Some International Examples (Lorraine Corner, Regional Economic Advisor, UNIFEM Asia-Pacific and Arab States). See website http://www.unifem-ecogov-apas.org/ecogov-apas/EEGProjectsActivities/TimeUseMeetIndia200210/ paperLC.pdf

  … Countries such as Australia, Cuba, Japan, and Republic of Korea have or are developing satellite accounts of the value of unpaid work. Australia integrated the monetary value of unpaid work into the analysis of the household sector in its national accounts for the first time in 1997.

- Policy Implications of Unpaid Work: Public Agenda for Gender and Development (UNESCAP)—http://www.unescap.org/stat/meet/wipuw/11. unpaid_module4.pdf (United Nations, 2003)

  Paid and Unpaid Work in Bangladesh.… Non-market work increase conventional GDP by 29%.

REFERENCES

APCAS (Asia and Pacific Commission on Agricultural Statistics). (1994). *Alternative data sources for women's work in agriculture* (Agenda Item No. 9, Fifteenth Session), October 24–28. Manila: Food and Agriculture Organization.

Aslaksen, J., & Koren, C. (1996). Unpaid household work and the distribution of extended income: The Norwegian experience. *Feminist Economics*, 2(3), 65–80.

Beck, T. (1999). *Using gender-sensitive indicators: A reference manual for governments and other stakeholders*. London: Commonwealth Secretariat.

Benería, L. (1999). The enduring debate over unpaid labour. *International Labour Review*, 138(3), 287–310.

Bos, F. (2005). Constancy and change in the UN manuals on national accounting (1947, 1953, 1968, 1993). In Z. Kennesey (Ed.), *The accounts of nations* (pp. 198–217). Amsterdam: IOS Press.

Budlender, D. (Ed.). (2010). *Time use studies and unpaid care work*. New York: Routledge.

Corner, L. (2002). *Time-Use data for policy advocacy and analysis: A gender perspective and some international examples*. New York: UNIFEM. Retrieved from http://www.unifem-eseasia.org/projects/eeg/ecogov-apas/EEGProjectsActivities/TimeUseMeetIndia200210/paperLC.pdf

ESCAP (Economic and Social Commission for Asia and the Pacific). (n.d.). *Information brief: Integrating unpaid work into national policies*. Bangkok: Statistics Division, ECLAC. Retrieved October 6, 2010, from http://www.unescap.org/stat/meet/wipuw/information_brief.pdf

ESCAP, & UNDP (United Nations Development Programme). (2003). *Integrating unpaid work into national policies*. New York: United Nations.

Folbre, N. (1991). The unproductive housewife: Her evolution in nineteenth century economic thought. *Signs*, 16(3), 463–484.

Gladwell, M. (2000). *The tipping point: How little things can make a big difference*. Boston, Massachusetts: Little, Brown and Company.

Horrigan, M., Herz, D., Joyce, M., Robison, E., Stewart, J., & Stinson, L. (1999). *A report on the feasibility of conducting a time-use survey* (1999 IATUR Time Use Conference) University of Essex, October 6–8.

ICP (International Comparison Program for Asia and the Pacific). (2003). *National accounts workshop 30–31 July*. Regional Inception Workshop Bangkok, Thailand, July 28–August 1. Retrieved October 6, 2010, from http://www.adb.org/Statistics/icp/files/Natl_Accounts_Workshop.pdf

INSTRAW (International Research and Training Institute for the Advancement of Women). (1995). *Measurement and valuation of unpaid contribution: Accounting through time and output*. Santo Domingo: INSTRAW.

————. (1996). *Valuation of household production and the satellite accounts*. Santo Domingo: INSTRAW.

ISWGNA (Inter-Secretariat Working Group on National Accounts). (1993). *System of national accounts*. Washington, DC: Commission of the European Communities, International Monetary Fund, Organisation for Economic Co-operation and Development, United Nations, and World Bank.

Lee, L. 2005. *Integrating women's unpaid work into economic indicators*. Kuala Lumpur: UNDP Malaysia. Retrieved from http://www.undp.org.my/uploads/unpaid_work_women.pdf

National Statistics Office. (1992). *Statistics on Filipino women*. Manila: National Statistics Office.

UNDESA (United Nations Department of Economic and Social Affairs). (2005). *Guide to producing statistics on time use: Measuring paid and unpaid work.* New York: UNDESA Statistics Division. Retrieved August 18, 2010, from http://unstats.un.org/unsd/publication/SeriesF/SeriesF_93E.pdf

UNDP (United Nations Development Programme). (2006). *Beyond scarcity: Power, poverty and the global water crisis* (Human development report 2006). New York: Palgrave Macmillan. Retrieved August 18, 2010, from http://hdr.undp.org/en/reports/global/hdr2006/

United Nations. (1985). *Report of the world conference to review and appraise the achievements of the United Nations decade for women: Equality, development and peace* (A/RES/40/108), Nairobi. Retrieved August 2010, from www.un.org/documents/ga/res/40/a40r108.htm

————. 2000. United Nations Millennium Declaration. Resolution adopted by the General Assembly. A/RES/55/2. September 18 .

————. 2003. Module 4. *In Guidebook on integrating unpaid work into national policies.* Bangkok: United Nations Economic Commission for Asia and the Pacific (UNESCAP) and United Nations Development Programme (UNDP). Retrieved from http://www.unescap.org/stat/meet/wipuw/11.unpaid_module4.pdf

Virola, R. A., & de Perio, S. M. (1998). *Measuring the contribution of women to the Philippine economy.* Convention Papers, Seventh National Convention on Statistics, Manila, Philippines.

Zambardi, P. (n.d.) *Stanford prison experiment.* Retrieved November 18, 2010, from http://www.prisonexp.org/

6

Poor Women Organizing for Economic Justice*

RENANA JHABVALA

Empowerment through organizing is the process by which the powerless, or disempowered, can change their circumstances and begin to have control over their lives. It results in a change in the balance of power, living conditions, and relationships. Most importantly, empowerment allows a person to say, "Now I do not feel afraid."

INTRODUCTION

The political economy of the world involves a complex web of relationships that drive economic systems toward increasing control by financial capital. Within this world dominated by finance exists a world of work in which most of the population survives, laboring for long hours merely to earn a livelihood. These billions of people have little power and face lives of increasing insecurity and vulnerability.

The quest for economic justice is dependent on change toward an economic system where people have a certain level of security, at least related

---

* As this chapter is based on the author's experiences organizing informal women workers in India, and is an attempt to interpret those experiences in the context of agency toward economic justice, most of the examples relate to the Indian context, although there is some evidence from international organizing.

to their basic needs, where work is fulfilling, and not back-breaking and exploitative, and where people feel a sense of community and empowerment. Such a change requires direction, and it is those who have the most to lose within the existing system—the most insecure, the vulnerable, and the poor—who can become the agents for this.

However, agency of the weak requires some form of coming together or organizing before people can feel empowered to act. People feel powerless in many ways. They feel at the mercy of forces over which they have no control; they are dominated by potent figures in their lives and groups far away that they cannot identify. Their powerlessness leads them to fear that their lives might be crushed, destroyed, or reduced at any time. This feeling of powerlessness kills the human spirit. It is very strong in the poor, because of their daily struggle for survival in the face of strong economic and social forces, and is increased in the case of poor women, who have to deal with not only external forces but also those within the household.

Empowerment through organizing is the process by which the powerless, or disempowered, can change their circumstances and begin to have control over their lives. It results in a change in the balance of power, living conditions, and relationships. Most importantly, empowerment allows a person to say, "Now I do not feel afraid."

A question that sometimes arises is whether there still needs to be a separate focus on women. We are told that although women were treated unequally until the last few decades, the women's movement worldwide had led to great advances, and in many European countries women are well represented in parliaments, business, and the professions. In South Asian countries too, women have attained higher levels of education, become prime ministers, presidents, and leaders of political parties, and are well represented in some professions and businesses.

But while it is true that there have been major improvements in women's position in India and other South Asian countries, the conditions for most women remain bleak. Poor women, women of lower castes, and women who work, especially in manual work, remain discriminated against and vulnerable. Two indicators will suffice to make the point. The first is the low female–male ratio in India, with 93 women for every 100 men (2001 Census), revealing that daughters are still considered a burden and less desirable than sons. In the words of Amartya Sen (1990), the country has to account for more than 100 million "missing women."

The second indicator is that the majority of women continue to work in the least remunerative and most physically demanding areas of the economy. An example is the feminization of agriculture. Whereas over 83.3 percent of rural women still work in agriculture, men are moving away from this sector to better paid work. Statistics show that 66.5 percent of rural males worked in agriculture in 2004–2005 compared to 83.2 percent in 1972–1993 (Srivastava & Srivastava, 2009).

THE WORLD OF WORK

Informal employment broadly defined comprises half to three quarters of nonagricultural employment in developing countries (see Box 6.1). In India, 92 percent of all workers and 96 percent of women workers are informal (or "unorganized," as it is called here). Yet the economic power is in the formal or organized sector, which is composed of public and private firms. The informal or "people's sector" covers most of the agricultural sector, including small farmers, marginal farmers, agricultural workers, forest workers, livestock herders, and so on. It involves a large part of the industrial sector as well, including small-scale industries, artisans, home-based workers, contract labor, and also a large proportion of the services sector, including domestic servants, barbers, rag pickers, and so on. Fifty-seven percent of this workforce is self-employed.

Box 6.1 Informal work the world over

Informal employment accounts for 47 percent of nonagricultural employment in the Middle East and North Africa, 51 percent in Latin America, 71 percent in Asia, and 72 percent in sub-Saharan Africa. If South Africa is excluded, the share of informal employment rises to 78 percent in sub-Saharan Africa; and if comparable data were available for other countries in South Asia in addition to India, the regional average for Asia would likely be much higher.

In the developing world, informal employment is generally a larger source of employment for women than for men. Other than in the Middle East and North Africa where the total is 42 percent, 60 percent or more of women workers in the developing world are in informal employment (outside agriculture). The comparative figures for informal employment as a share of nonagricultural employment by sex and region are: 84 percent of women workers compared to 63 percent of men workers in sub-Saharan Africa; 58 percent of women workers in comparison to 48 percent of men workers in Latin America; and 73 percent of women workers in comparison to 70 percent of men workers in Asia.

Source: WIEGO, 2002.

Workers in this sector face a number of problems that lead to their disempowerment. First, there is uncertainty with respect to their livelihoods. Employment is often not a year-rounder, especially among the poor, which creates a constant fear in people's minds as to whether they will actually get any or enough employment. Second, they generally do not earn enough to provide for a minimum basic standard of living. The National Centre for Labour has calculated that in order to meet minimum basic needs, a family of four requires a minimum wage of 125 INR per day, but in fact the daily income of a poor family may be as low as one-fifth of that amount (in 2010, 47 Indian rupees [INR] = 1 United States dollar [USD]). Third, the poor and many workers do not have access to social security, which means they have to pay for health care and other social security needs—if these are even available—at high market prices, so their earnings are drained away.

In most sectors of the economy, the tendency is to employ women in the lowest paid, most menial tasks, using the least technology. In agriculture, for example, women do not plough but engage in labor-intensive tasks such as transplanting and weeding. Bhatt (1988, p. iii) reported:

> … men refuse to do certain jobs. In Rajasthan, they refused the work of plucking chillies, which burns their hands, so women were the only ones doing it. And in Madhya Pradesh, Bihar and Rajasthan, women are the only ones carrying from 12–40 kgs of fuel and fodder on their heads every day, sometimes for the small sum it will fetch on the open market or from the trader. The job takes them anywhere from 4–6 hours a day, and carries the additional hazard of harassment by the forest guards.

In the construction sector, women do the hard work of carrying loads on their heads while men are masons. Women workers are more likely to be home based, while men engage in the same tasks in workshops or factories with better tools. For example, male garment workers, whether self-employed tailors or not, tend to make higher quality garments with better machines. Home-based female workers with access to only lower quality machines make products such as petticoats, which are in the lower-priced part of the market. Similarly, employees of the forest department who are paid regular wages tend to be men, while forest produce collectors are women.

Moreover, the tendency is to pay women less than men, even for the same work. For example, Bhatt (1988) reported that a tea plantation in Mandi, Himachal Pradesh, was the only place on a national tour by a Commission investigating women's work where women reported getting the same wages as men. Everywhere else men were earning from 30–150 percent more than women for the same tasks and working hours.

Work is central to the lives of both women and men. It takes up a substantial part of their daily activities, providing a source of identity and dignity as well as a livelihood. In general, men's identities as workers are more easily recognized and appreciated than women's. People will say of a man, "He is a miner, an accountant, a farmer," but women are described primarily in their roles as mothers or caregivers. Women often remain invisible and unrecognized as workers, both because they are women and because work in the informal economy is often hidden. The work and contributions of women to the economy, as well as to the family and community, are persistently undervalued, particularly when women are home-based workers, paid domestic or care workers, or unpaid contributing workers in family businesses or on family farms. Focusing on their role as workers, rather than as homemakers or childcare providers, serves to underscore the fact that women are economic agents who contribute to their households and the economy, and therefore should be considered a target of economic as well as social policies.

THE TRADE UNIONS AND *SHRAM SHAKTI*

The 20th century saw the rise of trade unionism as a powerful force of agency to correct the injustices of the industrial system. Although trade unions tended to exclude informal women workers, it was believed by both trade unions and policymakers that eventually these excluded workers would also get a voice in this way.

Twenty years ago Ela Bhatt, the founder of the Self-employed Women's Association (SEWA), submitted the first comprehensive report on working women in India to the Prime Minister of India (based on the work of the Commission). This report (Bhatt, 1988) was entitled *Shram Shakti*, which means "the power of labor" (*shakti* translates as female power). It detailed the working and living conditions of women workers in what today is being called the informal economy.

An important part of the report, entitled "On Organizing," identified trade unions and cooperatives, which were widespread all over India, as the most effective organizational types. It therefore recommended that there should be "an expansion of coverage of the co-operative movement in new and important areas like farm labor, artisans, cereal processing...." At the same time, the report said:

The Commission feels that unless the workers in these sectors whose need for unionisation and protection is the greatest, are brought into the mainstream of the labour movement, the latter has very little relevance to them. It is high time that the major labour unions took the workers of the unorganized sector into their fold. (Bhatt, 1988)

The report also recognized that the Government had a major role in all areas of life, and most of the recommendations concerned the need for various government policies.

Liberalization and the Decline of Voice through Trade Unions

In the 1980s and 1990s rapid changes were taking place internationally, with the ascendancy of the forces of globalization and trade liberalization. The macroeconomic changes in industrialized countries were supported by the rise of neoliberalism, which shifted the emphasis from security to growth. Regulations that promoted security were seen as inimical to economic growth, and "deregulation" was promoted in order to facilitate the working of the market.

In India, this school of thought gradually began to gain ascendancy in the mid- to late 1980s, and became dominant with the debt crisis in 1991. The main target of this new thinking was the public sector, the visible face of the socialist economy. In addition, there were persistent demands for de-licensing industry, lowering import and excise taxes, and removing quotas for categories such as small-scale industries. The popular image of the "License-Permit Raj" (complicated bureaucratic measures, or "red tape," associated with setting up and running a business) caught the imagination not only of the industrialists and the middle classes but also the poor, all of whom continually suffered under the high-handed treatment and corruption of an entrenched bureaucracy.

The statutory regulatory system for labor also came under attack with demands for an "exit" policy to increase the "flexibility" of firms and allow them to compete internationally. More and more came to be written about the privileged position of formal sector labor. Then the focus began to shift toward workers who were not part of the formal sector.

SEWA was able to see some of the effects of "informalization" very early in the process. Ahmedabad, where it is based, was a prosperous city, with more than 60 textile mills in production that employed a labor force of 150,000 workers. Over the course of the last century these workers had acquired a certain degree of security: they had stable jobs with a living wage; they were covered by social security schemes protecting their health and old age; and they had a strong union, which not only represented them in disputes but also ran activities for the welfare of workers and their families. The textile workers of Ahmedabad had begun to enter the ranks of the middle classes.

In the 1980s textile mills all over the country began to close down. In some places, such as Mumbai, the mills closed rapidly. In Ahmedabad, over a period of 10 years, nearly 80,000 permanent workers and more than 50,000 non-permanent workers—mostly men lost their jobs and were driven into the informal sector. The city experienced an economic recession and public disturbances, including communal riots. A whole class of workers was thrown from the middle class back into poverty. Alcoholism and suicides were widespread, and children were withdrawn from school and sent to work. Once the mill workers lost their jobs, they were no longer members of the trade union and no longer had a collective voice. The process of informalization of the workforce made workers and trade unions begin to realize the importance of organizing informal workers.

There has been a dramatic decline in the power of the trade unions in India, and as a result there are very few organizations actually representing workers. For example, I was asked by the Government of Madhya Pradesh to chair a task force in 2001 on the unorganized sector in that state. During visits to a large number of districts and discussions with workers, employers, traders, farmers, government officials, and many other people, we found that the employers were very well able to articulate their grievances at all policy-making forums, whereas the informal workers, who were equally aware of their own problems, had no method to voice or articulate them. The following passage is taken from my field notes:

> In Katni we visited the workers in the limestone factories. They do hard manual work but have weak and emaciated bodies, and more than half of them are women. They are covered in lime-dust and work in conditions where they are breathing in lime at least eight hours a day. Many of the women bring their children along. However, after our field visits we had a meeting of employers and workers in the circuit house. The employers were there in full force and they gave us a list of their problems. Representatives were there from various Government departments including the labor department. No one was there who wanted to tell us the problems of the workers and possible solutions.

Similarly, in Damoh, we found that the bidi [hand-rolled cigarettes] workers earned less than Rs15 per day. However, when we had a meeting of the employers and trade unions, we received many complaints against the government's bidi welfare programs, about the quality of leaves and the state government's forest policy as well many other grievances, like taxes, which were of more concern to the employers. Except for the SEWA representative (and that also hesitatingly), no one mentioned that the workers were receiving such low earnings.

When we met with the workers, in every place, they were very articulate about their problems and had many suggestions and solutions. But there did not seem to be any organization or association that could bring these issues to the notice of the relevant authorities.

WOMEN ORGANIZING

Although trade unions have lost a lot of ground, many new types of organizing have emerged. The issues around which women organize today cover a wide range, from environment-related issues to microfinance, to protests over land. This section looks at some of these issues to see what they mean for women and for organizing.

Just as women workers are often invisible, so too are their organizations. This is particularly true of organizations created by informal women workers. International and national forums, conferences, and seminars tend not to invite them directly, and not much has been written about them. This is partly because some organizations choose to operate "under the radar" in order to protect their members. However, it is largely owing to the fact that the working poor, even if they are organized, remain invisible in mainstream development circles, leading to the assumption that organizations of informal women workers do not exist.

The reality is very different. For example, when the United Nations Development Fund for Women (UNIFEM) and HomeNet, a regional network of home-based workers, mapped organizations that served these workers, they found that there were at least 508 in Bangladesh and 307 in Pakistan, all with a large percentage of women members. Similarly, when StreetNet International (a global network of street vendor groups) attempted to identify organizations of street vendors in Brazil, they learned of 770 associations of women and men street vendors in the city of São Paulo alone (UNIFEM, 2005).

It is important to recognize that women are not only the "followers" in the organizing process, but often the leaders. In fact there are many areas where it is the women, and especially poor women, who have taken the lead in articulating the issues and in organizing to deal with them. In this process women have brought into the national consciousness issues that have major relevance to society as a whole and, at the same time, invented new forms of organizing.

Women Take the Lead

In India, women have been the leaders in recognizing and preserving the environment. The well-known Chipko ("cling") movement, where women living in hilly and forest areas protected trees with their own bodies, stopping the contractors from using their felling equipment, was the start of a growing awareness of the importance of preserving forest cover. This movement, which began in the 1970s, spread spontaneously through the forest areas in the country in the 1980s. Indiscriminate felling had led to loss of wood used as fuel for cooking and fodder for cattle, caused the run-off of rainwater leading to shortages of water for drinking and irrigation, and was contributing to major climate change. All these changes affected women and their work; it took an increasingly long time for them to collect fuel, fodder, and water; their farms were no longer productive; and their men began migrating away. The women's lives became so hard that some even committed suicide. It was these circumstances of hardships that led women to organize their first protests.

The environment gradually became a major issue for government policies as well as for civil society and the private sector. Laws were passed to prevent indiscriminate felling of trees, major reforestation and watershed programs were implemented, and terms like "corporate social responsibility" became part of the mainstream.

Protest actions similar to the Chipko movement to preserve ownership of land, livelihoods, and rural environments—and against alcohol, the treatment of dalit movements and, in more recent times, industrial projects such as big dams—have always been important in the process of organizing and empowering women. Less dramatic, though perhaps more widespread, have been developmental movements that have changed people's lives for the better. One of these is now known as "microfinance."

The microfinance movement has become well-known worldwide, and has led to a Nobel Prize for Dr Mohammad Yunus and the Grameen Bank he founded in Bangladesh, for taking a bottom–up approach to making microloans. In fact, microfinance was started and led by women, with new organizing structures developed by them. After SEWA was founded in 1972, members came up with the idea of "a bank of their own" in December 1973, and 4,000 women contributed share capital of 10 INR each to establish the SEWA Cooperative Bank, which was registered in May 1974. The origins of the Grameen Bank, which was formally started in October 1983, can be traced back to an action research project in 1976 (Grameen Bank, n.d.). I visited it in 1980, when over 80 percent of the loanees were men. As their repayment rate began to drop, the Bank turned to women, and by 1990 over 90 percent of the loans were given to women.

In the 1980s, women were also spontaneously getting together into groups in rural areas all over India, saving their earnings, and taking loans from their own savings. Thus was launched the "Self-help Group" (SHG) model (see next section), which became the basis for the country's growing microfinance movement. In addition, women have taken the lead in urban slums, where they suffer most from the effects of lack of water and sanitation and from overcrowding and crime. Even worse has been the inhuman removal of slums, with people's shacks bulldozed along with their belongings. The struggle for water, sanitation, and tenure rights has led to shack-dwellers coming together to change policies.

Yet another area where women have taken the lead is in giving a new direction to the workers' movement. This had been dominated by male leaders and male workers and their concerns, and by the ideas of "labor" instead of work, of an employer–employee relationship, and of factories and formal workplaces. However, as noted above, the majority of workers today work in the informal economy in occupations that have never been recognized. As the economies around the world change, the employer–employee relationship is increasingly vanishing. Since most women workers are used to being in these insecure, "flexible," and informal types of work situations, they have been out in front in organizing informal workers, which include home-based workers, domestic workers, agricultural workers, and many more.

Women Create New Forms and Structures

As women in forests, in slums, and in informal employment emerged into the public sphere to address their issues, they created new forms and structures. These structures came out of their own experiences and their ways of working, and allowed them to feel comfortable as they entered new and unfamiliar territory.

The hundreds of thousands of SHGs (or their equivalent), based on savings and/or credit, are a way for women to come together in small homogenous groups and enter the public sphere and the financial markets without causing huge ripples in their family relationships. Women in South Asia still face almost crippling constraints in interacting with people outside their families. Most public dealings, including financial dealings, are carried out by men, leaving women feeling powerless and closed in. The SHG is a way in which a woman can begin to feel that she has a way out of the four walls of her home and that she has a support group outside her family.

Having money is empowering, and the fact that the SHG deals with money, that as time goes on there are sizeable funds belonging to the group, and that members have an independent source of loans, gives the women power that they have never had before. The success of the SHG depends as much, or perhaps more, on its empowering effects than it does on its much talked about potential for "group-guarantee pressure."

The women (and men) in the slums have also been organizing in loose groups that have come to be called community-based organizations (CBOs). These come together to get better access to basic facilities such as drinking water, toilets, electricity, or roads. They are formed because there are no structures through which slum dwellers can talk to the municipal authorities. Women feel comfortable in such CBOs because they rely on neighborhoods and neighborliness to work. For women in urban slums, the neighbors become their community, often closer than their extended family. Sometimes these CBOs register themselves as regular organizations—cooperatives or NGOs—and are able to approach the legal system for their rights.

Another new form of organizing is the "people's movement," which has no structure but is organized to protest against dispossession. The Chipko movement, mentioned earlier, was an early spontaneous people's movement, and as observed, was followed by people's movements against big dams and land acquisitions for big industries, which displaced thousands of people. These movements spring up as people in a particular area face extreme change that will disrupt their lives and perhaps bring them into a cycle of poverty. Women, whose way of life is rooted in the land and in their homes, feel the threat even more than men and are willing to take part in long drawn-out protests.

The changing nature of work has also given rise to new types of organizations. For example, although registered as a trade union, SEWA is different in a number of ways. First, rather than organizing workers of one trade, it brings together workers from many different trades, ranging from urban street vendors to rural livestock breeders. Second, it organizes workers who are generally in non-factory settings. Third, it organizes not only to gain higher wages or enterprise benefits, but for a whole variety of issues ranging from developmental needs such as skills-training and microfinance, to social security and childcare, to education; it follows an integrated approach. The form of organizing is dictated by what the women workers need. SEWA is the earliest example of this type of organization, and today there are many organizations in the same model (see Box 6.2).

Box 6.2 Some examples of women's unions around the world

Africa—Chad: Syndicat des Femmes Vendeuses de Poisson (Union of Women Fish Vendors) was founded in 2002 and currently has 500 members. Its aim is to protect the vendors' economic interests by increasing the price of fish and improving storage facilities. It also seeks to build women's solidarity through education and social activities.

Europe—The Netherlands: Vakwerk De Rode Draad (Red Thread Union) is a sex workers' union established in 2002, not long after sex work was legalized in the Netherlands. It is affiliated with the Netherlands Confederation of Trade Unions. In 2004 Red Thread established an organization for trafficked women and began negotiations with the Association of Brothel Owners for a national agreement. Negotiations stalled when the brothel owners insisted that sex workers were self-employed.

Latin America—Brazil: Associação do Movimento Interestadual de Quebradeira de Coco Babaçu (Interstate Movement of Babassu Coconut Splitters), founded in 1989, is a union of women who harvest, shell, and market coconuts in the Amazon region. The union has formed alliances with environmental protection groups to fight overexploitation of the crop by private and public companies. Members can join cooperatives set up by the union, which is linked to trade union federations.

Source: UNIFEM, 2005.

With Success Come Pitfalls

As the structures women create begin to succeed, they attract the attention of (often very well-intentioned) people who want them to become even more successful. In this way such structures tend to lose their essential nature, including leadership by poor women.

A good example of this is microfinance. A movement that started out with small groups of poor women getting together to save and get access to credit has, on the one hand, become a major government program, and on the other attracted big business. Likewise, the enthusiasm for and success of the SHGs has convinced state governments that all their programs should be channeled through these groups. Government officials are entrusted with the task of "forming SHGs" almost overnight, and ensuring that subsidies go through them. Thus, the SHGs lose their "self-help" and empowering character, becoming instead merely a means to obtain access to government programs.

Moreover, it has been found that making loans to SHGs and poor women is good business, because they are willing to pay high interest rates and repay on time. So microfinance has become a business controlled by financial systems and generally run by technical and professional men rather than poor women. As this business becomes more professionalized, banks and private investors have been investing and earning good returns.

MEMBER-BASED ORGANIZATIONS OF THE POOR

The trade unions, cooperatives, and political movements of the last century have given way to SHGs, NGOs, CBOs, and "people's movements." The trade unions of the last century were frankly political, with political parties having trade union wings and trade unionists aspiring to political power. The cooperatives in India also relied on political parties for protection, and in return provided a vote bank. But the civil society organizations and movements of today have become detached from political systems, operating in the spaces between the economy and electoral politics.

An important aspect of the trade unions, cooperatives, and political movements was their representative character. Trade unions spoke on behalf of their members, who confirmed their membership by paying dues. Members of a cooperative could be owners once they bought shares and adhered to its rules of relations and behavior. Political movements translated into membership of political parties and even further into legitimacy through the democratic electoral system. There were democratic structures within these organizations that (at least in theory) allowed members to exercise their voice in decision making, and the leaders were obliged to go through certain procedures of consultation before they took major decisions. These processes of accountability ensured that the organizations were truly representative, and that their leaders spoke on behalf of the members. The downside of these accountability processes was that often the rules and procedures became so detailed that these organizations began behaving like rather cumbersome bureaucracies.

Today's organizations have no clear methods of accountability, and it may not always be obvious who their members are and what rights they enjoy. Thus it is not always evident that these organizations can indeed be called "representative" of the people they claim to speak or act on behalf of. That is why there is a need to take another look at member-based organizations for poor women.

In 2005, Cornell University, SEWA, and the global action-research-policy network Women in Informal Employment Globalizing and Organizing (WIEGO) issued a joint call for papers on member-based organizations of the poor, and the selected papers were presented at a conference and then published in a volume (Chen et al., 2007). In the overview, the editors (including the author) developed their concept of member-based organizations of the poor (MBOPs), as distinct from NGOs and also from member-based organizations (MBOs) in general.

> It is useful to first distinguish MBOs from other NGOs, then MBOPs from other MBOs, and finally one MBOP from the other. MBOs are different from other NGOs. The democratic governance structures of MBOs are intended to provide both internal accountability (leaders are elected) and external legitimacy (leaders represent their constituency), characteristics not shared by other NGOs.... Turning now to MBOPs as a subset of MBOs, we have considered several alternative terms to try to capture what we had in mind, namely, that the poor need to be organized, need to be recognized, and need to have a "seat at the (policy) table." We finally settled on "membership-based organizations of the poor," putting an emphasis on "of " (not "for") and "the poor" (not "the non-poor"). (ibid., p. 5)

The conference also developed a related set of "characteristics of any organization that aspires to be an MBOP." Based on the traditions of trade unions and cooperatives, these are as follows:

- The organization's primary objective is to cater for the socioeconomic needs of its members.

- There is a well-defined constituency from which membership is drawn.
- Its members finance it.
- The highest decision-making structure is (or should be) the most representative forum of members.
- There is a strongly developed sense of ownership of the organization by the members, and of accountability of the leadership to the membership.
- It embodies values of cooperation and solidarity.

Within this broad framework, there is a wide range of MBOPs, including trade unions, cooperatives of various kinds (for example, production, service, marketing, credit, bank), worker committees, savings and credit groups/SHGs; community-based finance institutions, funeral associations, informal insurance institutions, producer groups, village or slum associations, community-based organizations, some of which represent traditional social groupings (based on kinship, caste, patron–client relationships), and clubs (for example, youth).

THE MAIN CHALLENGE: SCALING UP

Women's MBOs—owned by and accountable to poor women—can form the building blocks for both action and voice. However, being effective requires scaling up. For example, the effectiveness of small SHGs of 10 women each will be very limited, even in the lives of those women, and have almost no impact on society or policy. But hundreds of thousands of SHGs, acting together, can have a major impact on the women involved and on society.

How do women's organizations scale up? The original base of organizing is always local: the SHG, the CBO. These small organizations start as single issue groups—for example, around savings or loans, around a need for drinking water or toilets, protesting against displacement, coming together for better wages, or around finding a new market for their goods or services. Scaling up means expansion, replication, and higher forms of organization (see Box 6.3).

Box 6.3   Scaling up the SEWA way

There are a large number of experiences of different types of organization within the SEWA movement.

Scaling up the organization: SEWA started in Ahmedabad in 1972 as a registered trade union with 200 members. It behaved as a "general workers" trade union, taking in members from all different trades. It spread to other states, with SEWA Madhya Pradesh registered in 1985, followed 20 years later by SEWA Uttar Pradesh and SEWA Bihar. In 2005 SEWA applied to be recognized as a national trade union and, after a major struggle with the existing trade unions, obtained recognition.

Scaling up the movement: SEWA is not only a trade union but also a movement. The SEWA model became popular about 10 years after its birth and was replicated in other states with nine new SEWAs being set up. These replicated SEWAs formed a federation called SEWA Bharat whose task was to help the new SEWAs develop and also represent SEWA members at the national level. Membership has grown steadily from 1,070 in 1972 to 45,936 in 1992 and 1,256,941 in 2009.

Scaling up cooperatives: In addition to its activities in raising wages and confronting the police and municipalities, SEWA began linking women street vendors to banks for credit. In 1974 it started its own women's cooperative bank, which today has over 300,000 members and capital of 1 billion INR. In 1981 it started the first women producers' cooperative called Sabina Stitchers' Cooperative. The number of cooperatives has continued to increase, and in 1995 SEWA started a state level women's cooperative federation in Gujarat that now has over 100 women's co-op members.

Scaling up the SHGs: SEWA helped women in rural areas form SHGs of 10–20 women each. The SHGs then formed associations at the district level, which have become economic organizations owned by rural women

Scaling up companies: As neoliberal economic policies have become more prevalent in India, it has been increasingly difficult to operate cooperatives and easier to work with companies. SEWA has been forming women-owned producer companies that bring them up the value chain.

Scaling up internationally: Reaching across countries, SEWA is a founder of a number of international networks including HomeNet South Asia, WIEGO, and StreetNet.

Source: Author.

There are many ways for a small and local women's organization to go to scale. One way is to grow and deepen locally, involving more and more women and becoming more complex. A number of rural SHGs in a district—maybe 50—come together to form a federation and pool their savings. More groups join them and their pool of savings grows, as do their loans. They start a consumer store, they take out insurance, and they help each other through crises. Worried about the lack of proper education for their children, they approach the school authorities and insist that teachers be sent to the schools, and they form parents' groups. There is a cooperative milk dairy in the vicinity that they approach, and the federation gives loans to its members to buy cattle. As time goes on the organization becomes bigger and more complex, and yet remains local.

Some organizations deliver services and in so doing are able to expand and grow nationally, regionally, and even internationally. Within the SEWA family, the SEWA Trade Facilitation Centre (marketing), Bimo SEWA (insurance), SEWA Lok Swasthya (health services), and SEWA Housing Trust (infrastructure and housing) are strong locally where they started but have also grown nationally.

Growth also occurs through replication, and there are many ways of "replicating" an existing organization. For example, the Grameen Bank model has been replicated with the emphasis on certain basic structural features. The SEWA model, on the other hand, is replicated with more emphasis on the principles than on a particular structure.

Yet another way to grow is by the trade union method of simultaneous struggles around issues. In recent years a number of issues have led to the formation of small "struggle" organizations in India, as mentioned earlier, where women have taken the lead. These also include the struggles of women to obtain a right to work through the National Rural Employment Guarantee Act, and for a right to social security through the Unorganized Workers' Social Security Act. Many of these struggles have led to the formation of national or statewide organizations.

A more recent form of scaling-up is through networks of existing organizations. An interesting case is that of HomeNet South Asia, the regional network of home-based workers formed in 2000. In South Asia there are about 50 million home-based workers, 80 percent women, who were invisible and voiceless. The organizations working with these women felt that there was a need to bring them together to give them a national and international voice. The members of HomeNet South Asia are national (country) networks of organizations of home-based workers. These are expanding in India as well as Bangladesh, Nepal, Pakistan, and Sri Lanka. There are more than 600 organizations in the network.

The Growth Impetus

Women's organizations do not naturally scale up. Women seem to prefer small, compact units that they are able to control, or they feel that adding members will change the dynamics and spread the benefits too thin. In some ways there is no push from within the organization to go to scale or to replicate. So why do women's organizations scale up at all?

An important impetus comes from governments. Given the mandate to remove poverty, governments tend to look for successful models and to take them to scale. One of the successes of the women's movement and women's organizations has been to prove that women are willing to participate, innovate, and work hard in "anti-poverty programs," and the success of many programs such as microfinance or environment regeneration has been mainly due to the enthusiasm and continuing participation of poor women. So governments tend to rely on forming groups, preferably groups of women, as the medium through which to run programs, and developmental funds are then pumped into them.

The largest such initiative today is an organization promoted by the Andhra Pradesh government called the Society for the Elimination of Rural Poverty (SERP), which is a network of SHGs. The Chief Minister of the State is the Chairperson of the governing body, and the Minister for Rural Development is the Vice Chairperson. SERP is implementing Indira Kranthi Patham, a community demand-driven poverty alleviation project covering all rural poor households in the state. The project involves organizing poor women into SHGs and then forming these groups into federations ranging from village to district level. SERP also markets commodities—for example, maize, soyabean, and coffee—and distributes government benefits such as old-age pensions.

Between 1995 and 2005, more than 700,000 SHGs in India obtained approximately 20 billion INR in loans from banks under a program of the National Bank of Agriculture and Rural Development (NABARD) (Nair, 2005). The on-time repayment rate has been over 95 percent, and their savings are at least 8 billion INR (ibid.).

The private sector can also provide an impetus to the growth of women's organizations. In recent years Indian companies have been using women's groups to market their products and in some cases to create employment by subcontracting a part of the manufacturing process. For example, in 2000, Hindustan Lever, the Indian arm of multinational giant Unilever, set up Project Shakti, which works through women's SHGs. It started in a few pilot villages with presentations at the groups' meetings, where women were invited to become direct-to-consumer sales distributors. The company trains the women in selling, commercial knowledge, and book-keeping, teaching them to become microentrepreneurs. There are now 30,000 *Shakti* entrepreneurs in 15 states, and the project is responsible for 40 percent of the company's rural sales growth.

Yet another growth impetus comes from crises. As noted earlier, small organizations have networked to prevent uprooting or displacement. In urban areas, for example, slum demolition drives bring together small CBOs to demonstrate and attempt to protect their communities. Similarly, natural disasters may activate and promote groups both for self-help as well as to help their neighbors. The Gujarat earthquake in 2001, for inst-ance, saw a mushrooming of spontaneous groups to help the victims, and many of these groups then developed into networked organizations.

SEWA's growth impetus tends to come from its base structure as a trade union. When women *bidi* workers in Gujarat organized for higher wages, the employers shifted much of their work to the neighboring state of Madhya Pradesh, and so SEWA was compelled to follow and help *bidi* workers to organize there too. When women street vendors, who had organized to bargain with the municipality and police in Ahmedabad, shifted to Delhi, they found themselves in a disempowered position, so they started a SEWA in Delhi as well. SEWA's growth often relies on family and community networks. Women who organize in one state have relatives in other states who learn about their work; younger women marry and move to new areas, where they carry the messages of organizing.

Scaling Up: Opportunities and Dangers

Although scaling up is necessary for organizing to become effective, it car-ries with it both dangers and opportunities. As we have seen, scaling up can occur in a number of different ways, the most common being through the government or through the private sector. The danger in both these models lies in the erosion of women's autonomy and control. Organiza-tions promoted by the government tend to be run by the government. In the best cases, as in the SERP example earlier, hundreds of thousands of women may become empowered, and may in fact assert control at local levels and within families. However, it is not clear how the women's organizations—the SHGs and the federations—would run without the support of the government both in terms of managing the organization as well as financially. Furthermore, when good examples like SERP are replicated in other states, the experience may be a hollow shell, in that although the structure of the women's organizations may be replicated, the spirit is missing. It is well known that many SHGs that are formed for the purpose of getting government subsidies for a project close down once the project has ended.

Another major issue for organizations promoted and run by the government is that after some time, when the first spirit of innovation disappears and when there is no more "special funding" for them, they are absorbed into routine governmental programs and lose their self-help character and dynamism. At this stage the distinction between the government and the organization breaks down, the "members" become beneficiaries as in any other governmental program, and the managers and leaders of the organization begin to see themselves as government functionaries.

The entrance of the private sector into scaling up women's organizations is relatively new and there are as yet only indications as to the possible dangers. Private firms tend to operate only so long as it suits their business interests. When those interests change, or the profits in that sector decline, the firm will lose little time in withdrawing itself from its supporting role, leading to a quick collapse of the organization if it is totally dependent on the firm. The opposite danger is complete domination of the organization by the private agency. Businesses like to firmly control all parts of their operations, and at some stage they begin to think of the women's organization as a junior department of their business.

In India, microfinance is itself becoming a private business. Many microfinance agencies are controlled by shareholders and investors from the mainstream financial world. Although women are benefiting from the availability of credit, there is very little empowerment or activism involved.

Scaling up through the private sector or through the government also has the effect of crowding out self-grown women's organizations or those supported by NGOs. Very often the women who have built an organization, brick-by-brick, find that their members are no longer active as they join subsidized government programs that offer many concrete benefits including soft loans. The real danger is that the organizations that empower women do not get scaled up, and instead women remain "beneficiaries" of government programs or "clients" of private ones.

However, the interests of the government and the private sector have opened up many opportunities for women. First, it has been acknowledged that women, and especially women coming together into organizations or groups, are powerful agents of change and not just objects of action.

Governmental and business interests have also brought a large amount of resources into women's organizations. These include funds from institutions such as the World Bank, from country aid agencies, from business investments, from financial markets, and from large international philanthropies. They have also brought in human resources in the form of committed professionals and managers.

The scaling up of women's organizations has also resulted in changing policies to accommodate their aspirations and growth. These include new laws and structures to accommodate women's access to loans, new governmental policies that recognize women's need for ownership of assets, and new sector policies that target women as producers.

The question remains whether it possible to avoid the dangers and maximize the opportunities, so that women's organizations scale up and yet remain autonomous and effective.

Personal Growth and Mutual Trust

The success of a member-based organization depends on the capacity of the women who are its members and even more on the capacity of the women who run it, who are its managers and leaders. Running even the smallest SHG requires skills—to manage money, to manage the aspirations and fears of its members, to allay the suspicions of family members and village leaders, and to deal with bank managers, local leaders, and government officials. As these organizations grow and become more complex, specialized skills are required, and professionals such as accountants, sales persons, and teachers have to be hired. The members of these organizations remain the poor, semi-literate—or sometimes illiterate—women, and it requires a great deal of personal growth on their part to be able to work with these professionals.

Scaling up requires networking, advocacy skills, and an understanding of issues at the national—and sometimes the international—level. It requires understanding and communication among women, sometimes those who do not even speak a common language. In order to attain these levels of scaling up and still retain control of their organizations, women need to develop a capacity to understand and manage. It requires a great deal of personal growth, bonding, strong mutual trust, and partnerships. This process takes time as women develop leadership and managerial skills, and learn to trust and rely on each other, and to deal with the changes that begin to occur in family relationships. Sometimes the growth is inter-generational, as knowledge passes from older to the younger women. Box 6.4 offers two examples of personal growth in SEWA.

Box 6.4 Examples of personal growth in SEWA

Indiraben worked in a tobacco-processing factory in Chikodra, a village in Gujarat, and joined SEWA in 1985. She became a leader of the trade union in her village and then her district, and was responsible for building a strong voice for the tobacco workers in her area. Although Indiraben had not finished high school, she was determined to educate her children. In order to pay for an education, her daughter Jyoti worked in the factory and fields alongside her mother and used her earnings to finance a college degree. A few years later she joined SEWA to look after the childcare program. As SEWA grew, Jyoti had the background, the education, and the motivation to grow with it and in 2005 she was elected the General Secretary of SEWA, by then a large, complex, national trade union with nearly a million members.

Krishnaben joined SEWA Bihar in 2004 and became a leader in her SHG. She encouraged other women to form a cooperative for production of incense sticks, and in 2007 was elected its president. She and other members of SEWA Bihar learned from the experience of long-term members in SEWA Gujarat.

Source: Author.

The main lesson that emerges is that the process of personal growth cannot be hurried; scaling up organizations is an organic process that takes time to flower. Organizations that grow too fast tend to bypass the process and rely on professionals to take the organization forward. In such cases the women remain the "beneficiaries," and while this is also a worthwhile goal, it does not build organizations owned by the women.

Addressing Fear and Resistance

One of the most powerful barriers to organizing is fear. Women have been brought up in fear of their men, their employers, and their communities. They live in constant fear of losing their livelihoods, of starvation, of losing their children to illness, and of being thrown out of their houses. The problem is compounded by traditional attitudes toward women, which result in a lack of mobility, a lack of value of women's worth, and a position of deference to male opinions. All of this leads to a sense of helplessness among women, which must be overcome before they can begin to take their lives into their own hands.

Women have also grown up in a world in which others constantly cheat them and they are, therefore, distrustful of the motives of organizations that claim help them. A further barrier to organizing is women's lack of knowledge or skills. A low level of literacy has often made it difficult for them to take on full responsibility for the management of their own organizations. Thus, many NGOs and women's organizations have introduced literacy training or adopted other strategies (such as encouraging younger, better-educated women to join groups) to overcome this obstacle.

Since organizing, if done effectively, leads to a shift in power between women and men, and between poor and rich, it is hardly surprising that much resistance is encountered from vested interests in the home, the community, and the workplace.

Women's empowerment is much more likely to be achieved if women have total control over their own organizations, which they can sustain both financially and managerially without direct dependence on, or subsidies from, others.

Organizing Internationally

Globalization has allowed capital to overcome national laws and regulations and act across countries, while workers remain subject to local rules. In order to deal with international capital, it has become important for workers to organize beyond the local to the international level.

Over the last century the labor movement formed international organizations, which allowed it to confront industrial inequalities with one voice. Today the International Trade Union Congress and the Global Union Federations speak for workers at an international level. However, these structures tend to exclude the voice of informal workers and especially women. It has, therefore, become necessary for informal workers to organize internationally too. According to WIEGO, workers have expressed the following reasons as to why they find international organizing important:

- Sharing information and knowledge that inspires organizing and introduces new technical ideas and ideas for action (see the example of organizing waste pickers).
- Raising the visibility and value of informal workers.
- Developing common policies and laws, and sharing strategies on how to succeed in achieving change with policymakers.

- Having a united and strong voice in international forums—for example, domestic workers and street vendors at meetings of the International Labour Organization (ILO).
- Coordinating international campaigns—for example, the World Class Cities for All Campaign, which aims to challenge the traditional approach to building cities and creating a new, more inclusive concept with the participation of street vendors and other groups of the (urban) poor, with a strong focus on women.
- Enabling international solidarity action.
- Developing knowledge, experience, skills, and confidence to empower the working poor, especially women, to speak for themselves.

Some recently formed international networks bring together street vendors, home-based workers, waste collectors, and domestic workers. Membership-based organizations (unions, cooperatives, or associations) that include street vendors, market vendors, and/or hawkers (that is, mobile vendors) among their members are entitled to affiliate to StreetNet International. StreetNet's aim is to promote the exchange of information and ideas on critical issues facing these workers and on practical organizing and advocacy strategies.

StreetNet International currently has more than 35 affiliates from 27 countries, employs a wide range of strategies, and engages in a number of activities. It promotes national alliance building, and it encourages unions to organize street vendors. It also promotes the sharing of information between affiliates on their strategies, struggles, and successes. In addition, it develops common approaches, policies, and strategies and takes up solidarity activities in support of members. It engages in international forums such as the ILO and has taken up the international World Class Cities for All Campaign mentioned earlier.

Not only are domestic workers organizing locally, but they are also uniting regionally and globally. The Asia Domestic Workers Network (ADWN), for example, was formed in 2004. It consists of 12 local domestic worker organizations and supports NGOs from six Asian countries. In 2008 migrant domestic workers' organizations in Asia also formed a regional alliance, the Asian Domestic Workers' Alliance (ADWA). There is a long-established regional organization in Latin America, the Latin American and Caribbean Confederation of Household Workers, with member organizations in 13 countries in the region as well as in Canada, and an organization of migrant workers in Europe. In the United States, the National Domestic Worker Alliance, founded in 2007 at the US Social Forum, held its first Congress in June 2008.

In an important development, in 2007 the International Union of Food, Agricultural, Hotel, Restaurant, Catering, Tobacco and Allied Workers placed priority on support for domestic workers. It is establishing a network to promote domestic workers' rights and is leading a campaign for an ILO Convention on domestic work.

Although environmental issues, including the recycling of solid waste, are high on the world agenda, the voice of waste pickers is barely heard. A Latin American network to improve their lives was set up in 2005 (see Box 6.5). WIEGO has also embarked on a program to facilitate networking among groups of waste pickers across the globe. It is committed to help strengthen democratic, member-based organizations of informal workers—especially women—and in particular to help build solidarity and action at an international level.

Box 6.5 The Latin American Waste-picker Network (LAWPN)

LAWPN was created after the Second Latin American Waste-pickers Conference, held in Sao Leopoldo, Brazil, in February 2005. At the beginning there were organizations from four countries involved in the initiative: the Brazilian Waste-picker Movement (MNCR), the Bogota Waste-picker Association (ARB) from Colombia, some waste-picker cooperatives and associations from Argentina (Bajo Flores and Tren Blanco) and members of the Waste-pickers Trade Union (UCRUS) from Uruguay.

During 2005 LAWPN provided solidarity to waste-picker cooperatives when they faced repression by local governments and engaged in protest action. When the Inter-American Development Bank held a conference in Buenos Aires, Argentina, on "Improving the lives of Latin American and Caribbean waste segregators" LAWPN decided to participate in order to give voice to waste pickers at the event. An important parallel session took place where leaders involved in LAWPN shared information about the network with new organizations.

The Avina Foundation for Sustainable Development in Latin America has provided support to the network since 2006. LAWPN now has 12 members from 12 Latin American/Caribbean countries: Argentina, Bolivia, Brazil, Chile, Colombia, Costa Rica, Ecuador, Mexico, Paraguay, Peru, Puerto Rico, and Venezuela.

Source: Fernandez, 2009.

SEWA had been organizing home-based workers since 1975, and in the 1980s realized that if these workers were to be protected, a national law and an international convention would be necessary. Although the campaign for a national law did not succeed, the campaign at the international level took off, with many organizations of home-based workers all over the world getting together with the trade union movement, and in 1996 the ILO adopted the first International Convention on Home Workers. A network called HomeNet International was formed during the international campaign, but it was disbanded soon after the Convention was passed.

At the time of the campaign, it was noted that the Asian region has perhaps the largest number of home-based workers in the world. HomeNet Asia, consisting of HomeNet South Asia and HomeNet South East Asia, formed with the support of the Federation of Dutch Trade Unions (FNV) and UNIFEM in 2000, is a dynamic and vibrant network of 400 organizations representing home-based workers from six countries in South Asia and seven in South East Asia. Its strength lies in its grassroots membership and the technical support it extends to its members, while raising their voice at national, regional, and international levels to influence legislation, policies, and programs.

There are over 60 million unorganized home-based workers scattered in the region who are not visible and recognized as workers. Therefore, HomeNet is trying to help them to build membership-based organizations where they would represent themselves and speak about their own issues. At the same time, it is advocating for a national policy on home-based workers and campaigning for the ratification of the ILO Convention. HomeNet has drafted a policy on home-based workers around which regular dialogs with governments are in process.

The network focuses on four key areas: strengthening home-based workers' organizations and networks in Asia; supporting development of policy frameworks and advocacy on key issues affecting home-based workers; supporting pilot approaches for the provision of social protection for home-based workers; and promoting fair trade practices at the national level to ensure more favorable working conditions for women home-based workers. HomeNet is also working on strengthening the livelihoods of producer home-based workers in the region through a project with the South Asian Association for Regional Cooperation (SAARC). This is intended to upgrade their skills through various trainings and enable producer home-based workers to form their own companies.

Representation

Organizing alone is not enough to bring about the necessary changes, however. Workers need a representative voice in those institutions and processes that set policies and the "rules of the (economic) game." In a global economy, improving conditions for informal workers in general—and informal women workers in particular—requires a representative voice at the international level as well as the local and national levels. International, regional, and national policies and negotiations all need to include the voices and concerns of informal workers (see Box 6.6). Ensuring a voice for informal workers at the highest level requires supporting the growth of their organizations and building leadership capacity. This is not an easy road to travel, but it is a vital one.

Box 6.6   Where informal women workers need to be represented

Local level	Community councils (social, political, administrative) Collective bargaining bodies, tripartite boards Municipal planning, zoning, and advisory boards Rural planning bodies and resource allocation bodies
National level	Planning commissions and advisory committees Tripartite bodies Chambers of commerce Trade union federations Collective bargaining bodies Sector-specific associations or boards National negotiations on the Millennium Development Goals (MDGs) and poverty reduction strategy papers (PRSPs)
Regional level	Intergovernmental commissions Bilateral trade negotiations Development banks and agencies Trade union bodies
International level	UN specialized agencies and funds (for example, UNIFEM, ILO) International Trade Union Confederation (ITUC), global unions, worker networks Finance institutions such as the International Monetary Fund (IMF) and World Bank Trade negotiations Fair and ethical trade initiatives Codes of conduct and international framework agreement negotiations Civil society movements

Source: Author.

CONCLUSION

The question remains whether it is possible to avoid the dangers and maximize the opportunities so that women's organizations scale up locally, nationally, and internationally and yet remain autonomous and effective. There is enough evidence to show that small and local women's groups are empowering for their members and contribute toward changing local power balances. But at higher levels and in larger organizations, poor women tend to lose authority and be reduced to "clients" or "beneficiaries."

The SEWA experience shows that there are many ways in which organizations can begin to scale up and at the same time be owned by poor women and be their representative voice. There are certain factors that seem to be necessary. One is an appropriate organizational structure. In order for the ownership to remain with the poor women, it is necessary for them to be the owners—the shareholders or members—as well as the board. The organization should be member-based, no matter how large it is.

Another factor is that the women who own the organization must have the capacity to play their role in a meaningful way. So, a very important part of scaling up is building up the members' capacity so that they understand the issues they are dealing with and are able to communicate with those in power. As the world gets more complex, there is a need for people with advanced skills, in particular the skill to communicate and to use modern technological tools. This requires a certain level of education and professionalism. Although most professionals tend to prefer to work for the mainstream, there are many who also believe in the ideology of economic justice and are happy to work with and for poor women.

Funding for a scale up is important. By definition the poor have limited resources, often insufficient for a decent life for themselves, yet they are often willing to use these for their own local organizations. However, it is not possible to expect that they would be able to fund a scale up of their work. As we have seen, the main sources of funds for scaling up are governments and private corporations. Other sources of funding include philanthropy through private foundations and international aid. Although funding is needed on a large scale, it is necessary for the funders to recognize the importance of maintaining the autonomy of the organization and the ideology of empowerment. Recognition of the *shakti* of poor women is the basis for moving to a scaled-up, member-based organization that can work for change at local, national, and international levels.

References

Bhatt, E. R. (1988). *Shram shakti: Report of the national commission on self-employed women and women in the informal sector*. New Delhi: Government of India.

Chen, M., Jhabvala, R., Kanbur, R., Mirani, N, Osner, K., & Richards, C. (Eds). (2007). *Membership-based organizations of the poor*. London: Routledge.

Fernandez, L. (2009). Latin American waste picker network. In M. Samson (ed.), *Refusing to be cast aside: Waste pickers organising around the world* (pp. 44–48). Cambridge, MA: WIEGO.

Grameen Bank. (n.d.) *A short history of Grameen Bank*. Retrieved August 17, 2010, from http://www.grameen-info.org/index.php?option=com_content&task=view&id=19& Itemid=114

Nair, A. (2005). *Sustainability of microfinance self help groups in India: Would federating help?* Policy Research Working Paper No. 3516. World Bank, Washington, DC.

Sen, A. (1990). More than 100 million women are missing. *The New York Review of Books*, December 20.

Srivastava, N., & Srivastava, R. (2009). *Women, work, and employment outcomes in rural India*. Paper presented at the FAO-IFAD-ILO workshop on gaps, trends and current research in gender dimensions of agricultural and rural employment: Differentiated pathways out of poverty, Rome, March 31–April 2.

UNIFEM (United Nations Development Fund for Women). 2005. *Progress of the world's women 2005: Women, work and poverty*. New York: UNIFEM.

WIEGO (Women in Informal Employment Globalizing and Organizing). 2002. Retrieved August 17, 2010, from http://www.wiego.org/stat_picture/

7

Gender Dimensions of the World of Work in a Globalized Economy

NAOKO OTOBE

Evidence shows that when an economic crisis hits, it is often women who bear the brunt. This is therefore a critical time to focus on promoting women's status in the world of work, in order for past achievements and progress toward gender equality not to be completely undone.

INTRODUCTION

The world economy continues its integration on various levels under the forces of globalization, accompanied by market liberalization and economic reforms. The 2008–2009 global financial and economic crisis, which started with food and fuel price hikes, has caused massive job losses in many countries. The ILO (2010) estimated that during 2009 the number of unemployed in the world would rise by 34 million over the total number in 2007, to reach more than 212 million.

Evidence shows that when an economic crisis hits, it is often women who bear the brunt. This is therefore a critical time to focus on promoting women's status in the world of work, in order for past achievements and progress toward gender equality not to be completely undone. All countries, both developing and developed, need to respond with concrete, gendered socioeconomic policy and program measures to help their people cope with substantial job and income loss and diminishing purchasing power. The crisis is a stark reminder that much broader safety nets are needed, because even those who were once the haves have joined the ranks of the have-nots.

Against this ominous backdrop, this chapter discusses the gender dimensions of the world of work in a globalized economy in order to review overall progress during the last 15–20 years. It pays particular attention to the gender dimensions of economic policies, employment, and poverty. It also provides an overview of the ILO's instruments for poverty alleviation and advancing gender equality. The chapter concludes by looking at the implications of the global financial and economic crisis for policies and programs, and suggests measures for consideration.

THE WORLD OF WORK AND GENDER EQUALITY

Gender equality is at the heart of the ILO's Decent Work Agenda, the aim of which is "to promote opportunities for women and men to obtain decent and productive work, in conditions of freedom, equity, security and human dignity" (ILO, 1999). All workers—both women and men—should benefit from more "decent" jobs and income. True decent work can only be assured in a society that allows labor market outcomes to provide equal opportunities and equitable living incomes to individuals from various social groups regardless of their personal attributes, whether biological, social, or political. In all countries, however, social barriers and discrimination persist to varying degrees. More specifically, with respect to gender-based discrimination, despite substantial progress made in promoting gender equality and narrowing gender gaps in the world of work during the last half a century, much of women's work remains in sex-stereotyped occupations that are more precarious, vulnerable, and poorly paid than men's. As a consequence, women are disproportionately affected by decent work deficits, and hence poverty, than men. Women are also the main care providers to society, work that is largely unpaid and economically unrecognized.

The ILO addresses sex-based discrimination as one of the most important grounds of labor discrimination; others include race, color, religion, political opinion, national extraction, social origin, age, and sexual orientation. The first six of these—in addition to sex—are covered under International Labour Convention No. 111 on Discrimination (Employment and Occupation) (ILO, 1958). Evidence shows that the socioeconomic status of women and girls among those social groups that are discriminated against is worse than that of their male counterparts. When a woman is part of an ethnic minority in a society, she suffers from double discrimination, facing more barriers and difficulties in finding decent employment and income-earning opportunities and in accessing various social services. For instance, in urban Brazil, non-white women earn the lowest income on average, followed by white women, non-white men, and white men across all workers at different education levels (ILO, 2003a).

Improved access to labor markets and to decent and productive employment for women is crucial in the process of creating greater equality between women and men in society. Analysis of the latest data in ILO's 2010 *Global Employment Trends* shows that women's employment-to-population ratio in 2008 was 48.6 percent, compared to 48.3 percent 10 years previously—globally, therefore, the activity rate has not substantially changed. Women globally have a greater likelihood of being unemployed than men. Female unemployment increased slightly—after having gradually deceased between 2004 and 2007—from 6.0 percent (men at 5.7 percent) in 2007 to 6.1 percent (men at 5.6 percent) in 2008. The ILO estimated, however, that this might reach as high as 7.3 percent by the end of 2009 (ILO, 2010). The report shows clearly that most regions had been making progress in increasing the number of women in decent employment before the crisis hit. However, in general, full gender equality in the areas of labor market access and conditions of employment has not yet been attained. Box 7.1 provides an overview.

Box 7.1   Progress in advancing gender equality in the world of work, 1998–2008: Key facts

- Of all people employed in the world, 40 percent are women, and this share has not changed over the last 10 years.
- The female adult employment-to-population ratio worldwide was 48.6 percent in 2008 (73.3 percent for men). During the last 10 years, this ratio increased slightly in almost all regions, while the male ratio decreased in almost all regions, except in Central and South Eastern Europe and Central Asia.
- More women are gaining access to education, which is key to more access to and better employment, but equality in education is still far from the reality in some regions.
- Overall, there is not a significant difference between the sexes when it comes to young people (aged 15 to 24 years) searching for work. The unemployment rate of female youth at 12.5 percent is only slightly higher than the male rate of 12.2 percent. A young person's likelihood of being unemployed in 2007 was three times higher than an adult's.

- Whereas 10 years ago, the main employer for women was agriculture, it is now the services sector. Out of the total number of employed women in 2008, 35.4 percent worked in agriculture and 46.3 percent in services. Male sectoral shares, in comparison, were 32.2 percent in agriculture and 41.2 percent in services.
- The poorer the region, the greater the likelihood that women are among the ranks of unpaid contributing family workers or own-account workers. These two employment statuses make up the newly defined "vulnerable employment." Female contributing family workers, in particular, are not likely to be economically independent.
- While the share of vulnerable employment in women's total employment decreased from 56.1 percent in 1997 to 52.7 percent in 2008, the rate is still higher for women than for men (49.1 percent), especially in the world's poorest regions, and this was expected to worsen in 2009 in the aftermath of the global economic crisis.
- The share of women in wage and salaried employment grew from 41.8 percent in 1997 to 46.4 percent in 2007.

Source: ILO (2008a; 2009).

WORKING POVERTY AND GENDER

In 2007, of the world's three billion working population, 609.5 million workers still did not earn enough to lift themselves and their families above the USD 1.25 a day poverty line and 1.2 billion workers did not earn enough to exceed the USD 2 a day line (US dollars throughout). This means that despite working, more than four out of ten workers were poor (ILO, 2008b). The ILO estimated that these numbers were likely to increase by between 3 and 7 percent by the end of 2009 (ILO, 2010). Hence, in the worst-case scenario, the level of working poverty would have increased from 20.6 percent to over 26 percent to reach a total of 1.3 billion in 2009. Total female unemployment was also expected to increase from 74.9 million in 2007 to almost 90 million in 2009, and the level of female working poverty is likely to have worsened as well. While poverty incidence in terms of the level of consumption and income is measured at the household level, and it is not easy to break it down by gender, it is estimated that a large majority of the world's absolute poor are women (UNIFEM, n.d.), a situation that is likely to get worse (ILO, 2010).

Gender cuts across the household, community, society, labor market, and economy. The socially ascribed roles of women and men dictate the division of labor between the genders both within the household and in the labor market. Given such persistent social values in a large number of countries, it is not surprising that females are over-represented among the poor, especially in those developing countries where society is traditional and discriminatory against girls and women (Islam-Rahman & Otobe, 2005). However, even in rich and more egalitarian industrialized countries, women—particularly single mothers—are still overrepresented among the poor. Research in the United States has shown that families headed by a single mother made up the vast majority of welfare recipients in the early 1990s, and poverty rates among working single-mother families failed to decline between 1995 and 1999 (Porter & Dupree, 2001). Furthermore, other research has shown that black and Hispanic women were poorer than white women during the 1990s, with lower income and a higher risk of entering poverty, and black women were more likely to be in single-headed households than white or Hispanic women (Wadley, 2008).

Poverty is multidimensional and could be defined in various ways. Figure 7.1 shows a pyramid of poverty concepts as conceptualized by Baulch (1996). This is an attempt to illustrate the different poverty concepts ranging from the narrow conceptualization involving nutrition-based indicators (at the top of the pyramid) to a broader definition that includes access to assets, and concepts of dignity and autonomy. Although most poverty measurement methods, including the poverty line, are based on one type or another of income/private consumption measurement, participatory strategies challenge the implicit hierarchy of poverty concepts based on physiological needs and stress the concepts of dignity,

Figure 7.1 A pyramid of poverty concepts

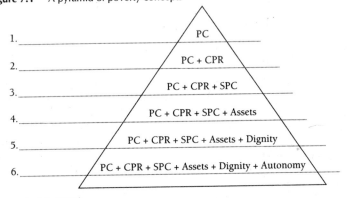

1.
2.
3.
4.
5.
6.

PC

PC + CPR

PC + CPR + SPC

PC + CPR + SPC + Assets

PC + CPR + SPC + Assets + Dignity

PC + CPR + SPC + Assets + Dignity + Autonomy

Source: Baulch (1996).
Note: PC = private consumption; CPR = common property resources; SPC = state-provided consumption.

self-confidence, and autonomy, which influence the ability of people to choose self-fulfilling and rewarding lifestyles.

Within the framework of the ILO definition of decent work, additional aspects of "freedom" and "security" could be added as the seventh and eighth levels, respectively. Gender dimensions intertwine with all these aspects of poverty, so that women continue to be overrepresented among—and form the bottom rung of—the poor in the world.

It is widely recognized that female children in a patriarchal society tend to receive less attention and resources than male children, even within a household. Girls tend to be educated less than boys in many developing countries, though much progress has been made toward gender parity in primary education. The disadvantages accumulated at early stages of life lessen the chances for a girl child to become employable when she grows up. Since much of common property resources (CRP) are owned under a patriarchal perspective of "men as the head (breadwinner) of the household," which determines the allocation of their usufruct rights, women tend to suffer from unequal access to the productive resources and assets needed to either earn an income in the market or cultivate food for subsistence in the informal economy.

As for the state-provided consumption (SPC), it is likely that women may benefit from this more than men, as they are usually the ones responsible for fetching water and fuel, and cultivating and preparing food for the household. However, if such publicly provided support as food and fuel subsidy and water supply is reduced, women are likely to be negatively affected first. Because patriarchal society generally provides women with less freedom of movement and intra-household decision-making power—not only to undertake economic activities outside the home, but also to allocate intra-household resources—their individual dignity and autonomy are also likely to be more suppressed in less egalitarian societies. An extreme example is the honor killing of Muslim women and girls by male family members (see Kazemi, 2000).

When women are employed in the formal sector, they tend on average to work fewer years and accumulate fewer social protection benefits and less income during their lifetime than men, due to their different life cycle. Women with young children may either reduce their working hours or stop working for a period, returning to the labor market once children grow up. This is one of the reasons why women tend to fall into poverty in old age.

Most workers among the poor are found in the informal and rural economies (ILO, 2002a) and include home workers and domestic workers—a large majority of whom are women. (For a detailed definition of home work, see C177 Home Work Convention, 1996, at http://www.ilo.org/ilolex/english/convdisp1.htm.)

Much of women's work in agriculture is unpaid, as is the case in sub-Saharan Africa and rural economies in South Asia, while some women are engaged in wage employment in the plantation sector. In the informal economy, women are employed as unpaid family workers, or are self-employed doing small-scale production, vending, or providing personal services. Their work often remains invisible and uncounted in national statistics; they are unorganized and unprotected (in terms of access to social protection, such as medical insurance or old-age pension); and they lack representation and a voice. Most of those working in the informal economy do not have access to any workers' rights, such as those on minimum wage, working hours, or a day of rest per week—let alone those on equal rights at work and maternity protection (Carr et al., 2000; Chen et al., 1999; ILO, 2002b). As a consequence, women are disproportionately affected by decent work deficits and poverty in the world of work, in particular in poorer developing countries.

Women's vulnerability to poverty also persists due to economic and political crises, civil strife, the pandemic of HIV and AIDS in a number of countries (especially in sub-Saharan Africa), an increasing number of environmental catastrophes, and diminishing social support in transition economies (see also Hemmings-Gapihan, 2008). Due to persistent poverty and the lack of alternative employment opportunities in originating communities, women are increasingly pushed into rural to urban and international migration. When they migrate internationally to work, they are mostly engaged in lower-end 3 Ds (dirty, demeaning, and dangerous) jobs that the nationals of the receiving countries no longer wish to do—for example, domestic work, supporting working women (and men) in these countries by doing their reproductive care work. There is also an alarming trend of exploitation, abuse, and violence against migrant women and children, especially trafficking into domestic work and the sex sector (ILO, 2003c; IOM, 2005).

This is the current situation after decades of development efforts made under the mainstream development economic thinking driven by the neoliberal macroeconomic policies advocated by key international financial institutions. Why has progress been so slow, not only in terms of the speed of development but also in reducing the level of abject poverty for millions of poor women and men in developing countries?

The World Bank does advocate for promoting gender equality in development. According to its 2001 report entitled *Engendering Development: Through Gender Equality in Rights, Resources, and Voice*, gender disparities in education and health tend to be greater in poor countries, and it argues that gender inequalities impose costs on productivity, efficiency, and economic progress. By hindering the accumulation of human capital in the home and labor market, and by systematically excluding women (or men for that matter) from access to resources, public services, or productive activities, gender discrimination diminishes an economy's capacity to grow and raise living standards (World Bank, 2001). This report puts forward the "efficiency argument" in gender and development—extending the concept of the human being as "economic" (wo)man—that is currently implemented through the Bank's gender mainstreaming strategy and action plan (World Bank, 2006).

Addressing gender discrimination—especially in the context of poverty alleviation—is crucial, since it manifests as structural poverty of women. It is often rooted in the existing social institution or value system, which is slow to change. The social institution determines who has access to and control over natural and financial resources, assets, means of production, education and training, employment, and income opportunities, as well as entitlements to social protection. So far as the social institution functions in a discriminatory manner, the "laissez-faire" and "neoliberal" macroeconomic policy aimed at economic growth, and total reliance on market forces under a "trickle-down" theory, will not automatically translate into the reduction of poverty of discriminated groups, especially poor women in traditional societies (Elson & Cagatay, 2000). We would, therefore, need a different macroeconomic policy framework aimed at development and poverty eradication, that is, one in which all humans can have the right (or entitlement) to work and live to their full potential in freedom, equity, dignity, and human security—or, as per the ILO's terms, in decent work and life.

In the wake of the global financial and economic crisis, many voices called for an increased role for the public sector, and G20 governments met in Pittsburgh in July 2009 to discuss ways to tighten regulations in the financial sector to increase the accountability and transparency of the operations of financial institutions. At the same time, the governments of key industrialized countries intervened in the financial sector on an unprecedented and massive scale to bail out large financial institutions that were "too-big-to-fail." This is an ironic outcome of the past market-driven and laissez-faire financial and economic policies that minimized the role of the government. A new macroeconomic paradigm is clearly needed for the world financial systems. Now is the time to call for a more inclusive new world economic order, or a "just economy," that can better foster more inclusive economic growth for poverty reduction and improved decent work opportunities for all. The global economic crisis has painfully proved that getting the macroeconomic environment right is also crucial for providing an enabling environment for gender justice in the world of work.

MACROECONOMIC POLICY, EMPLOYMENT, AND POVERTY: GENDER IMPLICATIONS

Promoting decent and productive employment is a very effective measure to reduce income poverty in a sustainable manner in general, and especially for poor women. There is a clear nexus between economic growth, employment growth, and poverty reduction. Currently, "pro-poor" growth is much debated in the context of development policies (Epstein, 2003; Islam, 2004). In order to make economic growth "pro-poor," we need to increase the employment content of growth in general, and for women in particular.

During the last 25 years, developing countries have been implementing economic policies driven by the neoliberal economic policy framework, especially under the aegis of the international financial institutions and the so-called Washington Consensus. The series of prescribed structural adjustment programs (SAPs), implemented in a large number of sub-Saharan African countries in the 1980s and 1990s, typically entailed emphasis on macroeconomic stability, freer markets, a smaller role for the public sector (involving reducing social expenditures, "right-sizing," and privatization of public enterprises, for instance), and liberalization of international flows of capital and goods—but not extending the same level of free movement to labor. The SAPs were subject to much criticism, not only by those who were concerned with the issue of poverty reduction in general, but also by feminist economists in particular (see, for example, Benería & Feldman, 1992; Cagatay & Korkurt, 2004). They have pointed to the negative social impacts of the programs on health and education, and the increased burden of women's unpaid work.

During the 1990s and into the 21st century, the globalization process further accelerated, with advanced communication technologies, increased volume of international trade, and a rising level of migration that is increasingly being feminized. Principally anchored by neoliberal economic policies that provided primacy to market forces and were implemented in most developing countries, it also coincided with increasing trends of income inequality. Between 1990 and 2005, approximately two-thirds of these countries experienced an increase in income inequality (as measured by changes in the Gini index). Likewise, during the same period, the income gap between the top and bottom 10 percent of wage earners increased in 70 percent of the countries for which data are available (ILO, 2008c). It is also important to note that the overall "feminization of the labour market" has taken place while the share of labor income has been declining in much of the world.

Public sector reform, or "right-sizing," tended to negatively affect more women than men in cases where the public sector had a relatively high proportion of women employees. Where public enterprises were privatized, however, the gender-specific impact on employment varied depending on where women and men worked. Sometimes the impact on female employment was more indirect, as loss of jobs for men pushed women to increase their level of economic participation, leading to "additional worker" effect (that is, when the primary worker's income is reduced, a secondary worker needs to supplement family income). Some empirical evidence shows that privatization has also contributed, in countries such as India, to increased "informalization" of labor (Gosh et al., 2008).

Regarding the gendered impact of trade on work, research shows that because the export sector in developing countries is often female labor intensive, the effect on women's employment is pro-cyclical; when exports expand, women's employment growth is more positively affected. However, trade liberalization involving import penetration in the import substitution sector could have an ambiguous impact on overall employment, and again the net gendered impact on employment could vary depending on where women and men work (Berik, 2000; Heintz, 2006).

In the case of specific sectoral changes in international trade, as seen in the post-Multifibre Arrangement (MFA) period in some countries, the impact differs depending on the expansion/reduction of the overall exports in the sector in individual countries. The MFA, a multilateral trade agreement on textile and clothing, expired at the end of 2004, enabling countries to export these items without trade restrictions. However, both the United States and the European Union have imposed some trade restrictions on imports from China, due to a sudden import surge immediately after the Arrangement ended. Under the current trading framework, least developed countries are still given preferential treatment, that is, they can export without importation taxes and fixed quotas, and also without restrictions on the sources of material used for production.

In those countries that lost competitive edge in the new, more competitive international trade environment—for example, Dominican Republic, Lesotho, and Mauritius (Ministry of Labour et al., 2007; Otobe, 2008)—a substantial number of jobs were lost. In Lesotho and Mauritius, because the ratio of women in the labor force in this sector was larger, more women were negatively affected by retrenchments, while in Dominican Republic, where the gender composition of the sector's labor was more even, both women and men were more or less equally affected.

In those countries that are now benefiting from the changed trade environment, such as Bangladesh (for its maintenance of duty-free privileges for exports to both EU and US markets), and China (from the lifting of restricted quotas for exports to the major markets), the initial net effect on employment in the textile and clothing sector has so far been more positive. However, it is possible that increased competition may be having a downward pressure on and worsened working conditions. In the wake of the recent global economic downturn, which has had a negative impact on exports to major markets, this situation may further deteriorate, and the medium- and long-term impacts on employment and labor conditions in these countries are yet to be seen.

As for monetary policies, reducing inflation frequently has a negative impact on employment growth in general, and when employment growth slows, women's employment is often disproportionately affected. Because women's formal employment is often concentrated in export sectors, maintaining a competitive exchange rate could also help counter the disproportionately negative impact on women's employment when total employment growth slows down (Otobe, 2008).

Evidence shows that for a given rate of economic growth, a higher share of government expenditures relative to GDP is associated with more employment. In the global financial crisis, the narrowing fiscal space for governments in developing countries could have more negative effects on women than men, as women often tend to be the last to be hired and first to be fired. It is important to be vigilant for the impact of the unfolding economic crisis on overall trends in this respect, given also that the recovery of labor markets takes several times longer than economic recovery.

Economic crisis and downturn tend to cause "informalization" of labor, and this has been increasing across many countries (Benería, 2001, 2008; Benería & Floro, 2005). It was also previously the case in the aftermath of the Asian financial and economic crisis in the late 1990s (Aswicahyono et al., 1999; Dejillas, 2000), and more recently, similar trends were also witnessed in the wake of the downturn in the textile and garment sector in Dominican Republic, Lesotho, and Mauritius, mentioned earlier. The increasing trend of decentralized production systems under the on-going globalization process is also likely to have contributed to this trend, as witnessed in the case of home workers (Carr et al., 2000). However, global trends are difficult to gauge, given the scarcity of comparable data on informal employment. More empirical study on this is needed to be able to understand the overall dynamics in the global trends (ILO, 2002b).

INSTRUMENTS FOR POVERTY ALLEVIATION AND ADVANCING GENDER EQUALITY UNDER ILO'S DECENT WORK AGENDA

What are the optimal forms of intervention by the ILO for poverty allevia- tion, especially with respect to disadvantaged groups? Promoting decent and productive employment is the most effective way of reducing poverty. Needless to say, enhancing the employment content (or social content) of economic growth through adopting a set of appropriate macroeconomic policies is also critically important. Recently, the nexus between economic growth, employment growth, and poverty reduction has been increasingly recognized. The macro policies and strategies must be such that growth yields efficient employment and income outcomes, and that special meas- ures are adopted to enhance the employability, participation, and voice of the poor (ILO, 2003b). The ILO (2004) has been engaged in a variety of policy-oriented research work on pro-poor growth. However, its eco- nomic analysis has been more focused on productive and remunerated work (market work) than on reproductive and unpaid work (non-market work), other than in the area of social protection—for instance, in relation to maternity protection and issues related to HIV and AIDS.

The ILO's interventions for poverty reduction include standard setting, technical cooperation, and research and advocacy in the areas of productive employment, social protection, legal and policy reforms, and organization building. These correspond to its four pillars of decent work: promoting rights; promoting decent, and productive employment; promoting the expansion of social protection for all; and promoting social dialog (among government, employers' organizations, and workers' organizations, plus other civil society groups such as women's organizations).

Poverty alleviation could be undertaken through various measures such as redistribution of capital and assets, enhancing human capital, promoting employment in rural and informal economies, increasing labor market access and reducing labor market vulnerability, providing social transfers, and supporting organizations of the poor. Over the past 30 years, the ILO has worked on poverty alleviation targeting poor women and other social groups, in particular through building self-help organizations, promoting women's entrepreneurship and self-employment creation, providing micro-credit for income generation, developing cooperatives, providing wage employment through public works programs, and extending social protection targeting informal workers, including home workers. A participatory approach developed in the 1970s was applied in various projects during the 1980s and 1990s, especially under a program that specialized in poverty alleviation for poor women in the rural and informal sectors through employment creation (ILO, 2000).

The ILO has set out International Labour Standards that have a direct bearing on the poor; for example, those on minimum wage, rural workers, and indigenous and tribal peoples (Nos. 131, 141, and 169). In more recent times, a special program has been implemented to follow up on the 1998 ILO Declaration on Fundamental Rights and Principles at Work (which commits member states to respect and promote principles and rights in four categories, whether or not they have ratified the relevant Conventions: freedom of association and the effective recognition of the right to collective bargaining, the elimination of forced or compulsory labor, the abolition of child labor, and the elimination of discrimination in respect of employment and occupation).

The Declaration covers two key equal rights conventions: Convention No. 100—Equal Remuneration (1951), and No. 111—Discrimination (Employment and Occupation) (1958). Thanks to the push by the ILO and its tripartite constituents for acceptance of the International Labor Standards, these conventions are almost universally ratified—reaching 90 percent of all the ILO member states (see Figure 7.2). However, due to persistent gender norms in society, weak enforcement mechanisms at the country level, and the high level of informality of employment in developing countries, this level of ratification has not yet been translated into real change.

In terms of developing new international legal instruments that have particular significance for poor women, the ILO adopted Convention No. 177 on Home Work (1996). The efficacy of this Convention was much debated during the 1996 International Labour Conference at the time of

Figure 7.2 Number of ratifications: Key equal rights conventions, 1952–2008

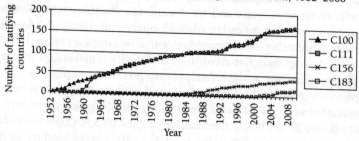

Source: ILO ratification tables. Retrieved February 2010, from http://www.ilo.org/ilolex/english/newratframeE.htm

Note: C100—Equal Remuneration (1951); C111—Discrimination (Employment and Occupation) (1958), C156—Workers with Family Responsibilities (1981); C183—Maternity Protection (2000).

discussion toward its adoption, but it was certainly a big milestone for millions of home workers, especially in the context of globalization and the decentralization of global production chains. Although the Convention has so far been ratified by only five countries—Albania, Argentina, Finland, Ireland, and Netherlands—it has been used as a tool to campaign for better working conditions for millions of home workers by organizations such as Women in Informal Employment Globalizing and Organizing (WIEGO) and the Self-employed Women's Association (SEWA) in India.

More recently, the Decent Work Agenda adopted in 1999 as an ILO strategic framework for its work is currently being implemented in four areas (rights, employment, social protection, and social dialog), with gender and poverty eradication as cross-cutting priorities. The ILO also adopted a Gender Policy and a Plan of Action in 2000, which aims at mainstreaming gender concerns in its institution, programs, and personnel. In all four strategic areas, there are programs that can contribute toward poverty alleviation, including for women. The ILO has also undertaken an active campaign called "Gender Equality at the Heart of Decent Work."

As for promoting employment opportunities for the poor, including for women, the ILO is committed to promoting decent and productive employment as a development objective and attaches importance to pro-poor economic growth, employment growth, and the promotion of social justice, placing employment and jobs at the heart of the development agenda. Convention No. 122 on Employment Policy (1964) provides an overall framework to promote freely chosen, productive employment and nondiscrimination in all countries. Accordingly, the ILO assists its member states in implementing the Global Employment Agenda (GEA), and gender concerns are also supposed to be mainstreamed across the board. The GEA seeks collective recognition and decision making on policies and regulations that enhance "freely chosen productive employment" and promote international labor standards and workers' fundamental rights simultaneously. The ILO's call for "making decent work a global goal," as endorsed by the World Commission's report (World Commission on Social Dimensions of Globalization, 2004) and ILO Declaration on Social Justice for a Fair Globalization (2008), is drawing increasing attention and support at the global, regional, and country levels (ILO, 2005).

More recently, the International Labour Conference in 2008 adopted a Resolution Concerning Promotion of Rural Employment for Poverty Reduction, calling for member states and the ILO to promote productive employment and decent work in the rural sector, where a large majority of the world's poor live and work. Particular mention can be made regarding the comprehensive nature of the resolution's policy and strategy guidance, including macroeconomic and sectoral policies, employment policies, promoting rights at work, and social dialog. In addition, providing adequate social protection, promoting gender equality, and strengthening labor market institutions form a part of this set of policy recommendations.

The ILO is currently following up on a Global Jobs Pact, adopted by the 2009 International Labour Conference in response to the global economic crisis, which gives top priority to jobs and decent work. The Pact also includes promoting gender concerns and making the crisis an opportunity to promote gender equality, in particular, in countries' stimulus packages.

In terms of addressing gender concerns in general, clearly there has been a paradigm shift in the ILO as in the UN system. While initially slow in coming, it has been distinct and steady, from "women-targeted only" and Women in Development (WID) approaches to the gender and development (GAD) approach, which calls for mainstreaming gender equality concerns across the board in various programs and activities. As a consequence, many more initiatives have been taken to promote gender concerns in the work of the ILO, particularly since the mid-1990s.

The question, however, is what economic policy paradigm orients the ILO's social policies. Certainly, the paradigm of decent work, with gender equality placed at its core, is strongly in line with the feminist economists' paradigm on development: that we need not only to promote decent and productive (paid market) work, but also to balance this with reproductive (unpaid) work in the lives of the world's working poor, particularly women. However, the current era of globalization continues to be driven by the neoliberalism of mainstream macroeconomic policy making in development, which is often gender blind. It is yet to be seen (at the time of writing) how the declaration adopted by the key 20 countries in Pittsburgh will be able to follow up on a different economic paradigm aimed at more inclusive and equitable economic growth, especially "decent job" creation, for all including women.

Addressing gender concerns requires not only a specific targeted approach but also efforts that ensure that all the interventions—research, technical cooperation, and standard setting (including promotional activities)—contribute to the achievement of gender equality and equity, mainstreaming these concerns in the entire work of the ILO. This will also contribute more effectively to poverty alleviation. The "operationalizing" of decent work programs at the national level, in this respect, provides an excellent opportunity, particularly within the context of the "Delivering as One UN" approach being implemented. This could entail interventions at different levels. National institutions and governance—and national policies including macroeconomic, labor market, and other social policies, programs, and projects—could integrate normative principles, combining both targeted and overall gender mainstreaming approaches. Creating synergy among various policy interventions, programs, and institutions would be indispensable for success.

CONCLUSIONS AND IMPLICATIONS: POLICIES AND PROGRAMS FOR POVERTY REDUCTION AND ADVANCING GENDER EQUALITY IN THE WORLD OF WORK

Despite substantive progress in promoting gender equality in the world of work and overall poverty reduction during the last 50 years, women continue to be disproportionately affected by decent work deficits and poverty. The goal of decent work—and the MDG target of halving poverty by 2015—can only be achieved when there is no longer gender-based discrimination and inequalities across countries, but there is still a long way to go in this respect. In particular, the global economic crisis can undo much of the progress made to date in the promotion of gender equality and the economic empowerment of women.

Integrating gender equality concerns in poverty alleviation is a sine qua non for various actors in development (governments, the donor community, the UN—including the ILO—and civil society organizations). Particular attention needs to be paid to the nexus between economic growth, employment trends (or work trends), and poverty reduction, especially the gender dimensions of the overall trends. Given that past economic policies have not yielded satisfactory results in development and poverty reduction, for women in particular, the crisis offers a golden opportunity to push for a feminist economists' perspective and an alternative paradigm of more inclusive development, increasing the social content of macroeconomic policies. This will need to entail more equitable resource distribution and appropriate rewarding of labor—those who work (both paid and unpaid)—in relation to capital, and enhanced consideration of those who are economically disadvantaged.

It is important to monitor the differentiated impacts of various macroeconomic policies on women and men in the world of work, as different policies could have different outcomes, depending on where women and men are—in which sectors they work and under which economic environment. In undertaking analysis of the social content of macro policies, it is fundamental that such analysis be gendered, and potential implications of such policies analyzed in a gender-specific manner, so that gendered policy implications can be drawn.

While there are both multilevel dimensions to poverty and multiple measures for reducing it, promoting better access to employment and economic opportunities for the poor, particularly women, is one of the most effective means of lifting them out of income and material poverty, and promoting their socioeconomic empowerment. However, in designing direct pro-poor interventions, gauging their potential impacts on women's both paid and unpaid work is key to ensure that the support provided would empower them, rather than disempowering them further.

Given the negative impact of the global economic crisis on poor working women, providing for the most vulnerable groups should be the most critical element of countries' response packages; they need to bail out the working poor and not just large banks. All the developing countries need to come up with additional safety-net measures, with attention to their gender dimensions. In addition to implementing effective fiscal measures to stabilize the financial market, and introducing tighter financial regulation, this will entail cash transfers to the poor, food and fuel subsidies, and regulating key commodities markets, as well as expanding both passive and active labor market measures. Such latter measures will include:

public provisioning for allocations for temporary, but well targeted, employment guarantee schemes (including creating jobs for women); expansion of credit schemes for the poor that can be equally accessed by women; extending/establishing insurance for the unemployed; and targeted training and job search facilitation for those who lose jobs in the formal sector, the unemployed, etc.

Under direct intervention at the program and project levels in development assistance that aims at poverty reduction, careful targeting of the most vulnerable and poorest should reach a far greater number of women. Gender mainstreaming across various existing programs, especially to redress gender disparities, is the right direction, and could potentially have a long-term positive impact on the world of work from the point of view of advancing equality and equity, though challenges are still enormous.

Since addressing the gender dimensions of poverty alleviation is critical for the promotion of the ILO's Decent Work Agenda and the achievement of the MDGs, it would be useful to have an integrated approach toward gender and poverty issues, specifically targeting the rural and informal economies. Such a strategy could combine the normative approach with other instruments of employment creation, social protection, and social dialog that can be implemented at multiple levels: macro, legislative, institutional, program, and project. This can be done by building on past experiences and lessons learned. Such an integrated approach could be tested within the framework of "operationalizing" decent work at the national level, and jointly implemented with donors and other UN agencies.

REFERENCES

Aswicahyono, H., Atje, R., & Feridhanuisetyawan. T. (1999). *Gender dimensions of globalization and modern sector employment in Indonesia.* SEAPAT Working Paper No. 5. ILO, Manila.

Baulch, B. (1996). Neglected trade-offs in poverty measurement. *IDS Bulletin: Poverty, Policy and Aid, 27*(1), 36–42.

Benería, L. (2001). Shifting the risk: New employment patterns, informalization, and women's work. *International Journal of Politics, Culture, and Society, 15*(1), 27–53.

———. (2008). *Globalization, labour and women's work: Critical challenges in a post-liberal world.* Mimeo submitted to United Nations Development Programme (UNDP), New York.

Benería, L., & Floro, M. (2005). *Labor market informalization, gender, and social protection: Reflections on poor urban households in Bolivia, Ecuador, and Thailand.* Paper prepared for the United Nations Research Institute for Social Development (UNRISD) research programme on Gender and Social Policy, Geneva.

Benería, L., & Feldman, S. (Eds). (1992). *Unequal burden: Economic crises, persistent poverty, and women's work.* Boulder, Colorado: Westview Press.

Berik, G. (2000). Mature export-led growth and gender wage inequality in Taiwan. *Feminist Economics*, 6(3), 1–26.

Cagatay, N., & Korkurt, E. (2004). *Gender and globalization: A macroeconomic perspective*. Geneva: ILO.

Carr, M., Chen, M. A., & Tate, J. 2000. Globalization and home-based workers. *Feminist Economics*, 6(3), 123–142.

Chen, M., Sebstad, J., & O'Connell, L. (1999). Counting the invisible workforce: The case of homebased workers. *World Development*, 27(3), 603–610.

Dejillas, L. J. (2000). *Globalization, gender and employment in the informal economy: The case of the Philippines*. SEAPAT Working Paper No. 8. ILO, Manila.

Elson, D., & Cagatay, N. (2000). The social content of macroeconomic policies. *World Development*, 28(7), 1347–1364.

Epstein, G. (2003). *Alternatives to inflation targeting monetary policy for stable and egalitarian growth: A brief research summary*. PERI Working Paper No. 62. Political Economy Research Institute (PERI), Amherst, Massachusetts.

Gosh, J., Sengupta, A., & Roychoudhury, A. (2008). *The impact of macroeconomic change on employment in the retail sector in India: Policy implications for growth, sectoral change and employment*. Geneva: ILO.

Heintz, J. (2006). *Globalization, economic policy and employment: Poverty and gender implications*. Geneva: ILO.

Hemmings-Gapihan, G. S. (2008). Climate change, subsistence farming, food security and poverty: The consequences of agricultural policies on women and men farmers in Burkina Faso and Cote d'Ivoire. *African Policy Journal*, 4 (Spring/Summer).

ILO (International Labour Organization). (1958). *Discrimination (employment and occupation) convention, C111*, August 25, 1958. Retrieved from http://www.ilo.org/ilolex/cgi-lex/convde.pl?C111

———. (1964). *Employment policy convention, C122*, July 9, 1964. Retrieved from http://www.ilo.org/ilolex/cgi-lex/convde.pl?C122

———. (1996). *Home work convention, C177*, June 20, 1996. Retrieved from http://www.ilo.org/ilolex/cgi-lex/convde.pl?C177

———. (1999). *Decent work*. Geneva: ILO.

———. (2000). *Modular package on gender, poverty and employment*. Geneva: ILO.

———. (2002a). *Decent work and the informal economy* (Report VI presented at the 90th session of the International Labour Conference). Geneva: ILO.

———. (2002b). *Women and men in the informal economy: A statistical picture*. Geneva: ILO Employment Sector.

———. (2003a). *Time for equality at work: Global report under the follow-up to the ILO declaration on fundamental principles and rights at work*. Geneva: ILO.

———. (2003b). *Working out of poverty*. Report of the director-general (91st International Labour Conference). Geneva: ILO.

———. (2003c). *An information guide: Preventing discrimination, exploitation and abuse of women migrant workers*. Geneva: ILO.

———. (2004). *Macroeconomic policies for growth and employment* (ILO Governing Body document GB291/ESP/1). Geneva: ILO.

———. (2005). *A stronger social dimension of globalization* (ILO Governing Body document GB.292/WP/SDG/1). Geneva: ILO.

———. (2006). *Implementing the global employment agenda: Employment strategies in support of decent work* (Vision Document). Geneva: ILO.

ILO (International Labour Organization). (2008a). *Global employment trends for women.* Geneva: ILO.

―――. (2008b). *Global employment trends.* ILO, Geneva.

―――. (2008c). *World of work report: Income inequalities in the age of financial globalization.* Geneva: ILO.

―――. (2009). *Global employment trends for women.* Geneva: ILO.

―――. (2010). *Global employment trends.* Geneva: ILO.

IOM (International Organization for Migration). (2005). *World migration 2005: Costs and benefits of international migration.* Geneva: IOM.

Islam, R. (2004). *The nexus of growth, employment and poverty reduction: An empirical analysis.* Geneva: Recovery and Reconstruction Department, ILO.

Islam-Rahman, R., & Otobe, N. (2005). *The dynamics of labour market and employment in Bangladesh: A focus on gender dimensions.* Geneva: ILO.

Kazemi, F. (2000). Gender, Islam and politics. *Social Research, 67*(2), 453–474.

Ministry of Labour, Industrial Relations and Employment, & UNDP. (2007). *Coping with retrenchment: Globalization, employment and livelihoods: Socio economic impact of the end of the multi fibre Arrangement on retrenched workers in Mauritius.* Mauritius: Port Louis.

Otobe, N. (2008). *The impact of globalization and macroeconomic change on employment: What next in the post-MFA era?* Geneva: ILO.

Porter, K. H., & Dupree, A. (2001). *Poverty trends for families headed by working single mothers, 1993 to 1999.* Washington, DC: Center on Budget and Policy Priorities. Retrieved February 5, 2010, from http://www.cbpp.org/8-16-01wel.pdf

UNIFEM (United Nations Development Fund for Women). (n.d.) *Women, poverty & economics.* Retrieved September 20, 2010, from http://www.unifem.org/gender_issues/women_poverty_economics/

Wadley, J. (2008). *Study: More frequent, but shorter, poverty spells among single mothers after welfare reforms.* University of Michigan News Service, Berkeley, California: University of Michigan and University of California.

World Bank. (2001). *Engendering development: Through gender equality in rights, resources, and voice.* Washington, DC: World Bank.

―――. (2006). *Gender equality as smart economics: A World Bank Group gender action plan* (fiscal years 2007–2010). Washington, DC: World Bank.

World Commission on Social Dimensions of Globalization. (2004). *A fair globalization: Creating opportunities for all.* Geneva: ILO.

8

Gender, Global Crises, and Climate Change

ITZÁ CASTAÑEDA AND SARAH GAMMAGE*

Climate change both responds to and heightens existing inequalities. Consequently, it is impossible to understand and meet the challenges it presents without taking on board the economic, social, and political context within which it occurs, that is to say, without addressing the urgent need to reduce poverty, secure sustainable development ... [and] understand that women and men experience the costs and consequences of climate change differently.

INTRODUCTION

The world is currently experiencing a period of profound change and instability. The coincidence of the ongoing financial, environmental, and food crises underscores an urgent need to interrogate our progress as a global community in search of sustainable human development and social justice for all. The financial crisis originating in the North has depressed demand, reduced private financial flows and remittances, and precipitated recession around the world. Unemployment and poverty rates are climbing, undermining human development, health, and well-being globally. Climate change remains largely unchecked, desertification

---
*The authors would like to thank Juliana Lazagabaster and Hannie Meesters for their valuable contributions to this chapter.

persists, water tables are falling, weather patterns are becoming more unstable, and greenhouse gas emissions continue to rise. Malnutrition and hunger are also increasing, exacerbated by the recent inflation in global food prices and the financial crisis. These crises are not mutually exclusive, however, but interlinked phenomena that call for coordinated action by states, markets, communities, and individuals.

This chapter focuses primarily on climate change as one of these ongoing crises with which we must grapple as a global polity. Climate change both responds to and heightens existing inequalities. Consequently, it is impossible to understand and meet the challenges it presents without taking on board the economic, social, and political context within which it occurs, that is to say, without addressing the urgent need to reduce poverty and secure sustainable development. Moreover, these challenges cannot be understood or overcome if we do not first understand that women and men experience the costs and consequences of climate change differently and have different resources available to enable them to respond and adapt.

Climate change poses both a development and a human rights concern because it imperils the resource base that secures development and undermines the realization of human rights. In this chapter, we analyze climate change from a gender and human rights-based perspective, concentrating on the fact that it cannot be tackled unilaterally in communities or by individual nations. Collaboration is required, and multilateral solutions need to be implemented. The existing normative human rights framework, which enables and supports the realization of community as well as women's rights, affords opportunities for realizing gender equity and women's empowerment while addressing this issue.

The principal objectives of this chapter are to explore how the key crises brought about by climate change may affect women and men differently, and how gender inequalities intersect with adaptation and mitigation strategies. It focuses for the most part on developing countries, given that the greatest costs of climate change and environmental degradation are likely to be felt there.

CLIMATE CHANGE AND INEQUALITY

Technological change and innovation mean that the planet has the potential to produce food for up to double the current population, and therefore that outdated Malthusian predictions can be dismissed. But the paradox remains that the poorest on the planet—some 830 million people—are hungry every day, while the richest spend billions of dollars on superfluous consumption items that are not essential for their well-being. This is what Kliksberg (2007) refers to as one manifestation of the "shameful gaps" that characterize the inequality that currently prevails.

In 2008, 100 million more people were driven into poverty as a result of the food and fuel crises, and the numbers affected continue to grow (UNDP, 2008a). The current economic and financial crisis could increase world unemployment by as much as 20 million women and men. As a result, the number of working poor living on less than USD 1 a day could rise by some 40 million, and those on under USD 2 a day by more than 100 million. There is evidence that such crises hit women hardest since they constitute the majority of the poor and frequently have the least resources available to mitigate the impact of rising poverty (Panel on Visible and Invisible Contributions, 2008).

Some 1.1 billion people in the developing world do not have access to clean water, and millions of infants die of malnutrition before they are five years of age (UNDP, 2006). Estimates are that almost 2.6 billion people do not have access to adequate sanitation, which greatly imperils health; for example, diarrhea in infants is three times higher in communities without sanitation (Kliksberg, 2007).

The planet is losing an average of 73 thousand square kilometers of forest a year, an area the size of a country such as Chile (UNDP, 2007). Illnesses that had been largely eradicated, such as cholera and typhoid, are on the rise and can be viewed as the product of the fatal combination of poverty, inequality, environmental deterioration, and climate change. In Central Mexico, for example, during the period 1998–2000, the probability of illness in children under five increased significantly when they suffered a weather shock—by 16 percent with droughts and by 41 percent with floods (ibid.).

Neumayer and Plümper (2007) analyzed disasters in 141 countries and concluded that gender differences in deaths from so-called natural disasters (in fact, most disasters are not natural) are directly linked to women's economic and social rights. In contexts where women's rights are not protected and substantial gender inequalities exist, often more women than men die in environmental disasters. Women accounted for 61 percent of deaths caused by Cyclone Nargis in Myanmar in May 2008, 70–80 percent of deaths in the 2004 Indian Ocean Tsunami, and 91 percent of deaths in the 1991 Cyclone in Bangladesh. Reasons vary. In Bangladesh, for example, women are not taught how to swim, warning information was spread only from men to men, and women waited for men to accompany them before evacuating (Aguilar et al., 2007).

As established by the independent and comprehensive analysis in *The Economics of Climate Change* (Stern, 2006), the distribution of the impacts of climate change will vary dramatically across continents and by context among developing countries. These impacts will be magnified by the prevailing economic and social inequalities that exist. Poor communities with a greater dependence on natural resources are likely to be disproportionately affected. Given the widespread differences in gender roles and responsibilities, women and men are also likely to be affected differently; as a result, climate change is not a gender-neutral process.

Climate Change as a Rights and Development Priority

The report of the Fourth Intergovernmental Panel on Climate Change (IPCC, 2007), the 2007–2008 *Human Development Report* (UNDP, 2007), and Stern (2006) underscore that we are on the verge of a disaster of cataclysmic proportions with profound implications for human development and the well-being of the planet and its ecosystems. Sea levels are set to rise along with increasing temperatures, glaciers are melting, and the global hydrological cycle will be radically altered. Weather patterns will become more extreme, and food security will be imperiled around the globe. As the *Human Development Report* exhorts:

> How the world deals with climate change today will have a direct bearing on the human development prospects of a large section of humanity. Failure will consign the poorest 40 percent of the world's population—some 2.6 billion people—to a future of diminished opportunity. It will exacerbate deep inequalities within countries and it will undermine efforts to build a more inclusive pattern of globalization and development, reinforcing the vast disparities between the "haves" and the "have nots." (UNDP, 2007, p. 2)

A human rights-centered vision of "progress" implies that we cannot choose between poverty alleviation, adaptation to climate change, and access to critical environmental goods and services such as water, food, and energy. These needs and rights are interlinked; they are all ultimately part of what we refer to as "development." To quote Rae (2008):

> The full realization of the right to food therefore depends on parallel achievements in the field of health, education, and access to resources. Although each right is worthy of achievement in itself, each has an instrumental value

in that different types of rights reinforce each other, and respect for one category may be essential to achieving another. (p. 17)

In the case of women's rights, we can readily see how intimately these needs and rights are linked, and we know from women's lives that unless a holistic approach is taken, the rights they are entitled to will not reach them. It is also important to note that states that are party to the different United Nations international covenants and agreements are obliged to implement the rights these enshrine in a timely manner.

Gender Equity and Climate Change in the International Framework

Gender equity, climate change, and development concerns should be considered in concert with one another as complementary concerns and not as competing interests. Furthermore, based on the common goals of achieving efficiency and equity, each of these three issue areas stands to gain from being mutually supportive, and all are given far less value if one is considered to the exclusion of the others (Dennison, 2003).

The formal principles guiding international action on gender equity and climate change are grounded respectively in the UN Convention on the Elimination of All Forms of Discrimination against Women (CEDAW) and United Nations Framework Convention on Climate Change (UNFCCC). These conventions—together with Agenda 21, the Beijing Platform for Action, Security Council resolutions 1325 and 1820, ECOSOC Resolution 2005/31, the Millennium Development Goals, and the Hyogo Framework for Action—provide a critical rights- and obligations-based framework for states to address the gender-differentiated impacts of climate change, mitigation, and adaptation. Yet, the various processes remain largely unconnected.

The information available on climate change, its causes and consequences, has increased considerably in the last few years. Yet a simple word search of the UNFCCC, the Kyoto Protocol, IPCC reports, and Stern (2006)—the most important treaties and reports related to global efforts to combat climate change—confirms that the words "gender," "women," or "men" are either not mentioned or appear so infrequently as to make their reference entirely marginal.

A review of key UN documents that refer to climate change, elaborated between 2003 and 2008 by diverse agencies, shows that in the majority of cases the words "gender" or "women" are mentioned in the initial few pages, together with "children" and "indigenous peoples," particularly when describing "vulnerable groups." However, a gender perspective is not integrated throughout the substantive analysis, the statistics reported are seldom if ever sex-disaggregated, and gender is mentioned only parenthetically in the recommendations. Other UN publications similarly neglect to include a gender analysis unless the publication is specifically dedicated to gender issues (Castañeda, 2008).

Moreover, the key accords and covenants associated with climate change also reveal a marked absence of attention to the gender dimension. One might ask whether the absence of references to gender considerations in treaties and protocols matters; they are, after all, legal documents designed to provide a general framework under which much more detailed plans have to be worked out (Skutsch, 2002). Yet, the failure to recognize differential effects of climate change on peoples and individuals by race, gender, and class contributes to the marginalization of these concerns and inhibits the commitment to the progressive and full realization of fundamental human rights.

A selection of key publications addressing gender and climate change, published by academia, civil society organizations, and donors, shows that in the last six years a number of important documents have been produced that propose an analytical framework and defined routes to follow to ensure the integration of gender throughout thematic areas related to climate change. Almost without exception, these publications call for a renewed commitment to producing data that are sex-disaggregated and that reveal the differences in how women and men experience climate change. They also call for greater participation of women's groups in decision-making bodies that deal with climate change, adaptation, and mitigation; and for gender budget initiatives that can facilitate gender integration as well as respond to the challenges of climate change (Lambrou & Grazia, 2006; Nelson et al., 2002).

Unfortunately, their analytical and policy research contributions remain largely unconnected to those that address the legal framework and the mechanics of international cooperation for adaptation or mitigation. At present, global negotiations on climate change are mainly focused on reducing greenhouse gases by means of the UNFCCC, IPCC, Kyoto Protocol, and other related mechanisms, none of which provides the rights-based approach needed to implement responses to climate change that are equitable for women and men.

Gender-differentiated Impacts

In order to explore the gender dimensions of climate change and environmental degradation, we must first identify a few of the key sectors and locations where climate change is likely to radically alter existing patterns of production and consumption. This section does not attempt an exhaustive description of women and men's relationship to the resource base, but instead focuses on key differentiated impacts on their lives in the context of climate change.

The scientific evidence that our climate is changing is now overwhelming, and the link between the traditional sense of "progress and modernity" and climate change is established. Progress and modernity are also associated with changed production and consumption patterns and individual and community relationships to the resource base worldwide. Yet, such progress has not necessarily brought about sustainable development, gender equity, or social justice. The deep biases in the monetary metric of progress have obscured the associated costs and allowed most of the wealthy members of the global community to ignore the profound inequities in the distribution of these costs.

Concerted efforts to measure environmental degradation and the economic costs associated with climate change are being made. For example, Stern (2006) concludes, "the risks and costs of climate change over the next two centuries could be equivalent to an average reduction in global per capita consumption of at least 5 percent, now and forever." Unfortunately, the human development costs associated with climate change cannot be measured in terms of quantitative outcomes nor disaggregated by sex.

At the same time, we now know with certainty that climate change entails impacts that are long term, persistent, and have serious risks of being irreversible. The direction of where we need to go from here is clear. We need to stabilize our climate consistent with the science, keeping likely warming below 2° Celsius compared to pre-industrial times. Reducing emissions would require that the power sector around the world be de-carbonized by about 60 percent by 2050, and extensive carbon sequestration and storage will be necessary to allow the continued use of remaining fossil fuels. It would also require that approximately 1 percent of global GDP be dedicated to actions to mitigate degradation and reduce greenhouse gas emissions (see UNDP, 2008b).

It is clear that people living in conditions of poverty worldwide and the majority of the populations of developing countries will be disproportionately affected by climate change for three reasons: their location in parts of the globe that will register the greatest rise in surface temperatures and sea level; their dependence on agriculture and environmental resources; and their limited institutional and productive resources to mitigate the costs (Stern, 2006). Table 8.1 shows some of the key and gender-differentiated impacts of climate change.

Table 8.1   Key impacts of climate change and its specific effects on women

Key impacts	Specific effects on women
Between 15 and 40 percent of species may be lost due to extinction associated with global temperature increases of only 1–2° Celsius. Strong drying effects from changes in the hydrological cycle and wind patterns could result in the die-back of extensive areas of the ecosystems with the highest biodiversity on the planet.	Increased time required for women's work on managing environmental resources (for example, collecting water and firewood) makes it difficult for them to engage in other tasks and negatively affects their health due to the increased work burden.
Rising temperatures, falling water tables, interrupted water cycles, and drought will drastically reduce crop yields, especially in Africa, and are likely to deprive hundreds of millions of people of the ability to produce or purchase sufficient food.	Decreased production and productivity in subsistence agriculture (a highly "feminized" sector in many parts of the world), fisheries, and forestry is likely to result in food insecurity and hunger.
Melting glaciers will increase the risk of flooding during the wet season and significantly reduce dry-season water supplies to one-sixth of the world's population—primarily in the Indian sub-continent, parts of China, and South America. Rising sea levels will contribute to land loss, coastal erosion, and population displacement (close to 200 million people by the middle of the century, according to Stern, 2006).	Where women have more contingent rights to property and depend on the global commons, their access to resources will be disproportionately restricted.
Loss of shelter, assets, family members, community networks, social capital, and jobs may result in relocation and transition to new livelihoods, and lead to increased conflicts and disasters.	Women's vulnerability to violence may be increased.
Climate-related health impacts are likely to include the spread of diseases such as malaria and cholera, as well as increased psychosocial problems.	This will not only affect women's own health but also add to their care responsibilities.

A gender and human rights-based approach to development that includes environmental sustainability will be essential if the global community is to confront the costs and coordinate the response to the urgency of climate change. Moving beyond narrow measures of economic progress to include multidimensional measures and maximize human well-being and environmental quality is going to be critical in the next phase of human development in the 21st century. Such an approach must consider women's rights and the gender dimensions of human progress both in the analysis of the distribution of costs and benefits and in the exploration of how vulnerable populations respond and adapt to climate change.

A gendered and rights-based analysis is likely to provide a richer understanding of the potential policy options in different countries and cultural contexts. What is more, without a gendered lens we are unlikely to harness the different contributions that women and men can make to mitigating environmental degradation, adapting to or compensating for climate change, and ultimately conserving ecosystems and ensuring human and animal survival and well-being.

Linking Climate Change, Global Crises, and Gender

There are four prominent crises that will be exacerbated by climate change: the food crisis, the water crisis, the energy crisis, and the emerging health crisis. These crises are interrelated, and their separation here is purely for expository purposes. They are not only attributable to climate change, but are also linked to the application of orthodox economic policies that privilege the market and price mechanisms over other means of allocating user and access rights.

To take one example, rising food prices also reflect changes in land use patterns in response to the combined pressures of urbanization, demand for alternative energy sources, environmental degradation, and competition for water resources. Climate change is likely to affect food production, storage, and distribution as water resources become scarcer, growing seasons are modified, and soils are affected by desertification and salinization. In many tropical and sub-tropical countries, growing seasons are likely to be significantly shortened, fertilizer prices will increase, and food production will be compromised. While growing seasons may lengthen in some temperate countries, it is estimated that the net impacts of climate change will be to reduce overall food supplies and raise prices (Stern, 2006).

Similarly, the energy crisis is in part a function of rising demand and greater dependence on petroleum products across the globe. Although new oil reserves are being discovered, it is generally thought that oil supplies are limited. The effect of rising energy prices on fuel efficiency and use, and the potential to substitute between different fuel sources, will determine how human populations respond. Climate change as well as adaptation and mitigation measures will also affect energy consumption and potentially could stimulate the more rapid adoption of alternative sources of energy and a greater dependence on biofuels.

Understanding how climate change affects these ongoing crises and how the measures of economic and social well-being capture these effects will provide information for determining how to adapt to and mitigate the effects, as well as how to tax and to transfer resources to reduce the impacts. Responses to these crises should include major investment in gender equality and women's empowerment.

This forward-looking strategy needs to take into account a number of issues. First, the focus on gender should not be on women or men but on gender relations in a context of unequal capabilities and opportunities. Second, the analysis should not essentialize women's and men's relationships to the resource base by arguing that their biology dictates their roles, responsibilities, and knowledge. Third, since women and men as groups or categories of individuals are not homogenous, the response must be carefully contextualized and focus on the key characteristics that differentiate women's and men's experiences and response to climate change, including their access to productive resources and their social and political position. Finally, women and men should not be viewed as passively affected by the crises, but seen as actors whose adaptive behaviors can exacerbate or mitigate the impacts of climate change.

The Food Crisis

The Food and Agriculture Organization (FAO) defines food security as a "situation that exists when all people, at all times, have physical, social and economic access to sufficient, safe and nutritious food that meets their dietary needs and food preferences for an active and healthy life" (FAO, 2008, p. 3).

Climate change will affect food security through its impacts on all components of global, national and local food systems.... It will first affect the people and food systems that are already vulnerable, but over time the geographic distribution of risk and vulnerability is likely to shift. Certain livelihood groups need immediate support, but everybody is at risk. (Rossi & Lambrou, 2008, p. xi)

Weather and "natural" disasters will have a lasting effect on agriculture, profoundly altering commercial and subsistence production (Parry et al., 2004; Parry et al., 2005; Stern, 2006). As patterns of production and consumption change and food prices rise, the right to food and adequate nutrition is likely to be compromised for many, with "negative repercussions in particular for poor households and vulnerable groups, particularly women and female-headed households, which tend to be particularly exposed to chronic and transitory food insecurity, due also to their limited access to income-generating activities" (Rossi & Lambrou, 2008, p. 17). A sudden rise in food prices can plunge households in developing countries even further into poverty because they spend an average of 70 percent of their incomes on food, compared to the 15–18 percent that households spend in industrialized countries (Women Thrive Worldwide, 2008).

More extreme weather patterns and the phenomenon known as El Niño, which has struck some Latin American countries, have already affected food production. For example, 90 percent of corn and bean crops in Mexico have been affected. Production of the latter was forecast to decline by between 50 and 60 percent in 2010 (Diario de Palenque, 2009). According to a recent report from the World Bank (2008), the rise in food prices has also been a result of increased biofuel production (discussed later under "The energy crisis").

According to the FAO (2008, p. 20), "persistently high prices force poor people to reduce consumption below the minimum required for a healthy and active life, and may lead to food riots and social unrest." It has identified 37 countries in crisis and requiring external assistance. Food riots occurred in at least eight developing countries between 2007 and the first half of 2008: Burkina Faso, Guinea, Haiti, Mauritania, Mozambique, Senegal, Somalia, and Yemen.

Even before the term "food crisis" became common parlance, an estimated 7 out of 10 of the world's hungry were women and girls (Women Thrive Worldwide, 2008). Particularly vulnerable groups, such as young children and pregnant women, are now at risk of becoming permanently malnourished—irreversibly affecting the well-being of the next generation. Women are also likely to be more vulnerable to food poverty because they have less access than men to credit, property rights, education, training, and good jobs. They own less than 15 percent of land worldwide and make up some 60 percent of the world's working poor, that is, people who work but do not earn enough to lift themselves above the $1 per day poverty line (Women Thrive Worldwide, 2008).

A marked gender division of labor characterizes much of the production, processing, and sale of agricultural products in developing countries. This is a result of a complex array of social, cultural, and religious norms and institutions that dictate women's mobility, mediate their ownership rights, and determine their family responsibilities (Warner and Campbell, 2000). Women are important stakeholders in food production in both irrigated and non-irrigated settings, and they produce an estimated two-thirds of the food in most developing countries (UNDP, 2006). Typically, although not exclusively, women are engaged in the production of domestic staples for household provisioning or in processing and sale of domestic foodstuffs in national markets, whereas men focus their activities primarily on cash crop production.

Where climate change induces significant losses in agricultural productivity, time and task allocation is also likely to alter in subsistence and commercial production within and beyond the household. How women and men respond will depend very much on gendered norms and expectations and the existing set of institutions that mediate their different access to productive resources. Falling farm incomes could increase the use of household labor engaged in subsistence production, reducing time dedicated to other activities such as education or leisure. Where women and the poor experience greater time burdens and greater time poverty, this could increase the costs of adaptation.

The relative impact of declining agricultural productivity is also likely to differ sharply by sex. As noted above, women typically have more limited access to resources—in the case of farmers, this translates into less access to agricultural credit, extension services, production information, training, technology transfer, transport, storage, and physical capital that would enable them to improve their productivity or switch into different crops and production methods (Mehra, 1991). Where climate change induces significant productivity losses, women's productivity may therefore be more adversely affected than men's.

Climate change can also induce rapid price rises in staples and locally produced foods. Under these conditions cheaper calories may be substituted for more expensive ones, and the nutrition and health of household members may be undermined. In circumstances where the intra-household division of resources is unequal, some household members may be privileged over others. Where male well-being is valued over female well-being, women and girls are likely to suffer (Ghosh & Kanbur, 2002; Hoddinott, 2004; Quisumbing & Maluccio, 2003; Sen, 1999).

Another factor that will affect the supply response in agriculture as well as productivity and food security is the absence of financial markets. These are typically poor or nonexistent in developing countries. The ability of most farming families to overcome the impacts of extreme weather conditions or events, such as drought and flooding, depends on their ability to have access to such markets and to save. Limited access to credit, crop insurance, or other types of loans greatly reduces the ability of these households to withstand the likely impacts of climate change, particularly in the case of women, who generally have reduced engagement in wage-earning activities and limited ownership or claims to productive resources that can be used as collateral.

Finally, in many contexts women depend disproportionately on common property for their subsistence, food production, and gathering activities. Their use of common property is frequently guaranteed through custom rather than statutory or de jure legal rights (Deere & León, 2002; Meinzen-Dick et al., 1997), and hence can be quite precarious. Where climate change brings about substantial changes in land-use patterns, land formerly defined as common property may be under pressure for conversion to private property or to other types of use. This may significantly undermine women's ability to provide for their households.

The Water Crisis

Water is essential for all human activity and is a key input for agriculture, industry, energy production, and transport as well as for domestic purposes. Individuals require approximately 20 liters of water daily to meet their basic needs. Europeans use an average of 200 litres per day and North Americans 400 liters per day. Yet, 1.1 billion people only have access to 5 liters per day. Furthermore, this limited quantity of water is largely contaminated. Contaminated water causes 1.8 million deaths per year. Climate change is going to radically alter water availability and usage since it is the most climate-sensitive environmental resource. Existing inequalities are likely to be exacerbated, contributing to further mortality and morbidity as the result of water scarcity (Arnell, 2004). Another, less visible, cost of drought, desertification, and falling water tables is the time dedicated to collecting, hauling, storing, treating, and distributing water.

For many households in the developing world, this means increases in time burdens for women, who have primary responsibility for household provisioning.

With scarcity, water will no longer be considered a free public good—a shift in how water is viewed and how water rights are conceived that will conflict profoundly with the understanding that access to water to meet basic needs is a fundamental human right. Increasingly, water management documents and policy papers mediate this conflict by recommending that the water sector be liberalized, allowing water to be priced according to its market value while creating targeted subsidies to provide a minimum amount of water to meet the basic needs of the poor (Walker, 2006).

Stern (2006, p. 98) points out, however, that most developing countries are in water deficit, lacking sufficient storage to manage annual demand. Moreover, it states, "inappropriate water pricing and subsidized electricity tariffs that encourage the excessive use of groundwater for pumping also increase vulnerability to changing climatic conditions". Under these conditions, water rights will become increasingly contentious.

Recent experiments with privatization and the creation of water markets have produced very mixed results—particularly in contexts characterized by pronounced income inequality, poverty, ethnic divisions, and the lack of viable public institutions (UNDP, 2006). Without a strong regulatory and institutional framework and an ability to guarantee minimum water requirements, privatization and liberalization can lead to highly unjust outcomes and provoke widespread civil unrest (see Fall's chapter this volume).

Extensive literature documents how property rights are central to irrigation and water-use debates (ibid.). Women and the poor frequently have more contingent or informal rights to water usage (Cleaver & Elson, 1995). In most informal systems there is a low recognition of women's specific water needs, particularly for production as opposed to domestic consumption. Under conditions of scarcity or rationing, water use and rights are typically prioritized for higher value activities. Where women and subsistence populations produce crops for own use and local markets, water is likely to be prioritized for cash crops for export, which may be disproportionately produced by men and by wealthier farmers.

Until recently much of the irrigation discourse has focused on using water rights as a mechanism for developing water markets. Water rights are viewed as a legal complement to infrastructures and institutions, which are necessary for efficient water allocation and distribution. Yet, narrow interpretations of water rights, based on formal state laws that do not take account of customary law or informal access rights, can exclude groups with marginal access to institutions that mediate or delimit water rights—women, pastoralists, and smallholders may be particularly vulnerable (UNDP, 2006). Furthermore, Zwarteveen (1997, p. 1339) notes:

> Having the legal possibility to take water in itself is meaningless without the adequate technology to subtract water from a source and convey it to irrigate fields; [and] the means (labour and resources) to operate (and maintain) the technology and distribute the water according to the agreed rules and rights.

Finally, under conditions of scarcity the institutions that govern local rights to water will become increasingly important. Supporting women's engagement in water users' organizations will be critical to ensuring that their access and use rights are not undermined. For example, under a locally devised water access scheme in Nepal, women were frequently unaware of their rights to water because the rotation schedules were devised in their absence at meetings where they were not formal members (Zwarteveen, 1997).

Merely declaring that water is a human right does not ensure that the water crisis will be resolved in the short or even medium term. There is a critical lack of institutions and an absence of mechanisms for stakeholder participation in determining how water will be allocated under scarcity, whether a price will be charged for water use (and what price is relevant for different sectors), how investment will be made and costs recovered, and the type and amount of services provided related to water use and quality.

The Energy Crisis

The energy crisis is linked to many other issues of global debate such as the production of liquid biofuels (fuels that can be produced from agricultural and forest products or by processing the biodegradable portion of industrial and municipal waste—see, for example, Addison et al. [2010]); the development of wind, solar, and nuclear energy; and the impact of war and conflict on the production of crude oil. Oil prices have reached unprecedented variability over the last decade. This implies serious consequences for a society that has largely depended for its development on the consumption of petroleum (fossil fuel).

Energy use is by far the greatest in the developed countries, and global CO_2 emissions are concentrated among the wealthier nations. For this reason, efforts to mitigate climate change focus on emissions reduction and stress the need for changes in production and consumption patterns in the developed world, including introducing more fuel-efficient machinery and providing incentives to switch to alternative fuels. In the development of alternatives, there has been an emphasis on biofuels because of their lower carbon content compared to fossil fuels.

A significant and rising share of biofuel production is occurring in tropical and subtropical developing countries, which have a comparative advantage in inputs such as sugarcane and palm oil. For example, in 2005 there were 12 million hectares under palm oil production worldwide, 5.3 million of which were in Indonesia and 4 million in Malaysia. These two countries have announced that they plan to set aside 40 percent of their palm oil output for biodiesel (Tauli-Corpuz & Tamang, 2007). Policies encouraging biofuels production and use are being established to pursue multiple aims: diversifying the energy supply and increasing energy security, reducing non-greenhouse gas emissions, stimulating economic growth and competitiveness, expanding exports, and promoting rural employment and development.

The potential socioeconomic costs and benefits of liquid biofuel production have been extensively reviewed at the micro and macro level, exploring the impact on household production and consumption as well as on exports, imports, and relative prices (Hazell & Pachauri, 2006). There is also a growing body of work that links biofuels production to changing the relative prices for food and fuels. Unfortunately, as Rossi and Lambrou (2008) observe, there is a general lack of understanding and consideration, within both the academic literature and as evidenced in the policy debate, of the differentiated outcomes and impacts for women and men at the household and intra-household level.

There are real concerns that women and subsistence populations may be displaced from marginal lands or lands to which they have customary rights in order to expand the production of biofuels inputs. For example, the Government of India, as part of its National Mission on Biofuels, aims to convert approximately 400,000 hectares of marginal lands for the cultivation of non-edible oil seed crops (mostly *jatropha*) for biodiesel production (Rajagopal, 2007). This potentially threatens the livelihoods of subsistence populations that depend on these lands for food, fodder, firewood, building materials, and so on (ibid.). Where women and subsistence populations depend disproportionately on common property resources and customary rights, their household provisioning may be greatly affected by such decisions.

Promoting biofuels does not necessarily mean that poor and subsistence populations will have access to these new energy sources. Most such populations across the globe have little financial capital to purchase stoves, are not connected to national energy grids, and do not have the disposable income to purchase energy. Most poor populations in rural and urban areas depend on biomass fuels such as firewood, charcoal, and dung for their domestic energy sources—particularly for cooking and heating water (Cecelski, 2004; Clancy & Roehr, 2003; Clancy et al., 2003; Smith et al., 2004). Across countries and continents women bear the greatest responsibility for cooking and household tasks, and in many contexts women and children are responsible for gathering these fuels.

Although most households in rural areas will use some biomass, poor households typically spend more time gathering these fuels than households in higher income groups (Reddy, 2000). As a result, the impact of environmental degradation, deforestation, or land conversion on gathering activities can be highly detrimental, increasing the time dedicated to gathering firewood. For example, the Population Reference Bureau (2002) documents that deforestation over the last decade in Sudan has contributed to quadrupling the time that women spend gathering firewood. In Malawi, UNDP (2008c) reports that 63 percent of urban households and 83 percent of rural households responded to drought by reducing expenditures on firewood and paraffin. The likely consequence of this was an increase in time spent gathering substitutes or the use of cheaper biomass fuels.

Using biomass fuels has a number of negative consequences for poor households. In general, the fuel quality is low and less efficient (Clancy et al., 2003). When these fuels are burnt they give off quantities of smoke and particulates that are recognized as having negative effects on health. A World Health Organization (WHO) analysis as part of the Comparative Quantification of Health Risks study (Smith et al., 2004) estimates that 1.6 million premature deaths and 3.6 percent of the global burden of disease can be attributed to indoor air pollution from the use of solid fuels.

Among the policy and program responses to the health concerns, and as part of a concerted effort to reduce the demands on specific ecosystems, there have been initiatives to develop appropriate technologies that use alternative sources of domestic energy or to improve the efficiency of existing biomass stoves (Cecelski, 2004; McCracken et al., 2007; Smith et al., 2004). It is clear, however, that such initiatives should also take into account the time burdens associated with their adoption and continued use (Gammage et al., 1999). Cecelski (2004) draws attention to the failure of many of these programs because they did not draw women into the design of the intervention or failed to consider the potential impact of the technology on the timing and sequencing of household tasks or women's time burdens.

The Emerging Health Crisis

The right to health is formulated in the International Covenant on Economic, Social and Cultural Rights (ICESCR) under Article 12 as: "the right of everyone to the enjoyment of the highest attainable standard of physical and mental health." This is not to be interpreted as merely a right to be healthy or to have access to health care services. Rather, it embraces a wide range of socioeconomic factors that promote conditions in which people can lead healthy lives, and extends to the underlying determinants of health such as food and nutrition, housing, safe and potable water, and adequate sanitation (FAO, 2008).

The WHO (2008) distinguishes five key health challenges as a result of climate change:

- Compromised food security will lead to increased malnutrition, which will be particularly acute in countries where large segments of the population depend on un-irrigated or rain-fed subsistence agriculture. Malnutrition, due in great part to periodic drought, is thought to already cause 3.5 million deaths per year (FAO, 2008).
- In situations where water is scarce—as well as in circumstances of excess water such as in floods and hurricanes—the burden of diarrheal infections rises. Diarrheal diseases are now a leading cause of child mortality, resulting in approximately 1.8 million avoidable deaths each year (ibid.).
- An increase in extreme meteorological phenomena contributes to greater mortality and trauma as a result of storms and floods. On the heels of floods and storms, outbreaks of disease such as cholera and typhoid are more frequent, particularly when water and sanitation services have been damaged or destroyed.
- Heatwaves, especially "islands of heat" in urban areas, can increase both mortality and morbidity, primarily among the aged or those with cardiovascular and respiratory problems. High temperatures can also increase ozone in the soil and accelerate the pollen season, precipitating attacks of asthma and other respiratory ailments.

- The variation in temperatures and precipitation will alter the geographic distribution of insect vectors that transmit infectious diseases. Among these illnesses, malaria and dengue are those that most alarm the public health community.

Thus climate change, exacerbated by the lack of adequate hygiene and sanitation services, will precipitate significant health challenges, especially in the developing world where they are more difficult to combat and are likely to bring about the avoidable deaths of millions (Gallup & Sachs, 2000; Patz et al., 2005). Stern (2006) echoes these concerns, noting that in the face of even moderate climate change, waterborne diseases are likely to increase, food insecurity will rise, and malnutrition rates will go up substantially. This report also estimates that if there is no change in malaria control efforts, an additional 40 to 60 million people in Africa could be exposed to malaria with a 2° Celsius rise in surface temperature (ibid.).

The gendered effects of these changes are likely to be registered through sex differences in rates of exposure and patterns of adaptation, and in gender roles related to caring for the sick and aged. The care economy, which is largely unremunerated, is where household members, frequently women and girls, care for infants, the aged, and the infirm. As disease burdens associated with climate change rise, increasing pressure will be placed on the care economy to provide for those who are affected. As income earners become sick and caring time burdens increase, vulnerable households are likely to be further impoverished and the health and quality of life of all members undermined.

BUILDING ON LOCAL KNOWLEDGE

While there are gender-differentiated effects of climate change, there are also gender-differentiated competencies and contributions that can be harnessed in measures for response and mitigation. Building on local knowledge and practices will prove essential as we try and conserve ecosystems; collect, document, and collectively bank genetic resources to avoid the loss of biodiversity; and develop programs and interventions.

Röhr (2006) reports that during a drought in the islands of Federated Micronesia women's ancestral knowledge of hydrology, passed on from generation to generation, enabled the community to identify where to dig wells to allow them to tap into reserves of portable water.

Similarly, women's knowledge of specific flora and fauna reflects their engagement with the resource base, and women often have specialized knowledge about "neglected" species. Estimates are that women provide close to 80 percent of the total wild vegetable food collected in 135 different subsistence-based societies (Aguilar, 2004). Women can often also better identify species' medicinal uses, value as fodder and fuel, and ability to withstand adverse environmental conditions such as pests, drought, or flood (Abramovitz, 1994; Dankelman & Davidson, 1988).

Howard (2003) describes how women predominate in plant biodiversity management in their roles as housewives, plant gatherers, home gardeners, herbalists, seed custodians, and informal plant breeders. As she observes, "because most plant use, management and conservation occurs within the domestic realm, and because the principal values of plant genetic resources are localised and non-monetary, they are largely invisible to outsiders and are easily undervalued" (ibid., p. 2). Yet, a pronounced gender bias has prevailed in scientific research about human–environment interactions, and conservation policies and programs largely ignore the domestic sphere and the importance of plant biodiversity for women's reproductive activities and, as a result, for household welfare. Building on gender-differentiated knowledge and practices will be essential if we are to conserve critical environmental niches, prevent biodiversity loss, and be alert to the incremental and cumulative impact of climate change.

A rights-based approach to securing environmental goods and services, and one that elevates women's rights as a priority, can be particularly beneficial for ensuring continued biodiversity. For example, ensuring women's access to land for agriculture and household use can lead to greater habitat protection. Achieving more gender equity in one realm can reinforce virtuous cycles that secure environmental resources and enable creative solutions to be found to support adaptation and mitigation activities.

WHERE DO WE GO FROM HERE?

Adaptation and Mitigation

It is clear that any strategy to adapt to or mitigate climate change globally must involve coordinate international action to reduce greenhouse gas emissions. There are multiple options for doing so, including a combination of carbon taxes, caps and permits, and sequestration initiatives

(UNDP, 2007). Since developed countries have greater resources and contribute the bulk of the emissions, they should disproportionately bear the costs of mitigation and adaptation.

At the micro level, the survival strategies adopted by poor households in the face of climate change may significantly affect human development and in some circumstances confine them to long-term poverty traps and an increase in the inter-generational transmission of poverty. For example, among the risk-managing and risk-coping behaviors that farming and subsistence households in developing countries can employ are those of switching to lower-return, lower-risk crops that are more likely to withstand climate change. Where such a strategy reduces total household income, little surplus may be available to invest in human capital and secure health and well-being. If households are forced to sell assets to maintain current consumption, longer-term survival and investment strategies may be compromised. Carter et al. (2004) document the case of households in Zimbabwe that sold their small livestock in times of crisis following the 1991–1992 droughts. Typically these assets were controlled by women and used for food, milk, and meat, and as savings to pay for their children's education. This coping strategy denied these households essential proteins and reduced their ability to invest in human capital or withstand future income or environmental shocks.

A gender analysis of the associated impacts and costs of climate change should inform adaptation and mitigation strategies at the micro and macro levels, providing information about financing and levying taxes and transfers to promote behavioral change and also revealing opportunities to build on local knowledge and participation.

For example, the community of La Masica in Honduras received training to monitor weather conditions and develop an early warning system that was managed and operated by women in the community. The disaster mitigation project took a gender-sensitive approach by disaggregating vulnerability assessments by gender, addressing gender in capacity-building programs, and emphasizing equal participation of women and men (Delaney & Shrader, 2000). Six months after the implementation of the project, the community reported no deaths attributable to Hurricane Mitch (Sánchez del Valle, 2000). Similarly, efforts to change resource use and promote biodiesel production and use should be accompanied by adaptive measures that maintain and enhance patterns of sustainability while avoiding negative impacts on the health and socioeconomic status of women. De la Vega (2005) documents the case of women using *jatropha* as a form of biodiesel, which has allowed them to diversify their income-earning activities and produce a variety of creams and lotions from natural fibres, nuts, and seeds.

At the macro level, countries may undertake specific policies to stimulate a shift in production and consumption. In some middle-income countries there may be a hasty push to reduce dependence on agriculture and expand other sectors such as manufacturing and industrial production. In those economies, where the majority of the population possesses low skills and little formal education, the types of manufacturing and industry are likely to demand lower skills and consequently be associated with lower value added. Where gender gaps in wages prevail and women form part of a flexible and relatively cheap labor force, they may be disproportionately absorbed into these sectors (Cagatay, 2001; Seguino, 2000; Standing, 1989, 1999). As a result, the shift to new patterns of production and consumption in the face of climate change could involve the continued sex segregation of labor markets and do little to erode gender inequalities in the terms and conditions of employment.

Both the developed and developing world will have to pay to change emissions or adapt to the consequences of climate change. How the funds are raised, taxes and subsidies designed, and policies and programs implemented will affect the distribution of costs and benefits across sectors, households, and individuals. When governments face financial constraints, they may have no recourse but to acquire more debt either through the private sector or through bilateral and multilateral loans. How this debt is financed, and over what time period, will affect who pays and for how long. The gender equality incidence of debt repayment may vary substantially depending on the extent to which women and men are engaged in formal employment, the size of the tax base, and the incidence of direct and indirect taxes.

While men and male workers may disproportionately bear the burden of direct taxation, indirect taxation typically affects all consumers of the goods or services in question. The gender dimensions of such taxes and the net effect on consumption can affect well-being. For example, levying an additional tax on fossil fuels can affect services such as transport. Where women have fewer cash resources, they may be disproportionately excluded from transport as the costs rise (World Bank, 1999). Understanding how taxes and transfers related to mitigating or adapting to climate change affect women and men differently will prove essential if we are to ensure gender equity and the fullfilment of human rights.

The Clean Development Mechanism (CDM) will form an essential platform for implementing mitigation and adaptation strategies. Although the primary purpose of the CDM is to reduce carbon emissions, it is also a mechanism for achieving sustainable development. In operation since the beginning of 2006, it has already registered more than 1,000 projects, which are anticipated to produce certified emission reduction (CER) amounting to more than 2.7 billion ton of CO_2 equivalent in the first commitment period of the Kyoto Protocol (2008–2012). The kinds of projects that are considered, and their impact on energy use and technology acquisition, will be particularly important for developing countries. The majority of these projects comprise large- and medium-scale investments that focus on renewable energy and technologies to reduce emissions. As Wamukonya and Skutsch (2002, p. 121) observe:

> The CDM offers a whole new opportunity to market technology to women on a large scale, mainly because the additional value of emission reduction may make investment projects attractive in cases where they otherwise might not have been. But this requires a marketing strategy that recognizes gender differences in needs and in acquisition possibilities.

Addressing Gender Concerns in Global Policy Documents

As noted earlier, the clear linkages between gender equality and climate change have so far not been recognized in any global policies on climate change, including under the UNFCCC. Over the past years, however, concerted efforts have been made by gender advocates and parties to the Convention to integrate gender language into the negotiations for a post-Kyoto Protocol. The work of the Global Gender and Climate Alliance (GGCA), a collaborative mechanism between over 38 UN and civil society organizations, has been particularly effective in this regard. Starting from no references in 2007, gender issues have been tabled by several parties and strong statements have been made in support of integrating gender language into these agreements, resulting in several references in the negotiation text to gender, women, and CEDAW.

During the Conference of the Parties (COP 14) UNFCCC that took place in Poznan, Poland, in December 2008, representatives of the GGCA and other civil society organizations met with the Executive Secretary of the UNFCCC and began to work together to incorporate gender considerations into the outcome of the December 2009 Conference of Parties in Copenhagen, in line with existing agreements on gender equality. However, although gender language remains included in the text of the outcome document of Copenhagen, little concrete progress has been made in implementing policies and programs that will actively address gender concerns (UNDP, 2009). Strong gender language in global policy is important as it will inform implementation mechanisms and policy at regional and national level that will be further worked out in the years to come (see Box 8.1).

Box 8.1   Addressing gender concerns in climate change policy documents

Gender advocates will continue to work to make sure the following are included at the global level:

- Concrete steps to include gender in policies and decision making with the explicit goal of supporting and complying with existing mandates and conventions on gender equity and human rights frameworks.
- Actions to ensure that financing mechanisms for mitigation and adaptation take into account the different needs of poor women and men.
- Commitments to develop global, regional, and local capacity to design and implement policies and programs to address climate change that take into account gender-differentiated needs and impacts.
- The participation and voice of women leaders, gender experts, women from local and indigenous communities, and women's affairs ministries in climate change and related decision-making processes, programs, and projects at community, national, regional, and international levels, including the Conference of Parties and subsidiary bodies of the UNFCCC.
- Sufficient resources to enhance the capacity of women at all levels, especially the poorest and most disadvantaged, to incorporate their contributions to mitigation and adaptation activities and foster their resilience to climate change and disasters.
- Gender disaggregation of data collected by governments, international organizations, and financial institutions in relevant sectors related to climate change, and its availability to all stakeholders.

CONCLUSIONS

What is clear from this analysis is that, as a global community, we urgently need to tackle the twin challenges of social inequality and environmental deterioration. The global crises affecting the world today are all intimately interlinked and are partly a result of the failure of the current model of production and consumption. This model is demonstrating signs of exhaustion, and climate change is but one manifestation of this failure.

The rights framework and foundational institutional architecture exist to develop and pursue a multilateral response to what is a multilateral challenge. The ICESCR and other agreements and conventions such as the UNFCCC, the Kyoto Protocol, and CEDAW together provide a comprehensive framework through which to contribute to reducing poverty, hunger, and gender inequality. Gender and environment documents and legal instruments should be revisited, however, with a strong commitment to integrating a gender perspective and a gender analysis throughout the amendments, protocols, and resolutions that are to be enacted as the global community engages in coordinated action to address climate change.

Additionally, to be consistent with the principal of "common but differentiated responsibilities" that are embodied in the UNFCCC—that is that all parties must contribute to the solution of climate change issues, but that the greatest contribution rests with the developed countries that generate most of the greenhouse gases and also possess the greatest financial and physical resources—the international community will need to revisit, modify, and adapt those conventional measures of progress and well-being that are reported in the system of national accounts. Any attempt to estimate the impact of climate change or to evaluate the costs of mitigation and adaptation will have to use these augmented measures as a basis for developing taxes and transfers, for devising joint implementation initiatives and costing emissions targets or CERs, and for trading emissions permits or calculating additional aid contributions for climate change mitigation and adaptation. These measures will need to incorporate all those anthropogenic activities that are negatively affected by climate change—evaluating the gender-differentiated impact on the reproductive and subsistence economies of communities and peoples whose livelihoods and well-being are interrupted or radically altered.

Financing mechanisms devised to meet the challenges of mitigation and adaptation will need to be creative. A combination of carbon taxes and permits, levies and auctions for carbon trading, ending fossil fuel subsidies and tax breaks, and taxes and transfers related to the consumption of goods that generate greenhouse gases or sequester carbon will need to be considered. Financing should be additional to and distinct from existing aid commitments; it should be based on estimates of the cost of mitigation or adaptation; it should be reliable, consistent, and readily forthcoming.

The livelihood costs and consequences need to be understood through a gender, age, and ethnic lens that values the contributions and time spent

by those whose labor is not remunerated and whose productive and reproductive activities are not marketized. Existing valuation methods rely on
parallel markets and prices, and as such transmit many of the biases in the
derived values that underestimate or make invisible the contributions of
women and subsistence populations. Particular attention should be paid
to those methodologies that modify existing prices by taking into account
these contributions. The estimates should be revised regularly where new
knowledge is forthcoming about the impacts and consequences of climate
change and the gendered incidence of costs and benefits. Furthermore,
these estimates should be used to inform the development of national
adaptation programs of action under the UNFCCC and the Global Environment Facility.

Finally, given that climate change is a development and human rights
issue, it should be addressed through existing development and human
rights commitments and informed by the multilateral covenants and protocols adopted to secure the pursuit of universal human rights to food,
health, adequate housing, water, and work. Gender equity and justice,
nondiscrimination, and non-retrogression are at the heart of these commitments and should play a central role in determining how we adapt to
climate change, who pays, how much of women's hunger, food insecurity,
and illness is a matter of climate change, and how this is compensated.

REFERENCES

Abramovitz, J. (1994). Women: A missing link in the evolution of the biodiversity and
sustainable development debate. In W. Harcourt. (Ed.), *Feminist perspectives on sustainable development: Shifting knowledge boundaries* (pp. 198–211). London: Zed Books.

Addison, T., Arndt, C., & Tarp, F. (2010). *The triple crisis and the global aid architecture.*
UN-WIDER Working Paper No. 2010/01. United Nations University-World Institute
for Development Economic Research, January.

Aguilar, L. (2004). *Biodiversity: gender makes the difference* (Fact Sheet). San José: IUCN (World
Conservation Union). Retrieved January 19, 2010, from http://www.generoyambiente.
org/admin/admin_biblioteca/documentos/Biodiversity_ing.pdf

Aguilar, L., Araujo, A., & Quesada-Aguilar, A. (2007). *Gender and climate change* (Fact
Sheet). San José: IUCN (World Conservation Union). Retrieved January 15, 2010, from
http://www.gdnonline.org/resources/IUCN_FactsheetClimateChange.pdf

Arnell, N. W. (2004). Climate change and global water resources: SRES emissions and
socio-economic scenarios. *Global Environmental Change, 14,* 31–52.

Cagatay, N. (2001). *Gender, poverty and trade.* Background Paper. United Nations
Development Programme (UNDP), New York.

Carter, M. R., Little, P. D., Mogues, T., & Negatu, W. (2004). *Shock, sensitivity and resilience: Tracking
the economic impacts of environmental disaster on assets in Ethiopia and Honduras.* Working
Paper. BASIS Collaborative Research Support Program, University of Wisconsin.

Castañeda, I. (2008). *A review of key United Nations documents that refer to gender and climate change elaborated between 2003 and 2008*. Mexico: UNDP.

Cecelski, E. (2004). *Re-thinking gender and energy: Old and new directions.* Energy, Environment and Development Discussion Paper. ENERGIA/EASE, Netherlands.

Clancy, J., & Roehr, U. (2003). Gender and energy: Is there a Northern perspective? *Energy for Sustainable Development,* 7(3, September), 16–22.

Clancy, J. S., Skutsch, M., & Batchelor, S. (2003). *The gender–energy–poverty nexus: Finding the energy to address gender concerns in development.* London: Department for International Development (DFID).

Cleaver, F., & Elson, D. (1995). *Women and water: Continued marginalization and new policies* (Series 49). London: International Institute for Environment and Development.

Dankelman, I., & Davidson, J. (1988). *Women and environment in the third world: Alliance for the future.* London: Earthscan/IUCN.

Delaney, P., & Shrader, E. (2000). *Gender and post-disaster reconstruction: The case of Hurricane Mitch in Honduras and Nicaragua.* Decision review draft presented to the World Bank, January.

De la Vega, J. (2005). *Jatropha y bio-diesel.* GVEP International (Global Village Energy Partnership). Retrieved January 19, 2010, from http://www.gvepinternational.org (membership site).

Deere, C. D., & León, M. (2002). *Empowering women: Land and property rights in Latin America.* University of Pittsburgh Press.

Dennison, C. (2003). *From Beijing to Kyoto: Gendering the international climate change negotiation process.* 53rd Pugwash Conference on Science and World Affairs Advancing Human Security: The Role of Technology and Politics. Canada: Halifax and Pugwash, Nova Scotia.

Diario de Palenque. (2009). *Sequía golpea a México, no a sus precios.* August 28, Retrieved on January 18, 2010, from http://www.wiego.org/stat_picture/ www.diariodepalenque.com/nota.php?nId=9673.

FAO (Food and Agriculture Organization). (2008). *Climate change and food security: A framework document.* Rome: FAO.

Gallup, J. L., & Sachs, J. D. (2000). *The economic burden of malaria.* CID Working Paper No. 52. Center for International Development at Harvard University, Cambridge, Massachusetts.

Gammage, S., Benítez, M., & Machado, M. (1999). *Appropriate technology and the challenge of sustainable development.* PROWID Working Paper. International Center for Research on Women (ICRW), Washington, DC.

Ghosh, S., & Kanbur, R. (2002). *Male wages and female welfare: Private markets, public goods, and intra-household inequality.* Working Paper 2002–15, Cornell University, Ithaca, New York.

Hazell, P., & Pachauri, R. K. (Eds). (2006). *Bioenergy and agriculture: Promises and challenges* (2020 Focus, 14). Washington, DC: International Food Policy Research Institute (IFPRI).

Hoddinott, J. (2004). *Shocks and their consequences across and within households in rural Zimbabwe.* BASIS Collaborative Research Support Program, University of Wisconsin.

Howard, P. (2003). *The major importance of "minor" resources: Women and plant biodiversity* (Gatekeepers Series no. 112). London: International Institute for Environment and Development (IIED). Retrieved January 10, 2010, from http://www.wiego.org/stat_picture/www.farmingsolutions.org/pdfdb/GK112.pdf

IPCC (Intergovernmental Panel on Climate Change). 2007. *Climate change 2007: Synthesis report.* Contribution of Working Groups I, II and III to the Fourth Assessment Report of the Intergovernmental Panel on Climate Change. *Geneva: IPCC.*

Kliksberg, B. (2007). *Paradojas inexplicables de un medio desigual.* Foro Para Una Democracia Segura. Retrieved January 12, 2010, from http://spanish.safe-democracy. org/2007/07/05/las-brechas-de-la-verguenza/

Lambrou, Y., & Grazia, P. (2006). *Gender: The missing component of the response to climate change.* Rome: Food and Agriculture Organization (FAO).

McCracken, J. P., Smith, K. R., Díaz, A., Mittlemen, M. A., & Schwartz, J. (2007). Chimney stove intervention to reduce long-term wood smoke exposure lowers blood pressure among Guatemalan Women. *Environmental Health Perspectives, 115*(7), 996–1001.

Mehra, R. (1991). Can structural adjustment work for women farmers? *American Journal of Agricultural Economics, 73*(5), 1440–1447.

Meinzen-Dick, R., Brown, L. R., Sims Feldstein, H., & Quisumbing, A. R. (1997). *Gender, property rights and natural resources.* Washington, DC: Food Consumption and Nutrition Division, International Food Policy Research Institute (IFPRI).

Nelson, V., Meadows, K., Cannon, T., Morton, J., & Martin, A. (2002). Uncertain predictions, invisible impacts and the need to mainstream gender in climate change adaptations. *Gender and Development, 10*(2), 51–59.

Neumayer, E., & Plümper, T. (2007). The gendered nature of natural disasters: the impact of catastrophic events on the gender gap in life expectancy, 1981–2002. *Annals of the Association of American Geographers, 97*(3), 551–566.

Panel on Visible and Invisible Contributions. (2008). *Gender equality, domestic revenues and ODA.* International Conference on Financing for Development, Doha.

Parry, M. L., Rosenzweig, C., & Iglesias, A. (2004). Effects of climate change on global food production under SRES emissions and socio-economic scenarios. *Global Environmental Change, 14*, 53–67.

Parry, M. L., Rosenzweig, C., & Livermore, M. (2005). *Climate change, global food supply and risk of hunger.* Philosophical Transactions of the Royal Society, B 360, pp. 2125–2136.

Patz, J. A., Campbell-Lendrum, D., Holloway, T., & Foley, J. A. (2005). Impact of regional climate change on human health. *Nature, 438*, 310–317.

Population Reference Bureau. (2002). *The gender dimensions of environmental policies and programs.* Washington, DC: Population Reference Bureau.

Quisumbing, A. R., & Maluccio, J. A. (2003). Resources at marriage and intrahousehold allocation: Evidence from Bangladesh, Ethiopia, Indonesia, and South Africa. *Oxford Bulletin of Economics and Statistics, 65*(3), 283–327.

Rae, I. (2008). *Women and the right to food: International law and state practice.* Rome: Right to Food Unit, Food and Agriculture Organization (FAO).

Rajagopal, D. (2007). *Rethinking current strategies for biofuel production in India.* Paper presented at the International Conference on Linkages between Energy and Water Management for Agriculture in Developing Countries, Hyderabad, India.

Reddy, A. K. N. (2000). *Energy and social issues. In world energy assessment.* New York: United Nations Development Programme (UNDP).

Röhr, U. (2006). Gender and climate change. *Tiempo, 59*(April), 3–7.

Rossi, A., & Lambrou, Y. (2008). *Gender and equity issues in liquid biofuels production: Minimizing the risks to maximize the opportunities.* Rome: Food and Agriculture Organization (FAO), Rome.

Sánchez del Valle, R. (2000). *Gestión local de riesgo en América central: lecciones aprendidas del proyecto FEMID.* Guatemala: FEMID and GTZ. Retrieved January 10, 2010, from http://cidbimena.desastres.hn/docum/crid/ASH/pdf/spa/doc12912/doc12912-a.pdf

Seguino, S. (2000). Gender inequality and economic growth: A cross-country analysis. *World Development, 28*(7), 1211–1230.

Sen, A. (1999). *Development as freedom.* New York: Anchor Books.

Skutsch, M. (2002). Protocols, treaties and action: The "climate change process" through gender spectacles. *Gender and Development, 10*(2), 30–39.

Smith, K. A. R., Mehta, S., & Maeusezahl-Feuz, M. (2004). Indoor air pollution from household use of solid fuels. In M. Ezzati, A. D. Lopez, A. Rodgers, & C. L. J. Murray (Eds), *Comparative quantification of health risks: Global and regional burden of disease attributable to major risk factors* (pp. 1435–1493). Geneva: World Health Organization.

Standing, G. (1989). Global feminization through flexible labor. *World Development, 17*(7), 1077–1095.

———. (1999). Global feminization through flexible labor: A theme revisited. *World Development, 27*(3), pp. 583–602.

Stern, N. (2006). *The economics of climate change: The Stern review.* Cambridge: Cambridge University Press.

Tauli-Corpuz, V., & Tamang, P. (2007). *Oil palm and other commercial tree plantations, monocropping: Impacts on indigenous peoples land tenure and resource management systems and livelihoods.* United Nations Permanent Forum on Indigenous Issues (UNPFII), 6th session. New York.

UNDP (United Nations Development Programme). (2006). *Human development report: Beyond scarcity—power, poverty and the global water crisis.* New York: Palgrave MacMillan. Retrieved January 15, 2010, from http://hdr.undp.org/en/reports/global/hdr2006/chapters/

———. (2007). *Human development report: Fighting climate change: Human solidarity in a divided world.* New York: Palgrave MacMillan.

———. (2008a). *Fast facts: Doha: A time of crisis and opportunity.* New York: UNDP. Retrieved January 15, 2010, from http://www.undp.org/publications/fast-facts/doha08-fast-facts.pdf

———. (2008b). *Kemal Dervis on "low carbon growth."* December 8. Retrieved August 25, 2010, from http://content.undp.org/go/newsroom/2008/december/kemal-dervis-on-low-carbon-growth-.en?categoryID=349469

———. (2008c). *Resource guide on gender and climate change.* Mexico: United Nations Development Programme (UNDP).

———. (2009). Women's organisations dismayed by lack of progress on climate change in Copenhagen. *Gender in Development, 37,* December.

Walker, M. (2006). *Women, water policy and reform: Global discourses and local realities in Zimbabwe.* Working Paper 287, Department of Anthropology, Michigan State University, May.

Wamukonya, N., & Skutsch, M. (2002). Gender angle to the climate change negotiations. *Energy and the Environment, 13*(1), 115–124.

Warner, J. M., & Campbell, D. A. (2000). Supply response in an agrarian economy with non-symmetric gender relations. *World Development, 28*(7), 1327–1340.

WHO (World Health Organization). (2008). *Protecting health from climate change.* Retrieved January 20, 2010, from http://www.who.int/world-health-day/toolkit/report_web.pdf

Women Thrive Worldwide. (2008). *The effect of the food crisis on women and their families.* Washington, DC: Women Thrive Worldwide, May. Retrieved January 18, 2010, from http://www.globalpolicy.org/component/content/article/217/46209.html

World Bank. (1999). *Gender and transport: A rationale for action* (Poverty Reduction and Economic Management Notes, 14). Washington, DC: World Bank.

———. (2008). *Rising food prices: Policy options and World Bank response* (Background Note). Washington, DC: Poverty Reduction and Economic Management, World Bank.

Zwarteveen, M. Z. (1997). Water: From basic need to commodity: A discussion on gender and water rights in the context of irrigation. *World Development*, 25(8), 1335–1349.

9

The Cost of the Commoditization of Food and Water for Women

YASSINE FALL

The vision of increasing trade to make corporations richer should be replaced by one where people, especially women farmers, producers, and caregivers, can first secure their basic needs of food, water, health services, and education, and where governments decide on the best policy mix that would ensure sustainable development as enshrined in international human rights law as well as the Millennium Declaration.

INTRODUCTION

Food and water are the essential elements for life to exist and are preconditions for the enjoyment of any other good or service such as health, education, housing, or durables. Food and water are considered human rights. The right to food recognizes that all human beings should live a dignified life free from hunger; it is guaranteed under various international human rights instruments including the International Covenant on Economic, Social and Cultural Rights (ICESCR, art. 11), the Convention on the Elimination of All Forms of Discrimination against Women (CEDAW, art. 12), and the Convention on the Rights of the Child (CRC, arts. 24 and 27). General Comment No. 12 (1999) of the UN Committee on Economic, Social and Cultural Rights states, "the right to adequate food is realized when every man, woman and child, alone or in community with others, has physical and economic access at all times to adequate food or means for its procurement." The Human Rights Council has defined the right to food as

> ... the right to have regular, permanent and unrestricted access, either directly or by means of financial purchases, to quantitatively and qualitatively adequate and sufficient food corresponding to the cultural traditions of the people to which the consumer belongs, and which ensures a physical and mental, individual and collective, fulfilling and dignified life free of fear. (United Nations, 2010, para. 17)

In 1992 the United Nations proclaimed that water should be regarded as a human right. The UN Committee on Economic, Social and Cultural Rights subsequently issued General Comment No. 15 (2002), which reinterprets articles 11 and 12 of the ICESCR and indicates: "Water is a limited natural resource and a public good fundamental for life and health. The human right to water is indispensable for leading a life in human dignity." It then adds:

> The right to water contains both freedoms and entitlements. The freedoms include the right to maintain access to existing water supplies necessary for the right to water, and the right to be free from interference, such as the right to be free from arbitrary disconnections or contamination of water supplies. By contrast, the entitlements include the right to a system of water supply and management that provides equality of opportunity for people to enjoy the right to water.

Despite these legal frameworks, competition for water and food has become more acute because they are increasingly controlled by market-driven policies and affected by climate change. According to the 2006 Human Development Report, more than 1 billion people lack access to clean water and an estimated 2.6 billion people do not have access to adequate sanitation (UNDP, 2006). This includes people in developing countries and poor people in industrialized countries. The justification for handing over water and agricultural sectors to market forces and the global private sector is the liberalization of trade and investment for growth acceleration, and the hope that the private sector will be more efficient than the state in its management and provision of services. However, this raises gender-equality questions, as water and food are at the center of the work that women do to sustain economic well-being and social welfare, and states are accountable for the provision of services to their citizens—especially those most in need.

The role women in developing countries play in water provision and management is at the core of the social construct of gender relations and inequalities between women and men. Women and girls provide water for domestic uses such as drinking, cooking, and personal hygiene; they also collect water for productive purposes such as small-cattle rearing or construction; and they fetch water for community-related activities such as weddings, funerals, and political events. Women also play a vital role in food production. Food crises have a tremendous impact on poor communities around the world, especially on women and children. So far, the world has not given due attention to its commitment to ensuring the right to food and gender equality (FAO, 2011).

Gender analysis of food and water policies provides a good entry point for examining public policies and understanding that the way market forces function matters a great deal for women's economic empowerment and sustainable livelihoods. This chapter analyzes how increased control by market mechanisms of water and agriculture policies contributes to curtailing the realization of the rights to water and food and to deepening women's economic insecurity. It looks at water privatization processes and access to water; it analyzes the current trends in food markets and productive assets like land; and it examines the interlocking dynamics between market forces and the work women do to sustain their families and their own well-being. Finally, it presents alternative policy responses proposed by development practitioners and organized actions undertaken at the local level by women and social-justice advocates.

THE LIBERALIZATION OF THE WATER SECTOR

Economic reforms leading to the liberalization of markets of goods, services, and financial markets often recommend privatization of public water sectors. Water privatization is frequently included in the list of conditions presented to the governments of least developed countries (LDCs) as a prerequisite for accessing loans from international lenders (Grusky, 2001). This has raised economic-governance questions.

In Africa, loans under the umbrella of the 1999 Poverty Reduction and Growth Facility (PRGF) were reported to be provided for several countries classified as Highly Indebted Poor Countries (HIPC) under conditions that included privatization of water or increased mechanisms reinforcing cost recovery under existing water-privatization agreements. For example,

Angola was required to review water tariffs to allow a rise in cost recovery. Benin was asked to privatize the state enterprise that distributed electricity and water. Guinea-Bissau had to transfer the management of its water and electricity utilities services to private hands. Niger's water, electricity, telecommunications, and petroleum had to be privatized and some of its profits used for debt payment. Tanzania was advised to transfer its Dar Es Salaam Water and Sewage Authority assets into the management of private companies. Some of these countries had to borrow more money to finance the cost of their water privatization. Tanzania, for example, would have had to borrow USD 145 million compared to the USD 6.5 million that the company buying the water authority would pay for installing standpipes (Mason & Talbot, 2002).

Citizens, workers, and civil-society organizations argue that they are excluded from decision making in this area. Water privatization is often the last stage of a process starting with years of disinvestment in the water sector due to budgetary cuts in public expenditure. The sector then falls into disarray following the deterioration of water delivery systems. After years of outcry and multiple calls for action, an international mission of Western experts is brought in to assess the situation. In the case of Senegal, for example, a team of Dutch consultants was hired to conduct the assessment of the water sector. In Ghana, it was a team of British and American consultants. These teams in most cases do not include local academics or national experts. The policy options they propose invariably lead to one form or another of privatization. Table 9.1 presents the different companies that hold ownership of drinkable water in Africa.

Privatization of water may be accelerated within the framework of the General Agreement on Trade in Services (GATS). GATS seeks to establish a multilateral framework of principles and rules for international trade in all forms of services with a view to the progressive liberalization and expansion of this trade. Defenders of GATS present it as a democratic arena for all countries. However, developing countries have been resisting in different ways attempts to push GATS implementation to its fullest extent, and there are some possibilities in this regard (see Box 9.1). Their concerns include the fact that their different levels of development, priorities, and political influence affect their ability to participate meaningfully in the World Trade Organization (WTO) negotiations. The Minister of Trade of Senegal, who was the spokesperson of a unified African group during the Cancun trade negotiations, eloquently underlined the un-level playing field of the negotiations (Mutume, 2003).

Table 9.1 Water privatization contracts in Africa

Country	Date	Company	Sector	Contract type	Lead investor
Côte d'Ivoire	1960	Société de Distribution d'Eau de la Côte d'Ivoire (SODECI)	Water	15-year renewable concession	Société d'Aménagement Urbain et Rural (SAUR)
Guinea	1989	Societé d'Exploitation des Eaux de Guinee (SEEG)	Water	10-year lease contract	SAUR, Electricité de France (EDF)
South Africa	1992	Water & Sanitation Services South Africa (WSSA)	Water	25-year concession (Queenstown) and 10-year concession (Fort Beaufort)	Suez-Lyonnaise
Central African Republic	1993	Société de Distribution d'Eau de Centrafrique (SODECA)	Water	15-year management leasing contract	SAUR
Mali	1994	Energie du Mali (EDM)	Water and electricity	4-year overall management contract	SAUR, EDF, Hydro Quebec International (HQI)
Senegal	1995	Société Sénégalaise des Eaux (SDE)	Water	51 percent ownership	SAUR
Guinea-Bissau	1995	Electricidade e Aguas de Guinea-Bissau (EAGB)	Water and electricity	Management contract	Suez-Lyonnaise, EDF
Gabon	1997	Societe d'Energie et d'Eau du Gabon (SEEG)	Water and electricity	20-year concession	Vivendi, Electricity Supply Board Ireland (ESBI)

Country	Year	Sector	Contract details	Company
South Africa	1999	Water	30-year concession Dolphin Coast	SAUR
South Africa	1999	Water	30-year service contract Nelspruit	Biwater Nuon
Mozambique	1999	Water	15-year concession (Maputo and Matola) and 5-year concession for the other cities	SAUR, Investimentos e Participações Empresariais (IPE)
Kenya	1999	Water	10-year management contract for water billing and revenue management	Vivendi
Chad	2000	Water and electricity	30-year management contract	Vivendi
Cameroon	2000	Water	20-year concession and 51 percent stake	Suez Lyonnaise
Burkina Faso	2001	Water	5-year support and service contract	Vivendi
Niger	2001	Water	10-year renewable lease contract—provision of water services to whole country	Vivendi

Source: Bayliss (2001) (citing the Public Services International Research Unit database and Campbell-White and Bhatia [1998] as sources).

Box 9.1 Protecting public services under the General Agreement on Trade in Services (GATS)

GATS applies to all services except public services—meaning "services supplied in the exercise of governmental authority." Such services are those not provided under a commercial process or a competition process between suppliers. It is up to WTO member countries to determine what sector they would like to include in their trade schedule and the level of market access they intend to set for the service. Countries are therefore free to take an entire sector—education, health, or water—out of their GATS commitments. WTO members are supposed to freely set the limitations they wish to establish, be it removing whole sectors out of the GATS commitments or selecting a few sectors to which they grant complete or partial market access (Council of Europe, 2002).

Given that each WTO member country has some space to determine its own obligations, States can use this provision to protect their citizens' rights to safe drinking water and sanitation as a necessary means to sustain their welfare, which could be threatened under the GATS. Without the use of such provision, the principle of Most Favored Nation (MFN) could apply. The MFN refers to a situation where the State agrees to give to another entity the same trading rights and advantages as those enjoyed by its own citizens. It must then remove any trade barrier, including safeguards against violations of workers' rights, environmental degradation, or women's marginalization in employment. This principle could curtail developing countries' chances to protect the basic rights of poor and marginalized people by surrendering provision of water and sanitation services to big foreign private businesses.

The Example of Senegal

In all the cases presented in Table 9.1, the water privatization process awarded the contract to multinational corporations that brought market-based water service delivery. Water privatization in Senegal, often cited as a successful good practice example to be replicated, merits further examination.

Senegal became independent from France in 1960. Right after independence the country's water and sanitation sector was put under the ownership of a French company called Compagnie Générale des Eaux (CGE). CGE was created in 1853 under an imperial decree of Napoleon III and later evolved, extending its activities to other sectors including transport services, energy, waste management, and telecommunications. It became Vivendi in 1998. CGE's ownership of the Senegalese water sector ended in 1972 with the Government's decision to nationalize the water sector.

The Société Nationale des Eaux du Senegal (SONES) was created and put in charge of the provision and management of water supply and sanitation. During this post-independence period, Senegal—like many developing countries coming out of colonialism—were receiving considerable earnings from the export of raw material as the terms of trade were not as unfavorable as they are today. In addition, the country had a substantial number of low-interest loans following the international financial crisis of excess Eurodollars, which had led to high outflow of lending to developing countries.

However, in the late 1970s the economies of developing countries such as Senegal started to decline. Factors include the global oil crisis, the rise of interest rates paid for servicing their debts, the deterioration of their terms of trade, and the fall in export revenues. Senegal lost substantial revenues because of decreasing returns from its groundnuts exports, while the price of its oil imports and their derivatives rose up. The country also experienced severe droughts and saw substantial increases in its debt service. These interlocking factors plunged the country into a serious crisis and made it unable to provide the essential services that had been made accessible to a large number of people since independence. These included education, health care, housing, water, sanitation, agricultural extension services, and transportation, which had been provided by state-owned enterprises that were suddenly unable to access state subsidies.

President Leopold Sédar Senghor stepped down in 1981. His Prime Minister Abdou Diouf succeeded him, and structural adjustment policies were introduced soon afterward. President Diouf attempted to introduce water-sector reforms and broadened SONES' responsibilities toward a more development-oriented role. However, public-investment resources needed for realizing the company's growth were not available because of restrictions in government expenditures implemented under stabilization policies. The water company severely lacked financing to respond to pressing challenges such as the increased demand due to population growth in Dakar, the capital city, and the diminished flow of water from Lac de Guiers due to drought and salinity of the groundwater. This set off a steady deterioration process of the water sector, leading to the arrival of consultants who recommended privatization.

In 1996 the World Bank Water Sector formally endorsed the privatization of SONES. The company returned to French hands, this time la Société d'Aménagement Urbain et Rural (SAUR), established in 1933. There were governance issues and even some conflict of interest in the sense that SAUR had been an advisor of SONES since 1980. The Government had attempted to exclude SAUR from the list of bidders, but it did not succeed because of the support the company received from the international institutions that backed the privatization. The Société Sénégalaise des Eaux (SDE), a subsidiary of SAUR, was set up and government oversight was reduced to a minimum.

Promises were made in Senegal that water leakages from pipes would stop and a larger proportion of the population would have access to water without a high increase in cost. As in many privatization schemes, the agreement with SDE was organized under the premise that water distribution and sale would be provided by the private company, while sanitation-service provision would be left under government management. This agreement formula is often the one promoted in Africa. Distribution and sale of water is the profit-generating enterprise. Sanitation-related activities are much less profitable because they require higher levels of investment and offer smaller returns.

Following the sale of the water sector, salaries that had been refused to Senegalese experts and engineers were multiplied at least fourfold to pay expatriates. The price of water included a cost-recovery scheme and had to climb to allow SAUR to recoup its investments and make appreciable profits, starting a situation leading to no affordability of water to poor households.

Social and Gendered Impacts of Water Privatization

Inequalities around access to water are aggravated by gender factors, rural–urban disparities, and poverty gaps. The WHO recognizes that women and girls are more negatively affected by lack of access to water and sanitation than men and boys. WHO also estimates that out of every 10 people lacking access to sanitation worldwide, 7 live in rural settings; and out of every 10 people lacking access to improved drinking water sources, 8 are rural inhabitants. In sub-Saharan Africa the richest 20 percent have more than double the chance to obtain water from an improved water source than the poorest 20 percent and close to five times the chance to access improved facilities for sanitation (WHO, 2010).

As stated by Bolivian social scientist Dr Carmen Ledo-Garcia (2005):

> The cycle of poverty is repeated every time lower income women are forced to invest an important part of their time in managing, using and getting water to their homes. Under these circumstances, improving their socioeconomic situation is almost impossible to them, the precariousness

of their lives is perpetuated and the systematic abuse of their human rights continuous .... At a world level the privatization of water sources and potable water systems stands as an additional obstacle since it makes the access to clean water more difficult for the lower income population, especially impoverished women.

Water privatization is promoted under the assumption that it will increase efficiency and improve the quality of water and other services. Promoters of privatization essentially measure its success on the basis of price-theory indicators—namely, the ability of the water distribution enterprise that bought the public-sector entity to minimize costs and improve its "financial health." This is specifically estimated through the ability of the company to install water connections or to recoup water-bill payments despite continuous increases for cost recovery. Given the essential nature of water, households often have to forgo certain other necessary goods and services to pay their water bills.

The African nongovernmental organization (NGO) Aid Transparency, which focuses on accountability issues and works with researchers and academics, undertook an investigation of the Senegal case. It looked into social factors that are not traditionally taken into account when assessing the success of water privatization; examined the institutional and juridical settings under which privatization of water should be undertaken; assessed challenges related to water and sanitation management; and analyzed the socioeconomic and gendered impact of privatization and access to water.

The study collected and analyzed quantitative and qualitative information from 1,200 male- and female-headed households in 11 neighborhoods of the cities of Dakar, Kaolack, and Diourbel. It found that privatization contributed to deepening inequalities because poor people paid relatively more for water than rich people. People living in poverty were faced with drastic increases in the cost of water. Price hikes and the need to use a substantial amount of income to pay for water increased negative health outcomes and malnutrition in poor households, which had to fetch water from unsafe sources and cut down on food and other necessary goods and services (Aid Transparency, 2004). There has been an eruption of waterborne diseases such as Guinea worm and cholera that have disproportionately affected children and women. Waterborne diseases also generate an increased work burden on women who have to care for the sick. In addition, WHO reported accounts from the Ministry of Health in 2004 of 861 cases of cholera and six cholera-related deaths (WHO, 2004).

Several years after water privatization in Senegal, other observers noted that anticipated results had not been met. It was reported that water distribution had not become more efficient (Gonzales, 2010). Poor neighborhoods were still experiencing water cuts that sometimes lasted for days (Diagne, 2009). Further, more than 10 years after the privatization of water in 1996, the share of the population in 2007 with access to safe drinking water in the capital city, where the bulk of the people live, had increased by only 2 percent (from 80 to 82 percent) and water leakage had been reduced by about 6 percent (from 36 to 30 percent) over same period (Keene, 2007).

Women are disproportionately affected by the unavailability and high cost of water because of the work they do. It is often overlooked that in developing countries women are the first providers and managers of water. They are the most present in reproductive arenas but are also active in water provision in the productive sphere. Many women in the global South are finding it difficult to access the bare minimum of 20 liters of water per day recommended by WHO. Lack of water represents a cost to women's work burden, girls' education, and women's income.

When community wells and/or sanitation projects are being established in low-income countries, women are mobilized to provide their in-kind contribution by transporting water to the builders. When water sources are remote, women remove their daughters from school and walk kilometers with them to fetch water from wherever they can find it, exposing themselves to many risks, including rape. When schools do not have running water, girls often stay home during their menstrual periods, and they sometimes end up dropping out because of long periods of absenteeism. When water prices rise, women forego other goods to pay for it (Fall, 2008).

In 2005 the African Women's Millennium Initiative on Poverty and Human Rights (AWOMI), a Senegal-based women's international NGO, conducted a study on the division of labor in water and garbage management in the suburbs of Dakar. In a sample of over 21,489 households, 77 percent of water provision was done by women. Water management also included waste-water disposal and cleaning of garbage containers. When municipalities do not take care of their responsibility for garbage management and disposal, this task is shifted into women and girls' unpaid-work arena. According to the AWOMI study, girls and women, respectively, transport and dispose of 36 percent and 32 percent of household garbage (AWOMI, 2005). In addition, 70 percent of the households surveyed by AWOMI found the cost of water extremely high and unaffordable.

Despite their central roles in water provision and management, women do not participate in water-policy formulation. The part they play in providing water is not valued and documented to inform water policies and programs. Their points of view are not requested when water privatization is being examined as an option for resolving a water crisis. Women are not consulted when hardware engineers are designing and installing bore holes that they, the women, will later use to fetch water.

In his foreword to the 2006 *Human Development Report*, the UNDP Administrator notes that some of the world's poorest people are paying some of the world's highest prices for water, and that this is due to the fact that poor people in general—and poor women in particular—do not have the political power to make equitable water allocation a development priority (UNDP, 2006). The participation of women in formulating public water policy is the best solution for ensuring that such policy is the main channel for providing water and realizing the right to water for all.

ENVIRONMENTAL CHANGE, BIOFUELS, AND THE FOOD CRISIS

Lack of access to food is also a human right violation. Food shortages and the rise in global food prices have increased economic insecurity throughout the world. The World Food Programme (WFP) has stated that the number of hungry people in the world passed the billion mark in 2009 for the first time in history, reaching almost one-sixth of humanity (WFP, 2009). The global South has the largest share and the fastest growing number of hungry people, rising from the mid-1990s over the following half decade by about 4 million a year.

Food prices have risen sharply, responding to increased demand and reduced supply of cereals. The World Bank (2008) reports that the global price of wheat increased 181 percent and the overall global food price rose 83 percent over the three years up to February 2008. US prices in wheat exports rose from USD 375/ton in January 2008 to USD 440/ton in March. Food inflation has surpassed aggregate inflation globally and even more than doubled it in a few countries, and prices were anticipated to remain high in 2009, well above their 2004 levels. This is one of the root causes of hunger and is curtailing the little progress made in reducing poverty in the global South.

Increases in food prices are the result of a combination of interlocking factors. Deforestation and climate change have made it very difficult for farmers in the global South to continue to respond to rising food demands. There have been years of neglect in placing food production at the center of the development engine. Dominant development models and consumption patterns have accelerated the impact of environmentally insensitive industrialization on eroding biodiversity and climate change. Human activities; change in precipitation patterns manifested through drought, flooding, and soil erosion; ocean-level variability; and disruption in the life cycle of many plants and animals are combined factors that have been threatening food security.

The survival of indigenous communities, people living in poverty, and those living on forest lands, especially women, depend a great deal on a sensitive ecological balance that is now endangered by climate change. Women in forest areas depend on gathering food products that are progressively disappearing because of excessive tropical mining and wood exploitation, as well as planting of rapid-growth monoculture plants. For example, women producers of shea butter in West Africa, who were moving from being small street vendors to exporters, face the challenge of increased loss of shea trees from the forest (Harsch, 2001). Deforestation has been accelerating at alarming rates. About 130,000 square kilometers around the world are deforested every year—an area four times the size of Belgium. Farmers, peasant organizations, scientists, and environmental groups point the finger at excessive industrial exploitation and unsustainable exploitation of forest and arable land for commoditization of agriculture and profit maximization (Collective Syllepse, 2008). This competition and pressure on land jeopardizes land-title ownership for rural farmers.

Furthermore, the world's growing dependency on oil, the political economy around oil supply, and the increasing pressure of the demand for energy have led rich countries and encouraged less-developed ones to invest in crops for fuel production. There is a conscious effort to progressively increase biofuel production by setting target levels of biofuels output. The United States has instructed that 28.4 billion liters of biofuels be used for transportation by 2010. The European Union (EU) plans to have motor oil use 5.75 percent of biofuels by 2010, while Brazil expects to have 5 percent biofuels content in its diesel oil by 2013. China and India introduced 10 percent ethanol blend in 5 provinces and 5 percent blend in 9 states, respectively. Thailand mandated that starting in 2007 all gasoline should contain 10 percent ethanol (World Bank, 2008).

Even though the production of biofuels is more advanced in the United States and middle-income countries such as Brazil, it is also gaining ground elsewhere. Africa, Asia, and the Caribbean are responding to the increasing demand for biofuels to obtain foreign exchange. There is more demand for raw materials such as wheat, soy, maize, and palm oil and increased pressure to convert land from food-crop cultivation. Efforts to diversify—to promote export-oriented agriculture and an alternative source of energy—can be beneficial for some and increase oil availability. However, there is a cost for subsistence farming, rural forestry, and the availability of food for many.

Developing countries are competing against each other to emerge as credible suppliers of alternative energy sources, distilling ethanol for energy from corn, sugar cane, and other crops. China, Nigeria, and Thailand are going into small-scale biofuel production using cassava leaves. As a varied nutritious diet is often out of reach of people living in poverty, many rely heavily on basic carbohydrates, and cassava leaves represent a major source of these. The multinational giant British Petroleum is investing in Mali in an indigenous plant, jatropha. Indigenous knowledge has taught generations of Africans how to use this plant to prevent erosion and keep destructive animals away from crops. In Fiji Islands and the Philippines, the potential to produce petrol from coconut oil is being seriously explored, especially since Virgin Atlantic inaugurated flying with partially coconut oil-based biofuel (Soguel, 2008).

Moreover, there is a recent phenomenon of "land grabbing," with land deals made between governments getting bigger and bigger. For example, *The Economist* (2009) reported that a Sudanese government official claimed that the country would set aside one-fifth of its land for Arab countries. This may prevent Sudanese indigenous people and small farmers, many of whom are women, from obtaining property titles. The International Food Policy Research Institute (IFPRI) confirms unprecedented acquisition of farmland in Africa, Latin America, and Central and South East Asia by corporations and by large and middle-income countries in pressing search of land (von Braun & Meinzen-Dick 2009). These deals focus on staples and biofuels—wheat, maize, rice, and jatropha.

Macroeconomic policies tend to favor promotion of market-oriented export farming at the expense of the food production sector, which is dominated by women. The disproportionate impact of the global food crisis on the agricultural sector of LDCs is the result of policy choices whose effects have been in the making for some time. Many development experts have warned for years about the negative impact that market-oriented agricultural policies would later have on food sovereignty and availability (see, for example, Amin, 1990; Dumont, 1966).

The increase in food demand from populous nations like China, India, and Nigeria has also contributed to the prices hikes. Nigeria, for example, which was once self sufficient in food, became a net importer of food following its oil boom. It relied on macroeconomic prescriptions that suggested a focus on oil exports as the country had a comparative advantage to gain from this trade and earn foreign exchange. Food production and women farmers were neglected in the process. There is now an alarming imbalance between Nigeria's national food demand, estimated at 4.64 million metric ton per annum, and its current consumption rate estimated at 2.3 million metric tons (All Africa.com, 2008). This means that large populations are not getting the minimum nutritional intake they need.

The policy prescribed to developing countries in the 1980s—to focus on sectors of high comparative advantage to generate export revenues—drove the process of commoditization of agriculture that is being promoted today under the auspices of the global trade regime. Structural adjustment and stabilization policies pushed for cuts in subsidies to farmers, often making this a condition of loans. Subsidy systems that provided seeds, fertilizers, extension training support, credit, and agricultural information were reduced or dismantled in order to impose fiscal restraint on government finances. Senegal is an example of those countries that have liberalized their agricultural sector. Policies put in place there toward eliminating agricultural extension services and gradually ending fertilizer subsidies left the farmers to survive on their own. According to the UNDP 2001 *Human Development Report for Senegal*, about 85 percent of the country's rural population live below the poverty line (UNDP, 2001). This is much higher than the rate of 60 percent for the country as a whole. Policies implemented during the early years of adjustments in Senegal set in place a progressive process of crippling the agricultural food sector.

During the United Nations Conference on Trade and Development (UNCTAD) XII, held in Accra, Ghana in April 2008, several UN officials highlighted the responsibility of macroeconomic factors in aggravating the impact of the food crisis on local communities in developing countries. They pointed at poorly conceptualized agricultural policies as major factors contributing to the painful impact that the crisis has had on poor farmers. In an interview, UNCTAD official Rolf Traeger blamed structural adjustment policies (SAP) and their conditionalities as the major factor that caused the demise of the LDCs' agricultural sector and consequently the inability of farmers to respond to the current food crisis (Fiakpa, 2008). He suggested that, "the production system of many developing countries underwent serious changes because, on one side, domestic support for production, that is subsidies to farmers, was generally cut. At the same time there was a very deep trade liberalization that was put in place by the developing countries as part of the SAP" (Fiakpa, 2008). Food imports at low prices initially created competition that led domestic producers to change what they were cultivating or the type of activities that they were undertaking; however, prices then rose again so that buying food began to represent the major part of the little income that developing countries had (UNCTAD XII Resource Center, 2008).

Women are Disproportionately Affected

Just as with water, the encouraged liberalization of agriculture does not have the promised positive effects. And again it is women who bear the largest share of the burden. The impacts felt on food production by rural women have been similar across continents.

The FAO presents a clear picture of the "feminization of agriculture" and the vivid reality of the level of discrimination against women farmers in access to and control over resources.[1] According to the 2010–2011 FAO report on the State of Food and Agriculture, women constitute, on average, 43 percent of the agricultural labor force in developing countries and 50 percent in Africa (FAO, 2011). The male population in Africa's rural areas is declining—due to factors such as sickness and death from HIV and AIDS and conflicts, as well as international and urban migration—while the female population is relatively stable. For example, the FAO notes that in Malawi the male rural population fell by 21.8 percent between 1970 and 1990 while the female rural population only fell by 5.4 percent. This increased representation of women among farmers helps explain why one-third of rural African households are headed by women.

Women produce the bulk of food consumed and ensure that each family member gets an adequate food ration and satisfactory nutritional level. Women work on farms and in fruit and vegetable gardens to earn an income. They invest a great deal of their time, energy, and income in resource management, purchasing or growing food, collecting fuel and water, and preparing ingredients to ensure a balanced meal. Women in South East Asia allocate up to 90 percent of their labor for rice cultivation. Sub-Saharan African women generate up to 80 percent of essential

---

[1] For much of the information in this section, see FAO's Gender and Food Security website at: http://www.fao.org/gender

foodstuff used both for sale and for household consumption. In Egypt 53 percent of agricultural labor is done by women, while in Colombia and Peru 25–45 percent of work in the agricultural field is undertaken by women.

Women are not only users of their agricultural environment but also its protectors and managers. They have invaluable knowledge about the biodiversity resources they use, yet access to and control over productive resources and assets is alarmingly discriminatory against women farmers (see Box 9.2).

Box 9.2   Women farmers protect biodiversity but have less access to resources

- In sub-Saharan Africa, some 120 different species of plants have been found cultivated by women in the spaces around plots allocated for cash crops cultivated by men.
- In the Andean regions of Bolivia, Colombia, and Peru, women are responsible for the generation and conservation of seed banks that constitute the backbone of food production.
- Rwandan rural women remain the traditional producers and custodians of beans from which rural people generate a quarter of their calories intake and close to half their protein intake.
- Less than 10 percent of Indian, Nepali, and Thai women farmers own land.
- Women got less than 10 percent of credits allocated to smallholders in farm credit schemes undertaken in five African countries.
- Women represent only 15 percent of agricultural extension workers worldwide.
- African rural female heads of households are less educated, younger, and have less access to capital, extra farm labor, land, credit training, and agricultural extension support than their male counterparts.

Source: http://www.fao.org/gender

Rural women in developing countries continue to struggle with triple work responsibilities in food crop production, family agricultural-export activities, and household non-market work. They are disproportionately affected by the food crisis because they are confronted with impoverishment, illiteracy, high health risks, inadequate access to productive resources, lack of financial market access, and inability to drive changes that affect their lives. Macroeconomic policy has not been supportive of women's work in food crop production and processing. The negative impact of economic policies hits women farmers harder because the work they do is not properly counted—often due to the fact that the labor is unpaid. Therefore, it is not properly recognized and factored in during the process of policy formulation to reflect program interventions.

The feminist economist Marilyn Waring, who pioneered work on women's unpaid work, reported her experience in an Asian country where 92 percent of women over 10 years of age were described as "inactive" and only 0.5 percent of women were counted as "active" in the agricultural sector. She reported a high official in the government statistical division as stating: "They expect me to count women who collect fodder, fuel, and water. That's just about every woman in [the country]" (Eberlee, 1997). Not properly counting and valuing rural women's work has serious implications for the way policies and programing respond to the multiple manifestation of their poverty related to resources, income, time, work burden, security, and leadership. As a result the productive and reproductive needs of women farmers in accessing a wide range of services, agricultural inputs, financing facilities, and extension-skill building become invisible and get relegated to a last-order priority behind market-related issues.

Even before the 2008 food crisis, inflation in food prices was a nightmare for women living in poverty, especially those heading households. Because they live below the income poverty line, they were already spending more than 50 percent of their income on food. These women have now reached a whole new level in foregoing expenditures on necessary goods and services such as safe drinking water, health care, or education in order to feed themselves and their families.

Because of liberalization, deregulation, and the rush toward crops for biofuels discussed earlier, indigenous plants—mostly produced and protected by women in developing countries—are being targeted for production. However, it is very unlikely that women farmers will benefit from biofuel production. That kind of farming requires intensive resources that go far beyond the precarious economic reach of rural women. Moreover, marginal land traditionally allocated to women farmers is now open for competition following increased farming for biofuel input (*New Scientist*, 2008). The more land is taken away by agribusiness and well-off farmers, the less opportunities women have to hold a land title.

Given that women are already among the poorest farmers, any cut in the little agricultural subsidy they receive has a negative impact on their farming systems and output, their cropping patterns and crop variety, and their nutritional quality and productivity. If free-trade ideology is to work for agriculture then it must first start with the removal of rich countries' farm subsidies, which represent the biggest challenge for developing countries. Questioning the commoditization of agriculture does not mean that developing regions like those in Africa do not need more equitable and more gender-sensitive land reform and a boost in productivity. However, these should happen as part of a serious scrutiny of the social justice issues generated under the present market-dominated process. It is time to counter the enormous pressure on developing countries and stop proposals that remove more tariffs and agricultural subsidies for domestic food production undertaken by women and small farmers. Agreeing to the basis of such a framework and rejecting distortions and dumping in agricultural trade for negotiations could constitute one of the answers.

Voices of Dissent, Organizing for Policy Change

Food and water resources and services are recognized as crucial for development and for addressing gender inequalities. They are increasingly placed in the political economy debates around globalization versus social-justice issues and around corporate power and competitive profit-seeking services versus government-supported policy in providing public goods (UNDP, 2007). Advocates for human rights and gender-equitable development argue that the vision of increasing trade to make corporations richer should be replaced by one where people, especially women farmers, producers and caregivers, can first secure their basic needs of food, water, health services, and education, and governments decide on the best policy mix that would ensure sustainable development as enshrined in international human rights law as well as the Millennium Declaration.

Social-justice advocates are organizing all over the world to question the handing over of human-rights entitlements to markets. In 2006, for example, women in the Handeni district in Tanzania organized themselves with the support of the NGO Peoples Voice for Development (PEVODE) to resolve health and work burden challenges associated with lack of quality drinking water. A participatory survey was undertaken followed by community mobilization, which led to the creation of Women Water User Groups. These groups elected leaders, established their constitution, and formally registered. The Handeni community saw an increase in agricultural productivity, a reduction in women's work burden, and improvement in hygiene and health, leading to replication of the good practice in other districts. This experience was made possible by the fact that the Tanzania national water policy stressed the need for water and sanitation projects to be managed by registered water users associations (Mulagwanda, 2008).

Following privatization of their drinking water in 2000, 90 percent of residents in the city of Cochabamba, Bolivia, demanded that water provision be returned into public hands. The company that purchased their public water system, Aguas del Tunari (a joint subsidiary of Italian utility Edison and Bechtel Enterprise), had immediately raised water rates up to 35 percent. This led poor people earning USD 100/month to pay about USD 20 a month for water, about the same amount as their food expenses. Cochabamba residents formed a coalition called Defense of Water and Life composed of local organizations, environmental groups, women's groups and leaders, lawyers, labor unions, economists, and neighborhood associations to defend local control of water management and finally saw Bechtel kicked out of the country (Schultz, 2000). Women also mobilized in 2004 in response to inability of the Aguas del Illimani water company to reach promised pro-poor targets in providing respectable quality and quantity of water service. A series of advocacy activities making clear demands helped lead to a situation where the government was obliged to listen and take action in line with the people's requests (Ledo-Garcia, 2005).

In 2001 in Ghana, a popular movement called Coalition against Privatization of Water in Ghana (CAP of Water) was formed when the Government opened the bidding process for privatization and short-listed five multinational corporations for selection. CAP of Water included students, women's groups, faith-based organizations, human rights groups, and trade unions. They organized an international fact-finding mission on the privatization of water and built a global solidarity network that put pressure on the government and its partners to be accountable. They developed a solid advocacy campaign and presented evidence and thoughtful argumentation regarding the lack of transparency in the bidding process and the bias in the agreements in favor of privatization at the expense of public-community partnership and local people. They managed to reverse the privatization process as several of the bidders reneged when they saw that owning the Ghana Water Company would be a risky business, given the issues raised by social forces in the country (Amenga-Etego, 2003).

Water Dialogues–South Africa (WD–SA) also involved a wide range of stakeholders included national and local government, the private sector, civil society, trade unions, water boards, and academic/research organizations. It came out of the international initiative of Water Dialogues, which were a series of national multi-stakeholder dialogues and research processes aimed at having a constructive discussion and better understanding of different approaches and models of water-service delivery, including the pros and cons of privatization. Other countries involved were Brazil, Indonesia, the Philippines, and Uganda (EMG, n.d.). WD-SA undertook studies and research and disseminated lessons learnt in promoting the most effective safe-water service delivery model. Although South Africa has recognized water as a human right, there were reports of poor and rapidly diminishing water quality. A high level of municipal dysfunction was revealed and the need for widespread changes to ensure effective, equitable, and sustainable delivery of water supply and sanitation (Water Dialogues, n.d.).

In March 2008 women living in Guediawaye, a poor suburb of Dakar, demonstrated in coalition with a youth group against the poor quality of water, water shortages, and high costs. They testified that the color of the water was the same as coffee; they went to municipality headquarters and called on their political leaders to ask the water company to answer to them. They expressed their anger of being discriminated against because of living in a poverty-stricken area. They also called on the Ministry of Health to conduct an investigation with a microbiological test of the water done by an independent and neutral laboratory in order to identify health hazards and demonstrate the links between the bad quality of the water and the presence of many waterborne diseases (Mbengue 2008). The pressure they exerted led the water authorities, which for many years had been quite silent, to reach out to the media and start responding to questions raised by local organized groups in communities.

Food riots in different parts of the world led by smallholder farmers and rural women will also be remembered among events that marked the year 2008. Hunger riots erupted in several countries from Egypt and Morocco to Indonesia and the Philippines. Haiti was obliged to name a new Prime Minister after food riots there, which killed six people, precipitated the early retirement of Jacques-Edouard Alexis (International Crisis Group, 2009). Sub-Saharan Africa was no exception as countries including Burkina Faso, Cameroon, Côte d'Ivoire, Mozambique, Mauritania, Nigeria, and Senegal also saw people demonstrating, sometimes holding up empty bags of rice to symbolize their hungry stomachs (Al Jazeera, 2008).

All these organized groups who are faced with water and food shortages and high prices have to be part of the search for solutions. They have answers to the challenges they face. Policy development would have a more balanced response to the water and food crises if policy choices were informed by the realities of and propositions made by local people and communities instead of relying so much on market mechanisms. Taking this direction could help start a genuine participatory process towards sustainable development based on human rights principles.

REFERENCES

Aid Transparency. (2004). *Enquête nationale sur l'accès a l'eau et sa privatisation au Sénégal.* Aid Transparency, Dakar.

Al Jazeera. (2008). Food costs spark protests in Senegal. April 27. Retrieved Janmuary 5, 2010, from http://english.aljazeera.net/news/africa/2008/04/2008614233848478410.html

All Africa.com. (2008). Global food crisis: World Bank ready to assist Nigeria. April 16. Retrieved January 6, 2010, from http://allafrica.com/stories/200804160205.html

Amenga-Etego, R. (2003). *Water privatization in Ghana: women's rights under siege.* Case Study Commissioned by UNIFEM for the 2003 World Social Forum.

Amin, S. (1990). *Maldevelopment: Anatomy of a global failure.* London: Zed Books.

AWOMI (African Women Millennium Initiative on Poverty and Human Rights). (2005). Genre et pauvrete au Senegal–etude diagnostique. AWOMI, Dakar.

Bayliss. K. (2001). Water privatisation in Africa: Lessons from three case studies. Public Services International Research Unit (PSIRU) School of Computing and Mathematical Sciences, University of Greenwich.

Berg, E. (1981). *Accelerated development in sub-Saharan Africa.* Washington, DC: World Bank.

Campbell-White, O., & Bhatia, A. (1998). *Privatisation in Africa.* Washington, DC: International Bank for Reconstruction and Development (IBRD).

Collective Syllepse. (2008). Déforestation: Causes, acteurs et enjeux. *Points de vue du Sud–Alternatives Sud, 15*(3).

Council of Europe. (2002). General information on the General Agreement on Trade in Services (GATS). Secretariat background document, item 5. Strasburg. June 3 . Retrieved March 17, 2011, from http://www.aic.lv/bolona/GATS/GATS_ovw.pdf

Diagne, M. (2009). Pénurie d'eau à Keur Massar: Diaxay 1 et 2 et la cité gendarmerie de Keur Massar privés d'eau depuis trois jours. October 5. Retrieved January 5, 2010, from http://www.seneweb.com/news/article/25791.php

Dumont, R. (1966). L'Afrique noire est mal partie False Start in Africa]. Le Seuil, Paris.

Eberlee, J. (1997). Sex, lies, and global economics: counting the 'invisible' workforce, International Development Research Centre (IDRC), Ottawa. Retrieved January 5, 2010, from http://archive.idrc.ca/books/reports/1997/25-01e.html

Economist, The. (2009). Outsourcing's third wave. *The Economist,* May 21 .

EMG (Environmental Monitoring Group). (n.d.) The water dialogues—South Africa: Enhancing delivery through dialogue. Retrieved March 16, 2011, from http://www.emg.org.za/index.php?option=com_content&view=article&id=33&Itemid=2

Estrada, D. (2007). Chile: indigenous and rural women demand rights, resources. *Inter Press Service English News Wire.* March 26.

Fall, Y. (1997). Social and gender dimensions of stabilization policies in Senegal: Testimony and advocacy. Paper presented by the Development Gap to the US Congress on Behalf of African Women, Washington, DC, April.

———. (2008). *Women's unpaid labour: A blind spot of gender equality in Africa*. Dakar: African Women Millennium Initiative on Poverty and Human Rights (AWOMI).

FAO (Food and Agriculture Organization of the United Nations). (2011). *The state of food and agriculture 2010–2011: Women in agriculture—closing the gender gap for development*. Rome: FAO.

Fiakpa, L. (2008). UNCTAD official blames food crisis on structural adjustment programme. This Day. April 23. Retrieved January 6, 2011, from http://allafrica.com/stories/200804230375.html

Gonzales, A. S. (2010). Sénégal: pénurie d'eau a Thiès—la SDE interpelle par les populations. Le Soleil. June 26.

Grusky, S. (2001). Privatization tidal wave: IMF/World Bank water policies and the price by the poor. Multinational Monitor, September. Retrieved January 6, 2010, from http://www.thirdworldtraveler.com/Water/Privatization_TidalWave.html

Harsch, E. (2001). Making trade work for poor women. *African Recovery*, 15(4). Retrieved March 17, 2011, from http://www.un.org/ecosocdev/geninfo/afrec/vol15no4/154shea.htm

International Crisis Group. (2009). *Annual report 2009*. International Crisis Group, Brussels. Retrieved January 5, 2010, from http://www.reliefweb.int/rw/lib.nsf/db900sid/SNAA-7RY4HR/$file/ICG%20annual%20report%202009.pdf?openelement

Keene, C. (2007). The politics of Senegalese water supply policy: Who bears the most influence? Senior Thesis, Columbia University, April 18.

Ledo-Garcia, C. (2005). Promoting and protecting women's water rights in the context of globalization: Household survey with a gender dimension in the cities of El Alto, La Paz and Cochabamba, Bolivia. Centro de Planificación y Gestión (CEPLAG), Bolivia.

Leonard, A. (2008). The Washington food crisis consensus. April 23 . Retrieved March 17, 2011, from http://www.salon.com/technology/how_the_world_works/2008/04/23/washington_food_crisis_consensus

Mason, B., & Talbot, C. (2002). What water privatisation means for Africa. International Committee of the Fourth International (ICFI). September 7. Retrieved March 17, 2011, from http://www.wsws.org/articles/2002/sep2002/wate-s07.shtml, cited March 17, 2011.

Mbengue, C. T. (2008). Contre la mauvaise qualité de l'eau: la banlieue va marcher. *SudQuotidien*, March 12.

Mulagwanda, M. J. P. (2008). Case study: Management of water and sanitation through women water user groups in Tanzania. Water Supply and Sanitation Collaborative Council. December 15. Retrieved March 16, 2011, from http://www.wsscc.org/resources/resource-peoples-stories/case-study-management-water-and-sanitation-through-women-water

Mutume, G. (2003). Hope seen in the ashes of Cancún: WTO trade talks collapse, as Africa and allies stand firm. *Africa Recovery*, 17(3). October. Retrieved November, 2010 from http://www.un.org/ecosocdev/geninfo/afrec/vol17no3/173wto.htm

New Scientist. (2008). Women farmers face eviction in biofuels boom. *New Scientist* 2654, May 6. Retrieved January 4, 2010, from http://www.newscientist.com/article/mg19826542.900-women-farmers-face-eviction-in-biofuels-boom.html

Schultz, J. (2000). Bolivia's water war victory. *Earth Island Journal*, Autumn. Retrieved March 17, 2011, from http://www.thirdworldtraveler.com/South_America/Bolivia_WaterWarVictory.html

Soguel, D. (2008). Rush to bio-fuel market bypasses female farmers. *WeNews*, April 27. Retrieved January 5, 2011, from http://www.womensenews.org/article.cfm/dyn/aid/3576/context/archive

UNCTAD XII Resource Center. (2008). *Official blames food crisis on structural adjustment*. United Nations Conference on Trade and Development. April 23. Retrieved October 28, 2010, from http://www.iatp.org/unctadxii/headlines.cfm?id=102421

UN Committee on Economic, Social, and Cultural Rights. (2002). Agenda item 3. *Substantive issues arising in the implementation of the International Covenant on Economic, Social and Cultural Rights. General Comment No. 15 (2002). The right to water* (arts. 11 and 12 of the International Covenant on Economic, Social and Cultural Rights). Twenty-ninth session, Geneva, November 11–29.

UNDP (United Nations Development Programme). (2001). *Human development report Senegal*. Dakar: UNDP.

———. (2006). *Human development report 2006—Beyond scarcity: power, poverty and the global water crisis*. New York: Palgrave Macmillan.

———. (2007). *UNDP water governance strategy*. A follow-up to human development report 2006. UNDP/BDP/EEG Water Governance Programme. February.

United Nations. (2010). *Report of the human rights council advisory committee—study on discrimination in the context of the right to food, including identification of good practices of anti-discriminatory policies and strategies*. A/HRC/13/32. January.

von Braun, J., & Meinzen-Dick, R. S. (2009). *"Land grabbing" by foreign investors in developing countries: Risks and opportunities*. Washington, DC: International Food Policy Research Institute (IFPRI).

Waring, M. (1997). *Three masquerades: Essays on equality work and human rights*. Toronto: University of Toronto Press Incorporated.

Water Dialogues. (n.d.) Retrieved March 23, 2011, from http://www.waterdialogues.org/

WFP (World Food Programme). (2009). *Number of world's hungry tops a billion*. Rome: WFP. June 19. Retrieved October 28, 2010, from http://www.wfp.org/stories/number-world-hungry-tops-billion.

WHO (World Health Organization). (2004). *Cholera in Senegal: Update*. Geneva: WHO. November 12. Retrieved January 5, 2010, from http://www.who.int/csr/don/2004_11_12/en/index.html

———. (2010). *Access to safe water improving: Sanitation needs greater efforts*. WHO Media Centre, Geneva. March 15. Rerieved March 17, 2011, from http://www.who.int/mediacentre/news/releases/2010/water_20100315/en/index.html

World Bank. (2008). *Rising food prices: Policy options and World Bank response*. Background note prepared by PREM, ARD, and DEC. April. Retrieved October 28, 2010, from http://siteresources.worldbank.org/NEWS/Resources/risingfoodprices_backgroundnote_apr08.pdf

10

Modernity, Technology, and the Progress of Women in Japan
Problems and Prospects

HIROKO HARA*

The global financial crisis stemming from subprime loan problems in the United States in 2008 has been having, albeit slowly, a profoundly adverse effect on the labor market and the national economy in Japan, and there are looming threats to the progress made toward gender equality.

INTRODUCTION

According to a survey by the Ministry of Health, Labour and Welfare (2008), as of September 2008, there were 31,213 women and 5,063 men aged 100 or more living in Japan. Compared to this, in 1963, when the survey was first conducted, there were just 153 women and men aged 100. Although some of this remarkable growth in longevity is attributable to a rise in the number of births in the country during the last years of the 19th century, the greater part is due to the increased probability of survival (Robine and Saito, 2003). It is a reflection of scientific and technological advances and improved social policies in contemporary Japan, as well as changes in the views and attitudes of families and communities toward the elderly. However, unfortunately, regarding women this phenomenon

---

*The author would like to thank Miwako Shimazu for her support in preparing and writing this chapter.

cannot be regarded as synonymous with their progress. This is because of the deeply rooted notion in Japanese society that a woman's primary role is to bear and raise children (as a good mother) and be obedient to men (as a good wife).

While Japan rates very highly on the Human Development Index (HDI), coming 10th in the world in 2007, it was only 57th on the Gender Empowerment Measure (GEM) (UNDP, 2009). Moreover, it ranked 91st in the World Economic Forum's 2007 Gender Gap Index, falling from 80th in 2006 (Hausmann et al., 2007). Among the obstacles to improving women's empowerment are traditional customs and stereotyped images that directly govern their participation in politics, business administration, and key decision making at home. Vogel (1979) hints that Japan's spectacular economic prosperity (what he calls "the Japanese Miracle") did not necessarily advance women's status. Among a list of serious problems for women he includes "the weight of social pressure ... to make adjustments to avoid divorce" (ibid., p. 240).

While it is true that women's participation in decision making has gradually increased in each field of society and in a wide range of occupations since 1975, but Japan's progress has been slow compared to other nations. Moreover, the global financial crisis stemming from subprime loan problems in the United States in 2008 has been having, albeit slowly, a profoundly adverse effect on the labor market and the national economy in Japan, and there are looming threats to the progress made toward gender equality.

In this chapter, I describe the factors contributing to Japan's high HDI but low gender empowerment rankings, with an emphasis on education and health since 1945. I shed light on the slow but steady headway made by women in the scientific and technological fields, followed by a discussion on the actions of women's nongovernmental organizations (NGOs) in relation to natural disasters, the enactment of women-related laws, and the international women's movement. Finally, I draw conclusions and present my outlook on the future progress of women in Japan.

FACTORS BEHIND JAPAN'S HUMAN DEVELOPMENT AND GENDER-GAP INDEX RANKINGS

Education

A new school system was established after World War II (WWII) that made education compulsory for nine years: six at elementary level and three at junior high level (Ministry of Education, 1980). Moreover, sex discrimination in education was abolished. This is evident from the change in the relevant law to make home economics compulsory for both girls and boys in primary and junior high schools.

During Japan's high economic growth era, from the mid-1950s until the beginning of the 1970s, there was a decrease in the number of workers in primary industries and of the self-employed. At the same time, the number of salaried male workers and full-time housewives increased in response to the growing industrialization and urbanization. Under the national pension system (basic pension), most men fell into the "type two" category (private-sector salaried workers, public-service personnel, and others insured under employee pension plans, as well as members of benefit societies, etc.), followed by women in the same category. However, approximately twice as many women as men were in the "type three" insurance category (dependent on a spouse with type-two insurance), including full-time housewives.

The change in the industrial structure saw a return to the division of subjects by sex from 1962 until the late 1980s, namely technical arts for males and home economics for females. Parents often advised their daughters to find employment or get married to men with a stable income rather than pursue education, and they tended to give their sons more advanced education than their daughters. In the wake of the government's move to sign and ratify the Convention on the Elimination of All Forms of Discrimination against Women (CEDAW), however, the curriculum was again revised in 1987 which made no distinction by sex in the range of subjects to be taken.

In 1969, girls for the first time exceeded boys in terms of the percentage of students going on to receive secondary education (Gender Equality Bureau, 2003). However, a White Paper on National Life also says that during the 1960s and 1970s female students usually went to colleges/universities to acquire a general education based on the premise that they would be full-time housewives (Economic Planning Agency, 1997). In particular, many female students who enrolled in humanities courses later "chose" to retire from companies before turning 25 in order to marry highly educated young men (with the potential to earn large incomes and receive generous pensions) and stay at home.

From the mid-1980s, the Japanese economy shifted its focus toward services and software businesses, and promoted the entrance of more women into the job market (often in lower positions with less salary than men), particularly in tertiary industries. As conditions became more favorable for women to work outside the home, including through implementation of the Equal Employment Opportunity Act in 1986, changes occurred in the field of higher education in two ways: "quantitative expansion" indicated by an increase in the number of women who entered colleges/universities and "qualitative changes" shown by the changes in the distribution of fields of study pursued by female students (Economic Planning Agency, 1997).

After 1995 more women began to opt for social sciences (Basic School Survey, 2008). This change in majors affected the growing diversity of employment among graduates. Nevertheless, not only have the job openings for those women who have completed master's/doctoral courses remained quite narrow, but even after they become employed, gender discrimination is still practiced—for example, in respect to participation in training courses abroad and joint-research projects (and opportunities to head those projects), as well as opportunities for promotion and salary increase. Many women are subject to sexual harassment.

In fiscal year 1996–1997, the author and others conducted a gender analysis of a survey on the careers of female and male researchers (Hara et al., 1999). The analysis focused on the correlation between the respondents' achievement index, as defined by the survey team, and the average number of children they had. There was a marked difference by gender. Whereas men with a high score tended to have more than the average number of children, women with a high score had very few or no children. This suggests that in the course of building up a research career, married life with children works advantageously for men but not necessarily for women (ibid.).

In response to the United Nations International Women's Year in 1975, when awareness was heightened that there were no women among its members, the Science Council of Japan (SCJ) began to address the issue of the advancement of women research scientists, albeit slowly. The number of women among the 210 members is gradually rising: in 1982–1985 there was one female member, whereas in 2008–2011 there are 11. Substantial improvements were slowly coming in until May 26, 1994, when the SCJ General Assembly adopted a "Recommendation on the Urgency of Improving the Research Environment for Women Scientists (Statement)." This made the point, "Allowing many more women to get involved in scientific research would likely lead to further advancement in science." Subsequently, women members of the SCJ and its satellite organizations, including the author, founded the Japanese Association for the Improvement of Conditions of Women Scientists (JAICOWS). Its main goal is to protect the human rights of women researchers, especially in relation to research conditions and security of livelihood, and to promote gender equality in the field of scientific research.

Health

In Japan, there is a tendency to prioritize children's health and welfare over that of mothers. Moreover, health policies are often not women friendly. They are a reflection of the principle of "men as breadwinners and women as good wives and wise mothers."

Infant and Maternal Mortality

Japan has successfully reduced both infant and maternal mortality rates; with the mortality rates for infants falling further than that for mothers. In fact, the infant mortality rate fell dramatically from 61.7 per 1,000 live births in 1948 to 30.7 in 1960, 13.1 in 1970, 7.5 in 1980, and 4.6 in 1990 (National Institute of Social Security and Population Research, 2008). The maternal mortality rate per 100,000 births decreased from 156.7 in 1951 to 108.2 in 1961, 42.5 in 1971, 18.3 in 1982, and 8.6 in 1991 (ibid.). According to statistics cited by the United Nations Development Programme (UNDP, 2005), Japan's infant mortality rate in 2005 was the second lowest among 176 countries, together with Czech Republic, Finland, Norway, Singapore, Slovenia, and Sweden, compared to a ranking of 16 in its maternal mortality ratio among 164 countries, the same as Hungary, the Netherlands, Slovakia, and Slovenia.

Causes of Death

There was no sex difference in the top three causes of death in 2007, namely malignant neoplasm (cancer), cardiac disease, and cerebrovascular disease (Ministry of Health, Labour and Welfare, 2007a). However, one cause of death that does exhibit sex differences is suicide, levels of which are higher for men than women (Ministry of Health, Labour and Welfare, 2007b). The fact that suicide-death rates peak at ages 55–59 could be interpreted as men choosing to commit suicide when suddenly confronted with dismissal from or lack of advancement at the workplace, having since childhood pursued the goal of what Osawa (2007) calls the "breadwinner model," or, to put it another way, men falling victim to Japan's cultural norms. To make things worse, men do not readily go for counseling or seek advice to relieve their anxieties about mental and physical health, although this situation is slowly improving (Ministry of Health, Labour and Welfare, 2007b, 2007c).

HIV and AIDS

Japan prides itself on its mother-to-child HIV and AIDS prevention policy. However, although pregnant women are tested for HIV and AIDS during medical checkups in the early period of their pregnancy, those who test positive can then be examined only at one of the 71 (as of March 31, 2008) AIDS Core Hospitals, though only some of these have obstetricians. Further, in some cases, women who have tested positive take second and third tests at an AIDS Core Hospital and are later told that the initial test result was wrong. Medical practitioners seem to lack the imagination to understand the distress pregnant women are bound to feel when informed of infection, and they need training in counseling methods. Many of the women who find themselves in this situation are hesitant to reveal it to their husband/partner, parents, or anybody else, and suffer in excruciating loneliness. In contrast, there is no requirement for husbands/partners to be tested. It seems as though there is a tacit belief in medical circles and the health administration that the foremost obligation of a mother is to give birth to a healthy baby; women who get pregnant knowing that they are HIV-positive are assumed to be evil and not to care about their responsibility to their children.

Reproductive and Sexual Health/Rights

Although, as noted earlier, maternal mortality rates have gone down over the course of time, the number of obstetricians/gynaecologists has fallen nationwide; in 2004, the number decreased in 35 of 47 prefectures (Social Security Council, 2007). This is due to a combination of factors including the long work hours, the heavy financial burden incurred by low wages, and the need for increased insurance against lawsuits (Ministry of Health, Labour and Welfare, 2007b). The number of private maternity clinics run by authorized midwives is also declining. Article 19 of the Medical Services Law provides, "the founders of maternity clinics ... shall designate commissioned doctors and hospitals/clinics." However, as fewer and fewer doctors accept the commission, maternity clinics are forced to close.

This situation makes it difficult for pregnant women to make an appointment for their delivery. In some cases, they move to another municipality in order to reserve a bed. Recently the nation has been shaken by a number of incidents involving women in labor who were taken to hospital by ambulance due to their exhibiting symptoms of a serious condition, but who were initially refused admittance for reasons ranging from no spare beds to no available doctors. Some of them lost their lives. There are only a small number of places where an appropriate network has been built among public hospitals, university hospitals, medical practitioners, and fire departments in charge of ambulances in order to minimize the occurrence of such incidents.

Contraception and Abortion

Thanks to the efforts of women's NGOs and concerned Diet (Parliament) members, the Ministry of Health and Welfare officially approved low-dose birth control pills in June 1999, nine years after the first application had been received by the Central Pharmaceutical Affairs Council. Nevertheless, medical products that are permitted for use are limited to those listed at the time of application in 1990. In 2008, public medical insurance was extended to a low-dose pill approved to treat complications of endometriosis, but it is banned for use as a contraceptive. Japan does not officially sanction emergency contraception.

Abortion is legal only if the conditions stipulated in Article 3 of the Mother's Body Protection Law are met—namely, doctors judge that continuation of pregnancy is undesirable for the health of the mother or for economic reasons—and both partners give consent. Since the 1970s, some politicians and religious groups have been claiming that the clause on "economic reasons" should be deleted. However, this threatens to restore the concept of "illegal abortion" found in the Penal Act, under which women who have had abortions, including rape victims, as well as medical doctors who have performed the operations, are penalized (while men who have made women pregnant against their will are not)—except as covered by the Mother's Body Protection Law. While opinions among women are not necessarily unanimous on this point, NGOs, obstetricians/gynaecologists, and midwives who support reproductive rights are endeavouring to prevent the revival of "illegal abortions."

Women and Scientific and Technological Advances

Although all seven national universities began to admit female students— at least in principle—in 1946, only an extremely small number of women majored in social sciences, natural sciences, and engineering. Women's employment opportunities after graduation remained heavily limited. Therefore, only a handful of women were able to contribute to Japan's scientific and technological advances during the 20th century. Those pioneering women who were fortunate enough to work with male researchers who acted as their mentors were able to lead a creative research life and obtain a doctoral degree in their specialized field of study so as to make significant contributions to academia both within and outside Japan. More recently, the number of women playing a prominent part in the field of natural sciences, and science and technology has increased.

Women Researchers

The *White Book on Science and Technology* (Ministry of Education, Culture, Sports, Science and Technology, 2008) gives special attention to "women researchers," including women engineers, reflecting its subtitle "Science and technology to overcome fierce international competition in the field." As previously pointed out, however, the percentage of women in science and technology research in Japan is extremely low; at 12.4 percent it is almost the lowest among developed countries, compared to Latvia with 52.7 percent and the United States with 32.5 percent (ibid.).

To offset the noticeable decrease in the number of male students choosing to pursue science and technology in the mid-1980s, the then Science and Technology Agency set out to prepare policies to encourage female junior high and high school students to enter these fields. After 2000, the Government began to actively recruit women research scientists as it became more difficult to secure enough human resources in science and technology. This is partly because of the rapidly aging population and declining birth rates, and partly because—as noted earlier—many more male students prefer the service industries to the manufacturing industries (Ministry of Labour, 1982, 1988). The Science and Technology Basic Plan for the third term (fiscal 2006–2010) introduced various measures to increase the active involvement of women researchers.

Spurred on by the enactment of the Basic Law for a Gender-equal Society in 1999 and the formulation of the Science and Technology Basic Plan for the second term (fiscal 2001–2005) among others, 29 academic societies in science and engineering fields (most of which are headed by men) joined together in October 2002 to organize an NGO called Japan Inter-Society Liaison Association Committee for Promoting Equal

Participation of Men and Women in Science and Engineering (EPMEWSE). Its committee board consists of both women and men, and its member associations take turns to function as the Secretariat.

EPMEWSE succeeded in having two important proposals adopted in 2004: one to improve childcare support systems appropriate for researchers in science and technology; and the other to expand the range of researchers entitled to apply for research grants. In 2005, the committee filed a "Request concerning Science and Technology Basic Plan for the third term——toward the realization of a gender-equal society," made up of the following:

- Create/continue a system for model projects to promote equal participation of men and women, and ensure its flexible implementation.
- Set numerical targets regarding the employment and promotion of women researchers, and introduce special subsidies.
- Put in place measures to narrow differences in the treatment of men and women.
- Promote specific measures for childcare support.
- Promote "Challenge Campaigns" for schoolgirls wishing to study science and/or engineering at universities/colleges.

Other organizations working to advance the status of women in the sciences include the Japan Scientists Association (JSA), set up in 1965, and the Japan Women Engineers' Forum (JWEF), founded in 1992.

Impact of Science and Technology Advances on Household Labor

The widespread diffusion of cars and home appliances—radios, TVs, washing machines, vacuum cleaners, dishwashers, and accompanying chemicals and related items (cleaners, detergents for windows and dishes, dust cloths)—as well as other products such as ready-made food was driven by marketing campaigns that emphasized a reduction in household chores, giving women more time for their own interests, such as lifelong learning and social participation in diverse fields (Amano, 2003; Amano et al., 2007). However, statistics indicate that working women still spend an average of 3 hours and 28 minutes per day on housework—less than full-time housewives (at 4 hours and 42 minutes) but far more than husbands who, whether their wife is working or not, spend only about

10 minutes (Ministry of Health, Labour and Welfare, Equal Employment, Children and Family Bureau, 2008). A few women choose to work part time instead of full time so as to supplement the income earned by their husbands and at the same time to fully perform their duties as housewives.

Since 1945, most Japanese households—except for the highest economic strata—have had no paid domestic workers, and household labor and childcare are mainly housewives' responsibility. In recent years, however, there has been an increase in the number of users of private services in which hourly paid housework specialists do cleaning, gardening, and other chores. Among the six leading companies in this field, all but one limit services to the Tokyo metropolitan area and its environs and/or major cities across the nation. The prices set by these companies range widely, from roughly JPY 2,000–3,000 per hour (at the time of writing, 84 Japanese yen [JPY] = 1 United States dollar [USD]).

The Government encourages companies and municipalities to enable working women and men to achieve work–life balance, but this is still far from becoming a reality. There have been some rare cases since 1990, some of them published in books that have caught the public's attention, where the wife earns a higher income than the husband and/or the husband does household chores and looks after children as a full-time househusband. Overall, however, Japan's progress in science and technology so far has hardly contributed to the equal sharing between husband and wife of household labor or to closing the income disparities between women and men.

NATURAL DISASTERS AND WOMEN

The Effects of Earthquakes on Women

The most common natural disasters in Japan are earthquakes and typhoons. In 1995 the Great Hanshin-Awaji Earthquake devastated the densely populated urban areas of Kobe. Nearly 1,000 more women than men were killed (Hyogo Prefecture, 2005), including elderly, low-income women who were living alone. There were also reports at the scene of the disaster and at evacuation sites, as well as via a telephone hotline, of violence against women and children. The privately run, toll-free hotline for women suffering from mental/physical problems received a total of 1,635 calls between February and June 1995 related to insomnia, fear, and anxiety; family and human relations; concerns about children, employment, and sexual harassment; and over 100 cases of child abuse (Council for Gender Equality, 2005).

Emergency measures put in place right after the disaster, as well as interventions by the national and local governments, imposed requirements based on the male breadwinner model, leaving women disadvantaged. For example, some full-time women employees who had to take leave after the disaster to care for injured or sick family members and/or clean their houses, lost their jobs, while many women in non-regular employment as part-timers or "dispatched" workers were refused renewed work contracts by managers attempting to reconstruct their damaged companies (dispatched workers are hired and fired by employment agencies).

Integrating Gender into Disaster Preparation and Relief

Based on the experiences of the catastrophic earthquake in 1995, Women's Net Kobe—a women's NGO that had been established in 1992 with the aim of upgrading women's status—published reports and books on the gender issues related to disaster relief, protection, and reconstruction of livelihoods. This, in turn, has meant that disaster measures put in place by other NGOs, and later by the national and local governments, have taken gender into consideration. Moreover, since 1995, the Japanese media have in general promoted the need for collaboration between women and men in disaster prevention, relief, and reconstruction, although not as much as they could have (Women's Net Kobe, 2005).

At the time of the 2004 Niigata–Chuetsu Earthquake, the Cabinet Office for the first time sent a woman official to the local support office of the Gender Equality Bureau to demonstrate its concern for women's needs in health and daily life. Immediately after the December 2004 Indian Ocean Tsunami, the Government also remitted funds amounting to USD 1 million to the United Nations Development Fund for Women (UNIFEM) for the support of victims (Cabinet Office, 2006).

At the World Conference on Disaster Reduction in January 2005, the Government proposed the "Initiative for Disaster Reduction through ODA [official development assistance]," which enumerates "gender perspectives" as one of its basic policies. As a result, this policy was incorporated into the revisions of Japan's Basic Disaster Management Plan (first drawn up in 1963) in July 2005 and February 2008. The Second Basic Plan for Gender Equality, adopted by Cabinet in December 2005, also cites "disaster prevention and relief" under the measure to "promote gender equality in fields requiring new initiatives." The Government was influenced by the actions mounted by Women's Net Kobe and other women's NGOs throughout Japan urging it to address the issue.

The 2007 Japanese Women's Conference in Hiroshima took up the issue of "disaster and women's policy." This annual conference, held in a different Japanese city each year, is designed and organized by local governments and women's NGOs. Three women NGO leaders debated with male staff from the Ministry of Land, Infrastructure and Transport and the Hiroshima Fire Department. The Conference concluded that there was an urgent need to promote gender equality before disasters occur, and that the mindset of every individual concerned was important (Working Committee for Japan Women's Conference, 2007).

In March 2008, almost a year after an earthquake struck the Noto Peninsula in Ishikawa Prefecture, the Conference on Disaster Prevention for Women was held in the Ishikawa Prefecture town of Anamizumachi, sponsored by local welfare groups and the town office. The "Anamizu Declaration," adopted by participants who gathered from all parts of Japan, called for ensuring that women participate in the operation of evacuation sites and the management of temporary housing; offering more support to women, who take key responsibilities in the community and at home and hence should play a major role in the recovery and rebuilding of livelihoods; and encouraging the participation of women in the process of rebuilding society to reduce disaster and work toward the creation of a society that gives due respect to diverse values and regional cultures without excluding minorities.

Women's NGOs have influenced the administration of local governments to look at disaster prevention from a gender perspective. For example, in a 2008 survey of 47 prefectures, 63.8 percent (30) answered "yes" when asked if they had held discussions on gender equality and how it should be integrated into policies in the field of disaster prevention (National Governors Association, 2008). However, when asked if there are any specific policies or systems to reflect women's opinions in the field of disaster prevention, only 23.4 percent (11), said "yes," which constitutes a major challenge for the future.

Laws for Gender Equality in Japan

Equality between women and men in Japan was specified for the first time in the Constitution enacted on November 3, 1946. Japanese women gained the right to vote in that same year through the revision of the Election Law for the House of Representatives (Lower House). Between signing CEDAW in 1980 and ratifying it in 1985, Japan overhauled its legal system, including revision of the Nationality Law (1984) and enactment of the Equal Employment Opportunity Act (1985). Later, following deliberations in the Diet, there was a partial revision of the Labour Standards Act (1997).

Women's movements in each field concerned played a crucial role prior to the enactment of dozens of other laws for gender equality, including the Labour Standards Act (1947), Equal Employment Opportunity Act (1985), Basic Law for a Gender-equal Society (1999), Act on Punishment of Activities Relating to Child Prostitution and Child Pornography, and the Protection of Children (1999), Law Concerning the Welfare of Workers Who Take Care of Children (1991) (revised in 1995), Food, Agriculture and Rural Areas Basic Act (1999), Law for the Prevention of Spousal Violence and the Protection of Victims (2001), and the Elder Abuse Prevention and Caregiver Support Law (2005), to name a few.

The Basic Law for a Gender-equal Society, passed unanimously by both the Lower and Upper Houses of the Diet, was a landmark:

> In essence, this Basic Law calls for a transition in social institutions and practices from a male breadwinner model to a neutral type social policy system (Article 4) and for support to ensure compatibility of home-related and workplace activities (Article 6). This is in accordance with the "gender mainstreaming" called for in the Beijing Platform for Action. (Osawa, 2007, pp. 88–89)

The Headquarters for the Planning and Promotion of Policies Relating to Women—established in 1975, under the Prime Minister's Office, to promote gender-equality policies and build awareness of the situation of women—was superseded by the Gender Equality Bureau, which was established under the Cabinet Office in 2001 as part of central government reform. The strengthening of the national machinery has given rise to the development of gender equality sections of local governments, albeit slowly. Again, the impetus for such favourable changes came largely from NGOs.

Under the existing laws, demands made by women can only be partially dealt with by legal means for two main reasons. One is the low percentage of female Diet members (9.2 percent for the Lower House and 18.2 percent for the Upper House as of 2009) (Gender Equality Bureau, 2009). Moreover, some female Diet members are against pursuing gender equality (although there are some male Diet members who are in favor). Another reason is that the majority of government officials and lawyers remain gender-insensitive. Hence, women's movements, together with autonomous organizations, have been seeking out Diet members who could support women and striving to gain the understanding of ministers and officials of related ministries toward the goal of revising the current laws.

Some women who have suffered discrimination—with respect to retirement systems, wages, loss of jobs, maternal protection, sexual harassment, domestic violence, and human trafficking, among others—have stood up as plaintiffs to bring the case to court, refusing to be brushed off by arguments in legal circles that such matters do not lend themselves to litigation. In pushing for the expansion of women's rights, many have mounted tenacious challenges and eventually won their cases, helped by the work of supporters in the women's movement and from the general public, as well as understanding lawyers and specialists, both women and men.

The Committee on Equality of Men and Women within the Japan Federation of Bar Associations (established in 1949) has been playing a significant part in advancing women's rights under the law. One of the Committee's activities is the publication of a 10-volume series detailing selected cases of discrimination against women, which was started in November 2008 and is expected to be completed in 2012. The series documents the experiences of people who have struggled against discrimination, with reprints of materials on related court cases, in order to examine the contemporary meaning of each case in the context of the development of women's rights.

However, while policies on women have been hammered out to some degree, in accordance with laws proposed by government ministries as well as those enacted through legislation drafted by Diet members, changes toward gender equality have been quite slow because of lack of understanding at the workplace and in communities, as well as recent harsh economic conditions.

Women's NGOs in Japan and the International Women's Movement

NGOs Active at National Level

The Japanese Association of University Women (JAUW) was founded in 1946, and up to 1978 it consisted of interested graduates from eight women's professional schools (transformed into women's universities/colleges between 1948 and 1949). In 1979, it began to accept graduates from four-year colleges and universities across Japan. Since its establishment, JAUW has been conducting fact-finding surveys on women receiving university education and making proposals to the Ministry of Education, Science, Sports, and Technology. Its Japanese name was changed to Daigaku Josei Kyokai in 2008, reflecting a change in the term for "women" from *fujin* to *josei*. The former is often associated with obedience, while the latter is more neutral.

The Japan Housewives' Association (Shufuren), set up in 1948, grew out of a nationwide campaign by housewives to stop the distribution of defective matches. Since then, it has taken the initiative in energetically campaigning against price hikes on rice, the staple food in Japan, and carrying out quality inspections on basic commodities, which has included advocacy with relevant government committees at national and local levels.

The members of the National Federation of Regional Women's Organizations (Zenchifuren) used to work in women's regional groups set up by residents within a village or town as a unit under the supervision of prefecture boards of education, before switching from top–down organizational management to decision making by all concerned members. In the early period of its establishment, it undertook nationwide campaigns in favor of fair elections and the enactment of the Anti-Prostitution Law, and against restoring the family system (see Box 10.1), raising train fares, and increasing the price of rice. In 1968, Zenchifuren started to manufacture and sell inexpensive "Chifure" cosmetics in order to provide quality products while cutting the cost of containers and advertising. During the 1970s, it expanded into a nationwide organization with the participation of all 47 prefectures. The present membership is estimated to be as many as 5 million (Kato, personal communication, 2009).[1]

In September 1982, the first symposium on women's self-support and aging was held and bore fruit with the formation of the Women's Association for a Better Aging Society (WABAS) in 1983. In 1994, WABAS adjusted its name to reflect Japan's transition from an "aging" society to an "aged" society (although its English name remains unchanged). Its message is that the long-held conviction that care for the elderly is one of the sacrificial roles of women (see Box 10.1) constitutes the principal cause of

---

[1] Sayuri Kato, head of the Secretariat for Chifuren, personal communication, January 4, 2009.

the low wages of care workers. WABAS asserts that respect for women's rights is essential for successful collaboration between women and men in caretaking, establishing a reasonable wage structure for care workers, and maintaining the dignity and autonomy of those being cared for.

Box 10.1 Increasing elder poverty and the burden of care

Although the percentage of women among the aged (those 65 years and over) is higher than that of men in Japan, life insurance benefits, including pensions, are generally more generous for men than women. Women on average have less savings than men, and the growing population of elderly women is propelling the trend toward the feminization of poverty. Moreover, women account for about 70 percent of those taking care of the elderly and the sick.

The family system, known as ie, traditionally set out specific roles for the family head, successors, children, and even the deceased. It was taken for granted that women, typically the wife of the oldest son or the daughters, should care for elderly parents. This social norm used to be deep rooted, as signified by "most dutiful daughter-in-law awards" presented by the head of local governments every year until the 1980s in some regions. In the case of Kochi Prefecture, only those daughters-in-law who had children of their own were entitled to apply for this competition; a childless woman, no matter how attentively she cared for her husband's parents (and sometimes an uncle and aunt as well), was excluded from consideration as a candidate. Although ie was legally abolished following WWII, and some of the burden of care for the elderly eventually shifted from families to society, it continues to influence attitudes.

In 1997, WABAS played a central role in the establishment of the Long-Term Care Insurance Act, which was a landmark law in its interpretation of caretaking as a public rather than a private responsibility. More recently, it has been making policy recommendations in cooperation with other NGOs working on the issues of Japan's aging society in response to a growing trend for care workers to leave their jobs due to unfavorable treatment at the workplace.

Mirroring the growing number of men taking on the responsibility of caring for sick wives, parents, grandparents, uncles, and aunts, there are men among WABAS' regular and advisory members. Male members include medical and social welfare personnel, voluntary social welfare workers, journalists, and social scientists engaged in empirical studies on caretaking. Currently, the Association has a membership of approximately 1,200 individuals and 100 groups and organizations from across Japan. WABAS has expressed support for an NGO of male caretakers and their supporters called "Man nursing and support persons nationwide networks," launched on International Women's Day (March 8) 2009.

Other important NGOs are the Asia-Japan Women's Resource Center (AJWRC), which engages in actions for the protection of the rights of women in Asia and Japan, and Japan's Network for Women and Health (WHJ), which was formed in advance of the International Conference on Population and Development (ICPD) in 1994. WHJ, working in cooperation with other organizations, including those of disabled people, achieved the revision of the National Eugenics Law in 1996 and the approval of low-dose contraceptive pills. Since 1994, it has been conducting dialogs with the Government on a regular basis in collaboration with other NGOs to facilitate the incorporation of gender perspectives into Japan's framework of international cooperation.

National Women's Committee of UN NGOs

In 1957, a year after Japan's accession to the United Nations, a member of the Diet Upper House and others founded the National Women's Committee of UN NGOs and requested the Government to allow women to participate in UN meetings and conferences as part of the official Japanese delegation. Thanks to this, from 1957 onward the Government has consistently allowed women NGO members to join its delegation to the Third Committee of the UN General Assembly and at times to deliver statements.Japanese government officials were designated as the official representative of the delegation at most of the annual sessions of the CSW between 1958 and 1976, but since 1978 women NGO members have been filling this role, although with the provision that every statement presented must follow the directions issued by the Government. These were important steps for preparing Japanese women for the world conferences on women as well as the series of international conferences on development beginning in the 1990s.

In the third Preparatory Committee meeting for the ICPD in 1994, the author, who served as an NGO advisory member of the government delegation, made an intervention concerning Chapter 7 of the draft ICPD Programme of Action. After that, other women members of Japanese NGOs joined government delegations as advisors at major UN conferences, including the ICPD itself in Cairo in 1994, the World Summit for Social Development in Copenhagen in 1995, and the World Summit on Sustainable Development in Johannesburg in 2002. In these processes, women's NGOs gained knowledge about the UN system, networked with many women and men across various countries/regions, and reported their experiences on the international stage back to their colleagues in Japan.

International Women's Year and the Women's Movement in Japan

Stimulated by the UN's designation of 1975 as International Women's Year, women's NGOs nationwide joined with women's departments of labor unions to form the International Women's Year Liaison Group (IWYLG) and held the International Women's Year Conference of Japan. This was followed by the UN Decade for Women Conference of Japan in 1980 and the Mid-term Year of the UN Decade for Women Conference of Japan in 1985. These three conferences, which top officials of government ministries and agencies as well as National Diet members attended as guests, discussed recent UN actions and activities, as well as related issues, relevant to women's NGOs.

Since its establishment, the IWYLG has submitted numerous requests concerning key issues to the Government. For example, in 1976, in meetings with top government officials, it called for the formulation of a national plan of action for achieving equality between women and men and also for making home economics compulsory for both female and male students. The IWYLG continues to be proactive, through submission of requests/demands and attendance at Diet sessions on the enactment/revision of laws related to a wide range of policies affecting women, including the tax system and the Government's formulation of the national plan of action.

NGOs and UN Conferences

Some 200 members of women's NGOs in Japan participated in the UN First World Conference on Women held in Mexico City (Hara et al., 1986). Until then, many Japanese women had believed that the country should try to attain the level of equality between the sexes achieved in Western countries. However, upon listening to the issues and challenges facing women in developing countries, some of the participants in this conference recognized the need for solidarity with those women as well.

At the Fourth World Conference on Women in Beijing in 1995, about 5,000 participants from Japan are said to have joined the NGO Forum on Women, held in Huairou (Office for Gender Equality, 1996). This large turnout was partly due to geographical proximity and partly to the relatively generous subsidies from each local government. Staff from the departments of gender equality in prefectures and municipalities called on the public to support participation in the Forum and led the trip. This experience prompted local governments to put more energy into measures for gender equality.

In November 1995, participants in the Beijing Conference from women's NGOs established a group called Japan Accountability Caucus, Beijing (Beijing JAC). Its mission was to set up a Ministry of Women and to formulate the Law for Equality between Men and Women and the Anti-Violence Law. Beijing JAC has local chapters throughout the country that network for joint action when the need arises. The Caucus initially had no representative or leader, preferring a more collective approach with all group members being responsible for consensus building and expression of opinions. However, after realizing that national and local governments would not accept petitions and written opinions without a representative's signature, it created a leadership position. Beijing JAC continues to advance the 12 Critical Areas of Concern in the Beijing Platform for Action and to address the emerging issues that have gained attention since then.

CEDAW and Japanese NGOs

As noted earlier, CEDAW was ratified by the Government in 1985, and it came into force on July 25 of that year. Seizing this opportunity, a group of women—primarily private lawyers and legal scholars who recognized the importance of the convention—established the Japanese Association of International Women's Rights (JAIWR) to elevate the status of women through research and dissemination of information on the convention. JAIWR publishes a number of periodicals on CEDAW, including the annual *Kokusai Josei* (*International Women*), and holds symposia and seminars. Every year since 1997 it has honored an individual who has made a substantial contribution to the advancement of women by promoting CEDAW.

However, in spite of JAIWR's appeals regarding the Optional Protocol to CEDAW, adopted by the UN General Assembly in 1999, Japan has not yet signed it. The Optional Protocol contains an individual communications procedure, and Japan has not accepted the communications procedures under any international human rights treaty. However, the Government has stated that it is giving consideration to this matter (Government of Japan, 2008).

After its first meeting in December 2002, the Japan NGO Network for CEDAW (JNNC) compiled a detailed input to Japan's periodic reports (JNNC, 2003), to be submitted by the Government to the CEDAW Committee's 2003 session (UN, 2003). It then began lobbying the Government, Diet members, and Committee members in charge of Japan's periodic reports at the UN. For the submission of Japan's sixth periodic report, the JNNC gained the active support of as many as 29 organizations from a variety of fields.

The Future of Women's NGOs

From the mid-1990s onward, women have been organizing in new networks that are focused on a particular issue (see Box 10.2). Of those groups that were established after 1945 and were most active during the period from around 1975 until 1995, some are dwindling due to the aging of members while some have no members in the 30–49 age bracket. The exceptions are those, few in number, with members in their 30s such as Zenkoku Josei Sheruta Netto, JNNC, and JAIWR. Many of the women's groups organized during the 1970s wave of women's liberation were characterized by equality without any hierarchy; that is, decision-making was collective. Although most of these disappeared over the course of time, those that remain now specify the division of duties to be assigned to posts such as representatives, vice-representatives, and secretaries.

Box 10.2 New types of women's groups in Japan after 1996

New women's networks in Japan are often organized around a specific issue. For example, Zenkoku Josei Sheruta Netto, formed in 1998, is a network of private grassroots shelters for survivors of domestic violence. It staged a successful campaign for the enactment of the Domestic Violence Prevention Law, contributing to the law's first and second revisions, and continues to exert an influence on the measures taken in each region to eradicate domestic violence. It is also making all-out efforts to improve the operation of various legal systems relevant to the elimination of violence against women.

Space Allies, which opened an office within the Allies Law Office in 2000, also focuses on domestic violence support activities as well as international collaboration in the areas of women's rights and women's health.

(*Box 10.2 continued*)

(*Box 10.2 continued*)

> Japan Women's Watch (JAWW) was founded in 2001 with the objective of expanding nationwide activities for the UN's 10-year review of the Fourth World Conference on Women (known as "Beijing+10") in 2005. Its major activities have included workshops on the themes to be covered, compilation of NGO reports, participation in CSW sessions, and lobbying the Government on various aspects related to CEDAW.
>
> The Women's Archive Center was opened at the National Women's Education Center in 2008. The Archive, comprising materials on activities by women NGOs in Japan (especially those organized immediately after WWII), recognizes the critical role of women's NGOs in promoting gender equality.

The future of women's NGOs in Japan hinges on three issues: First, they need to acquire skills in raising funds for their sustainability, including the ability to pay decent, if not high, salaries to the staff. Second, those NGOs established before and after 1995 should seek ways to form networks, however loose they may be. Third, NGOs established by younger generations (aged under 40) should also be given financial support. This would be possible if donations to support NGOs were subject to tax exemptions by revising the current regulations to cover a wider range of donors. For many women's NGOs in Japan, the road ahead is bound to be difficult due to extremely tight financing, which makes it almost impossible for women to engage in NGO activities as a profession.

CONCLUSION

The technological advances and economic growth Japan has achieved since WWII, along with its high HDI, do not directly correlate with an advancement in the status of women. This could be regarded as one of the downsides of "the Japanese Miracle." Instead, in the 1980s, the Government—together with industries—pushed forward the sexual division of labor, which maintains "men should work outside and women stay home," thereby establishing what Osawa (2007, p. 54) terms a "livelihood security system for the male breadwinner model."

Salaried men's wives used to enjoy various benefits, including exemption from income declaration up to a designated amount, family benefits and health insurance as a dependent of their husband, and payment of half the pension their husband would have received after his retirement or death. As a result, it was often the case that those wives who worked part-time adjusted their working hours so that their income would not exceed the specific amount that required income declaration every year. In other words, the pension premiums that single, working women and men paid every month were allotted to pension payments for full-time housewives whose husbands were salaried men. This system long constrained wives with abusive husbands from seeking a divorce.

Although the recession Japan experienced in the 1990s presented a threat to the male breadwinner model, the situation did not improve for women. In fact, employment opportunities were still extremely limited for those housewives who sought work outside the home when their husbands lost their jobs; even if these women could find a job, it was usually part-time or contract work at best, and they were compelled to accept low wages.

In accordance with the principles of the Basic Law for a Gender-equal Society, the 1999 Basic Plan for Gender Equality and the 2005 Second Basic Plan for Gender Equality provide for specific measures to be taken. These actions have been decided on by the Cabinet and thus are being introduced into the policies and budgets of government ministries as well as local governments nationwide. Since 2004, social security and tax systems have shifted from "household-based" to "individual-based," with the abolition of special tax deduction for spouses and the introduction of pension splitting on divorce as part of the pension reform.

According to the labor statistics on women issued since 1998 by the Ministry of Health, Labour and Welfare, the number of contract employees shows a steady increase every year, while the percentage of women among them remains at the 70 percent level. When it comes to the number of non-regular workers who have lost jobs, no sex-disaggregated data are available. Similarly, there are currently no government documents to confirm the high percentage of women leaving jobs and the low percentage of women re-entering the job market. Research is needed on the possible impact of the current crisis on the gender gaps in entitlement to social security benefits.

More women feel there is still persistent sex discrimination than men do, and, regrettably, a high percentage of men and women of all ages do not recognize sexual harassment and sexual violence as crimes. When asked about equality between the sexes, 63.4 percent said they feel women and men are "equal" in school education, which is exceptionally high in comparison with equality in terms of legal and social systems (39.5 percent), conventional wisdom/conventions/customs (20.2 percent), and Japanese society as a whole (20.9 percent). Conversely, the percentages of those who said they feel "men are treated more favourably than women" were 15.1 in school education, 48.2 in family life, 60.9 at the workplace, 67.9 in politics, 72.3 in conventional wisdom/conventions/customs, and 73.2 in the society as a whole. When classified by age group, more men (72.5 percent) and women (84.2 percent) aged 30–39 feel that men are treated more favorably than women and that women and men are not equal, than do men (62.5 percent) and women (75.8 percent) aged 20–29 years (Cabinet Office, 2007).

At the same time, based on my day-to-day experiences, an increasing number of men seem to feel that the realization of gender equality in Japanese and global society is essential to the solution of environmental problems, peace, and sustainability, although studies show that men are less concerned about the environment than women (see, for example, Fuji Global Network, 2009). Related to this, a Gender Equality Bureau report on communities proposes that various issues—such as a drop in the vitality of communities, childcare provision, domestic violence, women's reemployment, self-support and social participation of elders, and so on—are best solved through the linkage and collaboration of various actors incorporating the perspective of gender equality (Cabinet Office, 2008).

At the same time, some women and men of all ages still believe "male superiority over female" is the basis of a sound society and should be preserved. Overcoming this viewpoint is a serious issue to be faced, and necessitates the solidarity of all people—women, men, and children—who share aspirations to achieve gender equality.

References

Amano, M. (2003). *The development of "things" that helped working women.* Japan Association for the Advancement of Working Women. [In Japanese].

Amano, M., Ishitani, J., & Kimura, R. (2007). *The post-war history of things and children.* Tokyo: Yoshikawa Kobunkan. [In Japanese].

Basic School Survey. (2008). *Summary of the quick report of the survey result* (higher schools). Retrieved October 2, 2010, from http://www.mext.go.jp/b_menu/toukei/001/08072901/002.pdf [In Japanese].

Cabinet Office. (2006). *White book on disaster prevention.* Tokyo. [In Japanese].

———. (2007). *Public opinion poll on gender equality.* Press Release. Retrieved October 2, 2010, from http://www8.cao.go.jp/survey/h19/h19-danjyo/index.html [In Japanese].

———. (2008). *White book on an aging society.* Saeki-insatsu. Retrieved October 2, 2010, from http://www8.cao.go.jp/kourei/whitepaper/w-2008/zenbun/html/s1-1-1-01.html [In Japanese].

Council for Gender Equality. (2005). *Intermediate report on the basic direction of policy concerning the promotion of building a gender equal society*. Tokyo: Council for Gender Equality. [In Japanese].

Economic Planning Agency. (1997). *White paper on national life* (Part I, Chapter 4-1). Retrieved October 2, 2010, from http://wp.cao.go.jp/zenbun/seikatsu/wp-pl97/wp-pl97-01401.html [In Japanese].

Fuji Global Network. (2009). *A survey on environmental awareness*. Retrieved October 2, 2010, from http://www.fgn.jp/mpac/sample/_data/impacter/200908_27.html [In Japanese].

Gender Equality Bureau, Cabinet Office. (2003). *White book on gender equality* (fiscal 2003) Part I. Tokyo: National Printing Bureau. [In Japanese].

————. (2009). *White book on gender equality 2009*. Tokyo: National Printing Bureau. [In Japanese].

Government of Japan. (2008). *Sixth periodic report on the implementation of the Convention on the Elimination of All Forms of Discrimination against Women Japan*. Retrieved October 2, 2010, from http://www.mofa.go.jp/policy/human/women_rep6.pdf

Hara, H. et al. (Eds) (1986). *Mini-encyclopedia on the history of women in the world*. Tokyo: Esso Petroleum. [In Japanese].

————. (1999). *Female researchers: Career formation based on the gender analysis of a survey on research environments*. Ministry of Education, Science and Culture. [In Japanese].

Hausmann, R., Tyson, L. D., & Zahidi, S. (2007). *The global gender gap report 2007*. Geneva: World Economic Forum.

Hyogo Prefecture. (2005). *On the investigation into the dead at the great Hanshin-Awaji earthquake*. Press Release, December, 22. [In Japanese].

JNNC (Japan NGO Network for CEDAW). (2003). *NGOs' answers to the list of issues and questions for the consideration of the fourth and fifth periodic reports*. Retrieved October 2, 2010, from http://www.jaiwr.org/jnnc/japanngoanswersenglishfinal.pdf

Ministry of Education. (1980). *A hundred-year history of the school system* (14th edition). Gyosei. [In Japanese].

Ministry of Education, Culture, Sports, Science and Technology (Ed.). (2008). *White book on science and technology in 2008*. Nikkei Insatsu. [In Japanese].

Ministry of Health, Labour and Welfare. (2007a). *Vital statistics: Three most common causes of death by sex and age groups*. Tokyo. Retrieved October 2, 2010, from http://www.mhlw.go.jp/toukei/saikin/hw/jinkou/suii07/deth8.html [In Japanese].

————. (2007b). *White book on health, labour and welfare, fiscal 2007*. Gyosei. [In Japanese].

————. (2007c). *Survey on the health conditions of workers: Availability of counselors and advisors among workers*. Tokyo. [In Japanese].

Ministry of Health, Labour and Welfare, Equal Employment, Children and Families Bureau, (Ed.). (2008). *An analysis of women's labour 2007*. Japan Institute of Workers' Evolution. [In Japanese].

Ministry of Labour. (1982). *Analysis of labour economics 1981, part II–2*. Retrieved October 2, 2010, from http://wwwhakusyo.mhlw.go.jp/wpdocs/hpaa198201/body.html [In Japanese].

————. (1988). *Analysis of labour economics 1987, part II-1*. Retrieved October 2, 2010, from http://wwwhakusyo.mhlw.go.jp/wpdocs/hpaa198801/b0039.html [In Japanese].

National Governors Association. (2008). *Special committee on gender equality*. March 26. Retrieved October 2, 2010, from http://www.nga.gr.jp/news/bousai080326.PDF [In Japanese].

National Institute of Social Security and Population Research. (2008). *Tokei joho*. Retrieved October 2010, from http://www.ipss.go.jp/.youshika/site-ad/index-tj.htm [In Japanese].

Office for Gender Equality, Prime Minister's Office. (1996). *A report on the fourth world conference on women and its related projects*. Tokyo: National Printing Bureau.

Osawa, M. (2007). *Livelihood security system in contemporary Japan*. Tokyo: Iwanami Shoten. [In Japanese].

Robine, J-M., & Saito, Y. (2003). Survival beyond age 100: The case of Japan. In J. R. Carey, & S. Tuljapurkar (Eds), *Life span: Evolutionary, ecological, and demographic perspectives*. (Supplement to Population and Development Review), 29 (pp. 208–228). New York: Population Council.

Social Security Council. (2007). *Trends in the number of obstetricians/gynecologists and its number per 1,000 births*. Review for revising a system of medical treatment fees in fiscal 2008. 47th meeting for Medical Insurance Subcommittee, Social Security Council, Tokyo September, 27. [In Japanese].

UN (United Nations). (2003). *The fourth and fifth periodic reports of Japan*, CEDAW/C/ JPN/4 and CEDAW/C/JPN/5. Retrieved October 2, 2010, from http://www.un.org/ womenwatch/daw/cedaw/29sess.htm

UNDP (United Nations Development Programme). (2005). *Human development report: International cooperation at a crossroads—aid, trade and security in an unequal world*. New York: UNDP.

———. (2009). *Human development report: Overcoming barrie—human mobility and development*. New York: Palgrave Macmillan.

Vogel, E. F. (1979). *Japan as number one: Lessons for America*. Cambridge, Massachusetts: Harvard University.

Working Committee for Japan Women's Conference. (2007). *Hiroshima report*. [In Japanese].

Women's Net Kobe. (ed.) (2005). *Natural disasters and women: Necessity of women's participation in disaster prevention and relief*. Kobe: Women's Net Kobe. [In Japanese].

11

Equity in Post-crisis China
A Feminist Political Economy Perspective

LANYAN CHEN

Given the gendered slant to the economic slowdown in China, the Government needs to adopt a stimulus plan first to address disparity and vulnerability, while not adversely affecting the strong growth rate, and second to meet the long-term need in society for a more equitable approach to economic and social development.

INTRODUCTION

The aftermath of the financial crisis that began in 2008 has had similar features in both advanced economies and a number of emerging markets: the asset market crisis in terms of the decline of real housing and equity prices; the banking crisis, which is also associated with declines in output and employment; and the increase in government spending or accumulating debt while tax revenues contract (Reinhart & Rogoff, 2009). However, mainland China (hereafter, China) seems to be a different case from countries such as Indonesia, Malaysia, and the Philippines (ibid.). It shares only a few of the above features such as declined output in export sectors and increased unemployment.

For example, the housing market in China did not collapse as it did in many other countries in 2009. Although uncertainties in the market and the economy have caused loss of confidence in real estate in some areas, in other areas there has been a slight rebound because the Government intervened through its control of banks and state-owned corporations. With interest rates falling, banks ready to lend, and developers offering their apartments at lower prices, the Government has also taken steps to prevent the housing market from heating up by stopping issuing loans to individual purchasers of third apartments, especially in major cities like Beijing and Shanghai (National Bureau of Statistics of China, 2010a; Wang, 2010; Xinhua News Agency, 2009).

China has also so far been spared by the crisis in the banking sector, largely because the Government has kept the domestic financial market fairly insulated from international speculation and interference while it promotes the country's participation in the globalizing supply chains of nearly all productive sectors. Through the control of banking and the adoption of draconian labor regimes, especially in the export-oriented industries (where women form the majority of the labor force), it has been able to accumulate the largest foreign reserve in the world: USD 2 trillion (US dollars throughout), half of which is invested in the United States. While the Government is rich, however, the majority of Chinese still have relatively low incomes with little opportunity to save. The net per capita income of the rural population in 2007 was only 4,140 RMB (at the time of writing, 1 Chinese yuan [RMB] = 0.15 United States dollar [USD]), while the per capita disposable income of the population with urban residential status was 13,786 RMB (Hu, 2007). In 2006 56 percent of the population lived in the countryside or held a rural household registration (National Bureau of Statistics, 2007).

The negative effects of the financial crisis in China can be better understood in the context of its reforms toward globalization. Over the past 30 years, as it made vigoros moves to globalize and became a major economic player in the world, the country has been an archetypal model of "miracle" growth, with an average of over 10 percent growth each year. Since it has been largely focused on developing an export-driven economy, the contractions in world markets have thus affected its trade, output, and employment. Some 20 million migrant workers have lost their jobs in the manufacturing processing zones of southern China alone between the last months of 2008 and the beginning months of 2009 (Premier Wen Jiabao cited in Wen, 2009). Moreover, there are close to 50 million college graduates entering the job market every year (People's Bank of China, 2010; Wen, 2009).

While job creation is, therefore, high on the Government's agenda, labor demands for better pay and working conditions—as well as citizens' uneasiness at the rising prices of foodstuffs, costs of care, and income disparity—have encouraged it to take steps to live up to its promise of "building socialism with Chinese characteristics." The construction of a harmonious, socialist, "Xiao Kang" (well-off) society was adopted in 2006 as a Chinese goal in ideological and material preparation for the achievement of the MDGs agreed on by the international community. The construction of such a society—as Hu Jintao, the Chinese President, has stated—will require an approach to balance economic growth with social development and to orient China to people-centered governance based on principles of harmony, fairness, and equality as well as openness and participation (Hu, 2007).

To what extent will the Chinese intervention policies, as part of its "stimulus effort" to combat the impacts of the recent financial crisis, result in an increase in social well-being or economic stability? This chapter takes a feminist political economy perspective to identify shortcomings in the intervention, arguing that these largely stem from the existing systems that have buttressed the gendered nature of China's economic growth in the process of globalization over the past decades (see Chen, 2008; Gaetano, 2009). A gender equity strategy is needed both to overcome the gendered effects of the crisis as well as to rebuild progress based on more equality and fairness to underpin the attainment of physical, mental, and social well-being for all.

Such qualities of progress require not only equitable distribution of the rights to resources in a balanced approach to economic and social development, but also public policy-making that responds to the concerns of grassroots women and men and answers to shared commitments to international goals and standards. These rights to resources include goods and services as well as incentives and benefits to which one is entitled not only through inheritance and one's own capabilities but also through financial transfers from government and legal and moral recognition of one's contributions (see Elson this volume).

Therefore, key to the above requirements for rebuilding progress is the idea of integrating production and social reproduction in one process of post-crisis economics, which should be supported especially by policy-makers putting social justice first and by those (academics, researchers, professional associations, social organizations such as trade unions and women's groups, etc.) who may have an influence on policies. It also requires that grassroots women and men of different ethnic backgrounds and of disadvantaged or less favorable social and economic standing exercise agency to influence policies so as to have their rights respected and protected. These two aspects are at the core of the concern of the feminist political economy perspective, which it is suggested should help guide the Chinese response to the effects of the financial crisis. One may argue that there is also a racial overtone to the effects of the crisis, given the recent eruption of ethnic conflicts in the country; this chapter emphasizes gender as many have pointed out that gender cuts across race and class (see, for example, Kabeer, 2003).

A FEMINIST POLITICAL ECONOMY PERSPECTIVE

A feminist political economy perspective is an interdisciplinary study of society, which is a totality of political, economic, social, and cultural relations, all which are mutually interdependent and form an intersectional nexus. Underlying this nexus is a set of divisions of labor that are largely unequal and that separate social reproduction from production, though they are part of one process. Such separation is supported by a set of discourses around perceptions of existence including sexuality, gender, ethnicity, and class. These discourses are the institutionalized rules, norms, and values that govern the divisions of labor as well as the distribution of resources, responsibilities, and power within these divisions.

One such important institution (out of four—the state, the market, the civil society/community, and kinship/family), as Diane Elson (1991) first discussed, is the state, which occupies an overwhelmingly powerful position, subordinating women and the disadvantaged through policies that favor production for the market at the expense of social reproduction. Policy-making can, however, be a contested site when women and the disadvantaged exercise agency to influence policies to take into account their concerns for the equitable distribution of resources, fair recognition of their contributions, and due protection of their citizenship rights (Chen, 2008).

Such exercise of agency in different parts of the world has encouraged member states of the international community to recognize access to education, health, food, water, and housing—key in social development and central to reproduction—as legitimate rights claimable by all, including women, men, girls, and boys. These rights, sanctioned by internationally agreed standards, are fundamentally important for the goal of attaining a general state of physical, mental, and social well-being. This goal requires a multi-sectoral strategy by governments to protect multiple rights (especially dignity, equitable access to quality services, and participation in decision making), and the integration of production, distribution, and social reproduction (Chen, 2008).

An example of the norms that have been institutionalized in Chinese patriarchal institutions and state policies is the core Confucian value of "men governing the outside, while women govern the inside [of the house hold]." This norm has helped not only to establish men's superiority in authority and wealth but also to enforce women's subordination and their responsibilities for reproduction. These responsibilities include: biological reproduction and daily maintenance of the current and future generation of workers; transmission of skills, knowledge, and moral values; and construction of individual and collective identities and maintenance of cultures. Historically, women have also often had to bear the burden and stigma of selling sex to support themselves as well as their families.

As defined by the 1996 World Food Summit Plan of Action, food security "exists when all people, at all times, have physical and economic access to sufficient, safe and nutritious food to meet their dietary needs and food preferences for an active and healthy life" (FAO, 1996). While the roles that women play in agriculture vary from country to country, in general they play a major part in food production as well as food security, traditionally being those who care for the basic needs of the household. However, their reproductive responsibilities are unpaid, and are excluded from social recognition even though they are central to the production of the means of life as well as the use of these means to reproduce life itself on a daily and intergenerational basis. They are central in terms not only of food provision but also of education of the young and care of the old, the young, and the sick—apart from the care of men in the family, who occupy a superior position as "heads of households" or "breadwinners." This care, which can only be partially provided through public and commercial services, has been provided mostly based on personal volition. The fact that it is unpaid suggests "that much of the value of personal care for others comes from it being given as a gift, without immediate recompense, in a context of mutuality" (Elson this volume).

As women provide more care than men and receive less, Elson argues that a more viable way to achieve equality in care provision and reception, namely, symmetrical reciprocity of care, is through universal, state-based entitlements. That is because such entitlements, which operate on the principles of equality and fairness and would be made available to all members of a society, are likely to be more accessible, transparent, and effective. Most importantly, claiming them is not stigmatizing as it is not seen as a sign of failure or dependency (ibid.). Women benefit because these entitlements require the development of public policy-making that reflects the needs and interests of women and men and abides by international human rights standards. It is thus a mistake to separate social reproduction from economics as care matters not only for production but also for the well-being of people overall. This perspective of integrating production and social reproduction in one process is feminist as it argues for recognition in policy-making of women's contributions and their rights to food, water, jobs, and health as equal to men's. Such recognition requires a feminist political economic analysis to decipher not only the impacts of policies on women but also women's potential to influence policies.

THE GENDERED EFFECTS OF THE CRISIS

The effects of the financial crisis in China have a gender dimension. More women than men were employed in export-oriented industries, and now more women are unemployed, especially migrant women from the countryside and ethnic minorities who have not acquired fluency in Mandarin Chinese. Most of them tend to have a low level of education and had worked largely in low-skilled jobs (for discussions of conditions under which young migrant women work in manufacturing, see Chan, 2001; Gaetano & Jacka, 2004; Ngai, 2005). Many of these jobless women and men have become desperate and sought work in the informal, unprotected job market—including the growing service sectors, such as in domestic services and the sex trade—to make a living and support themselves and their families. Being part of the informal economy exposes them to abuse by employers, including withholding pay; harsh and dangerous working conditions; and, in the case of the sex trade, health hazards (including HIV and AIDS) and police raids and arrests (Associated Press, 2010; Chen, 2009; Wang, 2000). .

Moreover, similar to India in recent decades (see Jain this volume), there is a clear decline in formal employment in the informal sector even though reform liberalization has generated an increased GDP and more women's employment. In 2004, for instance, the total rural and urban employed population in China was 744 million, of which 337 million were women—which was 5.6 percentage points higher than the 319 million employed women in 2000 (Chen, 2008). Of these women, 79.8 percent worked in labor-intensive jobs and 60.1 percent (5.3 percentage points more than men) were in the agricultural, husbandry, forestry, fishery, and small, privately owned, and self-employed sectors, where jobs are often uncounted, unprotected, and precarious. The total number of urban women employed in 2004 was 114 million, which was 13.2 percentage points more than in 2000 (Chen, 2008). However, only 110 million (41.9 percent) of the employed urban population worked in the formal sector—a decrease from 140 million in 1990, when this was 95.4 percent of the total urban employed; and 42 million of them were women (38.1 percent), a decrease of 4.2 percent from 2000. This means that though women's overall employment increased, it declined in the formal sector where income, social benefits, and overall social protection are more secure.

In addition, most of those who have lost out during the reforms of the past 30 years are women, especially middle-aged and elderly women (ibid.). If they live in rural areas, women are burdened with the productive and social reproductive tasks of farming and caring for children/grandchildren at the expense of their own health and well-being. They are also excluded from access to social benefits provided by the Government to urban residents, such as schooling and social assistance. If they live in urban areas, many of them were laid off from state-owned factories during the privatization of the 1990s and are now vulnerable as they fall outside the protection of social security programs and form a majority of those who are in need of low-income housing support.

Recent reports on the Government's widespread attacks on sex workers are indications that, due to losing jobs as a result of factory closures in the coastal manufacturing zones of Guangdong and slowdowns in other areas, more women have entered sex work to make a living for themselves and their families (Associated Press, 2010; China Development Brief, 2010; Jacobs, 2010). Such attacks have clearly revealed that the nature of existing Chinese systems of political and economic control is oppressive and discriminatory against women. The dissent the attacks incited among women was also suppressed.

Given this gendered slant to the economic slowdown in China, the Government needs to adopt a stimulus plan first to address disparity and vulnerability, while not adversely affecting the strong growth rate, and second to meet the long-term need in society for a more equitable approach to economic and social development. A gender equity strategy would enable the Government to take advantage of the opportunity that such a plan offers for integration with the enforcement of the new Labour Contract Law and other legislation and regulations that promote equality and ensure fairness.

THE CHINESE RESPONSE TO THE FINANCIAL CRISIS

The Chinese Government announced a stimulus plan in February 2009 as its response to the effects of the crisis. According to Premier Wen Jiabao, who was answering questions from "netizens" through the government website on 28 February, the plan consisted of an investment package worth 4 trillion RMB (about USD 570 billion), one fourth of which would be used for the reconstruction of the earthquake-torn areas in Sichuan (Wen, 2009). The central government would contribute 1.18 trillion RMB (about USD 173 billion), and the rest would be raised from local governments, banks, and the private sector.

The goal of the plan was to have a growth rate of 8 percent in 2009 through the combined measures of raising productivity by restructuring major industrial sectors and increasing domestic demand by investing in social services, housing, and education. It was expected that 909 billion RMB would be used in 2009 for improving the quality of people's lives in these areas.

Increasing Productivity

The Government saw the crisis as an opportunity to upgrade the level of productivity through improving technology and management. Ten industries to receive special support through the stimulus plan were auto, steel, shipbuilding, textiles, machine manufacturing, electronics and information technology, light industry, petrochemicals, non-ferrous metals, and logistics.

Based on the measures adopted, there would be an opportunity for the Government to address issues of disparity and the imbalance between economic and social development that have marred the "miracle growth" of the past 30 years. If growth and the environment were used as the main indicators, restructuring the industrial sectors could be expected to provide mixed evidence of improvement. On the one hand, two of the aims of the restructuring are to upgrade technology, especially through the use of cleaner energy, and to create Chinese name brands. On the other hand, all levels of the regional governments have been given the task of providing support to small and medium-sized businesses and to those who are poised to start a business that creates jobs, especially among rural migrant workers. Past practice has shown that while small and medium sized-businesses have created jobs and contributed to economic growth, many of them have also added pollution to the local environment. They are by and large privately owned or jointly owned with foreign investment, are less observant of the labor standards stipulated by law, and are generally lower on the social responsibility index than state-owned enterprises (China Central TV, 2008).

In addition, local governments have been encouraged by the central government to provide assistance to the needy and to fund local projects that will generate jobs. Past experience has shown that loans and credits administered by government-influenced banks and government agencies that are charged with initiating projects and job creation are often more favorable to men than women.

Furthermore, in recent years local governments have used land to finance projects. Although land in China is owned by the state, villages in the countryside collectively manage the land within their boundaries. Since the economic reforms in the late 1970s villages have leased pieces of collectively managed land to individual households based on 30- or 50-year contracts. Village councils sometimes connive with local governments at the township or county levels to sell collectively managed but individually used land to the highest bidder for industrial use or commercial development; villagers have then been shortchanged as they are in many cases not properly compensated and are kept in the dark throughout the dealings. If they refuse and protest, they may be thrown out of their homes, witness their houses being leveled by bulldozers, or even run the risk of losing their lives in standoffs with police or thugs sent in by local governments and companies (Cohen, 2010; Wines & Ansfield, 2010). Women are often at the forefront of such protests by villagers as they form the majority of the agricultural labor force and their income is more tied to the land. Prominent cases where women residents refused to move and subsequently lost their lives shocked the country and led to law professors calling on the government to change the law on the management of land (Associated Press, 2009).

Theoretically, some of the listed industries on the Chinese stimulus plan (textiles, electronics and information technology, light industry, and parts of machine manufacturing) have employed women as their predominant workforce and hence investment in these industries would provide more jobs for women. In reality, however, these industries are often privately owned or established with foreign investment, and it is rare for there to be unionization or formal contracts to ensure labor standards. Moreover, investment in these industries promised by the stimulus plan is for the purpose of improving productivity through restructuring with the

use of advanced technology and branding. Past experience with industrial reform in China suggests that restructuring also means streamlining
in which less skilled jobs—many of which are held by women—are
eliminated.

Simply relying on the stimulus plan will not change much of women's
lives for the better in these sectors mainly because there are few ways for
workers to have their voices heard or respected. What is needed is to
enforce, possibly through the courts and the role of civil society, the Labour
Contract Law (adopted in 2008 and publicized as pro-labor), and other
legislation that promotes gender equality. What would also be helpful,
of course, is the adoption of a specific gender equity strategy to assure
participation of women in the establishment of a nationwide system of
social security programs that cover everyone, including migrant workers.
More substantial improvement can be achieved, as is discussed next, if
the creation of a basic universal health care system is combined with the
implementation and enforcement of gender-sensitive legislation, including the Labour Contract Law and the Law on the Protection of Women's
Rights and Interests.

Investing in Basic Health Care

As part of the stimulus plan, the Government is expected to invest 850
billion RMB (USD 120 billion) over three years to establish a basic health
care system. A special issue of *Feminist Economics* on "Gender, China, and
the World Trade Organization" in July/October 2007 included an article
on the Chinese health care policy reforms. The authors noted that in
2004 the coverage of health care insurance was only 20 percent, and the
majority of those who were not covered were women, especially elderly
women, as indicated by the 3rd survey of healthcare services (Chen &
Standing, 2007). In 2003, on average, a visit to the hospital cost 219 RMB
in urban areas (an increase of 85 percent from 1998) and 91 RMB in rural
areas (an increase of 103 percent from 1998). A patient paid 7,606 RMB
per year for hospitalization in urban areas (up by 88 percent) and 2,649
RMB in rural areas (up by 73 percent). The recent 4th survey of health
care services shows that 90 percent of the rural population now have
access to a health care system, based on a cooperative fund raised by the
Government and individual contributions (ibid.).

With the investment of USD 120 billion (about USD 55 billion from the
central government and the rest from local governments) in a universal

basic health care system, coverage is expected to increase to reach 90 percent of urban residents. This investment would also help build 29,000 rural medical centers, 5,000 rural clinics, 2,000 rural hospitals, and 2,400 urban clinics. Moreover, it would increase the average level of investment in each person's health services to 15 RMB in 2009 and is expected to raise the amount again to 20 RMB in 2011. It would also help increase government subsidies to each person's health care coverage from 100 RMB a year in 2009 to 120 RMB in 2011. It is thus clear that the government has decided to tackle health care disparities from both the demand and the supply side (Xinhua News Net, 2009).

To invest in the demand side, the government intends to initially create three health-care programs to cover three sets of populations: working people in urban areas, urban residents, and rural residents. The government will expand on a program that supports needy families who experience difficulty in paying for health-care costs related to serious illnesses. It is intended that, in three years, the three programs will be merged into a nationwide system of health care. This could help to address the concerns of the migrant population because individuals would be able to use their health plan to seek medical assistance outside their local provinces.

To invest in the supply side, the Government is paying more attention to improving the conditions of local clinics and hospitals, especially in rural areas. Chen and Standing (2007) strongly argue for a health-care reform agenda, under which the government creates a list of publicly funded medical facilities that can handle patients for a minimum registration fee and also underwrites a list of medicines and basic health-care services. Based on the preliminary information gleaned from reports on the Decision of the Central Committee of the Communist Party and the State Council to Deepen the Medical and Healthcare System Reform, issued on April 6, 2009, basic healthcare services will include preventive care, mother and childcare, health education and information dissemination, and public health services for communicable diseases such as HIV and AIDS. Preventive care will be free to children up to age 15, and post-natal healthcare and examinations will be free to children up to age 3 (Xinhua News Net, 2009).

It will be interesting to see how this basic health-care system takes shape. Of immediate concern are the rural-to-urban migrants who are currently covered by the rural cooperative medical plan at home but not in the urban areas where they are working and living. It would be desirable to include them in the 90 percent of urban residents whom the government pledges to support with healthcare over the next three years before the nationwide system is established. Also, women and men who lost jobs in the aftermath of the financial crisis and entered into casual work, including sex work, become excluded from social services due to stigmatization. These people are highly mobile, according to my own research, and are entitled to health care not only as members of society but also as concerned partners in safeguarding public health.

Increasing Social Assistance

Social assistance is extremely uneven across the country as it is determined by local resources and, being frequently based on the head of household system, has overlooked different needs among household members. Women have often not benefited as much as men from such initiatives, unless there is some involvement from agencies with a mandate to advance women's issues such as the Women's Federation, which has a presence nationally, regionally, and even at the grass roots (see Chen, 2008; Chen et al., 2008).

In September 2009 the government adopted a decision to establish rural pension programs based on a combined funding scheme of individual contribution, donation from society, and government subsidy. This would be implemented by first setting up pilot schemes in selected local areas. It is unclear how such programs would benefit rural women equitably as women and men have different needs, and the head of household system has been a limitation on government rural reform policies. The government has attempted to intervene in addressing the income disparity that is growing between rural and urban areas, demonstrated by the call for more equitable redistribution of income stated again by Wen Jiabao in his address to the UN General Assembly on September 22, 2010 (Shen, 2009; Xinhua News Agency, 2010). Setting up pension programs and health-care coverage based on cooperative principles in the countryside would help alleviate the problem of rural–urban disparity, especially if such programs promote equality and equity in meeting different gendered needs of women and men.

However, a concern related to the stimulus plan· is with respect to the absence of equitable support for women farmers and their role in agriculture. Women form 60–80 percent of the agricultural labor force across the different provinces, but they have experienced a slower growth of income compared to that from industries and services, due in part to international competition and rising prices of energy in the past years.

It remains a concern that the Government at different levels has not adopted a strategy to improve rural conditions based on more equitable participation of rural women, who are in the forefront of agricultural production and food security as well as social reproduction, in planning and decision making.

HOW A GENDER PERSPECTIVE COULD IMPROVE THE RESPONSE

China's response to the effects of the current financial crisis provides an opportunity to chart a new course and to invest in a balanced approach to economic and social development. A gender equity strategy based on a feminist political economy perspective is conducive to the government's goal of building a harmonious and well-off society, a goal that reflects its commitment to achieving the MDGs.

The feminist political economic perspective is highly relevant to China for the following reasons. First, it helps demonstrate that the rural reform policy of household land contract responsibility, adopted at the start of the Chinese economic reforms in 1979, has failed to respond to gender differences and instead has caused gender inequalities and an increase in rural women's isolation. This is largely because the government failed to promote social organization such as farmers' associations and women's cooperatives to help address the potential social impacts of the policy (Chen, 2008). As a result, this policy has contributed to the rise of "the three rural problems"—problems related to the peasantry, rural areas, and agriculture—and failed to improve rural living and welfare equitably. Policies to safeguard food security and advance agricultural production, adopted in the aftermath of the household land contract system, have failed to achieve their goals, as they continue to be insensitive to the different positions of women and men in food production and distribution.

Second, rural women continue to carry out the majority of housework and home-based care. Policies to improve health care and pensions in the countryside may help relieve some burdens of care by women—for example, with respect to care for patients and the elderly (as the latter may be able to receive more care provided by institutions such as clinics and home facilities). However, women workers who migrate from the countryside to work in cities are left out, as their rural benefits are inadequate to cover their costs of social reproduction (children's education and health care) in urban areas (Chen, 2009).

Third, women's burden of food security and care may have been increased by environmental challenges and male-dominated control of processing and distribution of foodstuffs in society. One example is the rising incidence of widespread poisoning among children from tainted food, such as milk products, and from lead in the environment caused by mineral refineries that are built near residential areas. Women face challenges due not only to lax regulation and enforcement of food safety standards but also to the impacts of policies favoring large enterprises—known as "dragon-head enterprises"—while marginalizing small farmers (the majority of whom are women), the middle-aged, and/or elderly (Chen, 2008).

Fourth, and most importantly, women's concerns with social reproduction—food security and safety and care—have been missing from the stimulus policy-making processes. For the stimulus plan to deliver the desired results of improving food security and recognizing women's burdens of care, there should be mechanisms to consult women—especially women farmers, migrant women workers, and women in minority groups. One outcome of such consultation would be the translation of the above aspects of women's reproductive responsibilities into policy concerns. The feminist political economy perspective calls for the construction of an alternative approach to food security and social security reforms with the participation of women, especially rural women and migrant women workers.

In a previous study (ibid.), I discuss a gender equity strategy that promotes the idea of government in a more open and participatory society as a contested site, over which women and disadvantaged groups can exercise agency to influence policies to reflect their interests. This discussion highlights the importance of active organization among women and the disadvantaged and their participation in social movements, elections, and party organizations. It also points toward a new political agenda for women's movements to include a demand for institutional mechanisms to facilitate their participation in public policy-making. A gender equity strategy therefore encourages the growth of grassroots organizations—be they women's associations, cooperatives, entrepreneurs' associations, or informal work organizations—that can provide a voice for their concerns and hold the government accountable for its commitments to international goals.

Such a strategy also calls for transformational leadership by the offices of women's federations and women's machineries to create mechanisms to transmit grassroots concerns to policy-making processes. These offices can help create gender units in public offices and organizations, and promote alliances of women and progressive men in the Chinese legislature and government, so as to facilitate the institution of public consultation or hearings with grassroots organizations on legislative issues and other matters of critical concern to women and the disadvantaged. Setting up and institutionalizing such consultations is in line with the next stage of democratic development for accountability and transparency already underway in China. It is desirable for the Chinese response to the recent financial crisis to also continuously remove barriers to mainstreaming the principle of gender equality in government and policy-making. In relation to this, there is a need to respect women's rights to dignity and equitable access to quality services through redistribution of income, formalizing their informal work based on universal social security coverage, and eliminating discrimination.

CONCLUSION

Recent statistics indicate that China was achieving over 8 percent GDP growth in 2009 in part due to its stimulus plan (for more on the economic assessment, see National Bureau of Statistics of China, 2010b; World Bank, 2010). Continuous growth is expected for 2010. It is hoped, however, that such growth will be achieved without the suffering inflicted recently on those women and men who either lost land to local governments during land grab schemes or were arrested in the widespread police attacks on sex workers, as mentioned earlier. China may be an exception in terms of Reinhart and Rogoff's (2009) discussion of the features of the recent financial crisis as the country did not exhibit an outright crisis in asset and banking sectors like the others on their list. However, if China does not live up to its commitment to build a harmonious, fair, and equal society—which Reinhart and Rogoff fail to discuss—and uses existing systems of political and economic control to respond insensitively to the impacts of the crisis, there could be social dissent and instability.

It is still too early to forecast accurately the outcome of the Government's decision to establish a public health-care program that will provide coverage of the entire population within the next three years, which is a gigantic stride toward balancing economic growth with social development. This balancing approach should be encouraged, as any equitable investment in social development benefits women.

A gender equity strategy based on a feminist political economy perspective would encourage policymakers, members of think tanks, and others who have an influence on policies to develop technical tools to respond, in a timely manner, to the needs and interests of all people, particularly those who are disadvantaged by gender, ethnicity, origin of birth, and/or social and economic standing. It would also promote grassroots organization that would help women and the disadvantaged to voice their concerns about integrating production and social reproduction through public consultation and make these concerns part of policy issues.

To encourage China as well as a post-crisis world to adopt a balanced approach to economic and social development will require the international community to also prioritize health and food security and reject the conventional course to growth in their stimulus efforts. Worldwide, feminist political economists have a responsibility to support a strategy that would promote redistribution of resources in both developed and developing countries.

This strategy might include a regime of taxation that would benefit from the behavior on the part of transnational corporations of maximizing profit, which has deprived the global labor force—especially women in developing countries—of their entitlement to proper labor protection, and irresponsible speculation, which has destroyed livelihoods in weaker economies. It might also include a lending regime that would help promote decent labor practices, agricultural production based on the cooperation of small farmers, and social services. Such a strategy would provide a step toward integrating production, distribution, and social reproduction and contribute toward building a general state of physical, mental, and social well-being for both women and men around the world.

References

Associated Press. (2009, December 27). China's demolition law criticized after protests. *Washington Times.*

———. (2010, August 2). Police detain China activists for sex workers' rights. *Beijing Globe.*

Chan, A. (2001). *China's workers under assault: The exploitation of labor in a globalizing economy.* Armonk, New York: M. E. Sharpe.

Chen, L. (2008). *Gender and Chinese development: Towards an equitable society.* London: Routledge IAFFE Advances in Feminist Economics Series.

———. (2009). The gendered reality of migrant workers in globalizing China. In E. P. Mendes, & S. Srighanthan (Eds), *Confronting discrimination and inequality in China: Chinese and Canadian perspectives* (pp. 186–207). Ottawa: University of Ottawa Press.

Chen, L., Hu, X., Lim, V., Arao, R. M., Francisco, J., & Yabut-Bernardino, N. (2008). *Gender dynamics in China's trade intensification. IGTN–Asia Economic Literacy Packet.* Quezon City, Philippines: International Gender and Trade Network–Asia. Retrieved September 23, 2009, from http://web.igtn.org/home/index.php?searchword=China+and+Trade& ordering=&searchphrase=all&option=com_search

Chen, L., & Standing, H. (2007). Gender equity in transitional China's healthcare policy reforms. *Feminist Economics, 13*(3&4), 189–212.

China Central TV. (2008). *Economic half an hour: Interview with Dan Zongdong.* December 26. Retrieved September 30, 2010, from http://finance.cctv.com/program/ jjxxlb/20081226/110023_1.shtml [In Chinese]

China Development Brief. (2010). *Aizhixing statement in support of women activists petition for sex worker rights.* July 27. Retrieved August 4, 2009, from http://chinadevelopmentbrief. org.cn/ngo_talkview.php?id=994 [In Chinese].

Cohen, R. (2010, January 26). A woman burns. *New York Times.* Retrieved September 30, 2010, from http://www.nytimes.com/2010/01/26/opinion/26iht-edcohen.html?_r=1

Elson, D. (1991). *Male bias in the development process.* Manchester: Manchester University Press.

FAO (Food and Agriculture Organization of the United Nations). (1996). *Rome declaration on world food security.* Rome, Italy: World Food Summit, November 13–17. Retrieved February 6, 2010, from www.fao.org/docrep/003/w3613e/w3613e00.HTM

Gaetano, A. (2009). Book review, gender and Chinese development: Towards an equitable society. *The China Quarterly, 197,* 220–221.

Gaetano, A., & Jacka, T. (Eds). (2004). *On the move: Women and rural-to-urban migration in contemporary China.* New York: Columbia University Press.

Hu, J. (2007). *Raise high the banner of socialism with Chinese characteristics to strive to achieve new victories in building overall a well-off society.* Beijing: People's Publishing House. [In Chinese].

Jacobs, A. (2010, July 27). China pushes to end public shaming. *New York Times.* Retrieved September 30, 2010, from http://www.nytimes.com/2010/07/28/world/asia/28china. html

Kabeer, N. (2003). *Gender mainstreaming in poverty eradication and the millennium development goals: A handbook for policy-makers and other stakeholders.* London: Commonwealth Secretariat.

National Bureau of Statistics of China. (2007). *Women and men in Chinese society: Facts and figures (2007).* Beijing: National Statistics Publishing House.

———. (2010a). *Quarterly briefings.* Retrieved July 2, 2010, from http://www.stats.gov.cn [In Chinese].

———. (2010b). *Monthly economic fcrecasts.* Retrieved September 21, 2010, from http://www. stats.gov.cn/tjsj/ [In Chinese].

Ngai, P. (2005). *Made in China: Women factory workers in a global workplace.* Durham, North Carolina: Duke University Press.

People's Bank of China. (2010). *China monetary policy report quarter four 2009.* Retrieved September 29, 2010, from http://www.pbc.gov.cn/image_public/UserFiles/english/ upload/File/ChinaMonetaryPolicyReportQuarterFour2009.pdf

Reinhart, C. M., & Rogoff, K. S. (2009). *The aftermath of financial crises.* Draft presented at the American Economic Association meetings in San Francisco, January 3.

Shen, J. (2009). No timetables for adjusting income disparity. *21st Century Business Herald.* October 23. [In Chinese].

Wang, J. (2010, July 1). System favours developers: An interview with a developer. *China Youth Daily*. [In Chinese].

Wang, Z. (2000). Gender, employment and women's resistance. In E. J. Perry, & M. Seldon (Eds), *Chinese society: Change, conflict and resistance* (pp. 62–82). London: Routledge.

Wen, J. (2009). *Interview by XinhuaNet*. February 28. Retrieved February 29, 2009, from http://www.gov.cn/zlft/page_2.htm [In Chinese].

Wines, M., & Ansfield, J. (2010, May 26). Trampled in a land rush, Chinese resist. *New York Times*. Retrieved September 28, 2010, form http://www.nytimes.com/2010/05/27/world/asia/27china.html

World Bank. (2010). *Chinese economy quarterly*. Retrieved May 20, 2010, from http://go.worldbank.org/DVYT1EA3N0 [In Chinese].

Xinhua News Agency. (2009, November 26). *To buy or not to buy: Chinese home buyers' dilemma*. Retrieved September 30, 2010, from http://www.beijingimpression.com/news/to-buy-or-not-to-buy-chinese-home-buyers-dilemma.shtml.

———. (2010). *Wen Jiabao presenting a real China at the UN general assembly*. Retrieved September 26, 2010, from http://news.hexun.com/2010-09-27/125002419.html [In Chinese].

Xinhua News Net. (2009, April 6). *Decision to deepening healthcare and medicine reforms*. Retrieved July 5, 2009, from www.xinhuanet.com [In Chinese].

12

Cuban Development Alternatives to Market-driven Economies
A Gendered Case Study on Women's Employment*

MARTA NÚÑEZ SARMIENTO

Cuba has been in permanent transition since 1959 toward a fairer society.... Being among the poorest, women benefited from the very beginning from the strategies put in place to change the social relationships that conditioned poverty.

INTRODUCTION

*T*his chapter critically examines the notion of "progress," which the processes governing the market have generally defined as a synonym for economic growth. Feminist social scientists have addressed this topic in various ways. I will do so by evaluating the Cuban experience of development to demonstrate that it is not necessary to be a rich country for society and women to advance and develop; rather, what is needed is the political will to comprehensively manage this process.

In the last 50 years Cuba has gone through several periods of social and economic transformation that I have divided here into two periods:

---

*A modified version of a paper originally prepared for a UNDP Colloquium on Assessing Development Paradigms through Women's Knowledge, October 25–27, 2008, Rabat.

1959–1989 and 1990–2009. First, to provide a historical background, the chapter summarizes the economic and social policies in Cuba between 1959 and 1989 and the results of integrating Cuban women into the workplace. This shows how much the situation of society in general, and of women in particular, differed in Cuba when the crisis of the 1980s hit, in comparison with other Latin American countries, which had adopted neoliberal policies. Second, the chapter turns to the effects of the crisis that hit Cuba and women's employment between 1990 and 2009. Both sections examine the actions taken to eradicate poverty, achieve equality, and promote female leadership by turning women into agents of their own transformation.

The feminist goal to promote women as agents of change has been one of the main instruments to advance women in societies. One of the purposes of this chapter is to summarize the complicated and unfinished ways this has been envisioned and experimented with in Cuba.

The Cuban idea of development is to meet people's material and spiritual needs. Progress therefore implies that economic transformation should provide material well-being to all and should contribute to changing ideological and cultural patterns of inequality and discrimination. The gender perspective that I use in this study has made me reflect on specific Cuban development strategies in order to:

- Evaluate their contributions to progress and their limitations in creating development models focused on human development.
- Understand the relationship between economic and social policies and the development of women in a specific historical and social context.
- Confirm whether these policies applied a gender-differentiated approach.
- Determine how the policies influenced gender relations, specifically power relations.
- Evaluate these processes from a historical perspective.

There are three main reasons why the economic goals set out as part of Cuban strategies for development have not been fully realized:

- First, the social policies were overly ambitious, since they attempted to lift the entire population out of poverty with immediate effect.
- Second, the Cuban economy was and continues to be an open one, and therefore the country needs to be part of the international

economy. However, the economic blockade by the United States since the 1960s has stopped Cuba from developing international economic relationships and prevented many of the transformations that had been envisioned.

- Third, Cuba's development strategies have been part of a socialist experience that was intended to take apart capitalist structures and establish new ones. Because it was the first attempt to do this in the Western hemisphere, errors were made in design and implementation that are still unresolved.

Yet although the goals have not been achieved in all respects—and differences persist in terms of incomes, gender, race, geographic settings, and other areas that are openly criticized by the population—the fact that there is universal and free access to basic benefits remains the pillar of popular support for the Cuban Revolution. Women's participation in applying, criticizing, and gaining from these policies has been a key factor in the gains made.

ECONOMIC STRATEGIES AND SOCIAL POLICIES REGARDING FEMALE EMPLOYMENT: 1959–1989

Cuba has been in permanent transition since 1959 toward a fairer society. Unlike other countries in Latin America in the late 1950s, Cuba explicitly incorporated social improvement into its economic development strategies (Pérez Villanueva, 2008). Moreover, it did not reproduce the economic liberalization policies that were widespread in the region in the 1970s and led to the debt crises of the 1980s. Another unique feature in Cuba was its repertoire of social policies and poverty management; this was the most extensive of all developing countries, which mainly understood poverty as a social situation that had always existed and would always exist (Espina Prieto, 2007). Being among the poorest, women benefited from the very beginning from the strategies put in place to change the social relationships that conditioned poverty.

Creating "Spaces of Equality"

Throughout these first 30 years, practical decisions were taken as needed, and at times under extreme pressure, to solve short-term development problems that required immediate solutions. From the beginning, the economic approach to development was discarded and the economy was organized in such a way that the growth of the GDP fed the social policies that universalized education, health, social security, social welfare, culture, and sports—areas defined by the Cuban sociologist Mayra Espina Prieto (2007) as "spaces of equality". These spaces are centrally designed by the state to implement activities that meet the population's basic needs and benefit everyone; therefore, they are offered free of charge, universal access is endorsed by legislation, and access is facilitated where necessary. But such a political choice in terms of development policies demands enormous financial resources that are difficult to attain in a developing country such as Cuba.

The Federation of Cuban Women (FMC) was established in 1960 to channel the participation of women as agents of their own development. There was a clear understanding that specific actions would be needed to overcome discrimination against women and have them join society fully, and the Government and the FMC declared from the beginning that the country could not wait for economic growth before ensuring that women made progress. This political will led to the implementation of economic strategies specifically geared at woman's equality as well as legal regulations, social policies, and actions mainly of an ideological nature to struggle against gender discrimination. A merely economic approach would have postponed these decisions and reduced the importance of women's participation, and the possibility for women to be the agents of change from the start would have been lost. These policies have been subject to constant modification in accordance with the unfolding conditions and needs of Cuban women and Cuban society as a whole. I characterize this trend as a process taking place both "top-down" and "bottom-up."

The spaces of equality were effective in breaking the cycle of reproducing inequalities in society and at home and were "feminized" almost immediately. Since discrimination had historically been exercised against women, the introduction of a lack of gender differentiation actually benefited them much more than men. For example, this was the case with the literacy campaign in 1961. Women made up 59 percent of the literacy teachers and 55 percent of those who learned to read and write (FMC, 1975). In just one year this helped inaugurate one of the most important spaces of equality: education. The nationalization of schools that took place that same year also favored the feminization of education because girls and young people became teachers and increasingly remained in the educational sector. Within 20 years, by 1980, girls outnumbered boys in enrolment and their attrition rate was much lower in grades 7 to 12.

Educational programs also included campaigns to help working adults advance their schooling, and by 1978 working women began to have higher educational levels than working men—5 percent of working women and 3.5 percent of working men were university graduates, while 23 percent of working women had a grade 12 level of education in comparison with 13 percent of working men (calculations made by the author from Comité Estatal de Estadísticas, 1988). This had an impact on their labor performance since it enabled women to be promoted in their jobs toward more complex and better-paid occupations. The nationalization of education in 1961 provided mothers with a feeling of security, because their children were guaranteed free and universal education from primary school through to university. The provision of lunch in primary schools, together with a double school session led by teachers' aides, contributed to allowing women with children to keep their jobs. The first day-care centers (and schools to train staff for such centers) were established in 1961, followed by the setting up of kindergartens in the mid-1960s, although these met the needs of only some working mothers.

In Cuba before 1959 there had been no state social security system. During the 1960s and 1970s legislation was passed to make social security and social welfare universal, benefiting working women and single mothers. Working women had guaranteed retirement and invalidity benefits and pensions on the death of their spouse. The Maternity Law was included in the Labour Code in 1974 to regulate maternity leave. Single mothers received small stipends that helped them raise their children while they were unable to work. Fathers were required to pay child support if divorced or separated from their spouses or partners, although many still did not do so. The Family Code approved in 1975 specified the rights and legal duties of all family members to contribute to eliminating the inequalities and discriminations that took place at home. At that time it was a very advanced legal instrument that insisted on the participation of all family members in domestic work to relieve women from this burden. However, although two of its articles stated that husband and wife must share all duties at home, even legislation was unable to make this a reality.

Promoting Full Employment

Full employment was one of the social policies promoted by Cuban development strategies in the first years. The participation of women in this policy was an example of how they were both involved in the transformation of society and transformed themselves. Very early in the 1960s measures were implemented that, though not described in that way at the time, can be seen in retrospect as having worked as "affirmative actions" toward eliminating the social disadvantages of women regarding employment. Thus once the literacy campaign concluded, the Ana Betancourt Program of schooling for rural girls transferred thousands of girls from the most backward areas of the country to the capital for courses on cutting and sewing. The objective was to train them in a short time in a remunerative activity and to both enable them to have their own income and broaden their vision of the world. Another program was implemented for domestic helpers so that these girls could study in night school, and girls were also trained as taxi drivers, bank employees, and telephone operators.

In addition there were several programs to integrate women from urban areas into agricultural employment, which mostly failed but provided useful lessons for the future. The FMC also promoted the inclusion of sanitary brigade members—who had been trained in first aid to help in the event of an invasion and to carry out health prevention campaigns—in studying and working as nurses and health technicians. Lastly, during 1969 and 1970 Cuban women replaced men in their jobs when the latter participated in the "10 million-ton sugar harvest," which aspired to break previous sugar production records. When this huge mobilization concluded and men returned to their previous jobs, women still continued to work and did not go back to being housewives, in contrast with similar events in other countries (FMC, 1975).

The value of these experiences was that they tested in practice different ways in which women could have access to employment during the first 10 years after 1959, and from then on could integrate into the active labor force in a permanent and increasing manner. The 1953 census showed that women were only 17.6 percent of the labor force, and only 16 percent of employed women had professional and technical jobs while 2 percent held executive positions. By the time of the 1981 census, however, women were 31 percent of the labor force, out of whom more than half (55 percent) held professional and technical occupations, 12 percent were in commerce and social food services, and 10 percent worked in industry. While 74 percent of women of working age were full-time housewives in 1953, this proportion decreased to 47 percent in 1981 (ONE, 1999). Actions to promote female employment were complemented by legislation, social policies, and actions to transform the patriarchal ideology. They also contributed to breaking the cycles that reproduced the disadvantages of Cuban women materially and spiritually—and not only those with the lowest incomes.

Together with the policies of full employment in public administration, the state created the conditions for more equality at work and at the same time guaranteed equal pay for equal work. As a result there was very little disparity between salary groups or wage scales: in 1988 the ratio between the highest and the lowest was 4.5 to 1. For 93 percent of the jobs the difference was 2.3 to 1 (Nerey and Brismart, 1999, cited in Espina Prieto, 2007). Salary became an element that contributed to the homogenization of social strata due to the minimal differentiation among them.

The participation of woman in the workforce increased steadily to 38.7 percent in 1989. The absolute number also increased (Núñez Sarmiento, 1988a). Women became salaried workers under the same legal conditions as men, however, in practice they earned less than men as they tended to hold jobs with lower salaries and were also absent more often because they had to take care of children, the sick, and the elderly, and because they had higher morbidity than men. Together with the burden of household chores, these were obstacles to women's progress and key issues in the fight against gender discrimination. Cuban women demanded equal participation in all branches of the economy, in all occupational categories—especially in senior administrative positions—as well as in the home.

Another of the economic policies of the first 30 years of the Revolution consisted in creating the bases of industry that would make the rest of the economy more dynamic. In these first years industry had a relatively high weight in the economy in order to offer commodities to the population, to create an administrative culture, and to train the workforce. However, despite their increasing numbers in the workplace, women did not initially integrate with the same dynamism into certain basic areas of industry or into agriculture, forestry, transportation, and construction.

This changed in the 1980s, with more than half the growth in the female workforce between 1981 and 1986 concentrated in the productive sphere. The industrial sector absorbed a quarter of the total, while public health, social welfare, sports, and tourism accounted for 15.6 percent, commerce 14.1 percent, and education 12.7 percent (Núñez Sarmiento, 1988b). From 1953 to 1970, 40 percent of the growth of the female workforce was in commerce. Between 1970 and 1981, 54.8 percent of the increase was in specialized social services, namely education and health, while industry accounted for 20 percent of the increase and agriculture for 11.9 percent (calculations made by the author with Dania Rodríguez, from the State Committee of Labour, for the FMC Seminar on the Application of the Nairobi Strategies, Havana, September 1988).

My intention is to demonstrate that even in conditions of underdevelopment there are actions that can be implemented to integrate women into the labor force, thereby assuring their independent place in society. Rather than waiting for economic growth, such actions were taken at the same time that the conditions for growth were implemented, so that women at work contributed to development. At the core of this concept was the exercise of political will to promote the participation of the whole population. There was also a comprehensive vision in the areas of economic and social policies, legislation, and ideology that looked for mechanisms to promote women to jobs as part of actions to break the cycle of social disadvantages, to ensure full equality for women that enabled them to participate in production as well as reproduction, and to promote them as agents of change not only for themselves but for all members of society.

Professional Training and Leadership Skills

The most important investments made in Cuba in the 1970s and 1980s came from the member countries of the Council of Mutual Economic Assistance (CMEA), which granted Cuba its main line of credit because the US embargo had practically closed the island's access to financial transactions with the rest of the world. (For an analysis of the effects of Cuba's relationships with the European countries that were members of CMEA, see Monreal, 2007; Pérez Villanueva, 2007.) Due to this cooperation and, above all, to its bilateral relationship with the Soviet Union, Cuba was able to send students to the universities of these countries. From 1962 up to 1990 when the CMEA ended, its member countries produced hundreds of thousands of Cuban graduates, most of them in specialties favored by those countries. Many of them were women, which contributed to the fact that by 1978 they made up half the category of professionals and technicians in Cuba, a proportion that went up to 56 percent in 1986 (Comité Estatal de Estadísticas, 1988).

The leadership aspect of the empowerment of women was an express purpose from the 1970s that has still not been fully achieved. At the end of the 1980s, several things suggested that Cuban woman would soon be in top positions. For example, women workers had higher levels of education than men, which allowed them to solve complex tasks; they were employed in all the sectors of the economy, even in those not traditionally female; and they were found in all occupational categories. But the burden of the "second shift" (see the next section), the lack of housing, and the patriarchal features of managerial policies thwarted this aspiration.

From the 1960s to the 1980s, Cuban social policies proposed to rationalize consumption as well as the needs of the population, not only as a way to solve the problems of poverty but also as an alternative to consumerism (Espina Prieto, 2007). This notion led to a system of distribution and consumption that operated in an egalitarian way and was capable of satisfying a set of basic needs for the entire population. However, it did not take into account two indispensable requirements in order to comply with the Marxist axiom "from each according to his/her capacity, to each according to his/her work": first, recognizing that there are differences regarding needs and the ways to satisfy them in the various groups of the population; and, second, acknowledging the imperative to provide differentiated treatment to the more disadvantaged sectors of the population.

A paradoxical situation resulted due to the influence exerted by these policies on the female population. As women were included in the most disadvantaged sectors of the population, this "homogenization" benefited them because they had access to consumer goods they had not had before. This meant improvements in nutrition, toiletry, clothing, footwear, and even domestic appliances for them and their families. Following the patriarchal tradition, women were those who managed the commodities distributed in an egalitarian manner by the state. Whether as salary earners who headed their homes and provided the main earnings, as providers additional to the man as the head of the home, or as housewives, they were the ones who managed on a daily basis the results of the social policies regarding consumption. This contributed almost invisibly to their abilities as decision takers, especially working women who took care of the home. Women also participated as agents of change in these transformations of consumption as part of the struggle against poverty. Therefore, it is important to understand women's role at the intersection of production and reproduction as part of the efforts against poverty and inequality and also as a way to promote their empowerment (Elson et al., 2008).

The Burden of the "Second Shift"

Early in the 1970s, the second congress of the FMC acknowledged that the instability of the female labor force was due, above all, to the pressure of household chores, to the nonexistence in many labor centers of work conditions suitable for women, and to the lack of economic incentives (FMC, 1975). Female workers were encouraged to qualify and requalify as a means of increasing the number of women who became professionals and technicians. However, the burden of a work at home continued to be a great difficulty. Moreover, working conditions fit for women were set up slowly, and in accordance with the ideas of the men who designed them rather than the real needs of women. This demand was progressively satisfied when women started to have access to senior positions in the mid-1980s.

However, there were two issues that called not only for solutions on the part of the state but also for the contribution of women and men. First, housework was very time-consuming as women did not have modern appliances or resources (laundries, semi-processed food products, etc.), and there were also problems with housing, including overcrowding and structural deficiencies. All this was taking place in the context of a very strong patriarchal ideology in women as well as men that prevented the latter from participating in housework. People tended to expect the state to solve all their difficulties, and women demanded more solutions from the state and not from their husbands to avoid marital conflicts.

Second, there were not sufficient day-care centers or kindergartens to meet the needs of working mothers during the first 30 years after 1959. The care of the elderly was not such a heavy burden at this time as the mothers of women who were first-generation workers were housewives who could take care of preschool children and the elderly. This started to change at the end of the 1960s and the beginning of the 1970s when those mothers started to grow old. Today women workers over 40 include in their second shift the care of the elderly at home, since there are not enough residential facilities for older people in the country (and furthermore Cuban culture rejects sending the elderly away to institutions). This problem has thus not been resolved and falls on the shoulders of women workers. As will be seen in the second half of this chapter, this has negatively affected the access of woman to senior administrative positions.

The Situation of Women by 1989

Women's participation in Cuban society has been part of the socialist transition and of its fight against all types of discrimination and in favor of social justice. This process has been subject to criticism, aimed at redressing aspects of programs that are not consistent with the realities that they want to transform, perhaps because they have been unable to interpret them or because the specific situation no longer exists. This critical conscience has operated at the highest levels of the political hierarchy, among academics, intellectuals, and artists, as well as in the daily life of women and men although, as with all critical thought, it has been hindered occasionally by persisting patriarchal currents and also by dogmatic stands.

The underlying concept of progress in this process did not have an economic or a welfare connotation. It was a participatory process, rather than women and men being treated as objects of change or as "victims" that should be assisted. This notion of progress granted importance to transformations at a global level and to the small details of daily life.

The changes that took place in female employment in the first 30 years involved both women and men, and both had to adapt to the new realities. Consequently Cuban social sciences evolved and began to study the problems of women to explain gender relations. For example, the limited female participation in senior administrative positions brought out the obvious reasons that hindered access and also the more subtle ideological arguments used by professional women with ample capacity to become leaders as to why they would not accept such positions.

In these years, women were the driving force of transformation in gender relations. They had to make greater efforts than men to conquer sexist inequalities, because they had to dismantle the cultural patterns of patriarchal ideology that existed in the society and in themselves. Moreover, they did not stop there because they also had to build new, non-sexist ideological patterns. In this endeavor they advanced more than men. Contrary to what has happened in other countries, where women have been revolutionized but society has stagnated as regards gender relations, in Cuba both women and the society changed.

To give an approximate idea of what Cuban working women were like at the beginning of the 1990s, I dare to describe them as women in the 22–55 age group who had either concluded ninth grade or had a university degree, from which we may infer that they had approximately 9–17 years of education; they had one or perhaps two children; their knowledge of health included the use of contraceptives and prenatal care as well as basic medical care for themselves, their children, and the rest of the family; they had a labor culture that allowed them to appreciate, among other things, the independence obtained by earning a salary; they had a sense of discipline that emanated from their presence in classrooms and in labor activities; they shouldered housework but understood that men should also participate (and openly criticized them for not doing so);

they began to care for the elderly in the family who could no longer contribute to domestic chores; and they were capable of taking decisions in their jobs and at home.

CRISIS, READJUSTMENTS, AND WOMEN'S EMPLOYMENT: 1990–2009

The Economic Crisis of the 1990s

In the mid-1980s Cuba started the process known as "rectification of economic errors and negative tendencies," aimed at correcting mistakes that had been made during the 1970s by uncritically copying Soviet economic recipes and applying them to the local situation. This "rectification" process was interrupted in 1990 due to the crumbling of so-called real socialism in Eastern Europe and the disappearance of the Soviet Union. Cubans therefore arrived at the crisis of the 1990s acknowledging that economic mistakes had been made—and the consequences these had had in the political, social, and economic arenas—without being able to implement the solutions that had already been designed to address them. Thus the country plunged into its worst years of transition to socialism.

In one year Cuba lost 85 percent of its foreign trade and exchange, which had been developed for 30 years with Eastern European countries on mutually advantageous terms. In the changed circumstances of the 1990s, it had to search for new trade and economic partners based on market laws ruling the international economy. At the same time, the United States toughened its 30-year blockade in order to aggravate the crisis and overthrow the Revolution. In 1992 the US Congress passed the Torricelli law, which added more obstacles to Cuba's foreign trade activities, and in 1996 passed the Cuban Liberty and Democratic Solidarity Act, known as the Helms-Burton law, which summarized all previous legislation on the blockade and added extraterritorial actions against Cuba. It attempted to compel third countries to adopt the same economic and trade restrictions implemented by the United States, or else those countries and their citizens would be penalized. These actions raised even more difficulties for Cuba's access to credit and markets when these were badly needed.

From 1989 to 1993 Cuba's GDP fell more than 33 percent, leading to a devastating decrease in social consumption (Perez Villanueva, 2008). This reduced the supply of rationed goods and services subsidized by the state to cover the basic needs of the population, while other non-rationed products practically disappeared. Black market dealings increased, which elevated the prices of goods and caused the value of salaries to plunge, affecting the more than 90 percent of the labor force employed in the public sector (Perez Villanueva, 2008). Two events show how hard the crisis hit food consumption: first, there was an epidemic of neuropathy, partly caused by acute nutritional deficiency; and second, the low birth weight index went up to 9 percent (Álvarez and Máttar, 2004).

Women, particularly female workers, had to fulfill their duties at the "crossroads of production and reproduction" in conditions of huge shortages. The frame of mind in which they demanded that the state solve their problems instead of working out local and personal solutions began to be overcome in the difficult years of the 1990s, as they devised daily strategies in their homes, neighborhoods, and work centers to survive the crisis and move beyond it. They were working a double shift in difficult conditions, being worn down physically and emotionally.

Economic Recovery Measures

Despite the crisis, the Cuban leadership guaranteed the basic needs of the population and made sure that the readjustment measures affected all citizens equally with no discrimination toward women. Its conception of development led to very different economic strategies and social policies from the neoliberal ideas that ruled readjustment policies in other countries in the region, as it maintained universal access to education, health care, subsidized food, social security, social care, sports, and culture.

The economic recovery measures of the 1990s included:

- Reform of state enterprises.
- Reintroduction of the economy into the world market with new trading partners.
- Decentralization of economic functions.
- Enlarging of the private sector.
- Increased importance given to tourism, telecommunications, and mining, with tourism acting as the "engine" that mobilized the other economic sectors.
- No devaluation of the Cuban peso and free circulation of the US dollar (with stores accepting only the latter opened to collect flows coming through remittances).
- Efficient use of a qualified labor force with technological learning abilities.

These measures were the result of adapting development ideas valid in Cuba up to that moment in order to incorporate the country into the global world economy. They continued the path of transition to socialism and were designed under enormous pressure, in a short period, flexibly, and with a practical approach (Monreal, 2007). Cuba began to come out of the crisis in 1994, and by 2004 GDP had reached 99 percent of the 1989 GDP (Pérez Villanueva, 2008). In 2007 the economy grew 7.5 percent, showing its gradual consolidation following a 42.5 percent increase in GDP since 2004 (Rodriguez, 2007).

All through the 1990s Cuba pursued industrialization as a way to substitute imports and to advance its long-range development plans. The country's economic connections with the rest of the world changed because its exports had to compete in different conditions than those prevailing in CMEA member countries. "The purpose was to keep the industrial structures existing previous to the crisis and to modernize them partially in order to wait for the moment when new investments appeared. Tourism, nickel and pharmaceutical industries received the highest investments" (Monreal, 2007, p. 130). The goal was to intensively exploit the country's natural resources, advanced technologies, and highly qualified labor force to reinsert Cuba into world markets with products of high aggregate value.

In these conditions tourism grew by 20 percent annually, pushing forward the rest of the economy while the basic social policies were retained. Tourism not only created direct and indirect jobs for 300,000 persons, but its growth stimulated the recovery of other areas such as agriculture and the food industry, beverages and liqors, construction, communications, and transportation. By 1994 it had replaced the sugar industry as the main earner of hard currency (García Molina, 2004). It dynamically influenced the so-called upward technological learning that took place in the fields of business administration—including marketing and advertising—and in-job training and retraining. The aviation, pharmaceutical (based on biotechnology), medical equipment, and telecommunications sectors also felt the effects of implementing this highly professional training.

One of the readjustment measures consisted in reorganizing part of the industrial structures previously designed for the CMEA integration scheme to produce for the Cuban domestic hard currency market. The purpose of this was to increase the amount of hard currency in the country, use it to restore the economy, and invest it in sectors aimed at covering the basic needs of the population. The potential purchasers of these goods were state enterprises, joint ventures, and Cubans with access to hard currency (those working in enterprises that paid their employees with hard currency, the self-employed, small land owners, and remittance receivers). These "inside–frontier–exports" helped reactivate and modernize those industries that were producing for domestic markets and selling their goods in Cuban pesos. The products initially lacked export quality, but some of them developed to levels of excellence and were purchased by tourist enterprises.

Women and the Labor Force

There are four main reasons that explain why Cuban working women stayed in their jobs during the crisis and readjustment years:

- First, approximately, one-third of Cuban women wage earners headed their households. Either they were the sole "bread winners" in their homes, or theirs was the highest income. This proportion would be even greater if one included working women who remarry or establish new marital unions, who are not the "official" heads of their household, but who consider themselves responsible for their children's economic support. This is typically the case with remarried women who live with their own children from previous marriages or marital unions.
- Second, women accounted for two-thirds of all Cuban professionals and technical workers. They thus represented the majority of a highly qualified labor force that is needed in a country that has a development strategy based on promoting economic activities requiring highly sophisticated technology and efficiency.
- Third, women wage earners had dramatically increased their participation in the Cuban labor force beginning in 1970. They therefore included a considerable proportion of younger women workers whose mothers had also worked and provided them with an example.
- Fourth, Cuban legal and political regulations and frameworks promoting women's participation in the labor force remained during the crisis years and were adapted to the changes taking place. For example, in 1993 maternity leave was increased from three to six months, and subsequently this went up to one year (and from 2,000 fathers were also granted the right to stay at home for up to one year taking care of their baby). In 1997 the Council of State passed the National Plan of Action Following the Beijing Conference of 1995, which included 90 articles to be enacted by state

institutions to continue promoting women's progress (República de Cuba, 1999).

While there was a small decrease in the number of women in the workforce, from 38 percent in 1996 to 37 percent in 2006 (ONE, 1999; 2006), their presence among technicians increased, with 39 percent of working women in 1996 and 44 percent in 2006 in this category. Thirteen percent of all working men worked as technicians in 1996, and 10 years later this figure was 17 percent. By 1996 women made up 64 percent of all technicians, and although this went down slightly in 2006, they were still the majority at 60 percent (ONE, 2006). Women's predominance in this area is due to the fact that since 1978 they have had higher educational levels than working men considered as a whole. From 1996 to 2006 women's participation in the category of blue-collar workers went down from 22 percent to 17 percent. There were fewer male blue-collar workers too: in 1996 they accounted for 51 percent and in 2006 for 49 percent of all workers.

However, women had very low representation in senior administrative positions, with only 6 percent of all working women at this level. Participation by gender among senior administrators showed stable quotas in 1996 and 2006: 71 percent and 70 percent for men and 29 percent and 30 percent for women. The latter were present in non-traditional sectors—steel manufacture, the sugar industry, sciences, telecommunications, and computers—as well as in traditional ones.

In spite of the role played by tourism in reinserting Cuba in the world economy as well as promoting other sectors with high aggregate value, exports continue to be mainly driven by natural resources (mining, tobacco, and fishery) where men have higher rates of employment. On the other hand, in those areas that produce exports based on high levels of technology, and that must lead Cuban exports in the future (telecommunications, the pharmaceutical industry based in biotechnology, and sciences), women are highly represented, particularly among professionals and technicians. Women are therefore key players in terms of Cuba's main economic asset: a qualified labor force with training capacities.

Levels of Salaries and Income

As mentioned earlier, consumption plunged with the decrease in GDP and the decline in the real value of salaries. Although salaries started going up in

2005, they have not regained their value because the consumer price index is still high. The labor force that on the threshold of the crisis accounted for 95 percent of the public sector reoriented toward the private, joint venture, and cooperative sectors as well as to those state enterprises that paid workers in hard currency. This led to a restructuring of the workforce between the public and non-public sectors. At present the former employs 75 percent of the total labor force, and includes those jobs that pay workers in Cuban pesos. These are the people, together with those depending on social security pensions and on social care, whose incomes have been most affected by the crisis.

Based on the scarce information available on income by gender as well as on the several case studies dealing with this topic, it seems that women have been more affected than men by the decreased values of salaries and pensions in the last years. They represent only one-tenth of self-employed citizens who belong to the private sector, only one-third of personnel in joint ventures, and are the majority of the beneficiaries of social care (Instituto de Investigaciones y Estudios del Trabajo, 2007).

According to official calculations in 1997, 50 percent of all citizens had access to hard currency, an index that grew to 62 percent in 2001 (Pérez Villanueva, 2008). While there were no available data on gender distribution, men represent 88 percent of the self-employed, 66 percent of those in joint ventures, and the absolute majority of small land owners—all categories with access to hard currency. As to which Cubans receive foreign remittances, the basic means for individuals to obtain hard currency, case studies indicate that women are the majority here. It would be worth studying this process of receiving and administering remittances from a gender perspective.

The crisis and reform processes that took place in the 1990s halted the trend of extending social equality to all and of eliminating the conditions that generated social disadvantages. An extremely complex situation developed that demanded rethinking state actions. Social policies were kept, but incomes and consumption seriously declined. An excellent study by the Research Institute of the Ministry of Labour, which analyzed gender differences in salaries among workers in the public sector, concluded , "Differences found in incomes, although small, disfavored women, who received 2 percent less in salaries than men" (Instituto de Investigaciones y Estudios del Trabajo, 2007). It also showed that women on average worked fewer days than men—and consequently were paid less—due mainly to sickness (60 percent), taking care of children and other family members (22 percent), and maternity leave (18 percent).

Of all registered absences, 77 percent were taken by women. Men rarely took leave from their jobs for reasons other than their own sickness. Only 4 percent of men categorized as technicians and blue-collar workers took leave to take care of their children and other family members, though 27 percent of men working in service categories—where salaries are lower—did so (Instituto de Investigaciones y Estudios del Trabajo, 2007). The reduction in the real value of salaries meant that these could no longer support families. Additionally, when goods that used to be part of the subsidized family basket started being sold for hard currency, large sections of the population were unable to access them. These events particularly affected women and men who worked in the public sector and women-headed households, which made up 32 percent of families in 2002 (ONE, 2002). All women had to find strategies to confront limited consumption while performing the second shift. Many people took on other jobs in addition to those that supplied their main salaries. Working women also undertook activities that provided them with additional income on top of their salaries. This multiple employment had not been practiced before the crisis.

The reduced income from social security and social care affected families with pensioners. Older people's contribution to the family budget shrank precisely when they needed additional care. This was a new situation compared to the first years of women's incorporation into the workplace and up to the crisis of the 1990s. As noted earlier, the mothers of these women workers had usually been housewives and taken care of their grandchildren. As time passed and they grew older, their daughters had to invent strategies to fulfill these additional duties known as the "ethics of care." Women workers now had to ask for unpaid work leave, or simply had to abandon their jobs, to look after their elderly family members on either their own or their husband's side. This also decreased family budgets.

The poverty level rose. In 1985, 6 percent of the population lived in poverty. Ten years later in 1995 this had risen to 15 percent, and at present 20 percent of the population in urban areas is considered to be in this category (Espina Prieto, 2007). While there are no national statistics measuring the gaps among population groups according to income, recent case studies indicate that differences may be as high as 1 to 24. This index is very different from the one calculated in 1978 that showed differences in income as 1 to 4 (ibid.). In neither case is there any information concerning gender.

The Role of Women in Tackling the Crisis

What role should women play in relation to economic strategies and social policies concerning employment in order to continue struggling against poverty and inequality, a process that was severely affected by the crisis of the 1990s? How must this be done without using neoliberal patterns, and in a world economy ruled by the market? Different proposals have been put forward, but all agree that the Cuban population is a fundamental asset to lead the way out of the crisis for it is already highly qualified and has great potential to continue its training.

Cuban women are very well educated. In 2006 19 percent of employed women had graduated from tertiary education, compared to 11 percent of employed men; and 56 percent of employed women had completed high school compared to 44 percent of men. In 2006–2007, 65 percent of all those that graduated from tertiary level were women. They accounted for 74 percent of graduates in Medical Sciences, 71 percent in Economics, 48 percent in Natural Sciences and Mathematics, 37 percent in Engineering and Architecture, and 34 percent in Agricultural Sciences, just to mention those programs related to basic economic activities that were traditionally considered male oriented (ONE, 2006; 2008). Many women have master's degrees and doctorates, and they enroll in graduate courses and study languages more than men do. Women are the majority of teachers and professors at all stages of the educational ladder—from pre-primary to graduate studies—and account for 57 percent of faculty members in the universities (Ministry of Higher Education, 2008).

Women workers are present in all economic sectors. As already noted, they make up the majority of the country's professionals and technicians—the most qualified members of the labor force. In those sectors that should spearhead the production of new exports with high aggregate value—the pharmaceutical industry based on biotechnology and computer programming—they surpass men. In the sugar industry, which is working to develop sugarcane derivatives, in aviation, and in tourism they are well represented among technicians and professionals, and they account for 52 percent of all those employed in the science sector (ONE, 2006).

Another requisite to participate in technologically advanced economic activities is to have leadership or decision-making abilities. In my research on women and employment in Cuba during the last 25 years, I have tried to show that changes in gender ideology have developed working women's decision-making abilities in all spheres of their lives: at their jobs, in their families, and with their partners. Living in a society that has been fundamentally transformed, and where they have been more subject to these changes than men, women have trained themselves to combine several tasks at their jobs and at home. Deeper studies have to be developed to understand how working women, whether they are professionals or not, have constructed decision-making know-how for all spheres of their lives, including the workplace and their traditional role in the household. In doing so, it should be noted that there are generational differences, with younger women more likely to "persuade" men in their families to perform domestic activities.

By exercising their decision-making abilities, women not only develop a sense of empowerment as human beings but also confirm their right to act independently. This is a basic civil right that Cuban women have not yet fully exercised. As mentioned earlier, less than one-third of all senior administrators in 2006 were women, and of all women workers only 6 percent were managers. These numbers—a trend for the last 15 years—are very low considering that women are the majority among professional and technicians, who should be considered the "natural" source of senior administrators.

In recent studies in which I interviewed professional women and men, the majority of the latter held senior administrative positions or had held them in the past. All of them were willing to perform leadership roles. On the other hand, only one-fifth of the women in my case studies had been and/or were willing to be senior administrators. The men considered that they were qualified for these responsibilities or were capable of being trained as such. They were "seeking" these posts. In contrast, most of the women claimed that they were not sufficiently trained. Some answered that it would take too much of their time, paying very little; others considered that it would be "an extra burden for the second shift"; while still others said that they preferred to continue upgrading their professional knowledge instead of being trained as managers. All of them believed that they were already decision makers in their jobs.

It is a mistake to interpret these answers to mean that these professional women lack self-confidence. What happens is that they know what they want to achieve in their fields of employment, and becoming managers is considered an obstacle to their projects. The few women in the sample who held senior administrative posts at the time of my study, or who had occupied them in the past, declared that they had not "looked" for these responsibilities, which had been assigned to them. Some of the women had been union leaders at the grassroots level. They acknowledged that their co-workers respected their authority; that they were capable of solving problems; and that although they were not completely satisfied performing managerial posts, they had exercised them responsibly. The fact that a majority of the Cuban women who are capable of becoming senior administrators do not want to become such reflects an unfinished area of gender ideology.

I suggest that there are a number of reasons why women have not yet attained leadership roles in the workplace, although these hypotheses need further research. One is that during the crisis years all women workers, including professionals, had to stay employed to keep their salaries in order to contribute to the family budget, whether they had a stable partner or were single and headed their households. As the value of the Cuban peso decreased, they were compelled to find a second job to contribute to their household incomes. If they had assumed a leadership post, it would have been difficult to obtain the necessary additional income. When managerial posts are capable of fulfilling the material needs of those that perform them, then more women will be interested. Moreover, Cuban managerial culture has been designed by and for men, and this has to be changed in order to get women to become managers.

However, all conditions are present at the social level to accomplish this goal, and the existence of six women ministers at present in so-called hard ministries proves that this is possible. Professional women have the ability to perform in leadership posts in the workplace. Women managers started at the basic levels of employment and have risen with constant feedback and learning in their job experience. They are familiar with all the complexities of the jobs they will direct. As discussed earlier, they are present in all sectors of the economy; they have made up the majority of professionals and technicians for the last 30 years; their educational levels are high; they perform complex tasks simultaneously; they are decision makers at their jobs and in their homes; and their curricula vitae are relatively long, beginning from the grassroots levels and making them familiar with their job environment.

Case studies comparing women and men's managerial methods show that the former introduce new concepts into the traditional, male-dominated managerial culture; they promote the upgrading of education levels among their subordinates; they do not fear competition; they use consensual methods in decision making; they have a personalized way of treating the people around them; and they direct their work by objectives. When all the needed conditions to promote women to managerial posts flourish in Cuba, it will be an irreversible process.

Patriarchal Holdovers ... and New Approaches

The wide access of women to leadership posts at the workplace cannot wait until the patriarchal cultural patterns in Cuba are completely transformed. It needs to be constructed both by assigning them to such posts as well as by making their leadership more socially acceptable in order to increase their willingness to take on such roles. This is what happened with the incorporation of women into the labor force in the 1960s and 1970s. Patriarchal ideology is a continuing social phenomenon that allows discrimination against women to endure, as important as the shortages in infrastructure at the household level and in the workplace.

Whether Cuban women are judges, engineers, doctors, scientists, or professors, they still carry the burden of the second shift. Studies show that they spend three times as many hours a week as working men doing household chores. A recent example underlines this point. Since 2004 Cuba has engaged in the "energy revolution," one aspect of which aimed at substituting both high-energy consumer appliances from the previously socialist Eastern European countries and very old ones that were bought before 1959. This "substitution" process was made in one year under the guidance and control of women working as professionals, technicians, and heads of departments at one of the ministries led by a woman: basic industry. Nevertheless, recent studies show that, although younger male family members tend to share household chores made easier by these new appliances, women keep performing the majority of these tasks, now pushing the buttons. They argue that men were not trained to use the appliances and fear they would spoil them.

Thus though some 70 percent of the Cuban population was born after 1959, and so has been exposed to the struggles against gender discrimination in the last 50 years, patriarchal ideologies permeate them "to the bone."

There are also examples of non-patriarchal approaches to politics in terms of gender. The way in which the project for the new law on social security has been introduced illustrates this. Cuba has experienced a decrease in its population from 2006 to 2008 due to the influence of multiple socio-demographic variables. It has an aging population: 17 percent of Cubans are 60 years old or more, and it is estimated that by 2025 they will account for 26 percent; life expectancy is 77 years. Birth rates have been low since 1978, with a fertility rate of 1.43 and reproduction at −0.69. The existence of family planning programs since 1964 and sex education programs has led to sexual health and the avoidance of unwanted pregnancies. The incorporation of women into the labor force since the early 1970s has also played a role. Prognoses for 2025 predict that the absolute number of Cubans of working age will decrease, as will the number of women of fertile age.

The new social security law therefore proposed to extend retirement age for women from 55 to 60 years and for men from 60 to 65. It also puts forward new calculations for pensions in order to increase them beginning from 2009 (Ministry of Justice, 2009). None of the arguments used to modify the law has "blamed" women for decreases in fertility rates or for staying in the labor force. On the contrary, the causes of low birth rates have been linked to questions concerning women and men alike, and changes in the law will benefit both. For example, at present widows have the right to decide which pension to keep: their own or their late husband's. When the new law is enacted, they will be able to keep both. Widowers will have the right to decide between their late wife's pension and their own.

CONCLUSION: THE NEED TO KEEP RETHINKING AND INTERROGATING CUBAN REALITIES

The following quotation from Mayra Espina Prieto (2007, p. 273) summarizes some important ideas:

> Cuban experience in the struggle to eradicate poverty has suggested to underdeveloped countries that this quest can only be efficiently developed if it departs from the perspective of merely "assistance" policies and puts itself in the dialectics of poverty, inequalities and development, understanding that poverty is not a social situation but is basically a social relation.

Policies aimed at women's equality in Cuba since 1959 shared this conception because of a conviction that women had to strive against the disadvantaged social relations that fostered their discrimination. They had to participate in ending the conditions that created their inequalities to become agents of their own transformation. To sustain women's development policies and struggle against inequalities and poverty, it has been indispensable "... to reactivate production and public services, to finance social policies that insure the well-being of the population, and to legitimize the state as responsible for this dynamic process" (ibid.).

Espina Prieto also writes that it is important to "reach a new understanding of equality as an essential characteristic of social relations and, basically, of distribution procedures and actions to satisfy material and spiritual needs, based on the understanding of diversity" (Espina Prieto, 2007). Differential criteria therefore need to be incorporated in policies to create goods and to distribute them. As noted earlier, socialism according to Karl Marx must be led by the principle "from each according to his/her capacities, to each according to his/her work," which means there will be inequalities depending on each person's contribution to society—for example, in terms of differences in jobs and differences in salaries. It could also warn against a mistaken notion of a totally "equalizing" society. Espina Prieto's suggestion that social scientists use a differential approach in their research could be fulfilled in studying Cuban experiences of promoting women in the workforce by using a gender perspective. This would mean analyzing women's leadership at work by considering their differences to men not only in the area of employment (or public sphere) but also in the home (or private sphere).

Policies aimed at promoting women's employment have been constantly updated based on the understanding that as women kept changing themselves through their roles as agents of social transformation, policies that promoted these changes had to be modified to adapt to the new women and to the new social conditions. This has been the case with the experiments with women's jobs in the 1960s, with the maternity law since the mid-1970s, and at present with the social security law.

The maternity law provided for differentiated treatment of working women during their pregnancy and during the first months after they gave birth. Although, as mentioned earlier, there have been legal and ideological means in place since 2000 to promote fathers' sharing in the care of their newborn, very few men have so far used paternity leave. So even when rights among women and men are equated, each one's reaction will differ according to her or his generation, zone of residence, occupation, educational level, and gender consciousness.

The way in which scholars and politicians have approached women's equality has changed over the last 50 years, basically because they incorporated a gender sensibility and did not stop at the point of considering only women. This was the case when legal conditions were created to ensure equal pay for equal jobs, and afterward, when it was necessary for women and society as a whole to eliminate the rest of the inequalities prevailing in social production and reproduction, as was the case of struggling against patriarchal decision-making patterns at the workplace and in families. It is also evident in the way that low fertility rates are being approached, that is, as a matter concerning both women and men.

However, the new visions of women and of gender relations have not been followed by the necessary transformations in the patriarchal subjectivities of men and women. There are still many traditional discriminatory attitudes. For example, the ideology that depicts men as the main breadwinners of their households keeps them from studying at the university level because of a belief that they must work to provide the main incomes of their "future families." Yet in fact research on women's employment in Cuba has shown that men have stopped being the main breadwinners (see, for example Safa, 1995). There is also a need to make the decision-making abilities of women workers an accepted component of the gender ideology, and to ensure that women's leadership is part of the social imagination as well as a reality.

REFERENCES

Álvarez, E., & Máttar, J. (coords). (2004). *Política social y reformas estructurales: Cuba a principios del siglo XXI.* Mexico City: ECLAC Subregional Headquarters in Mexico/ National Economic Research Institute (INIE)/United Nations Development Programme (UNDP).

Comité Estatal de Estadísticas. (1986). *Anuario estadístico de Cuba 1986.* Havana: Comité Estatal de Estadísticas.

———. (1988). *Anuario estadístico de Cuba 1988.* Havana: Comité Estatal de Estadísticas.

Elson, D., Chacko, S., & Jain, D. (2008). *Interrogating and rebuilding progress through feminist knowledge* (Note prepared for the UNDP project Assessing Development Paradigms through Women's Knowledge).

Espina Prieto, M. (2007). Efectos sociales del reajuste económico: igualdad, desigualdad y procesos de complejización de la sociedad cubana. In J. I. Domínguez et al. (Eds), *La economía cubana a principios del siglo XXI.* Mexico City: El Colegio de México.

FMC (Federation of Cuban Women). (1975). *Memoria: II National Congress of the Federation of Cuban Women.* Havana: Editorial Orbe, Instituto Cubano del Libro.

García Molina, J. M. (2004). Reformas económicas, políticas macroeconómicas y desempeño económico reciente. In E. Álvarez, & J. Máttar (coords), *Política social y reformas estructurales: Cuba a principios del siglo XXI.* Mexico City: ECLAC Subregional Headquarters in Mexico/National Economic Research Institute (INIE)/United Nations Development Programme (UNDP).

Instituto de Investigaciones y Estudios del Trabajo (2007). *La presencia femenina en el mercado de trabajo, en las diferentes categorías ocupacionales y sectores de la economía, la segregación horizontal y vertical, los salarios e ingresos en general.* Havana, November.

Ministry of Higher Education. (2008). *Prontuario estadístico educación superior, curso 2007–2008.* Havana, January.

Ministry of Justice. (2009). Decreto Ley de Seguridad Social No. 283/09, Gaceta Oficial de la República de Cuba. No. 13, 24 de abril de 2009. Año CVII. http://www.gacetaoficial. cu, accessed October 20, 2009.

292 Marta Núñez Sarmiento

Monreal, P. (2007). La globalización y los dilemmas de las trayectorias económicas de Cuba. In J. I. Domínguez et al. (Eds), *La economía cubana a principios del siglo XXI*. Mexico City: El Colegio de México.

Nerey, B., & Brismart, N. (1999). *Estructura social y estructura salarial en Cuba: encuentros y desencuentros*. Diploma paper for a master's degree in sociology.

Núñez Sarmiento, M. (1988a). *La mujer cubana y el empleo en la revolución*. Havana: Editora de la Mujer.

——. (1988b). *Case study of Cuba: women and the economic crisis*. United Nations Interregional Seminar on Women and Economic Crisis, Vienna.

ONE (Oficina Nacional de Estadísticas). (1999). *Perfil estadístico de la mujer cubana en el umbral del siglo XXI*. Havana: ONE.

——. (2002). *Censo de poblacion y viviendas de la República de Cuba*. Havana: ONE.

——. (2006). *Anuario estadístico de Cuba 2006*. Havana: ONE.

——. (2008). *Dirección de estudios sociales, inicio del curso escolar 2007–2008 y resumen del curso escolar 2006–2007*. Havana: ONE.

Pérez Villanueva, O. E. (2007). La situación actual de la economía cubana y sus retos futuros. In J. I. Domínguez et al. (Eds), *La economía cubana a principios del siglo XXI*. Mexico City: El Colegio de México.

——. (2008). *La evolución del modelo económico cubano*. Seminar on the 50th Anniversary of the Cuban Revolution, Havana.

República de Cuba. (1999). *Plan de acción nacional de seguimiento a la conferencia de Beijing de la República de Cuba*. Editorial de la Mujer, Havana.

Rodriguez, J. L. (2007). *Report on 2007 economic results*. Granma: National Assembly of the Popular Power.

Safa, H. (1995). *Myth of the male breadwinner: Women and industrialization in the Caribbean*. Boulder, CO: Westview Press.

13

Challenges for African Feminism in the Contemporary Moment

PATRICIA MCFADDEN

Activists and scholars [might] consider the notion of "introspection" as a possible conceptual facilitator for new thinking in terms of beginning to respond to the intellectual and ideological challenges with which many feminist and gender activists are currently faced, within their specific locations as radical women and as anti-capitalist/anti-patriarchal women.

THE JOURNEY THUS FAR: HOW WE ARRIVED AT THIS MOMENT

The moment that we have arrived at—those of us who are consciously engaged in transforming our worlds and the larger universal spaces of human habitation—is one that is riddled with tremendous contradictions and threats to the security and future of humankind, whilst bearing at its core the unique possibilities for transformation that have accompanied such "instances of change" throughout the human narrative (Tandon, 2009).

Most of what could be described as "negative" energy at the national and global levels is directly linked to the century-old systems of human and environmental exploitation and oppression (Kovel, 2002; Seager, 1999;

Shiva, 1989), while much of the hope for social and individual renewal remains embedded in the struggles of women and working people in every society. Speaking of the process of researching and documenting women's lives in communities in South Africa during the early years of independence, Taylor and Conradie (1997) had this to say: "More importantly, in reading aspects of their stories and in discussions with the women it was evident that through their many struggles women believed that the miracle of political democracy could be attained and that in this process their own liberation would become possible."

This fractured reality of human existence presents a particular set of challenges for feminists, and I would like to consider some of the tasks that lie ahead as we strive to navigate our paths forward by mobilizing the knowledge and visions of women (and men) who are dedicated to the celebration of life in all its diverse forms.

In each of our social locations as feminist activists who participate in the crafting and dissemination of radical knowledge, we are confronted with the consequences of inequality in ways that are deepening and expanding with such rapidity that our abilities to respond in credible and sustainable ways have come under severe pressure. For almost a decade, across the global and national theaters of our social landscapes, feminist thought and activism has increasingly reflected this deepening crisis of "response-ability." Many if not most of the conceptual and activist tools and strengths that we brought to our work at the close of the last millennium have fallen short of the challenges and tasks that await us as we step more firmly into this 21st century. Our movements, our assumptions about the state and its ancillary structures, and our understandings of class and the practices that accompany privilege and power have all come into question and urgently require closer and more radical scrutiny.

Every community of feminists is being challenged, whether they like it or not, by the realities that the crisis of capitalism and bourgeois democracy is throwing in our faces. Regardless of what we thought we had achieved and/or acquired, and what we had assumed would be "in place" in more definitive ways--within the state or in major institutions in our respective societies—this moment has become a "wake-up" call for us all, and we have to recognize this imperative and respond accordingly (Alexander & Mohanty, 1997). This is where I would like to make the entry point for my contribution to this collective moment of feminist introspection and renewal.

THE DIFFERENCE MADE BY WOMEN'S KNOWLEDGE AND AGENCY IN TRANSFORMING OUR WORLDS

There is no doubt that we have transformed our worlds and our lived social spaces in individual and collective ways that speak loudly to the value and intrinsic necessity of a dynamic women's presence in human societies. This is not new knowledge among women (see, for example, Brill, 1995; Friedlander, 1996; Kerr, 1993; Mayo, 2005; Taylor et al., 2000). However, in terms of the social construction and public recognition of women's intellectual traditions and inputs that we have made in all our societies, we have had to "break down walls and climb over fences" everywhere in order to initiate the processes of minimal inclusion into the academy, state policy arenas, and wider societal informational sites. (For a range of discussions and debates on the making of African feminist intellectuals on the continent, see *Feminist Africa*, 2002, 2008.)

In Africa, and particularly in eastern and southern Africa, women began the process of redefining and transforming the very notions and practices of freedom and personhood through their engagement in struggles against colonialism and racist supremacy. In the course of a century, women of all ages and class locations brought to the African experience of that centennial moment the long and arduous traditions and legacies of anti-patriarchal resistance and agency (Gasa, 2008; McFadden, 2005).

This historic fact may not be socially or politically recognized and, in the current context of the continental shift toward postcoloniality and deepening state-led repression through more nuanced and often fetishized forms, women's knowledge is becoming less and less visible and/or remembered. However, the truth of this fact cannot be erased.

Certainly, we see the reemergence, in the global and national media, of the tired stereotyped representations of African women (and their communities) as being in need of rescue, presumably from their governments and from those who now make up the state on the continent. The "politics of rescue" is being played out through the discourses and practices of humanitarianism and human rights scrutiny—initiatives that in and of themselves are not repugnant, just deeply problematical and eventually disastrous for all Africans (Shivji, 2006).

Increasingly, African women's voices are becoming an echo, filtered through the larger voice of international nongovernmental and United Nations structures and the media forms that they have created, that they control. While these institutions have often been a recourse that Africans can turn to—given the dire state of the continent's structural, ideological, and material conditions—this reality actually goes to the heart of the matter for feminists and all those who are engaged in social transformation (McFadden, 2007; Silliman, 1999).

We need to return to the moment when women initiated the political, social, and legal processes that resulted in the energies that remain central to the transformation of their lives and worlds. We have to return to the pivotal moment of change that marked the beginning of independence and initiated our journey toward postcolonialism. The notion of a "postcolonial moment" remains largely untheorized and barely considered as a distinctive political concept within either general political economy analysis or African feminist discourse. Most scholars use the notion of postcolonialism synonymously with neocolonialism, and often it is in reference to the state in Africa rather than to the relational terrain between citizens and the state—and additionally, for women, their struggles against patriarchal repression and exclusion. In my own work around citizenship and entitlements for African women, I have begun to explore the possibilities of conceptualizing postcolonialism and postcoloniality as sites of struggle and moments of political opportunity for fundamental transformation.

For women on the African continent, in the main, that moment was ushered in through their participation in struggles for freedom from colonial domination and exclusion. By bringing their agency to the struggles for liberation, African women transformed—in a limited sense, of course, given the narrowness of nationalism as a transformative ideology—the meanings and expressions of freedom, especially as they relate to women. This profound possibility is most dramatically reflected in the presence of African feminist intellectuals at every level of the international community. At the more real-life levels of women's daily struggles for entitlements and protections, these possibilities remain largely unrealized and often unimagined in a collective sense. This is not to imply or even claim that working women and their communities do not imagine an alternative life. Rather it is meant to draw our attention to the need for feminist scholars to scrutinize more closely the implications of neoliberalism for the consciousness and imaginations of working people, given its deeply reactionary ideological and practical impacts.

The postindependence years witnessed the emergence and consolidation of civil society movements that were crafted as vehicles of entitlement—facilitating the relocation of Africans, in their diverse statuses, in the public realm, and in a direct relationship with the neocolonial state. At the same time, the radical edge of women's politics, which was necessary to take them to the next level in their relationships with the state (in national, regional, continental, and global terms) and with the patriarchal institutions that inhabit and constrain their realities, remained muted and was often consciously blunted.

Through colonization, the relationship between the state and various categories of people within African communities had been shunted to the margins of the political and economic landscapes of their societies, with women and young males experiencing the most dramatic forms of such exclusion. Through the restructuring of social and economic relationships within these communities and across geographical spaces, the category of "African women" became "flattened" and homogenized—collapsed into feudal notions of womanhood and motherhood that were systematically exploited to create a reservoir of superexploited black labor across regions of the continent for several hundred years. Often African males colluded with such politics and practices, in desperate attempts to retain their beleaguered masculinity in the face of economic and political domination. There is an immense reservoir of historical and political economy analysis that has been produced on this process, which clearly shows how African communities were economically, legally, politically, and socially excluded from the colonial project, except in terms of capitalist exploitation and severe state and racial repression. For specifically feminist/gendered work see, for example, studies by Teresa Barnes, Merle L. Bowen, Jean Davison, Mark Epprechet, Lynette Jackson, and Elizabeth Schmidt.

As "breeders" for colonial capitalism, African women, especially in eastern and southern Africa, were kept outside any direct relationship with the state and/or public institutions (besides the missionary churches and later the white family household as worshippers/volunteers and domestic labor, respectively). This created a civic gap between African women in particular (and African communities in the main) and the state as the repository of rights and protections in all our societies. The colonial state and this "frontier capitalism" were embedded in racist supremacy and vicious, institutionalized systems and practices of violence, particularly sexual violence (which was not recognized by colonial state officials and was treated as shameful by black men, who often blamed women for its occurrence). Through the act of challenging and rejecting colonialism, African women began to shift the relationships of power between themselves and black men, while also initiating a more direct relationship between themselves and the neocolonial state to which black nationalists had ascended at the moment of independence. They instigated a consciousness of anti-patriarchal entitlement, which moved them and millions of their sisters (across class and social divides) into the public spaces of our societies—shaping the moment of independence as a radical moment for all women (Mohanty et al., 1991; Yuval-Davis & Werbner, 1999).

However, the class and social status differences that had initially been suppressed by colonial sexist and racist hegemony, and which had been aggravated over time by limited access to education and religious indoctrination, resurfaced soon after independence and posed critical challenges in terms of the formation of alliances and resistance strategies by women vis-à-vis the neocolonial state.

Deep-seated tensions surrounding issues of identity and aspired-to statuses—particularly in terms of class, ethnicity, race, age, ability, sexual orientation, and social location—simmered under the surfaces of the plethora of women's movements that sprung into action in the public spheres of all the countries of the continent over the past four decades. This was facilitated in large degree by the internationalization of "gender" as an analytical concept and later as a neoliberal tool for the deradicalization of women's movements and their political agendas. The depoliticization has occurred at several levels, largely in response to the increasing hegemony of neoliberal conservatism, instigated in the main by UN agencies, international humanitarian organizations, and donor agencies. Beginning with the insistence that "gender" was about equality for all and the imposition of "gender mainstreaming" as a requirement in the procurement of funding support to women's and other civil society organizations, such "global partners" have systematically depoliticized women's activism and rendered women's organizations largely humanitarian and/or pro-neoliberal structures.

As the neocolonial moment has progressed, women's movements have increasingly been rent asunder by struggles over their ideological directions. These civil society structures have been appropriated to a large extent by cliques of middle-class, professional women to further specific class interests and agendas (whether they pose as representatives of "the girl child" or "HIV and AIDS sufferers" or "women in politics"), and/or by opposition movements that rapidly transform themselves into political parties that treat women in typically sexist and misogynistic ways. The lessons for radical women—for feminists—have thus become ever more glaring. The case of Zimbabwe over the past 10 years is most instructive in terms of the appropriation of women's movements by both the neocolonial state and the opposition movements "for democracy."

While much has been written on the crisis and ongoing transition in the country, barely any critical analysis exists on how women's organizations were mobilized and reoriented to suit the interests of what has become the "Unity Government," which has the regular token female appointments at the level of the state and government. The time of "feminist reckoning" stands firmly at the doorstep of those women who define themselves as engaged individuals who are members of radical communities.

POSTCOLONIAL TRANSITION, GLOBAL CAPITAL, AND RIGHTWING AGENDAS

In eastern and southern African, the imperatives that neocolonialism is posing for radical women encompass the entire spectrum of women's politics as we had imagined, crafted, experienced, and performed it—whether in the academy, in our personal/private lives, or in the public institutions and state-controlled sites of power that radical women have been contesting for over five decades of "independence." Feminist intellectual–activists, who straddle the divide between the academy (and the various sites of knowledge production in our societies) and the vibrant—yet increasingly economically and politically repressed—sites of their communities and national spaces, are having to imagine new notions and strategies in responding to this intractable moment of postcolonial transition (see Chigudu, 2002 and the work of Yvette Abrahams, Amanda Gouws, Shareen Hassim, Mary Haymes, Desiree Lewis, and other feminist academics based in southern Africa).

It is a moment that is deeply contested and exceptionally uneven in historical, gendered, and class terms, with most aspiring citizens having been driven further away from the state and the resources that it controls. In most societies on the continent, the gap between "the state"—which controls the most critical resources in the society—and "the people," who constitute largely economically, politically, legally, materially, and structurally excluded communities, was deliberately recreated through the implementation of structural adjustment programs (SAPs) over the past three decades (Caffentzis & Federici, 2001; Maramba et al., 1995).

In fact, the vibrancy of the independence moment, which was most poignantly encompassed by the engagements that African people entered into with those who assumed occupancy of the state, has been shattered by a globalized neoliberalism that has deepened economic exclusion and widened the social distances between and among Africans everywhere. The discursive and combative relationships among "ordinary" Africans (be they intellectuals, working people, women activists, environmentalists, or queer and/or disability activists)—which are essential for the emergence of a new and substantially different notion and practice of citizenship—were systematically and often brutally usurped through the imposition of policies that were designed to "put Africans in their place." I mean that the colonial project mapped the world and its peoples in particular classed and raced ways that still frame the underbelly of current neoliberal policies and practices. As the literature on this strategy clearly shows, this forced removal of the people from the public sphere as a contested arena of power was achieved most efficiently through the complicity of the newly emergent black ruling classes everywhere on the continent, in collusion with globalizing capital (Elich, 2006; Shivji, 2006; Tandon, 2009).

Where people attempted to resist this capitalist imperative, they were taught brutal lessons through military interventions, the imposition of sanctions, and systematic exclusion from the "global community." See, for example, the literature on Angola and Mozambique in southern Africa and on Grenada in the Caribbean, and analysis of the impacts of economic sanctions and the use of military and economic blockades on Cuba and Zimbabwe over the past five decades. While controversy rages concerning the "right" of the so-called international community to impose sanctions on any government that does not respect the human rights of its citizens (which is code for US/UK and EU hegemony in the international sphere and a defense of their economic and military interests), historical memory should be surfaced on how these very present-day guardians of "human rights in the world" resisted—and in the case of the United States refused outright—the imposition of sanctions on the Apartheid regime during the years of struggle for freedom by the people of southern Africa.

This recent history is often obfuscated by loud hegemonic voices and messages that insist on homogenization through "globalization" as the inevitable present and future of all humans (and that claims that history has ended and that we are all now postcapitalist, postmodern, and postfeminist). In terms of a more intersectional analysis of rightwing strategies like SAPS, however, it throws up several challenges that feminists and radical women in general need to acknowledge and begin responding to.

We need to ask how neocolonialism interfaces with global capitalist interests and agendas and scrutinize the rightwing agendas that are being imposed on the lives of working communities. More specifically, how have these agendas translated into very conservative discourses and notions of womanhood, wifehood, and person-hood for women via the plethora of HIV and AIDS programs in all our communities on the continent? For example, most if not all HIV and AIDS programs and the discourses that accompany them in Zimbabwe are pushing a very conservative, rightwing agenda on women's bodily and sexual rights. This reflects a deeply reactionary notion of community that separates out working people, particularly those who are located in remote rural spaces, marking them with a unique cultural and social identity (by deploying remnants of feudalism and conservative notions of gender identity), and further exoticizing them through the invention of a "unique voice"—which in reality is a conservative stance on women's and people's realities (for an excellent example, see SAfAIDS, 2009a). They are questioning the relevance of certain laws (such as the law criminalizing marital rape) and also claiming that women "in communities" want to be able to "choose" on issues of inheritance after the death of a husband (SAfAIDS, 2009b). This is only one example of what is clearly a reactionary trend within civil society in Zimbabwe to push for more religious-inspired, tradition/culture-centered discourses on women's issues and the laws and rights that activists had put in place during the past three decades of independence.

We need to ask how such exclusionary policies have affected the abilities of women to be in the public sphere; how they have restructured women's political (class) orientations and boomeranged back onto these movements in ways that are recreating conservative, reactionary, and even feudalistic notions and discourses about women and their futures. How have these exclusionary strategies affected the ability of women activists in terms of how they conceptualize freedom and its articulation/translation into real changes in women's lives? Are women activists who had acquired a radical consciousness about women's entitlements and interests in the recent past now shuffling their intellectual feet in the presence of a reactionary discourse about women because they do not want to be seen to be "radical" and "unreasonable?" After all, donor guidelines now determine the ideological and political orientation of research and discourse in a society such as Zimbabwe—and these guidelines are conspicuously and blatantly reactionary, given their neoliberal foundations and orientations.

How does exclusion continue to be reinscribed and reinvented at all the levels at which women struggle for basic livelihoods and a sense of life with dignity, considering that neoliberal capitalist ideology and policies are the order of the day across the societies of the continent?

BRINGING INTROSPECTION TO HOW WE ARE DOING OUR FEMINISM

There is no doubt that feminists everywhere in the crisis-ridden capitalist world understand that the time for us to regroup and take stock of our recent and current political herstory is upon us. Feminists in Africa, in Latin America, in Europe and Asia, in the Caribbean and Oceania are beginning to ask new and difficult questions about where the feminist movement is; how it needs to be strengthened and/or rebuilt; and what directions and positions feminists will have to adopt in order to respond in more long-term ways to the phenomenon of capitalist globalization—which is much more than the hyper-corporatization of finance capital and a concomitant expansion of Western-driven militarism (see Riley et al., 2008; Tax, 2008; Wilson et al., 2005).

I would like to propose that activists and scholars consider the notion of "introspection" as a possible conceptual facilitator for new thinking in terms of beginning to respond to the intellectual and ideological challenges with which many feminist and gender activists are currently faced, within their specific locations as radical women and as anti-capitalist/anti-patriarchal women.

Introspection is appealing to me for several reasons—some of which might not be immediately explicable and are still largely "felt" in terms of my own search for new radical thinking tools (I have been exploring some of these concepts in more recent work—for example, McFadden, 2008, forthcoming) I think that by adopting an introspective stance, one is able to revisit the feminist landscape and approach particular moments, events, and ideas that shaped one's understanding of what occurred in a more continuous manner. By reconnecting the thread of understanding about particular conjunctures and the significances that they are endowed with for us as radical women (such as the moment of independence and our entry into the public spheres of our societies as formerly excluded, raced subjects in colonial capitalist landscapes), one can retrace the discourses and ideas. Sometimes, one is able to reclaim those intellectual possibilities that the moment "threw up," but that fell between the cracks of our understanding amid the urgencies that drove the moment. It is interesting that several feminists in the Western academy are also calling for this retrieval of our feminist herstory in order to better understand the current moment (see, for example, Hesford, 2009; Plate, 2008).

By being introspective, we are able to mine and excavate our resistance traditions and narratives and energize those legacies and expressions of our knowledge that have been consistently and systematically under attack (through the backlash) for the past five decades—in fact, as soon as we stepped into the public realm and became political women in anti-patriarchal, antiracist, and antihomophobic ways in particular.

In eastern and southern Africa, we are faced with a situation where the transition to postcoloniality is characterized by a deepening economic and political crisis that is most manifest in the increasing inability of working people to reproduce themselves socially and otherwise. The crisis of social reproduction is directly linked to the global crisis of capitalism, as well as to the seemingly unstoppable consolidation of state and economic power by emerging black ruling classes across our continent. Militarism, neoliberalism, blatant plunder of the natural resources of a society—often accompanied by the imposition of sexual and other forms of coercion and impunity—continue to characterize the process of transition from neocolonial malaise to postcolonial rule as an active and directed intention by most African ruling classes.

In the wake of this class and state reconfiguration, women's and civil society movements have all but vanished from the public and political landscape—replaced structurally and ideologically by UN and donor (read Western state) agencies and discourses. Everywhere across the continent, vibrant, autonomous movements (composed of structures, discourses, knowledge systems, skills, and radical political agency) have been systematically absorbed into regional, continental, or international organizations. Silliman (1999, p. 134) makes this point very clearly when she argues:

> Women's NGOs are among the fastest-growing groups within the NGO sector. While one may expect that women's NGOs differ from other NGOs, in fact they mirror what is occurring throughout the NGO sector. Many women's NGOs too are being restructured in keeping with the dictates of a neo-liberal political and economic agenda.

The African civil landscape is being carefully refashioned in ways that exclude radical ideas about anything: women's health, rights, ideologies, knowledge, demands, entitlements, protections—the entire gamut of issues and agendas that should rightfully be defined and envisioned by African citizens through their publicly situated movements and institutions.

This is the reality that faces us as radical women in our regions and continents. We urgently need to engage in a deep interrogation of the knowledge systems that we have created; ask new sets of questions about our relationships with the state and resistant patriarchal institutions that are reshaping the African political and sociocultural landscape; challenge the reemergence of revanchism and feudalism, especially in societies such as South Africa that were supposedly "more developed"; and craft new intellectual and activist strategies and practices in order to rebuild the feminist movement—without the conservatism and narrowness of nationalism as an ideological prop.

The tendency to adopt defensive attitudes toward a critique of neo-colonialism and the conservative implications of nationalism for African women's movement politics generally does not assist feminist and/or gender activists and scholars to further the conceptual and practical agenda for women. Nationalism has undoubtedly served certain positive functions for women of all classes, and it must be highlighted and celebrated. However, as an ideology and as a practice it is fundamentally androcentric and limited in its ability to realize a more radical agenda in terms of the interests of working women in particular, and of other excluded groups in all our African societies. Therefore, women who name themselves feminist and who aspire to transform their respective societies will have to delink their personal and national identities from the established notion of nationalism and craft new elements of identity and political activism in order to move forward with a sustained agenda.

We must reclaim our political agency by exposing the fetishized forms that repression and exclusion have assumed through the manipulation of neoliberal discourses of inclusion and openness. We have to take back our discourses and the meanings of rights and entitlements from the hegemonic agencies that are not only silencing the vibrant, young, and diverse voices of African women everywhere, but are replacing them with an echo that is composed of media-generated, generalized stories about African women; stories that are written quickly and without depth or acknowledgement of the political struggles and tensions that shape and often undermine the efforts of African women to change their worlds; narratives that are usurping the abilities of African women to speak for themselves.

We have to question the re-homogenization of African women's "voices" and identities—the flattening of our identity landscapes through the imposition of conservative notions about our relationships with the state in our respective countries; about our understandings of rights and entitlements; about disease and health; and about our views on who we are in the world. These are the imperatives that face us as intellectual, activist, radical women—on our continent and across the face of the planet. We have to take our lives back now.

REFERENCES

Alexander, M. J., & Mohanty, C. T. (1997). *Feminist genealogies, colonial legacies, democratic futures.* New York: Routledge.

Brill, A. (Ed.). (1995). *A rising public voice: Women in politics worldwide.* New York: The Feminist Press.

Caffentzis, G., & Federici, S. (2001). A brief history of resistance to structural adjustment. In K. Danaher (Ed.), *Democratizing the global economy* (pp. 139–144). Monroe: Common Courage Press.

Chigudu, H. (Ed.) (2002). *Composing a new song: Stories of empowerment from Africa.* Harare: Weaver Press.

Elich, G. (2006). *Strange liberators: Militarism, mayhem and the pursuit of profit.* Tamarac, Florida: Llumina Press.

Feminist Africa. (2002). *International politics.* Issue 1. Retrieved from http://www.feministafrica. org/index.php/edition_one_editorial

———. (2008). *Researching for life: Paradigms and power.* Issue 11.

Friedlander, E. (Ed.). (1996). *Look at the world through women's eyes.* New York: NGO Forum on Women.

Gasa, N. (Ed.). (2008). *Women in South African history: Basus'iimbokodo, bawel'imilambo/ they remove boulders and cross rivers.* Cape Town: Human Sciences Research Council (HSRC).

Hesford, V. (2009). The politics of love: Women's liberation and feeling differently. *Feminist Theory, 10*(1), 5–33.

Kerr, J. (Ed.). (1993). *Ours by right: Women's rights as human rights.* London: Zed Books.

Kovel, J. (2002). *The enemy of nature: The end of capitalism or the end of the world?* London: Zed Books.

Maramba, P., Olagbegi, B., & Webaneno, R. T. (1995). *Structural adjustment programmes and the human rights of African women.* Harare: Women in Law and Development in Africa (WiLDAF).

Mayo, M. (2005). *Global citizens: Social movements and the challenge of globalization.* London: Zed Books.

McFadden, P. (2005). Becoming postcolonial: African women changing the meaning of citizenship. *Meridians: Feminism, Race, Transnationalism, 6*(1), 1–22.

———. (2007). *The women's movement in the SADC region: Recommendations and strategies for revitalization, lobbying and advocacy.* Harare: HIVOS.

———. (2008). *Challenges and possibilities in crafting a contemporary feminism in southern Africa.* Paris: Cité University.

———. (Forthcoming). *Re-crafting citizenship in the postcolonial moment: A focus on southern Africa.* Paper presented at the Cité University of Paris, April 2009. Cité University, Paris.

Mohanty, C. T., Russo, A., & Torres, L. (1991). *Third world women and the politics of feminism.* Bloomington, Indiana: Indiana University Press.

Plate, L. (2008). Remembering the future; or, whatever happened to re-vision. *Signs: Journal of Women in Culture and Society, 33*(2), 389–412.

Riley, R. L., Mohanty, C. T., & Pratt, M. B. (Eds). (2008). *Feminism and war: Confronting US imperialism.* London: Zed Books.

SAfAIDS. (2009a). *Changing the river's flow series: Challenging gender dynamics in a cultural context to address HIV.* Harare: SAfAIDS.

———. (2009b). *Cultural attitudes, perceptions and practices on HIV infection: A baseline towards challenging gender dynamics in a cultural context to address HIV in Seke Zimbabwe.* Harare: USAID and SAfAIDS.

Seager, J. (1999). Patriarchal vandalism: Militaries and the environment. In J. Silliman & Y. King (Eds), *Dangerous intersections: Feminist perspectives on population, environment and development* (pp. 163–188). Cambridge, Massachusetts: South End Press.

Shiva, V. (1989). *Staying alive: Women, ecology and development.* London: Zed Books.

Shivji, I. (2006). Lawyers in neo-liberalism. *Pambazuka News,* Issue 266, August 24. Retrieved August 17, 2010, from http://www.wiego.org/stat_picture/www.pambazuka. org/en/category/comment/36468

Silliman, J. (1999). Expanding civil society, shrinking political spaces: The case of women's nongovernmental organizations. In J. Silliman & Y. King (Eds), *Dangerous intersections: feminist perspectives on population, environment and development* (pp. 133–162). Cambridge, Massachusetts: South End Press.

Tandon, Y. (2009). Political, economic and climate crisis of Western civilization: Dangers and opportunities. *Pambazuka News,* 426. Retrieved August 17, 2010, from http:// pambazuka.org/en/category/features/55334

Tax, M. (2008). *Why we need a feminist left.* Paper presented at the Left Forum, New York.

Taylor, V., & Conradie, I. (1997). *We have been taught by life itself: Empowering women as leader—The role of development education.* Pretoria: Human Sciences Research Council (HSRC).

Taylor, V., Mager, A., & Cardoso, P. (Eds). (2000). *Cracks in the edifice: Critical African feminist perspectives on women and governance.* Cape Town: University of Cape Town/SADEP.

Wilson, S., Sengupta, A., & Evans, K. (Eds). (2005). *Defending our dreams: Global feminist voices for a new generation.* London: Zed Books.

Yuval-Davis, N., & Werbner, P. (1999). *Women, citizenship and difference.* London: Zed Books.

14

"Progressive Masculinities"
Oxymoron or Achievable?

JAEL SILLIMAN*

It is imperative for women's movements as well as feminist scholars to engage the developing body of research on masculinities and seek out more partnerships and collaborations with nascent activities led by men to reach other men, for greater synergy between these two movements.

INTRODUCTION

Over the last decade, there has been a dramatic increase in research and programming from different global locations that interrogate, reimagine, and challenge what it means to be a "man" in the 21st century. Some of this work is a direct outcome of mandates that came out of the United Nations International Conference on Population and Development (ICPD) in Cairo (1993) and Fourth World Conference on Women in Beijing (1995), which called for greater male participation in promoting

* The author would like to thank the Ford Foundation for support of this work through a study leave program, Lory Harbison for her assistance with the presentation of the chapter and with gathering materials, and Larry Harbison for his suggestion of an appropriate title; and is also deeply grateful to the groups mentioned in the chapter who provided insights and comments as well for the careful reading and critical comments of Riki Wilchins, Willy Mutunga, Nikky Naylor, Esta Soler, and Gary Barker. Their insights were invaluable.

sexual and reproductive rights. These have been supported by initiatives such as the affirmation by the 48th Session of the Commission on the Status of Women (CSW) in 2004 of the need to engage men and boys in questioning and confronting gender-inequitable norms, and the WHO underlining of the need to challenge gender inequities to improve health (see, for example, WHO, 2007).

These global mandates and initiatives, together with over four decades of feminist organizing, have shifted the discourse from woman's rights to a focus on gender and gender relations. The development of gay rights activism and queer theory, the rapid spread of HIV and AIDS, the work of some women's rights groups and activists, and the invisibility of men or "men as problem" in the international development literature have contributed to the burgeoning field of study and action. The assumption is, and evidence is increasingly finding, that social constructions of manhood can and do change. Advances in public health, greater gender equity, and improved well-being for men, their families, and communities can be attained through challenging ideals of "hegemonic masculinity."

Anandhi et al. (2002, p. 2) define "masculinities," both their "hegemonic" and "subordinate" forms, as follows:

Masculinity—both an ideological construct(s) and a set of practices—is not homogenous across time, space and social groups ... we need to differentiate between the "hegemonic" variant of masculinity and its subordinate forms. The dominant model or hegemonic masculinity in any society is often an ideal realizable (if at all) by a very small group of men who control power and wealth. Such a hegemonic variant emerges as the norm against which other "subordinate" variants of masculinity are placed and assessed. The "subordinate" variants of masculinity are valid for most of the population who remain powerless, even while they remain complicit in sustaining the hegemonic masculinity at a broader level by desiring to imitate it .... Those men who do not or cannot conform to the hegemonic masculinity are treated by those who do as effeminate and inferior. Thus, any study of masculinity needs to explore the complex inter-relationship between competing notions of masculinities and femininities.

Riki Wilchins notes:

In No [North] American society, there certainly are forms of masculinity (think Donald Trump) related to alpha male status of power and wealth. However, there are equally dominant forms that don't fit this: rappers who combine displays of hyper-musculature and aggression either with economic deprivation or (think 50 Cent) with the acquisition of status symbols (if not real power); the "Rambo" model of hyper-militarism and violence, and the cowboy model (think John Wayne) of the classic American West. All of these are some version of hegemonic Western masculinity, but only some are linked in any direct way to wealth, or even broad social power. (Personal communication, 2009)[1]

The intersection between masculinities and other axes of power is underlined. Clearly, women too are enmeshed in the process of defining and sustaining masculinities—as mothers, relatives, friends, sexual partners, and coworkers. It is the political and theoretical agendas of feminism that have enabled this new discursive category to emerge.

Feminist movements that have been weak in reaching out to men, and have had some difficulty in attracting young women in some countries, could be reenergized by embracing the efforts of progressive masculinity (also called "feminist masculinity") (see Mutunga, 2009). Activist–scholar Andrea Cornwall has suggested that alliances with men's groups could help move the debate and action of the progressive masculinity movement from a narrow focus on addressing violence against women and issues related to sexuality and fatherhood, toward issues of equal pay and leave entitlements, parental rights and benefits, men sharing housework, and addressing masculinities in the political arena and the economy (IDS, 2007). Furthermore, as efforts to deconstruct masculinities expand to include concern with and for marginalized men, marginalized sexual identities, and the subjugation of "weaker" men in patriarchal systems, opportunities emerge to work together with the growing sexual rights movement as a partner in feminist struggles, which broadens the base and reach of women's movements.

This chapter is intended to provide a road map for feminists in considering the work on masculinities that is grounded in gender equality, which I am calling progressive masculinities, and in seeing how best to respond to these efforts. I briefly introduce intellectual work on issues of masculinity, highlighting a key work from each analytical category, and note some of the important activities in the field. I then categorize the types of programs being implemented and refer to some innovative local projects. The chapter closes with a discussion of recent attempts by both women's organizations and men's groups working in the area of

---

[1] R. Wilchins, founding Executive Director of the Gender Public Advocacy Coalition (GPAC), personal communication, 2009.

masculinities to take their various local efforts to the global arena. These struggles seek to bring about policy changes at national and international levels to relieve men from the burdens of hegemonic masculinity, which has been oppressive for many men, and simultaneously creates greater gender justice.

FEMINISM, MALE MOVEMENTS, AND GENDER JUSTICE

Despite its foundation in feminist theory, literature on masculinities is rarely written by, referred to, or engaged with by feminist activists and scholars. An anomaly is the work of feminist writer Barbara Ehrenreich, whose early book, *The Hearts of Men* (1983), explores the conundrum of the relationships between women and men in America since the early 20th century and tracks the instabilities inherent in this relationship through time. Here, Bell Hooks (2004, pp. 114–115) is another exception; she insists that redefining maleness is essential for feminists:

> Undoubtedly, one of the first revolutionary acts of visionary feminism must be to restore maleness and masculinity as an ethical biological category divorced from the dominator model. This is why the term patriarchal masculinity is so important, for it identifies male difference as being always and only about superior rights of males to dominate, be their subordinates females or any group deemed weaker, by any means necessary. Rejecting this model for a feminist masculinity means that we must define male-ness as a state of being rather than as performance. Male being, maleness, masculinity must stand for the essential core goodness of the self, of the human body that has a penis. Many of the critics who have written about masculinity suggest that we need to do away with the term, that we need "an end to manhood." Yet such a stance furthers the notion that there is something inherently evil, bad, or unworthy about maleness ....

Besieged by the backlash against women's rights as well as the lack of funding for their critical work, feminist movements pay scant attention to this upsurge of scholarly work, to men's organizing efforts, and to the support of several UN and bilateral agencies and large international NGOs on the topic of masculinities. These have included the United Nations Children's Fund (UNICEF), United Nations Development Fund for Women (UNIFEM), United Nations Population Fund (UNFPA), and WHO, as well as bilateral agencies including the Swedish and Canadian

International Development Agencies (Sida and CIDA), and NGOs such as CARE International, Save the Children Sweden, Engender Health, and the International Center for Research on Women (ICRW).

When women's organizations and feminist thinkers and leaders have paid attention to this nascent movement of men that seeks to transform men's subjectivity and roles and/or seek gender justice, they have often been quite skeptical. The African Women's Development and Communication Network (FEMNET)—one of the few key feminist networks that does work with men and leads several men's groups, including a program called the Regional Network of Men for Gender Equality Now—explains how "... other feminists feel that working with men and boys is diluting, diverting and trivializing our struggle ... many doubt that men and boys can commit to changes that would mean them losing the privileges they now enjoy" (Mutua, 2009).

By and large, there has been an unspoken and untheorized reaction that assumes men's organizing efforts reframing gender relations could compete with efforts of women's movements to attain gender justice, take the leadership away from women, or challenge feminist priorities. There is also grave concern that the paltry sums of money available to advance women's rights could be siphoned off for these initiatives.

Male scholars and men's organizations have engaged feminist scholarship and practice, despite critiques both from other men and from feminists. (See Mutunga, 2009 for a fuller discussion of the risks men face due to their involvement in gender justice.) Some of the leaders of these organizations cut their teeth in women's organizations and follow their leadership. A few of the key men's organizations have reached out to younger feminists or hired feminists to work with them to interrogate and challenge definitions and ways of being a man. Some have aligned themselves with women's organizations working with men to advocate for women's rights and to reduce gender-based violence and sexually transmitted diseases, resulting in a few working partnerships between women's organizations and male-led efforts around this set of concerns—one example is Women for Women International's work in the Democratic Republic of Congo. However, this rather narrow focus may preclude deeper analysis among collaborating partners regarding underlying issues of power and privilege.

Only very recently was a full-scale effort launched to gather up key organizations and leaders in the male movement for gender equity to go beyond individual projects and advance a bold policy agenda for men's efforts to transform gender roles. I contend that it is imperative for women's movements as well as feminist scholars to engage the developing body of research on masculinities and seek out more partnerships and collaborations with nascent activities led by men to reach other men, for greater synergy between these two movements. Organizers of women's movements also need to clarify the terms on which it would be useful to include men in their work to advance gender justice and question patriarchal structures.

On a parallel note, the expansion of studies and research in "queerness" is also not being addressed by NGOs pursuing greater gender equality. Any true movement for "gender justice" will have to integrate analysis of "queerness," of nonbinary forms of gender that are not simply new iterations of femininity and (less toxic forms of) masculinity. Riki Wilchins states,

> Put another way, from the feminist perspectives I'm familiar with, reforming gender roles is a shorthand for redistributing power and privilege more equally between the two binary genders, rather than any wholesale attempt to attack that system as a whole. Not meaning to diminish its importance for many woman, for that small group of us who live "off the binary" this seems a limited project indeed. (Personal communication, 2009)[2]

This is not to suggest that integrating an analysis of "queerness" would result in the successful promotion of nonbinary gender. Rather, I assert that:

- Feminism would seem to have much to gain from deeper engagement with gender that interrogates rather than simply redeploys the binary.
- Redistributing power and privilege more equally between two "allowable" genders will leave a small but substantial minority still deeply oppressed.
- There remains significant doubt whether the current "separate but equal" approach to gender—which still depends on binary regulation of the sexes—can ever work in the long run.

Perhaps before using the term "gender justice" we ought to define what kinds of justice we want and for whom.

---

[2] R. Wilchins, founding Executive Director of the Gender Public Advocacy Coalition (GPAC), personal communication, 2009.

Engaging progressive movements of men is urgent because counter movements, seeking to reconstruct "manhood" in moulds that are more traditional, are gaining ground. These movements emphasize the need for men to "take back their manhood," shoulder their patriarchal responsibilities, better provide for their families, and in doing so, extend male authority and privilege. Fundamentalist movements all over the world are reasserting traditional patriarchal norms—the Promise Keepers in the United States, for example, seeks to reassert male leadership of the family in order to "protect" women.

There have also been broader, decentralized movements of men, sometimes dubbed "mythopoetic movements" in the Western world that, while deconstructing masculinity, have been less mindful of male privilege (Magnuson, 2007). This therapeutic model, launched largely by white men of privilege, has had an overriding emphasis on personal growth and healing and been less concerned with issues of social justice, which includes reducing inequities among men. Additionally, an element in the men's movement has been antifeminist in some of its stances. For example, one wing in the United States has reacted very negatively on issues where the women's movement has made gains relating to family law and the laws on domestic violence as well as child custody. In this political context, partnering with progressive efforts relating to masculinities is critical so that more conservative or less gender justice oriented movements do not gain ground and determine how the "new man" is defined.

Overview of Research on Masculinities

Research and literature on masculinities from various parts of the globe is growing, including a number of studies on particular issues as they relate to black masculinities, from industrialized countries as well as countries on the African continent. This is characterized in three analytical categories. The first category includes studies exploring the meanings and practice of masculinities in different cultures, the ways in which these masculinities change over time, and their tensions and instabilities. This has been referred to as a "gender-specific" approach. The second category of work explores masculinities as a way to end patriarchy and promote gender justice and/or meet broad development goals—an instrumental approach. Much of the work in "development" is focused more on issues of economic development and less on issues of systemic change that redefining masculinities would entail. The third category perceives hegemonic or patriarchal masculinity as onerous to many young men, especially marginalized ones, who cope with the inability to be "real men" by unleashing violence on others.

In addition to these three analytical frameworks, there is a challenge mounted from the perspective of those who are "gender non-conforming," most prominently the transgender perspective. This is the most subversive of all the approaches to interrogate masculinities, as it uses the standpoint of the transgender or "genderqueer" person to destabilize the very category of gender itself. By challenging normative heterosexuality as well as homophobia, this intellectual inquiry cuts at the very heart of masculinity and binary gender. Because it threatens gender itself as a category, as well as the category of woman—in both of which feminists have a longstanding investment—many theorists and advocates have been highly reluctant to engage it.

To grasp the key features of these categories of literature, the following sections look at one book in each, with the understanding that bodies of scholarship are not neatly divided but draw on each other and overlap.

The Gender-specific Approach

The approach referred to as "gender specific" focuses on the health, human development, and specific needs of mostly young men. For example, research in sub-Saharan Africa suggests that there are many versions of masculinity in the region. Achieving some level of financial independence and subsequently starting a family are key in attaining manhood. An older man socially recognizes one's "manhood," and there are numerous rites of passage throughout the region to socialize boys. Rapid social changes as a result of urbanization, political upheavals, and the AIDS crisis as well as armed conflicts have had profound impacts on this socialization. Understanding and coming to terms with what it is to be a man in these contextualized and changing circumstances drives this body of work (see, in particular, Barker & Ricardo, 2005). Perhaps its main thrust is to articulate how young men—as one category of "weaker" or less powerful men—express their discontent with patriarchal systems, and elaborate how rigid forms of socialization lead to vulnerabilities for young men (as well as young women).

Victor Seidler's book, *Young Men and Masculinities* (2006), is indicative of this category of literature. It explores responses of young men to the massive changes that have occurred since the 1970s. Many young men are in the process of forging new understandings of themselves and in so doing are questioning dominant notions of masculinity prescribed by religion and tradition. Seidler narrates how women's movements have led men to rethink their inherited masculinities and encouraged them to create more open, loving relationships with their partners and children. Young men today have numerous challenges, which include understanding the relationships between colonialism and masculinity, responding to the global nature of media and the messages it circulates, and coming to terms with modernities that have fundamentally altered the composition of families.

Young men are still constrained by dominant masculinities that treat emotions and desires as weaknesses and as threats to male identities, conceive of sexuality as sin, and promote the authoritative role of the father in male lives. In many parts of the West—and countries colonized by the West—young men who have lived by the dictates of hegemonic forms of masculinity find it difficult to listen to women and to express themselves without guilt about their unspoken desires. This tension is a source of anxiety for young men struggling to define themselves and their relationships in a world of growing inequities and insecurities. Literature in this category, including the book by Seidler, is sympathetic to the future of young men in their struggle to assert themselves in liberatory ways.

An Instrumental Approach

Using a gender equality or rights-based approach that engages men to address inequality is not that dissimilar from efforts to deal with women's issues as a way to meet broader development goals. The considerable body of work taking an instrumental approach, where masculinity is interrogated in the service of a goal (namely, to reduce violence against women and challenge patriarchy) includes writing from developing as well as industrialized countries. Actions are proposed to meet four main objectives: improving reproductive and sexual health, ending violence against women, encouraging responsible fatherhood, and changing gender norms. There is increasing emphasis on issues of safe sex due to the high levels of HIV and other sexually transmitted diseases, especially among vulnerable youth, as well as on reducing violence, especially violence in intimate relationships (with partners/families). Research is emerging on the relationship between salient versions of masculinity and armed and unarmed conflict, especially in the African context (Baker & Ricardo, 2005).

Jackson Katz's powerful book, *The Macho Paradox* (2006), exemplifies this more instrumental category. Katz is a feminist who has taken cues from the women's movement to analyze how violence against women is a men's issue. He describes the ways in which men are socialized into violence, how they are bystanders to violence, and how and why men seek and need to get validation from other males to show their "manliness," which often leads to greater violence. He discusses these forces as the components of a "rape culture." Katz underlines the importance of men listening to women, internalizing the statistics regarding male violence against women, and talking with other men about these issues of domination and violence. If they are not made to feel self defensive, men can come to grips with how violence affects them and those they love. Katz reminds us that men are not violent, nor do they have a predilection for violence; our culture perpetuates violence.

Katz also presents a treatise on pornography in which he argues that it contributes to sexual violence by desensitizing men to women's real sexual desires. Porn, a multibillion dollar industry, limits sexual expression and freedom and sets women up to be sexually victimized by men, and it plays a powerful role in defining heterosexual male sexuality. Violent porn normalizes violent sex and has the same dynamic that underlies the rape culture in which the threat of violence is always lurking beneath the surface. Katz pays particular attention to the athletic culture as exemplary of traditional masculine success, highlighting the important roles that athletes can play in redefining what it means to be a man. Katz also surveys the "men against violence" efforts that have empowered men to confront abuse, and proposes numerous recommendations on how to address violence. The book ends with a useful discussion of male antiviolence programs, primarily in the United Kingdom and the United States, and the challenges and pitfalls men's groups face.

The important work that feminist scholars like Cynthia Enloe and Joni Seager have contributed on the violence of male institutions like militaries, and the ways in which militarism reinforces systems of violence, provides valuable extensions to this (see, for example, Enloe, 2000; Seager, 1994).

Marginalization and Violence

The third line of inquiry addresses masculinity in the context of marginalized communities by juxtaposing "hegemonic masculinity" with the failure of many men and boys to live up to its dictates in the context of globalization and rapid change. This work responds to the impact that onerous notions of masculinity have on disenfranchised young men who are vulnerable to violence, which leads to further violence and behaviors that intensify their marginalization. It brings to light the factors that keep young men from living up to expectations of hegemonic forms of masculinity and explores their coping and accommodation strategies as well as their more negative responses. It seeks to identify the factors that "protect" young men from negative forces impinging on their lives. It is this body of work that most critiques and engages the state and its role in upholding and determining masculinities—what it means to be a man in different societies. The relationship between manhood and the state and these interactions are less theorized in the literature on masculinities to date.

Gary Barker's book, *Dying to be Men* (2005), belongs to this third category of intellectual engagement. Barker focuses on shantytowns in Brazil, Nigeria, and the Caribbean and, through a series of case studies, shows that as a result of socialization young men between the ages of 15 and 25 die more violently and at rates far higher than their female counterparts due to traffic accidents and homicides. Young men aspire to live up to models of manhood that endanger them, while at the same time they continue to victimize young and adult women. As large groups of young men come of age in settings of social exclusion—that is, with few opportunities and lack of jobs—they are finding it increasingly difficult to be breadwinners and supporters of families.

Their vulnerability and marginalization leads these young shantytown dwellers to become involved in gang-related activities, often the only source of income and recognition. Such involvement combines with peer pressure to enmesh them in violent lifestyles. Gangs adhere to a specific version of manhood characterized by the use of armed violence to achieve goals, a willingness to kill, callous attitudes to and violence against women, an exaggerated sense of male honor, and a propensity to use violence in minor altercations. These young men seek to be standard-bearers for the most "visible and fear-inspiring versions" of what it means to be a man, with grave consequences for their interactions with young women, their ability to be good fathers, and their sexuality and reproductive health. It often leads to violence in intimate relationships. Barker concludes that, as part of the solution, there is a need to address individual, community/peer group, and family relationships as well as structures of social inequality, unemployment, deficient public education systems, among others, and question why there is an incomplete inclusion of gender relations in all these sectors and policies.

The Transgendered Perspective

Building on the scholarship of queer as well as women's studies is the challenge to gender binaries that comes from a transgendered perspective. Riki Wilchins's *Read My Lips: Sexual Subversion and the End of Gender* (1997) is at once a personal and political account that chronicles the shame, depression, and trauma that transgender people experience as they try—and sometimes fail—to neatly fit into either the prescribed "female" or "male" category. While some "transpeople" want nothing more than to be accepted and regarded as "normal" males and females, others choose to live in alternative nonbinary genders. Wilchins argues that gender is socially constructed and constricts both women and men from being their full selves by arbitrarily drawing hard lines between the two genders—borders we transgress at our own peril. S/he argues, in other words, for a more radical approach to gender justice that looks beyond simply reapportioning power between two opposing and binary genders. As long as men are restricted to masculinity and women to femininity, s/he doubts that real gender liberation is possible.

According to Wilchins, "the regime of gender is an intentional, systemic oppression" and must be challenged systemically; doing so shatters conventional notions of masculinity and femininity, enabling people to express, be, and enact their full selves. In this, s/he echoes some early feminist theorists, such as Sandra Bem (1994), who contested the idea that a sign of healthy psychological adjustment in boys and girls was their learning to fulfill masculine and feminine roles. Bem argued that this binary restriction impoverished individuals, and that a fuller version of self was to be found when individuals were able to successfully integrate qualities of both genders.

Literature from a transgendered perspective critiques hegemonic forms of masculinity that subordinate, co-opt, or marginalize other forms of masculinity, and explores the varied ways in which masculinities get constructed in different social contexts. The role of national projects as well as various religions in buttressing masculinities is addressed. There is also an understanding of the role of empire in constructions of masculinity, as European empires were established as gendered systems, and in the process changed the formations of gender for the colonizer and the colonized.

Deconstructing Masculinities

Just as the workings of gender went unnoticed until feminists deconstructed them, what it means to be a man is not visible in society. The structures of masculinity are hidden from men, as is the "invisible backpack of privileges" that derives from being male (see McIntosh, 1990). What the literature on masculinities makes clear is that there is no universal form of masculinity and, as scholars such as Lynne Segal have affirmed, masculinity is always and constantly in transformation (see, for example, Segal, 1990). Differences exist across race, class, age, religion, and disability, as well as sexual orientation, and over time and in specific relationships and contexts.

Although masculinity carries with it enormous personal and social privileges, it also exacts a tremendous personal toll. For instance, in North America where men enjoy many privileges that are denied to women, they also have shorter life expectancies. They are more likely to die violently or from a host of deadly "lifestyle" diseases (lung cancer, diabetes, coronary heart disease), suffer from depression, contract a host of illnesses related to tension and aggression (high blood pressure, adrenal disorders, etc.), and take their own lives (also violently).

Masculinities are collectively constructed and enacted within groups and institutions—such as the factory, the sports field, the military, and corporations—that amplify and weigh them with meaning. The gendered nature of these institutions is not always apparent, and it is what these studies make evident. Seager (1994) does an excellent job of deconstructing the ways in which government, militaries, and corporations are gendered and reproduce patriarchy. Men in subordinate groups feel entitled to the "patriarchal dividend," but often do not benefit from it. In many instances, marginalized men carry the burden of masculinities and its concomitant responsibilities, which they are unable to withstand and which lead to aggression and hostility. The literature notes how definitions of masculinity are actively constructed, dynamic, and subject to change. It is precisely in the potential to disrupt these social constructions of manhood that the possibilities for change emerge, especially for men who are marginalized and for sexual minorities who do not conform to strict gender categorization.

The literature challenges restrictive forms of masculinity and deficit models that are confining. It challenges "the men as problem, women as victim" discourse and the essentialisms therein (IDS, 2007). Activist men in this movement are searching for more complicated understandings of vulnerability and violence that take into consideration men's gendered subjectivities and particular identities, as well as their exercise of male privilege. Much of the literature draws on case studies and specific pilot interventions in order to document advances. The areas of theorization now needed, according to scholars in this field, are gendered subjectivities and relationships to structures of male power, as well as men's complicity and accountability within such regimes.

As scholarship and interest in the subject of masculinity has grown, so has the number of meetings and conferences on the topic. In October 2007, academics, policymakers, practitioners, and activists gathered in Senegal to debate issues of men, gender, and power, and to "inform and inspire a greater engagement in the struggle for gender justice and broader social change." The symposium sought to go beyond innovative work at the local level geared to transform men's sexual behavior, attitudes toward violence against women, and fatherhood to the broader realms of development work. Participants focused on how they could move beyond the personal to shape policies and transform institutions, in part through activism and movement building. Sexual rights struggles were embraced as a strategy to politicize masculinities, and critiques of "heterosexuality" used to challenge social norms and serve as a bridge between lesbian, gay, bisexual, transgender, and inter-sex (LGBTI), women's rights, and men's movements.

MASCULINITY PROJECTS ADVANCING GENDER JUSTICE

I see five kinds of actions being undertaken in this burgeoning progressive masculinities movement. By far the majority of projects fall into the first category of those that are instrumental in nature—that is, the intervention seeks to interrogate masculinity to achieve another objective, such as reduce violence against women, reduce HIV and AIDS, lead to better parenting by fathers, promote gender equity, and so on.

Second, there are a few efforts to engage men to come to terms with issues of masculinity and its redefinition, but only individual men and small numbers of progressive masculinities activists have been engaged and galvanized by this self-reflective focus. The socially more conservative efforts, as well as the mythopoetic movements, have been successful in drawing small groups of men together to reflect on the meanings of manhood, to redefine it, and to work toward self healing. However, workshops for men to deal with tensions they feel regarding what it means to be a man are not sufficient to sustain the development of an organizational framework.

The third thrust of work on masculinities seeks to empower marginalized men and reduce their vulnerability and risk of violence. Fourth are efforts by women's organizations to reach men and engage them in work to reduce violence against women and challenge male bastions of power that perpetuate masculinity—for example, working within sports culture to reshape definitions of manhood. Finally, some new work is emerging that employs a transgendered critique to destabilize gender categories.

The following are examples of projects in some of these different areas of action. Almost all of the work described has been going on for a decade or slightly longer.

Conscientizing Male Adolescents (CMA) (Nigeria)[3]

CMA, founded in 1995, engages young men on issues of masculinity to dislodge gender oppression—a prevalent type of work. It uses long-term group education and reflection. From a pilot project structured to address 25 young men, it now reaches approximately 700 students a year who are recognized as leaders among their peers. CMA has developed a two-year group education curriculum emphasizing dialogue, reflection, and logical argument. In the first year, the young men participate in weekly two-hour discussions focused on gender and sexism as social constructions, discrimination, sexual and reproductive health and awareness, and understanding violence. The second year is dedicated to reinforcing these concepts and further developing critical thinking, communication, and mediation skills to challenge sexism. CMA has more recently developed a Level 3 group that meets regularly and engages in community activities and discussions facilitated by trained field officers. It also distributes a newsletter in local primary and secondary schools to promote women's rights and prevent violence.

Employing an educational format, CMA is developing a movement of progressive men to work as allies in the promotion of gender equity. The program is considered successful in enabling young men to perceive

---

[3] For information on CMA and other similar projects in Africa, the author relied on Barker and Ricardo (2005).

their misconceptions and biases, become self-reflective, and transmit lessons learned to their peers. The young men also indicate changes in their relationships with sisters and parents. Numerous initiatives like CMA all over the world have been put in place to work with young men to reduce violence, improve public health, and achieve other positive outcomes.

Instituto Promundo (Brazil)

Founded in 1997, Instituto Promundo in Rio de Janeiro, Brazil, is a good example of an organization addressing the needs of marginalized youth, with a focus on young men—in this case, the disenfranchised youth of the favelas of Rio. Given the degrees of poverty, social exclusion, unequal income distribution, and racism in many urban settings, it is perhaps surprising that young men in low-income neighborhoods of Brazil are not even more violent. Promundo explores the dimensions of social exclusion that young men face and examines the ways in which race works to compound their marginality. Through action-oriented research, it tries to understand the challenges that young men confront as they come of age in such difficult settings. It also identifies the factors that most protect them from getting involved in pervasive violence. Promundo works with policymakers and the media to discuss the structural violence that underpins lack of educational and employment opportunities and that can propel young men toward dangerous lifestyle choices.

Promundo also conducts research to identify innovative ways of producing positive social change in the lives of marginalized young men. Pilot projects, implemented in partnership with community groups, inform the research and reach young men who might otherwise be attracted to violent versions of manhood. Partners promote positive images of young men from marginal communities to counteract the "glory" and attention bestowed on gang-involved men. Adults from the community are involved as mentors and group coordinators for youth at risk.

Promundo has recognized the limitations of a "short-term, project-oriented approach" to engaging men, and findings and policy recommendations are adapted and replicated by a consortium of partners working nationally and in other parts of Latin America and the Caribbean to improve the lives of marginalized youth. The consortium develops educational materials, such as the Program H manuals that are widely used in workshops to help young men question gender roles, and conducts public campaigns in local languages to promote alternative ways of being a man. Educational activities enable young men to reflect critically on the "costs" they bear by adhering to traditional views of manhood. It was found that those who participated in such educational activities had greater empathy, and that conflict and violence were reduced. Participants' attitudes to women changed positively, and there was greater reflection among participants regarding how they treated their female partners. Controlled research findings showed that condom use increased with regular partners, and there was a decrease in the rates of self-reported symptoms of sexually transmitted diseases.

Promundo is also seeking to work in partnerships on broader advocacy issues and to contribute to a global agenda on progressive masculinities, including through a new alliance called MenEngage (discussed in the following paragraph). Currently, it is taking its programs and research findings to international agencies and health ministries for integration in national HIV and AIDS prevention programs and public health budgets. Sonke Gender Justice in South Africa is doing similar work, in close collaboration with Promundo. It conducts community activism and works with marginalized, low-income men in the townships to challenge destructive notions of masculinity and reduce risky and violent behaviors in the context of the HIV epidemic.

Family Violence Prevention Fund (FVPF) (USA)

FVPF is an example of a women's organization that reaches out to men to address violence against women and to challenge systems of male power and privilege. This work is based on the premise that boys are swamped with negative messages about manhood, which involves having to be in control and to boss others—including their girlfriends—to assert their manliness. It is interesting to note that many of the efforts to reach out to young men to reduce violence against women were started by women's organizations. They saw the necessity of not only taking care of victims of violence and empowering them, but also stopping the violence—which required working with the perpetrators. While working with women is still its primary focus, FVPF has two innovative approaches to include men in its efforts: it has reached out to fathers through a media campaign, and it has also enlisted coaches in its antiviolence work.

FVPF pays public homage to "courageous men," who make a public commitment to work in partnership with women to create a new society and use their status and influence to make a significant financial contribution to its work. This campaign also invokes the status of fathers as a reminder to men of their unique position as role models for the next generation in building a world free of violence.

The other successful FVPF public education campaign is its Coaching Men Into Boys initiative. Men, especially coaches, are enlisted to be mentors to young boys. They talk with boys about violence and about appropriate ways to express anger and frustration. They also listen to what boys have to say about how they and their friends talk about girls, popular music, and the media they watch. To guide mentors, FVPF has developed brochures, posters, campaign ads, other awareness materials, and leadership development activities to facilitate dialog about domestic and dating violence. In this way, it engages coaches to help shift negative attitudes and behaviors of young males that can perpetuate gender-based violence and inequality, and they teach boys that violence does not equal strength. FVPF relies on and works with organizations across the United States and increasingly in other parts of the world to support and implement the campaigns at local and global levels.

Gender Public Advocacy Coalition (GPAC) (USA)

An interesting variant of the work being done to challenge masculinities comes from a transgender location that seeks to destabilize the meaning and practice of gender stereotypes. GPAC, a human rights organization formed in 1995 in Washington DC, works to ensure that classrooms, campuses, and communities are safe for children and youth to learn, grow, and succeed—whether or not they meet expectations for "appropriate" expression and performance of "masculinity" and "femininity." This work is a response to widespread gender-based violence and rampant bullying among young people. GPAC is particularly committed to advancing the rights of transgender people and fighting hate crimes targeted at them. It makes apparent the connections between gender stereotypes and all forms of discrimination.

GPAC's Community Partners initiative works with youth groups to strengthen their efforts to combat the "crisis of masculinity" among young men, especially those in communities of color, and to help them integrate an analysis of gender into programs, policies, and materials. Through its Gender YOUTH Network, GPAC empowers youth leaders on 106 campuses in 29 US states to combat bullying and harassment of students who are not considered appropriately masculine and feminine. GPAC also has a program, Children As They Are, which helps create environments where children can be themselves and develop all their interests, skills, and talents whether or not these are deemed socially "right" for girls or boys. By challenging homophobia and the notions of what it means to be a woman or a man, GPAC destabilizes gender binaries and hierarchies. It highlights the lack of safety experienced by nongender conforming youth, helps them organize, and upholds the human rights of all people without reference to their gender identity or gender claims.

The MenEngage Alliance

In an effort to seed a global movement with a focus on policy activism, MenEngage has been formed. An alliance of more than 400 NGOs in Latin America, South Asia, Europe, North America, and sub-Saharan Africa, it seeks to build on evidence-based activism to ensure integration of masculinity issues into public health and social development agendas. A second goal is to provide feasible and practical strategies to have a large-scale impact in changing social behaviors relating to sexual and reproductive health, gender-based violence, fatherhood, and maternal and child health. MenEngage overviews the programmatic and policy landscape in each country where it has partners, and articulates appropriate legislative and policy interventions to support changing attitudes and behaviors of men—for example, in relation to their roles in the family and as sexual partners.

To contribute to this effort, ICRW and Promundo, together with local partners, are carrying out the multi-country International Men and Gender Equality Survey (IMAGES), to gather information on men's and women's attitudes and behavior on a wide range of issues related to gender relations (violence, health, work–life balance, and caregiving, among others). In this way it is anticipated that legislation in one country can serve as a guidepost in another. Several Nordic countries have already launched policies that encourage fathers to participate in parenting—for example, through the provision of parental leave for both partners. Family friendly policies that enable new definitions of manhood are examined in the development of a global agenda to encourage policymakers to involve men in health and development agendas. Survey findings will be launched at key global meetings.

Parallels with the Women's Movement

The progressive masculinities programs discussed earlier work from culturally specific definitions of manhood. They seek to create safe spaces and materials for men to "unpack" their male identities through self-reflection, use trainers to facilitate dialog to critically assess prevailing norms and attitudes, and provide men and boys with opportunities to model new behaviors in safe settings. They tap into men's sense of responsibility and create enabling environments to support individual and group changes. They draw men into broader alliances and campaigns and have them reach out to their peers to develop alternative notions of manhood. These processes are still at the individual/community level, and it is understood that change will take time. They are very much like those of the early feminist consciousness-raising movement, where change was directed at the personal level with the expectation that those who went through the process would be forebearers of broader social change. Just as what it means to be a woman has changed through the work of feminists who started in this personal, conscientizing way, what it means to be a man may evolve through similar strategies, judging from trends emerging in men's movements.

There are hundreds of small organizations and individuals carrying out work like this in various parts of the world, some of them building on pioneer efforts, others making it up along the way.[4] They are also seeking to engage broader audiences beyond individuals and communities through media programs and public education campaigns that challenge dominant norms of hypermasculinity. For example, sreeking to change social norms, Soul City in South Africa has developed a television series on how men are socialized that has been very popular with young men. Using the musical video format, Let's Breakthrough in India has produced "What kind of man are you?" videos and public service announcements that challenge men to alter their male behaviors and reduce HIV infection and violence. E-technologies are also used to communicate positive masculinity messages. At the individual level, Byron Hurt, film director and antiviolence activist, provides a critical perspective of hip-hop and its portrayal of norms for men. His film, *Beyond Beats and Rhymes*, has resonated in the United States and overseas as a basis from which to

---

[4] The author acknowledges the insights of Gary Barker for this sense of the scope of the organizations and people involved in this burgeoning set of activities as well as for his very useful comments and suggestions on this chapter.

explore masculinity and its tensions, and to move to gender relations that are more equitable.

CONCLUSION

> ... working with men is critical for developing partnerships and common visions between young women and young men. (AWID, 2004, p. 2)

The field of masculinities is coming into being and developing its own constituency. While the research and intellectual base is expanding, key activists and organizations are working to deconstruct what it means to be a man in the 21st century through project-based work and the elaboration of policy goals and objectives. The interrogation of masculinities provides more "complex accounts of vulnerability and violence" and allows for an exploration of men's "gendered subjectivity as well as their exercise of male privilege, and (in) men's multiple locations within systems of oppression together with their patriarchal power...." (IDS, 2007, p. 7). For some it offers the potential to "break out" from the work on gender that "seems inadvertently stuck in reconstructing or reinforcing essentialist and het-ero-normative gender binaries" (ibid., p. 6).

International agencies are attuned to compelling evidence showing that

> ... well-designed programs with men and boys ... lead to change in behavior and attitudes relating to sexual and reproductive health, maternal, new-born and child health, their interaction with their children, their use of violence against women, questioning violence with other men and their health seeking behavior as a result of relatively short-term programs. Approaches that sought to transform gender roles and promote more gender equitable relationships were more effective than those that distinguished little between the needs of men and women (gender neutral) or those that recognized the specific needs and realities of men (gender sensitive). Integrated programs and those with community outreach, mobilization and mass media campaigns show greater effectiveness in producing behavior change highlighting the importance of reaching beyond the individual level to the social context that includes relationships, social institutions, gatekeepers and community leaders. (Barker, 2005, pp. 4–5)

It is important to engage men in terms of their emotional and personal lives and have safe spaces to do so. Fatherhood interventions are ideal points of leverage, as men are better able to unpack their emotions and behaviors in relation to their children, as this is less contested than their relationships with women.

This transnational movement is poised to scale up the mostly small pilot programs that currently exist to have an impact on structures and policies that could lead to major changes in defining and being a man. The progressive masculinities movement is clearly an unanticipated outcome of four decades of feminist theory and organizing, which more recently has drawn from the LGBTI field. Whereas the women's movement has been very successful in reaching out to other women and national and global policymakers, it is only very recently that some women's organizations have reached out to men as allies in the struggle, initially to reduce gender violence. For the most part feminist movements have not sought to conduct outreach to men, nor have they been successful in attracting men to their cause. What has transpired is that a movement of men is evolving in a parallel space that has many goals that are similar to, and overlap with those of the global women's movement: a desire to rethink rigid gender hierarchies in favor of more equitable relationships between women and men; a reduction of violence among men and against women; greater sexual responsibility among men to reduce exposure to HIV and AIDS; and more responsible fatherhood and partnering with women on issues of maternal and child health. While the objectives and mission of the masculinities movement are to date narrower than those of the women's movement, there is clearly common ground from which to start working together on common goals. There is growing recognition among leading women's networks that working with men is critical for developing partnerships and common visions between young men and young women (see, for example AWID, 2004).

I believe that the progressive masculinity movement can help complete much of the work that remains to be achieved by feminists in critical areas. Clearly, men are often better able to reach other men on issues of violence, sexual and reproductive health, parenting, and equitable gender roles. This work should not compete with the work done by women but rather complement and augment it by reaching out to constituencies that the women's movement cannot. Furthermore, it enables feminists to take on wider challenges related to economic and political equity, while men who are disenfranchised, or privileged men willing to question privilege, can become allies. A key conclusion from local organizing and "local practice" has been that at times it is useful and strategic to work with boys and men only, and at other times to work with women and girls only or collaboratively. This micropractice offers important insights into how these "movements" might work in conjunction—at times apart, at times together, but ultimately seeking common cause.

Much of women's work on issues of gender equity and gender justice got waylaid by the backlash on issues of sexual and reproductive health, which absorbed a disproportionate amount of the energy of feminist organizing efforts all over the globe. If men's movements take on some of these burdens, women's movements could recoup and refocus some of their energies without giving up the important work they have catalyzed and continue conducting. Feminists still need to work to name and define issues, such as violence against women, as well as to expand definitions and theoretical approaches and move beyond issues of domestic and sexual violence, now being taken up by male organizers, to challenge systemic violence, and then have men engage that effort too. In other words, feminists must continue to be trailblazers in the struggle for gender justice while accommodating and partnering with progressive masculinity efforts, thus facilitating the creation of spaces for dialog and exchange and joint action efforts. In so doing, together they can move forward feminist agendas even further. As the Association for Women's Rights in Development (AWID, 2004, p. 4) points out:

> Involving men does not mean that our fundamental strategies of women's empowerment are discarded, but instead that additional strategies are considered in order to bring about real gender equality.... Women-only spaces for awareness raising and organizing are still essential and should be protected.

There are opportunities for the women's, masculinity, and LGBTI movements to work together, from their distinct vantage points, to topple gender hierarchies and binaries from multiple locations. Their collective power could reenergize feminist and sexuality struggles that have clearly been key social movements of the latter part of the 20th century.

REFERENCES

Anandhi, S., Jeyaranjan, J., & Krishnan, R. (2002). Work, caste and competing masculinities: Notes from a Tamil village. *Economic and Political Weekly*, 37(43), 4397–4406.

AWID (Association for Women's Rights in Development). (2004). Working with men for women's rights. *Young Women and Leadership*, no. 2, February.

Barker, G. (2005). *Dying to be men: Youth, masculinity and social exclusion*. New York: Routledge.

Barker, G., & Ricardo, C. (2005). *Young men and the construction of masculinity in sub-Saharan Africa: Implications for HIV/AIDS, conflict, and violence.* Social Development Papers, Conflict Prevention and Reconstruction paper 26. Washington, DC: World Bank.

Bem, S. (1994). *Lenses of gender: Transforming the debate on sexual inequality.* New Haven, Connecticut: Yale University Press.

Ehrenreich, B. (1983). *The hearts of men: American dreams and the flight from commitment.* Garden City, New York: Anchor Press/Doubleday.

Enloe, C. (2000). *Maneuvers: The international politics of militarizing women's lives.* Berkeley, California: University of California Press.

Hooks, B. (2004). *The will to change: Men, masculinities, and love.* New York: Washington Square Press.

IDS (Institute of Development Studies). (2007). *Politicizing masculinities: Beyond the personal.* Report of a meeting held in Dakar, Senegal, IDS.

Katz, J. (2006). *The macho paradox: Why some men hurt women and how all men can help.* Naperville, Illinois: Sourcebooks.

Magnuson, E. (2007). *Changing men, transforming culture: Inside the men's movement.* Boulder, Colombia: Paradigm Publishers.

McIntosh, P. (1990). White privilege: Unpacking the invisible knapsack. *Independent Schools,* Winter, 31–36.

Mutua, M. (Ed.). (2009). *Human rights NGOs in East Africa: Political and normative tensions.* Philadelphia, Pennsylvania: University of Pennsylvania Press.

Mutunga, W. (2009). Feminist masculinity: advocacy for gender equality and equity. In M. Mutua (Ed.), *Human rights NGOs in East Africa: Political and normative tensions* (pp. 112–130). Philadelphia, Pennsylvania: University of Pennsylvania Press.

Seager, J. (1994). *Earth follies: Coming to feminist terms with the global environmental crises.* New York: Routledge.

Segal, L. (1990). *Slow motion: Changing masculinities, changing men.* London: Virago Press.

Seidler, V. (2006). *Young men and masculinities: Global cultures and intimate lives.* London: Palgrave Macmillan.

WHO (World Health Organization). (2007). *Engaging men and boys in changing gender-based inequity in health: Evidence from programme interventions.* Geneva: WHO.

Wilchins, R. (1997). *Read my lips: Sexual subversion and the end of gender.* Milford, Connecticut: Firebrand.

About the Editors and Contributors

The Editors

Devaki Jain is Founder and former Director of the Institute of Social Studies Trust New Delhi, India. She was previously a lecturer at the University of Delhi, member of the South Commission (chaired by Julius Nyerere), founding member of Development Alternatives with Women for a New Era (DAWN), and member of the Advisory Council of the intergovernmental NAM (Non-aligned Movement Institute for the Empowerment fo Women (NIEW) in Kuala Lumpur. In 2006 Dr Jain was presented by the President of India with the Padma Bhushan Award for exceptional and distinguished service. She has been a member of a number of Indian Government policy committees and has published several books and articles on Indian development and women's status. Her most recent publication is *Women, Development, and the UN: A Sixty-year Quest for Equality and Justice* (2005).

Diane Elson is Professor of Sociology, University of Essex, United Kingdom. She is the former Chair in Development Studies at Manchester University. She worked on the United Nations Development Fund for Women (UNIFEM) report on *Progress of the World's Women 2000*, and was named one of 50 key thinkers on development in 2006. Her current research and teaching interests are global social change and the realization of human rights, with a particular focus on gender inequality and economic and social policy. Professor Elson has been Special Advisor to the Executive

Director at UNIFEM, a member of the UN Millennium Project Task Force on Education and Gender Equality, and has provided consultancy services to many development agencies including the UK Department for International Development (DFID), the Swedish International Development Agency (Sida), and the Dutch Ministry of Foreign Affairs. She has published widely on gender, development, and human rights. Her recent publications include "Macroeconomic Policy, Employment, Unemployment and Gender Equality" in Ocampo, J.A. and Jomo, K.S., ed., *Towards Full and Decent Employment* (2007) and "Emerging Issues with a Focus on Economic Decision-Making" in UN Economic Commission for Europe, ed., *Gender Gaps and Economic Policy* (2007).

THE CONTRIBUTORS

Lourdes Benería is Professor of Gender and Economic Development, Cornell University, United States. Her research centers on gender and development, labor markets, women's work, globalization, European integration, and Latin American development. She is on the Advisory Board of the Technological Change Lab at Columbia University, served on the International Advisory Committee for the UNIFEM report on *Progress of the World's Women 2000*, and is a member of the International Advisory Board for the Global Programme on Socioeconomic Security of the the International Labour Organization (ILO). Professor Benería has been a member of the Research Advisory Council of the Economic Policy Institute in Washington, DC, and is a current member of the United Nations Development Programme (UNDP) Directory of Appointed Experts on Poverty in Latin America and the Caribbean. Her forthcoming book, with D. Strassman and A.M. May, is titled *Feminist Economics for the 21st Century*.

Itzá Castañeda is Senior Gender Advisor, UNDP Country Office, Mexico City, Mexico. An expert on gender and the environment, she was the Director of Gender Equity in the Secretariat of Environment and Natural Resources of Mexico, and has vast experience in environmental research and local capacity building in communities in Mexico and Central America. Her publications include: "Resource Guide on Gender and Climate Change" (coordinator); "In Search of the Lost Gender: Equity in Protected Areas"; "About Fishermen, Fisherwomen, Oceans and Tides: A Gender Perspective in Marine Coastal Zones"; and "The Unavoidable Current: Gender Equity Policies within the Mesoamerican Environmental

Sector." She is a member of the Global Gender and Climate Alliance (GGCA) and the Gender and the Environment Network of Mexico.

Lanyan Chen is Assistant Professor, Social Welfare and Social Development, Nipissing University, North Bay, Ontario. She helped found the Institute of Gender and Social Development at the Tianjin Normal University, the first of its kind in China that supports a Master's program in Gender and Development. She has a PhD in sociology from the University of British Columbia, with a strong emphasis on political economy. She taught sociology, gender, and international development at the University of Victoria in Canada for many years before she was appointed by UNIFEM as the Gender Advisor for Northeast Asia. As such, from 1998 to 2003, she initiated, among several projects and programs, an HIV and AIDS research/advocacy project, a research project on assessing the impacts of China's entry into the World Trade Organization (WTO) on women and men in agriculture and industry, and a white ribbon campaign against violence against women. She has published research on poverty alleviation, women's cooperatives, health care policy reforms in China, and HIV and AIDS in China. Her book on *Gender and Chinese Development: Towards an Equitable Society* (2008) is in the International Association for Feminist Economics (IAFFE) book series.

Solita Collas-Monsod is Professor of Economics, University of the Philippines Diliman, Manila. She is also the convener of the Philippine Human Development Network and was its Chair for 11 years. Her international involvement includes having been a member of the UN Committee on Development Policy (UNCDP), the South Commission, the Advisory Board of the South Centre in Geneva, Switzerland, and the Board of Trustees of the International Food Policy Research Institute (IFPRI) based in Washington, DC. Professor Collas-Monsod is frequently asked to serve on the Advisory Board of the UNDP Human Development Report. She served as Minister and later Secretary of Socio-economic Planning in the Philippine Government, and as Vice-Chair of the Department of Agriculture Senior Scientist Advisory Committee. She is currently Chair of the Advisory Board of the Southeast Asian Ministers of Education Organization–Southeast Asian Regional Centre for Graduate Study and Research in Agriculture (SEAMEO–SEARCA) and a member of the high level Task Force of the UN High Commissioner for Human Rights. She also writes a weekly column for *Business World* and *Philippine Daily Inquirer*, and is co-host of "Unang Hirit," an early morning TV show dealing with current socio-political and economic issues.

Yassine Fall is Senior Economic Advisor, UNIFEM, New York, United States. She is an economist with 18 years of field and policy experience. She is UNIFEM Senior Economic Advisor on secondment to the UN Millennium Project as Senior Policy Advisor on Gender Equality, and was previously UNIFEM Regional Programme Director covering Francophone and Lusophone countries in West and Central Africa. As Executive Director of the Association of African Women for Research and Development (AAWORD for five years, she played an important role in facilitating policy dialog between African governments and different women's constituencies within Africa and during major UN international conferences. She is a founding member of distinguished organizations including the Open Society Institute for West Africa, Gender and Economic Reforms in Africa, International Gender and Trade Network, and Network of African Women Economists, and is the President of the African Women's Millennium Initiative on Poverty and Human Rights (AWOMI). She has been a consultant to both donor and UN agencies on issues such as gender and development, macroeconomic reforms, international trade, poverty reduction strategies, emergency relief operations, natural resources management, and land tenure. She is the author of several publications in French and English.

Sarah Gammage is an Economist at the ILO in Chile. She has written academic and policy research articles on gender and trade, poverty, labor markets, migration, and environment. She has a Masters degree in Economics from the London School of Economics and Political Science and a PhD in Development Economics from the Institute of Social Studies, The Hague. She has worked with a number of international and multilateral organizations including the International Center for Research on Women (ICRW), Washington, DC; the International Institute for Environment and Development (IIED), London, England; the UN Economic Commission for Latin America and the Caribbean (ECLAC), and UNDP.

Hiroko Hara is Professor, Graduate School, Josai International University, and Professor Emeritus, Ochanomizu University, both in Tokyo, Japan. In addition, she is Convener of Japan Women's Watch, Vice Representative of Japan's Network for Women and Health, and member of the Councils for Gender Equality, Prime Minister's Office Council for Gender Equality, and Special Committee on Violence against Women. Previously she was Professor at the University of the Air (now The Open University of Japan), and Director and Professor at the Institute for Gender Studies, Ochanomizu University. Her various activities have also included being a member of the Japanese Government delegation as an NGO advisor for the ICPD+5

Preparatory Committee in New York. Professor Hara received a PhD from Bryn Mawr. She has produced more than 250 publications in Japanese. Major works in English include "Environment, Resources, Population and Human Rights: Views as a Japanese Woman" (paper presented in 1999), and "Women's Participation in Various Areas of Higher Education in Japan" in National Women's Education Center, ed., *Women in a Changing Society: The Japanese Scene* (1990).

Renana Jhabvala is Chair of the Executive Committee of Women in Informal Employment: Globalizing and Organizing (WIEGO) and President of the Self Employed Women's Association (SEWA), New Delhi, India. She is also Chair of the Task Force on Workers in the Unorganized Sector, Government of Madhya Pradesh, and of the Group on Women Workers and Child Labour, National Commission on Labour, Government of India. In 1990, she was awarded the Padma Shri by the Government for her distinguished contribution. Some of her publications include *The Unorganised Sector: Work Security and Social Protection* (2000) and *Speaking Out: Women's Economic Empowerment in South Asia* (1997), both co-edited. She has also contributed several articles on the issues of social security and women's economic empowerment to journals such as *Seminar* and *Economic and Political Weekly*.

Patricia McFadden is Visiting Professor, Women's and Gender Studies Department, The College of Arts and Sciences, Syracuse University, United States. She was the editor of the *Southern African Feminist Review*, the Endowed Cosby Chair in the Social Sciences in the Women's Research and Resource Center at Spelman College, Atlanta, head of the Southern African Regional Institute for Policy Studies (SARIPS), Harare, and the Zimbabwe Visiting Scholar/Affiliate at the Five Colleges Women's Studies Research Center, Mount Holyoke College Massachusetts, United States. In the United States she has taught at Cornell, Smith, Spelman, and Syracuse Universities, and in Europe, she served as international dean in the International Women's University from 1998 to 2000 in Hannover, Germany.

Marta Núñez Sarmiento is Professor at the Center for Studies of International Migrations, University of Havana, Cuba. She teaches in the University's Department of Sociology and is also a researcher at the Center for Studies of International Migrations (CEMI). She has been an adviser to the Embassy of Cuba in Russia and has served as a consultant for several agencies of the UN, for the Association of Caribbean States, for the Canadian International Development Agency (CIDA), Cuba, and for UN

ECLAC. She is currently a Visiting Scholar at the David Rockefeller Center for Latin American Studies in Harvard University.

Naoko Otobe is Senior Gender and Employment Specialist, ILO, Geneva, Switzerland. She is a strong advocate of promoting social justice for the working poor, in particular for women in developing countries. She has over 26 years of professional analytical and operational experience in the UN system in the areas of development, employment, poverty, and gender. She has previously worked for the United Nations Environment Programme (UNEP) in Kenya and UNDP in the Philippines. She has substantial professional experience in a large number of developing and transition countries in Africa, Asia, and Europe. Her involvement in research and publications encompasses such countries as Bangladesh, Estonia, Indonesia, Kenya, Mauritius, the Philippines, United Republic of Tanzania, Viet Nam, and Zimbabwe. Her recent publications include *The Impact of Globalization and Macroeconomic Change on Employment in Mauritius: What Next in the Post-MFA Era?* (2008).

Stephanie Seguino is Professor of Economics, University of Vermont, United States. She holds a PhD from American University Washington, DC. She is Research Scholar at the Political Economy Research Institute University of Massachusetts Amherst; Associate Editor of *Feminist Economics*, board member of Eastern Economics Association, and member of the The International Working Group on Gender, Macroeconomics and International Economics (GEM-IWG) Over the past several years, Professor Seguino has worked with a number of international organizations and research groups: the US Agency for International Development (USAID), UNDP, United Nations Research Institute for Social Development (UNRISD), and the World Bank. In March 2009, she presented a paper on "The Global Economic Crisis, Its Gender Implications, and Policy Responses" to the 53rd session of the Commission on the Status of Women, United Nations.

Jael Silliman was the Program Officer for Women's Rights and Gender Equity in the Human Rights Unit, Peace and Social Justice Program, Ford Foundation, New York, United States. She was Associate Professor in the Women's Studies Department at the University of Iowa, Iowa City, United States. Her areas of interest include transnational feminist movements, population and reproductive rights, women of color, and environmental justice. She has been the recipient of numerous awards and the author of many books and articles, including (with M. G. Fried, L. Ross, and E. Gutiérrez) *Undivided Rights: Women of Color Organize for Reproductive Justice* (2004).

Index